DISTANCE FROM THE BELSEN HEAP

Allied Forces and the Liberation of a Nazi Concentration Camp

The Allied soldiers who liberated the Nazi concentration camp at Bergen-Belsen in April 1945 were faced with scenes of horror and privation. With breathtaking thoroughness, *Distance from the Belsen Heap* documents what they saw and how they came to terms with those images over the course of the next seventy years. On the basis of research in more than seventy archives in four countries, Mark Celinscak analyses how these military personnel struggled with the intense experience of the camp; how they attempted to describe what they had seen, heard, and felt to those back home; and how their lives were transformed by that experience. He also brings to light the previously unacknowledged presence of hundreds of Canadians among the camp's liberators, including noted painter Alex Colville.

Distance from the Belsen Heap examines the experiences of hundreds of British and Canadian eyewitnesses to atrocity, including war artists, photographers, medical personnel, and chaplains. A study of the complicated encounter between these Allied soldiers and the horrors of the Holocaust, *Distance from the Belsen Heap* is a testament to their experience.

MARK CELINSCAK is an assistant professor in the Department of History at Trent University.

Distance from the Belsen Heap

Allied Forces and the Liberation of a Nazi Concentration Camp

MARK CELINSCAK

UNIVERSITY OF TORONTO PRESS
Toronto Buffalo London

© University of Toronto Press 2015
Toronto Buffalo London
www.utppublishing.com

ISBN 978-1-4426-4762-6 (cloth)
ISBN 978-1-4426-1570-0 (paper)

Library and Archives Canada Cataloguing in Publication

Celinscak, Mark, 1978–, author
Distance from the Belsen heap : Allied forces and the liberation of a Nazi concentration camp / Mark Celinscak.

Includes bibliographical references and index.
ISBN 978-1-4426-4762-6 (bound)   ISBN 978-1-4426-1570-0 (paperback)

1. World War, 1939–1945 – Concentration camps – Liberation – Germany – Personal narratives – History and criticism.   2. Bergen-Belsen (Concentration camp).   3. World War, 1939–1945 – Concentration camps – Liberation – Germany.   4. Canada – Armed Forces – History – World War, 1939–1945.   5. Great Britain – Armed Forces – History – World War, 1939–1945.   6. World War, 1939–1945 – Canada.   7. World War, 1939–1945 – Participation, British.   I. Title.

D805.5.B47C45 2015   940.53'1853593   C2015-905390-0

This book has been published with the help of a grant from the Federation for the Humanities and Social Sciences, through the Awards to Scholarly Publications Program, using funds provided by the Social Sciences and Humanities Research Council of Canada.

University of Toronto Press acknowledges the financial assistance to its publishing program of the Canada Council for the Arts and the Ontario Arts Council, an agency of the Government of Ontario.

To Colleen and Ivan

It is painful to recall a past intensity, to estimate your distance from the Belsen heap, to make your peace with numbers. Just to get up each morning is to make a kind of peace.

Leonard Cohen

Contents

Illustrations xi

Preface xiii

Acknowledgments xix

1 Experience, Narrative, and Meaning: Encountering Bergen-Belsen   3
2 The Rhine, the Heath, the Wire   23
3 The Distance of Presence: Inside Seventy-Two Hours   44
4 A Camp on Exhibit: Workers, Witnesses, Visitors Descend   78
5 The Impossible Real: Bergen-Belsen in Art and Photography   116
6 Padres, Patients, and Pathologies: Medical and Spiritual Relief   160
Conclusion: A Past Intensity   191

Notes   195

Bibliography   251

Index   293

Illustrations

Map 1   The establishment of new camp sections   32
Map 2   The advance of British Troops to Bergen-Belsen in April 1945   32

A road sign at the entrance to the village of Bergen, Germany, near the Bergen-Belsen concentration camp.   55
RCAF public relations officer Fred Hopkinson and Sergeant Joe Stone of 39 Wing stand before the dead at the Bergen-Belsen concentration camp.   58
A Hungarian sentry monitors the perimeter of the Bergen-Belsen concentration camp.   70
Former Bergen-Belsen concentration camp personnel lined up in front of a mass grave.   72
Schutzstaffel (SS) Irma Grese, left, and Josef Kramer, right, await trial.   73
Citizens of Minden, Germany, gather to view a film about the Bergen-Belsen concentration camp.   89
Canadian servicemen and Bergen-Belsen child survivors, 1945.   93
Survivors attack a former guard at the Bergen-Belsen concentration camp.   97
Former camp guards and military personnel dig a mass grave.   98
An untitled painting by leading aircraftman Henry S. Abramson, RCAF, depicting the dead at the Bergen-Belsen concentration camp.   128
Belsen by Flight Officer Donald K. Anderson, official Canadian war artist.   130

Dying Girl at Belsen by Mervyn Peake for *Leader* magazine.   133
Bodies in a Grave, Belsen, by Lieutenant Alex Colville, official Canadian war artist.   135
Human Laundry, Belsen: April 1945 by Doris Zinkeisen of the St John Ambulance Brigade.   137
One of the Death Pits, Belsen: SS Guards Collecting Bodies by Captain Leslie Cole, official British war artist.   138
Fritz Klein, a former SS doctor in Auschwitz and Bergen-Belsen, makes an announcement for British newsreels.   139
Belsen Concentration Camp, Malnutrition Wards, by Flight Lieutenant Aba Bayefsky, official Canadian war artist.   141
A Living Skeleton at Belsen Concentration Camp, 1945, by Sergeant Eric Taylor of the Royal Engineers.   142
Remembering the Holocaust by Aba Bayefsky.   144
Young boy walks by corpses in Bergen-Belsen, photograph by George Rodger.   151
A frame of film shot by Lieutenant Mike Lewis of the Army Film and Photo Unit.   154
The bodies of former prisoners lie on the ground in Bergen-Belsen.   155
Former camp staff throw corpses into a mass grave at Bergen-Belsen.   164
A photograph of burials by Corporal A.P. (Pete) Holborne, RCAF.   180

Preface

This book retraces the relief efforts at the Bergen-Belsen concentration camp in northwest Germany following its surrender in the weeks before the end of the Second World War. Of utmost importance are the responses of not only British but also Canadian military personnel. While it is well documented that Bergen-Belsen was surrendered to VIII Corps of the British Army, hundreds of Canadians also assisted and hundreds more encountered the camp through informal visits and authorized tours. Like their British counterparts, though arriving at the camp in smaller – and yet no less significant – numbers, were Canadian airmen, paratroopers, soldiers, doctors and nurses, padres, nutritional and agricultural experts, war artists, and photographers. The central focus of this study is on the language, metaphors, and narratives offered by both men and women in the British and Canadian forces. This work scrutinizes the stories communicated with special attention afforded to the roles performed by military personnel and to the point in time that they entered the camp.

Scholars must make defined choices in their work. The decision to focus this study on Allied military personnel comes at a cost. The voices of Bergen-Belsen's wounded, its survivors, are largely and regrettably silent in this book. The gulf between inmates and Allied military personnel at liberation was often, although not always, pronounced. This work maintains that divide. When Allied forces first entered the camp, Fania Fénelon, a French pianist, composer, cabaret singer, and survivor of Bergen-Belsen observed:

> A new life breathed in the camp. Jeeps, command cars, and half tracks drove around among the barracks. Khaki uniforms abounded, the marvelously

substantial material of their battle dress mingling with the rags of the deportees. Our liberators were well fed and bursting with health, and they moved among our skeletal, tenuous silhouettes like a surge of life. We felt an absurd desire to finger them, to let our hands trail in their eddies as in the Fountain of Youth. They called to one another, whistled cheerfully, then suddenly fell silent, faced with eyes too large, or too intense a gaze. How alive they were; they walked quickly, they ran, they leapt. All these movements were so easy for them, while a single one of them would have taken away our last breath of life! These men seemed not to know that one can live in slow motion, that energy was something you saved.[1]

As this work demonstrates, in the days and weeks immediately following the surrender of Bergen-Belsen, that separation, that distance – at least from the perspective of Allied military personnel – was indeed profound. Perhaps a future study will examine the relationships and exchanges between inmate and liberator, but for now, this book attempts to expand our knowledge of the words and actions of Britons and Canadians at the camp. While any serious communication between inmate and liberator is left unexamined, other links are traversed.

The connections between Britain, Canada, and Bergen-Belsen are complex and extensive, stretching back to even before the camp was formally entered during the late afternoon of 15 April 1945 by the 63rd Anti-Tank Regiment under the authority of VIII Corps. Indeed, men from a section of the (British) Special Air Service, which also included a Canadian, entered the camp ahead of the 63rd Anti-Tank Regiment under the command of Lieutenant-Colonel R.I.G. Taylor. Remarkably, even before Allied forces arrived, there were inmates in the camp with British and Canadian connections. For instance, Petty Officer Alfred John Roe and Able Seaman Keith Mayor both died while being held prisoner in Bergen-Belsen. Captured in May 1943 during a commando raid in Norway called Operation Checkmate, the men were first taken to the Sachsenhausen concentration camp, and later, to Bergen-Belsen. According to International Tracing Service (ITS) records, Roe died of typhus on 13 April 1945.[2] Multiple witnesses at the Bergen-Belsen war crimes trial testified that Mayor had been executed in early April 1945.[3] In addition, there was an inmate named Harold Osmond Le Druillenec, a schoolmaster and Channel Islander from Jersey, who later provided testimony at the Bergen-Belsen war crimes trial.[4] After the war and to the present day, associations with the camp, on both sides of the Atlantic, persist in myriad ways.

In the aftermath of its surrender, Bergen-Belsen was, and continues to be, a name, a site, and a symbol frequently evoked in the Western world. While not a killing centre or extermination camp – thus making it a less than accurate representation of the worst of the horrors of the Holocaust – Bergen-Belsen was still a terribly frightful place and became one of the most filmed, photographed, and discussed camps of the entire war. For many people the name "Belsen" became synonymous with the crimes of the Third Reich. Accordingly, the camp and the images associated with it, are widely known, recognized, and employed.

In Britain, Bergen-Belsen occupies a distinct position in the remembrance of the Second World War and it continues to feature prominently in different aspects of both its popular culture and counterculture. From Leonard Cottrell's *The Man from Belsen* (1946), a dramatic account about daily life in Hitler's camps that aired on the BBC, to the recently completed and restored film *German Concentration Camps Factual Survey* (1945), directed by Sidney Bernstein with assistance from Alfred Hitchcock, Bergen-Belsen has long lingered and lurked in British art, music, film, and literature.[5] While the aforementioned representations were initially conceived immediately following the camp's surrender, reference to Bergen-Belsen continued unabated in the ensuing decades. Perhaps most notoriously, in late 1977, the English punk band the Sex Pistols began performing a song written by their bass player, Sid Vicious.[6] Titled, "Belsen Was a Gas," the record was objectionable to many, not to mention historically inaccurate, as there were no gas chambers at Bergen-Belsen. The camp was likely selected by Vicious because the name was well known throughout Britain and the Western world, and thus he recognized it would warrant controversy.[7]

Decades later, Bergen-Belsen would continue to be evoked and discussed in British culture, albeit in a starkly different manner. What has been called a "Holocaust lipstick motif" frequently appears in a number of works by Banksy – the English-based graffiti artist, painter, film director, and political activist.[8] Accordingly, for a period of time on Banksy's personal website under a section titled "Manifesto," Lieutenant-Colonel Mervin Willett Gonin is quoted at length. It was Gonin, an officer commanding the 11th Light Field Ambulance, who while assisting the inmates at Bergen-Belsen, noted the positive effect a shipment of lipstick had on the female survivors.[9] Perhaps Banksy chose the quote as some kind of reflection on the human condition.

More recently, the dramatic film *The Relief of Belsen* (2007) premiered, first airing on Channel 4 throughout the United Kingdom. Directed by

Justin Hardy, in association with the Wellcome Trust, the movie features Iain Glen, Corin Redgrave, Jemma Redgrave, Nigel Lindsay, and Tobias Menzies. The film recounts the humanitarian efforts that took place at the camp in the weeks following its surrender. More than seventy years after Allied forces entered Bergen-Belsen, the camp continues to be a focal point for Britain.

While the significant Canadian involvement at Bergen-Belsen has gone largely unacknowledged, the camp has made its mark both culturally and socially in the country. The National Film Board of Canada documentary *Memorandum* (1965), directed by Donald Brittain and John Spotton, follows Holocaust survivor Bernard Laufer on his journey back to the former site of Bergen-Belsen – the camp from which he was liberated twenty years earlier. Making appearances in the film are Glyn Hughes, the former deputy director medical services of VIII Corps and one of the first Allies to enter the camp; Josef Rosensaft, a fellow survivor and former president of the World Federation of Bergen-Belsen Survivors; and Herbert Weichmann, a German-Jewish lawyer and the then mayor of Hamburg. The film received a number of honours, including awards at the Venice Film Festival and the San Francisco International Film Festival.

Contemporary artist Herzl Kashetsky has made reference to Bergen-Belsen in some of his work. Born in 1950 in Saint John, New Brunswick, Kashetsky created the exhibit *A Prayer for the Dead* (1996) as a work of remembrance for those who died in the Holocaust.[10] Kashetsky was motivated to create this series of paintings based on photographs he saw of Bergen-Belsen and through his own contemporary visits to camps in Poland.[11] Moreover, Canadian poets such as Irving Layton and Leonard Cohen, among others, have also uttered the name of Bergen-Belsen and used the camp as a symbol in their own respective works.[12]

Of late, Solo Mobile – part of Bell Canada's Mobility subsidiary, which sells wireless service throughout the country – made international headlines because of an unintentionally controversial advertisement campaign. During the autumn of 2007, numerous billboards on display in both Toronto and Vancouver featured a young woman dressed in punk rock attire and wearing a button that read "Belsen Was a Gas" – a reference to the notorious Sex Pistols song from thirty years earlier.[13] The campaign received complaints from around the world, prompting Bell Canada to offer apologies. Consequently, even seventy years later, the name Bergen-Belsen is familiar to many and, when used negatively, deeply unsettling and contentious.[14]

While this is the first large-scale study to examine the Canadian involvement at Bergen-Belsen, priority is given to what was said rather than to the work that was done. The central question asked of the numerous letters, diaries, memoirs, and interviews presented by military personnel is the same: what messages are being offered and what does this mean? Additional questions are also presented, such as: How did Britons and Canadians view those who had been starved and who were suffering from a variety of illnesses? How does one maintain a sense of humanity when dealing with those who had been dehumanized for days, weeks, months, and, quite often, years? Indeed, these questions are as relevant today as they were during the spring and summer of 1945 at that dreadful camp on the Lüneburg Heath in northwest Germany.

The following chapters present a series of arguments that frequently push against conclusions previously made about the liberation and relief of the Bergen-Belsen concentration camp. When we broaden our view of Allied military formations in northwest Germany, it becomes evident that many more units were involved at and came across Bergen-Belsen than have been previously discussed. Furthermore, this work attempts to make clear that Bergen-Belsen, and thus the Holocaust, should be considered as part of both British and Canadian history. Thousands of Allied military personnel descended upon the camp in a variety of capacities.[15] For many in the armed forces, the camp became their defining moment of the Second World War. As this work illustrates, for some Bergen-Belsen was an awful, recurring memory, while for others it altered the course of their lives. Accordingly, the situation often became one of extreme ambivalence: an absorbing curiosity which prompted a closer gaze mixed with sheer horror and thus forcing one to turn away; an obligation to help those in need alongside a disgust for the sounds, sights, and smells of those same people; a desire to recount the scenes aligned with the struggle to locate and find suitable words and metaphors. It was an experience that remained long after the war.

The following study consists of six chapters and a conclusion. The first chapter explains the theoretical and methodological foundations of this book. Chapter 2 provides an overview of the British and Canadian approach on Bergen-Belsen, starting with the crossing of the Rhine River through to the takeover of the camp. In addition, it illustrates the locations of other British and Canadian military groups that also became involved at the camp in the ensuing weeks and months. The third chapter explores the responses of those military personnel who came across or entered the camp during the first three days of its capitulation.

Chapter 4, meanwhile, surveys the accounts of British and Canadian military personnel in the weeks and months following the handover of the camp. Here, the individuals under examination either worked at or visited the camp during the spring and summer of 1945. The fifth chapter scrutinizes the interpretations of the war artists, photographers, and some photojournalists who attempted to depict and interpret Bergen-Belsen. Chapter 6 examines the medical and spiritual relief efforts at the camp. Finally, the conclusion provides a brief summary and assessment of the overall themes of this work.

During a speech marking the fifty years that had passed since the end of Hitler's camp system, Sam E. Bloch, then president of the World Federation of Bergen-Belsen Associations, offered a tribute "to the allied soldiers that liberated the camps 50 years ago, and especially the British and Canadian soldiers that liberated Belsen." He then added, "Our commandment of 'Remember' implies not only memory, remembrance, but a warning that such tragedies should not be repeated to anyone, anywhere in the world."[16] It is to the subsequent Allied responses to these tragedies at Bergen-Belsen that this book will now attend.

Acknowledgments

This work is indebted to the British and Canadian liberators, as well as the Holocaust survivors, who shared with me their stories about their encounters at the Bergen-Belsen concentration camp. While many individuals offered their insight over the years, I would be remiss if I did not recognize at least a few of the men and women who offered so much of themselves.

Survivors from Hungary, Leslie and Eva Meisels spent many hours with me discussing their experiences during the Holocaust. As a child, Mrs Meisels and her mother were sent to the Budapest Ghetto. They eventually obtained false papers from Swedish diplomat Raoul Wallenberg and in January 1945 were liberated by the Red Army. Meanwhile, in December 1944, Mr Meisels and his family were sent to Bergen-Belsen. One week before the Allies arrived, Mr Meisels, his mother, and two brothers were taken by train towards the Theresienstadt concentration camp in German-controlled Czechoslovakia. Recognizing that the war would soon be over, their captors abandoned the train. On Friday, 13 April 1945, twenty kilometres north of Magdeburg, Mr Meisels and more than 2,000 other prisoners were liberated by soldiers from the 743rd Tank Battalion of the United States Army.

During one of our interviews, Mr Meisels told me of his reunion, nearly sixty-five years later, with some of the men who liberated him. In 2009 at a symposium in Hudson Falls, New York, seven liberators and seven survivors met again for the first time since that memorable day in April 1945. As I sat in his condo in Markham, Ontario, Mr Meisels told me of his admiration and respect for the men who – as he phrased it – gave him back his life. While there was no grand strategy put forward by any nation to rescue Mr Meisels or the other prisoners of Hitler's

Third Reich, his story illustrated a salient point: the achievements of Allied forces in Europe during the Second World War made it possible for such events to occur. Moreover, these moments altered forever the lives of not only survivors, but also liberators.

Not long after hearing this story, I was privileged to meet some of the liberators of Bergen-Belsen. The first was Ronald Ford "Andy" Anderson, a sergeant in the 1st Canadian Parachute Battalion. I came across an article in a local newspaper about a speech Mr Anderson gave at an event marking the sixtieth anniversary of the liberation of the camps and the end of the Second World War. The speech he gave at Earl Bales Park in Toronto detailed his brief but haunting encounter in the liberation of Bergen-Belsen.

When we spoke on the phone for the first time, Mr Anderson noted that the efforts of the battalion at Bergen-Belsen had largely been overlooked. Indeed, upon arriving at the camp, the men offered their food rations, some of the medical personnel tended to the sick, and the photographers attached to the battalion documented the crimes. While this encounter, like so many others, has generally been passed over in the annals of history, it was a moment the liberating men never forgot. Mr Anderson's narrative became a reminder of the challenges scholars face in the retelling of the past. It demonstrates that history, no matter how thorough, is always to some extent incomplete.

I have spent nearly ten years researching, writing, and revising this book. It has benefited from the support of many people. In my endnotes, I have tried to acknowledge all those individuals – survivors, veterans and their families, colleagues, archivists, and the like – who assisted me in its completion. Over the years, hundreds of people offered me their time, opinion, encouragement, and rare documents. I am forever grateful. I most sincerely apologize in advance if I have overlooked the help of anyone.

This publication has received generous financial support from a number of institutions. It has been published with the help of a grant from the Federation for the Humanities and Social Sciences, through the Awards to Scholarly Publications Program, using funds provided by the Social Sciences and Humanities Research Council of Canada. In addition, this book was made possible in part by funds granted to the author through a Pearl Resnick Postdoctoral Fellowship at the Jack, Joseph and Morton Mandel Center for Advanced Holocaust Studies of the United States Holocaust Memorial Museum. The statements made and views expressed, however, are solely the responsibility of the author. I am also grateful to the Emerging Scholars Program at the Mandel Center for Advanced Holocaust Studies for its support in the preparation of the manuscript and of the book proposal.

I have been rather fortunate to have worked with many insightful and thoughtful colleagues at both York University in Toronto and Trent University in Peterborough. Accordingly, I would like to acknowledge the ongoing support of Sara Horowitz, Marlene Kadar, Suzanne Langlois, Markus Reisenleitner, Bernard Lightman, Joan Steigerwald, Tom Cohen, and Carolyn Kay. Your kindness over the years will not soon be forgotten. To my many colleagues at the United States Holocaust Memorial Museum in Washington: your expertise, feedback, and criticism have vastly improved this work.

Lastly, I must thank my family. The journey has been a long one; their love, patience, and reassurance mean much to me. My parents have always provided their unconditional support. My sisters have kept my spirits up and my ego grounded. To my wife: thank you for opening my eyes and helping me see that which is essential.

DISTANCE FROM THE BELSEN HEAP

Allied Forces and the Liberation
of a Nazi Concentration Camp

Chapter One

Experience, Narrative, and Meaning: Encountering Bergen-Belsen

Far from being one code among many that a culture may utilize for endowing experience with meaning, narrative is a meta-code, a human universal on the basis of which transcultural messages about the nature of a shared reality can be transmitted.[1]

Hayden White

Experience is at once always already an interpretation *and* something that needs to be interpreted ... Experience is ... not the origin of our explanation, but that which we want to explain.[2]

Joan W. Scott

For years I've been trying to face up to this. But my mind is like a jigsaw puzzle with many of the pieces either so fuzzy they won't fit into place or are lost ... As I now ponder how to handle this, with the same shudder I have had for ensuing years, I find I'm able only to put swatches of scenes together – never the whole picture.[3]

Pilot Officer Ron Laidlaw, Royal Canadian Air Force

During the late afternoon of 15 April 1945, the Bergen-Belsen concentration camp was formally surrendered to the British Army. That same day a Canadian battalion arrived at the camp and provided medical assistance to the sick and starving inmates, as well as documented the crimes. In the ensuing weeks and months, Canadian military personnel worked alongside their British counterparts. Both nations sent doctors, nurses, padres, nutritional and agricultural experts, artists, photographers, along with many others, to assist survivors and to witness the crimes first-hand. By entering the Bergen-Belsen concentration camp, military personnel crossed into another realm and struggled with an assault on the senses. Many understood that they were important eye-witnesses to tragedy, yet they also felt the burden of relating what they had seen, smelled, touched, and heard to those back home.

This book reveals in detail, for the first time, the considerable Canadian involvement during the surrender and relief of the Bergen-Belsen concentration camp. In addition, the following chapters examine personal narratives of both British and Canadian military personnel as they responded to the dreadful situation at the camp. Employing an interdisciplinary approach that uses historical, cultural, and narratological analysis, this study will evaluate the form and content of the accounts and assess the impressions the experience made on British and Canadian personnel. The focus of this book is then twofold: to contribute to the historical understanding of the surrender and relief of Bergen-Belsen by revealing the – as of yet – untold Canadian involvement, and second, to survey the responses, both oral and written, of British and Canadian military personnel.

This introductory chapter aims to explicate the theoretical and methodological foundations of this work. Accordingly, this chapter is divided into five sections. The first section will outline how a variety of sources will be employed to illuminate the history of the British and Canadian involvement at Bergen-Belsen. The second section will reflect on the complex relationship between experience and narrative. How is language employed by individuals in order to represent experience? The third section will present the value and limitations of the autobiographical in the study of the past. How can scholars employ narratives of the past in scholarly work? The fourth section will assess the various forms and genres of the personal accounts analysed in this project. Do certain genres better lend themselves to experience than other forms? The fifth and final section will offer a meditation on the moral claims of these narratives.

Personal Accounts as Historical Sources

In writing about the past, evidence is critical. Historical researchers seek sources not only to illustrate but also to substantiate specific interpretations of events. The study of history takes the past as its object, and the knowledge subsequently gained must then be verified. And yet, historical narratives can never be definitive. The past is constantly being challenged, rewritten, amended, corrected, and supplemented. Indeed, the value of any historical account is often the result of recovering a view of the past that had long been lost, forgotten, or even ignored.

Without the aid of sources from the past, the writing of history could not take place. Historical sources or traces are thus essential to the practice of history. Whenever there is an event or an experience, there will be a trace, an imprint, or a remnant of that event. That which remains in the form of a trace can materialize in written form, perhaps later housed in an archive, or remembered, in the minds of individuals. Furthermore, people have a basic desire to narrate past experiences. Indeed, personal narratives are potential source materials for the historical researcher. And yet, as Dan Stone has observed, "the lack of dialogue between theorists of narrative and historians of the Holocaust ... remains striking."[4] While some historians view narratives of personal experience with doubt, quite often they become an indispensable source.

For instance, the Canadian involvement at Bergen-Belsen has never before been fully documented. Indeed, in the decades following the war the Holocaust was not a significant part of public discourse or scholarly study in Canada. Even in the Canadian Jewish community the Holocaust had, as a serious topic of discussion, a "delayed impact."[5] While hundreds of Canadians became involved at Bergen-Belsen in various ways, the vast majority have been ignored or relegated to a mere footnote in history books. While official documents such as military reports, war diaries, and operations record books (ORBs) have noted, albeit sparsely, that Canadians assisted at Bergen-Belsen, it is often the abundant personal responses that offer a fuller, more detailed account of events. Perhaps the Canadian involvement had not been previously detailed because some personnel left their units to assist at the camp or some were simply loaned to the British Army, and thus, it was not formally documented. Nevertheless, the sheer number of Canadian responses is immense. Therefore, how can we engage personal accounts in a serious, accurate, and attentive manner?

The work of Christopher Browning offers insight into how the historical researcher can employ testimony, first-hand accounts, in scholarly work. Browning has written numerous books that rely heavily on eyewitness testimony.[6] He is interested not only in the authenticity of an individual's testimony, but also in its factual accuracy. His methodology often involves gathering a sufficient mass of testimonies that can be weighed against one another.[7] Accordingly, when Canadians – as well as Britons – left their squadrons or units to assist at Bergen-Belsen, this was not always noted in the official ORB or war diary. Thus, when multiple accounts exist, experiences and encounters can be verified and corroborated with one another. Moreover, these accounts can be supplemented by records establishing the time and specific location of a battalion and unit. As the following chapter will reveal, for example, Royal Canadian Air Force squadrons, during the spring and summer of 1945, were scattered across the Lüneburg Heath. These squadron airbases were often only a few kilometres away from the Bergen-Belsen concentration camp.

Browning's approach involves looking at testimonies, "not in the collective singular but rather in the individual plural, not collective memory but rather collected memories."[8] As is sometimes the case, when other historical sources are lacking, such as reports and personnel lists, a researcher must then rely on first-hand accounts or eyewitness testimonies. Nevertheless, personal accounts must be handled with the same scrutiny and analysis as any other forms of evidence. Yehuda Bauer advises that "the principle should be that one testimony is interesting but not persuasive; two converging testimonies create a basis for consideration; ten converging testimonies are proof."[9] And while one can argue that even ten converging testimonies do not always offer incontrovertible proof, multiple accounts can be used to narrow the gap on empirical certainty. Indeed, one must recognize and assess the problems that can arise from employing first-hand accounts in any study of the past. This does not mean however, that first-hand accounts should be ignored.

Those cautious of employing personal narrative – such as autobiography, memoir, or other life-writing texts – in any objective study of the past often argue that it is because of the genre's perceived self-reflexive, unstable, fictive properties. Historians in particular are concerned with the gap involving the past and its representation, or as Paul Ricoeur has expressed, between "ce qui, un jour, fut."[10] Moreover, experiences, especially those involving particularly moving or crucial events, often motivate individuals to narration. People attempt to make sense of experience through language. Our encounter with the world and with each other is often mediated through language. Accordingly, personal accounts can expose critical encounters, revealing what individuals both thought and understood at certain points in time. These texts demonstrate not only what was known, but also what *could* be known at a given time. An individual's actions can be better grasped when we take into account how someone perceived his or her role in history.

The manner in which a historical event is remembered will inevitably be influenced by the responses to it. For historical researchers who ignore witnesses to an event, as Walter Laqueur notes, "however thorough their research and innovative their explanations, are missing one whole dimension."[11] Structure, style, substance, and strategy come together in shaping narratives of personal experience. What is needed then, in any serious study involving first-hand accounts, is a narratological critique. How an individual shapes, and is shaped by, narrative is a central focus of this study.

Experience and Narrative

Hayden White, a historian in the tradition of literary criticism, acknowledges that to focus on narrative is to think about the very nature of culture and about the spirit of humanity itself.[12] All narratives, to some degree, are dependent on culture. A narrative that recounts a real event can expose patterns of an individual's personal identity as well as something about their respective culture. Moreover, an individual does not remember in isolation. Sociologist Maurice Halbwachs observes that individuals evoke, distinguish, and focus their memories from the social framework of which they are a part.[13] In other words, individuals remember the past as members of a group. While narratives can be attributed to the individual, they are also socially and culturally determined. Being a subjective, internal aspect of human life, culture thus symbolically maps the external world. Individuals come to terms with themselves and their experiences as agents in history through culture.

The responses of British and Canadian men and women who encountered the Bergen-Belsen concentration camp during the spring and summer of 1945 reveal not only aspects of their own characters, but, when collected together, also reflect something of their particular viewpoints and communities. The testimony of Allied soldiers offers a perspective on the way individuals both think and act when confronted with incredible anguish. Consequently, their encounters, which can be viewed as an event, can lead us to contemplate the narratives of that event. In other words, examining multiple accounts of an event can reveal the narrative practices and meaning-making patterns by members from particular cultural groups. The men and women who assisted at Bergen-Belsen did so both as individuals and as members of different nations and militaries, as well as from a multitude of cultures and communities.

Our encounter with a past experience, and the manner in which we represent it, is always mediated in some way through memory, language, or narrative. We comprehend our past experiences from a culturally and historically specific present. Barbara Kirshenblatt-Gimblett recognizes the importance of mediation to the understanding of any form of representation, stressing that we pay attention not only to form and content, but also to the relations among creators, audiences, critics, as well as to the medium and genre.[14] Our vision of the past is much more than an isolated, personal act. There are significant layers to any vision of the past. We become subjects through experience, or, as Joan Scott suggests, "it is not individuals who have experience, but subjects who are constituted through experience."[15] As subjects, an individual's experience is shaped in terms of how one views their status and identity in society.

Language and narrative are fundamental to our relationship with experience. Edward Sapir demonstrates that people are "very much at the mercy of the particular language which has become the medium of expression for their society ... We see and hear and otherwise experience very largely as we do because the language habits of our community predispose certain choices of interpretation."[16] In other words, individuals are shaped by and subsequently draw from the culture or cultures they inhabit whenever they communicate. For example, doctors learn the languages, metaphors, and narratives produced by medical institutions; this medical discourse becomes a manner in which doctors both understand themselves and their experiences. The stories they tell, the narratives they offer, are invariably shaped by these discursive domains.[17] But what exactly do narratives communicate? What can they reflect? The work of three scholars – Hayden White, David Carr, and Paul Ricoeur – provide a number of insights regarding the value of narrative.

Hayden White considers that, to some extent, all forms of narrative are fictional. For White, a narrative is "always a figurative account, an allegory."[18] His work is significant because he reminds historians of the narrative dimensions of their work. Indeed, the *writing* of history certainly belongs to the genre of narrative. Accordingly, historical narratives share commonalities with fictional narratives, such as emplotment and the presentation of the temporal character of experience. White recognizes that historians deal with events that are located specifically in time and space and which are clearly discernible, while imaginative writers can work with both real and imagined events.

White is at his most controversial when, moving beyond the similarities between the two, he assimilates history with fiction. He refuses to concede the difference between knowledge gained through historical research and the knowledge brought about by fiction. He calls historical narratives "verbal fictions, the contents of which are as much invented as found and the forms of which have more in common with their counterparts in literature than they have with those in the sciences."[19] For White, the very idea that the sequences of real events are contained in the narratives we tell is nothing more than "wishes, daydreams, reveries."[20] As a result, while historical narratives are still able to convey a form of truth, White views them as a type of fiction.

In well-known debates concerning historical objectivity and truth, historian Carlos Ginzburg confronted White in conferences in 1989 and 1990, and then again in print in Saul Friedländer's edited collection titled *Probing the Limits of Representation: Nazism and the "Final Solution"* (1992). Ginzburg charges White with absolute relativism and argues that even "just one witness" can move us closer to the reality of historical truth.[21] In an essay in the same volume, White looks for a compromise to this charge of "relativism." In the search for historical truth, White comments that, as accounts of factual events, "competing narratives can be assessed, criticized, and ranked on the basis of their fidelity to the factual record, their comprehensiveness, and the coherence of whatever arguments they may contain."[22] Thus, White concedes that historical events differ from fictional ones and that the former can be evaluated through documentation and records. Nevertheless, he insists that while narrative accounts can contain factual statements, they will also invariably contain poetic or rhetoric elements.[23]

Philosopher David Carr presents a differing view from White's and one that unites life and narrative. While White emphasizes a discontinuity between life, its real events, and narrative, Carr stresses the continuity between them.[24] Theorists like White argue that historical and fictional narratives are distinct from the real world they claim to represent. This, they maintain, is due to the particular form of narrative itself. Narratives in this view are distortions of reality. Conversely, Carr considers narrative the principal manner in which an individual organizes experience. While White insists that real events do not have an inherent narrative structure, Carr suggests that "narrative structure is not 'imposed' on anything. It constitutes the principle of organization for our action and experience ... it is the structure of our very being."[25] In Carr's analysis, real events, in terms of both experience and action, are narrative in nature. Therefore, narrative encompasses all human existence, in the way we experience time and in how we relate to one another.

According to Carr, historical and fictional narratives should be considered as "extensions and configurations" of reality.[26] Narrative is not then an exaggeration of reality, but an accompaniment to it. "[Stories] are told in being lived and lived in being told," he writes. "The actions and sufferings of life can be viewed as a process of telling ourselves stories, listening to those stories, and acting them out or living them through."[27] Our actions are based on the way we narrate our experiences and, consequently, our lives. Our relationship with time in our present draws its significance from the way we think of the past and the future. Thus, Carr wants us to grasp that narrative is at the "structure of our very being."[28]

In his three-volume *Time and Narrative* (1985), philosopher Paul Ricoeur recognizes and integrates some of White's insights, but, like Carr, stresses that life is not alien to narrative. In the debate between the discontinuous (White) and continuous nature (Carr) of narrative, Ricoeur appears to fall somewhere in between. His work highlights the connections between narrative and life, but he also acknowledges the differences. Thus, for Ricoeur, it is not a case of either/or; rather, it is a situation of and/but in the contemplation of life and narrative. In other words, there are continuities and discontinuities between life and narrative.

A gap will always exist between the past as it happened and its representation in the present. Ricoeur acknowledges the possibility of narrowing this gap between narration and action in historical narratives. He emphasizes that there is a difference between discussing the past "as" it happened, to which the historian strives, and "as if" it happened, which is the domain of the imaginative writer. While historical narratives can never offer a completely precise account of the past, it is closer to the real world "as" it happened because it normally deals with claims that can be measured and verified. If it were otherwise, there would be no way to repudiate Holocaust deniers. "If we do not resolutely maintain the difference between history and fiction," Ricoeur insists, "[it] is an insult to the dead."[29] Therefore, while sharing commonalities, the intention of history is to offer a type of knowledge distinct from literature.

In addition, and similar to the analysis of Carr, Ricoeur recognizes narrative as a part of our being, an element of our lived existence. "Time becomes human time," he remarks, "to the extent that it is organized after the manner of a narrative; narrative, in turn, is meaningful to the extent that it portrays the features of temporal existence."[30] Thus, narrative is the manner in which individuals endeavour to comprehend the intricate relationship between time and life.

In response to Carr, Ricoeur does not place narrative, life, and history for that matter, on the same plain. Indeed, Carr's continuity thesis makes it difficult to claim that there are narratives that recount real events. Or as Richard Kearney succinctly puts it, "If *life*, *history* and *story* are placed on the same narrative continuum, how do we answer the revisionists that our narrative is not just *any* narrative but one which makes a claim to truth, which tells it as it really was?"[31] This presents a dilemma that also challenged White. In response to this predicament, Kearney points to what he calls a "trans-narrative truth" claim, something that would emerge from a "plurality of narrative interpretations."[32]

For a "trans-narrative truth," and drawing from both the theories of Carr and Ricoeur, Kearney offers three criteria in order to orient and anchor claims to historical truth. First, he points to "narratives referring back to prior narratives."[33] All historical narratives are mediated to some degree by narratives of witnesses to the events described. Historical researchers look to verify their claims with first-hand documents. What is more, personal narratives can, in turn, be measured and compared with other first-hand accounts to the same event. Kearney's second criterion is narratives corresponding with facts.[34] Personal narratives, stories of real events, need to be supported, wherever possible, with verifiable facts. For example, narratives that falsely claim that there were gas chambers at Bergen-Belsen can be compared with empirical evidence, such as camp plans and maps, reports, and other accounts, which prove otherwise. Stories and empirical evidence are thus both essential in uncovering historical truth. Finally, the third criterion Kearney elicits is what he calls the "thing," which is that which defies description and comprehension. More specifically, Kearney suggests that this brings forth a "move from a first-order reference to 'facts' and a second-order reference to 'life-stories' to a third-order reference to a reality deeper than words."[35] In the context of Bergen-Belsen and the Holocaust, this might mean somehow acknowledging the great challenge of adequately narrating a horror that defies any cogent, rational understanding.

The work of White, Carr, and Ricoeur helps us to appreciate the relationship between narrative, experience, and history. White's work illustrates the importance of narrative to the writing of history. However, and as Ricoeur discusses, recognizing the importance of narrative to the enterprise of historical writing does not mean that history and literature are the same. As Sara Horowitz advises, "Without narrative, history becomes unknowable; but when narrative displaces history, the real events become inaccessible."[36] Ricoeur has gone to great lengths to show the ways history is distinct from literature. Carr's theory, which corresponds with some of Ricoeur's work, stresses the importance of narrative to all human experiences and suggests how narrative negotiates our way of being in and relating to time. Narrative is a record of our lived existence. It is now necessary to review the various forms personal narratives can take and that are available as source material for the historical researcher. For our purposes, the generic term "personal narrative" will be used in broad reference to the different types of accounts discussed below. Therefore, personal narratives are accounts – both written and oral – offered by participants who have first-hand experience of the events under discussion.

The Fictional, the Autobiographical, and the Historical

While many military personnel from the British and Canadian forces did not talk in any way about their encounters at the Bergen-Belsen concentration camp, thousands of them did in fact discuss it. Thus, the historical researcher is left with a myriad of oral and written accounts. Some of the men and women documented their experiences as they were happening, while others waited years, and, in some cases, decades, before revealing their thoughts and feelings about the camp. Therefore, it is important to recognize the time that has passed in the telling and the different forms taken in these written and oral accounts.

The personal narratives discussed in the following chapters can and should be classified as autobiographical or life-writing texts. The first-hand accounts concerning Bergen-Belsen that are available to researchers include primarily journals-diaries, letters, memoirs, and oral interviews. All can be considered life-"writing" texts and are examples of narrative in different forms. According to Marlene Kadar, life writing is "more or less" autobiographical and embraces narratives "by an author who does not continuously write about someone else, and who also does not pretend to be absent from the text ... life writing is a way of seeing."[37] Accordingly, life writing is a particular type of expression, distinct from both historical and fictional narratives, but sharing some commonalities between the two forms.

German philosopher Wilhelm Dilthey, in his work concerning historical methodology, underscores the significance of autobiographical writing for the study of culture and history. Dilthey considers autobiography as "the most direct expression of reflection about life."[38] He contends that autobiography is highly selective and that one's view of the past is inevitably influenced by the present. Instead of viewing this as a distinct weakness, Dilthey views this as the potency of autobiography. "The person who seeks the connecting threads in the history of his life," he reveals, "has already, from different points of view, created a coherence in that life which he is now putting into words."[39] Through autobiography and other life-writing forms, the individual reflects on and evaluates the past, which can bring a meaning and coherence to it.

Like the historian who contemplates the past in search for meaning, the autobiographer considers the events he or she has experienced in an attempt to gain insight about existence. This can have implications for the historical researcher. Individuality and historical understanding depend on each other. "Therefore," Dilthey explains, "autobiography can, ultimately, widen out into a historical portrait; this is only limited but also made meaningful by being based on experience, through which the self and its relation to the world are comprehended. The reflection of a person about himself remains the standard and basis for understanding history."[40] For Dilthey, autobiography, like self-reflection, is an ongoing process. It is always incomplete, since the individual cannot remember his or her birth and will not be around to respond to his or her death. Nevertheless, Dilthey concludes that reflecting on the self is at the root of historical consciousness.

Dilthey's insights on autobiography have influenced a wide range of scholars. James Olney, who counts Dilthey as a source, insists that autobiography can offer knowledge of what man has been or what man is.[41] Rather than looking for names, dates, and places from an autobiographical account, Olney suggests that what we really seek is a "characteristic way of perceiving, or organizing, and of understanding, an individual way of feeling and expressing."[42] How did British and Canadian military personnel "see" Bergen-Belsen and its victims? What is being communicated in these innumerable accounts? Indeed, a writer reflecting on the self strives for coherence out of the instability and confusion of past events.

Two relatively recent works of scholarship illustrate the value of autobiographical texts for the historical researcher. In *Artful Histories* (1996), David McCooey contends that autobiography is much closer to history than it is to fiction and thus can be a valuable source for historians. A major difference between fiction and autobiography is that the former cannot be empirically verified. "Autobiography, however, is an inherently discursive act of writing," McCooey remarks. "Like other forms of history, it is a form of testimony and as such it is not autonomous the way fiction and poetry are ... [it is] open to all the checks and limitations of testimony."[43] Since an autobiographer, like a historian, can lie or distort the truth, this is precisely what separates both genres from fiction. Consequently, McCooey underlines that, like historians, autobiographers become responsible for the points they make in their works.[44]

In *History, Historians, and Autobiography* (2005), Jeremy D. Popkin acknowledges some of McCooey's insights but also strives to distinguish autobiography from history. He observes that autobiographies offer a distinct perspective concerning how individuals see themselves and grasp past experiences. He agrees with McCooey that both history and autobiography aspire to shape the past into a comprehensible narrative.[45] Moreover, both genres claim to recount real events, and neither can be entirely absorbed as works of fiction.

However, Popkin, who is a historian, also sees important distinguishing characteristics between history and autobiography. According to Popkin, autobiography is not "bound by history's requirement for documentation and its emphasis on collective, as opposed to individual, experience, and since no autobiographer can tell his or her story all the way to the end, autobiography has an open-ended character that separates it from both history and fiction."[46] Thus, understanding these differences is paramount for historical researchers who employ autobiography and autobiographical texts in their work.

Genres of the Autobiographical

Autobiographical or life-writing texts appear in a variety of forms and genres. Sidonie Smith and Julia Watson remind us that the term autobiography has been highly contested due to its broad historical reach and the sheer range of life-writing genres and practices.[47] For our purposes, an autobiographical text does not necessarily mean an autobiography. As Smith and Watson note, autobiographical or life-writing narratives are a "historically situated practice of self-representation" in which "narrators selectively engage their lived experience through personal storytelling."[48] Consequently, it will be necessary to briefly examine the conventions that diaries, letters, memoirs, and oral interviews typically follow. While the following chapters focus more on the content than on the form of personal narratives, it is necessary to keep in mind that each genre operates within certain restrictions and boundaries.

A number of personal accounts to be examined appear in the form of journal entries or diaries. Philippe Lejeune, who does not, incidentally, distinguish journals from diaries, has spent much of his career focusing on the practice of diary writing. His work has helped differentiate diaries from other forms of autobiographical writing.[49] Typically, entries in diaries appear chronologically and can demonstrate patterns of what individuals value in life. However, the reflections within often focus on specific moments in time. Moreover, as Sandrine Arons demonstrates, while diaries are generally unedited, diarists are often aware that their writings may be read posthumously.[50] Karl J. Weintraub comments that the diary is "governed by the very fact that a day has its end."[51] The diarist does not have the benefit of extended hindsight and does not know what tomorrow will bring.

In addition, the author of a diary often writes in the very moment that the events, which are being reflected upon, are taking place. Similar to letter writing and immediate eyewitness reports, the diarist often writes from the perspective that action can still affect change concerning the event being described. James Young highlights that this type of writing does not necessarily call out for "reflection or contemplation of the events' meaning (even as they suggested meaning) so much as they are demands for immediate action and justice."[52] Diary and journal entries, while generally written privately and without much consideration of outside sources, are thus more "faithful" in their recounting. It is then a document of "dailiness": a written record of the emotional reaction of an individual's everyday experiences. Furthermore, due to its proximity to the events being recounted, diaries can be restricted by inadequate or inaccurate knowledge of those events or by an idiosyncratic viewpoint.

Letters, like diary entries, are documents frequently written in the moment being reflected upon. Accordingly, opinions, thoughts, and feelings can shift widely over a collection of letters. Gathered together, letters can reveal patterns of attitudes, thoughts, and feelings, not only about the self but also about others. As Robert McGill notes, letters are "both artifacts of existence and commentaries upon it."[53] The correspondence is generally, although not always, directed or addressed to someone else. Thus, there is often an intended audience in mind and letters usually remain unpublished. In addition, letters are useful, and particularly for the following chapters, in establishing the where and the when from which the subject is writing.

Janet Malcolm observes that letters constitute the "great fixative of experience ... they are the fossils of feeling."[54] Thus, the fissure between experience and text is typically narrowed in letter writing. When a letter writer recounts a recent occurrence, the memory of the experience does not have the opportunity to ripen. As McGill explains, "a distinguishing feature of letters is their potential for proximity to the life-events they narrate – thus their conventional claim to be 'true' to those experiences. In this respect they share a close kinship with the diary form. The further convention of dating them foregrounds their occasional quality and confers upon them the status of events in their own right."[55] Of course, immediacy does not necessarily imply that letter writing will provide a closer image of the event itself. Nevertheless, letters do present the subject's initial responses, unrefined emotions, and prime thoughts.

In contrast, memoir writing is characteristically an edited narrative of an individual's past experiences. Memoirs are more frequently published than letters and diaries. There is often a larger gap between the event and writing in a memoir than, for example, in a diary or letter. A memoir is not, as Mary Jean Corbett posits, "an autobiographical text that tells a story about a centered self, but one in which the writing subject recounts stories of others and events or movements in which she and/or her other subjects have taken part."[56] Therefore, it is less "of the moment" and based more on lengthy retrospection. In addition, memoirists can employ narrative devices that are often associated with novelists, such as point of view, character, structure, and voice.

The memoirist has travelled beyond the experience being reflected upon, and knows its outcome. The writer can consult historical sources, which might aid in understanding. For example, a soldier writing about Bergen-Belsen in a letter home or in a diary entry would not use the term "Holocaust," a word not commonly employed until the 1960s after the Adolf Eichmann trial. Conversely, the scope and conceptualization of the "Holocaust" would be available to the memoirist writing decades after the event. As Weintraub brings to light, "the fact once in the making can now be seen together with the fact in its result. By this superimposition of the completed fact, the fact in the making acquires a meaning it did not possess before. The meaning of the past is intelligible and meaningful in terms of the present understanding; it is thus with all historical understanding."⁵⁷ Memoirists bring with them facts, knowledge, and historical understandings not accessible at the time of the experience under consideration.

Oral accounts – also referred to as oral histories or oral narratives – which were once considered suspect and highly controversial, are now a widely used source for scholars. The eminent Holocaust historian Raul Hilberg had long been cautious and at times even critical of the use of oral accounts as evidence in historical research. In reference to establishing the historical record of Nazi policies and methods of persecution, Hilberg states that German documents were more reliable than postwar memories.⁵⁸ Over time, many historians have been willing to employ testimonies in their work, notably Christopher Browning, Omer Bartov, and Israel Gutman. Browning affirms the value of testimony in historical research, as long as it is used carefully and met with critical analysis.⁵⁹ Any thorough historical account of the Holocaust requires a recognition and employment of the numerous oral accounts available.

Indeed, the sheer number of oral accounts concerning the Holocaust is enormous. While the vast majority of oral responses dealing with the Holocaust are rightfully survivor accounts, there are significant numbers of liberator accounts available. The accounts of Allied military personnel were among the first attempts at a response by those not themselves victims of the camps. Predominately, these accounts are conducted through the interview process. Thus, the interviewee and the interviewer both have a role in shaping the narrative of the account.

Henry Greenspan comments that oral accounts are not only oral history, but also oral psychology and oral narratology.⁶⁰ Even when a response departs from verifiable fact, it can still be a repository of meaning, revealing the teller's insecurities, thoughts, and feelings. Moreover, the accounts are not always only oral, but can also be visual, such as in video interviews. Thus, while the listener has to focus not only on tone, cadence, and interruptions in speech, one might also have to be aware of visual cues, such as performance, gesture, and emotion. Julia Creet draws attention to the fact that gesture can be both a "historical act and a reenactment in the present."⁶¹ Thus, oral accounts are quite distinct from diaries, letters, and memoirs, and yet each offers the reader or listener a meaning of some kind in each of the narrative's point, purpose, and direction.

Furthermore, oral responses can certainly be used as a historical source. Like any source, it must be examined on its own terms. Oral accounts should not necessarily be considered defective when compared to other sources. Written documentation, sources most historians regularly rely on, can certainly be susceptible to deception. For instance, there is the well-known case of the Wannsee Protocol, whereby the minutes of the meeting discussing the annihilation of European Jews was distorted at the behest of SS-Obergruppenführer Reinhard Heydrich. At his trial, Adolf Eichmann testified to how the protocol was written and altered. His oral account ultimately revealed more of what was actually discussed at the meeting.[62] For many, the oral account exposed greater, more precise details than the written report. It is, of course, always possible that a letter or an oral testimony can be relied upon as one would depend on a formal report or document. As Jacques Derrida reminds, "Every text participates in one or several genres, there is no genreless text; there is always a genre and genres, yet such participation never amounts to belonging."[63] In other words, the forms or genres examined above not only have disparate elements from one another, but also share similar qualities. Each form reflects on the past and can offer knowledge or information pertaining to that past. Nevertheless, the historical researcher must observe all sources with concern and a degree of scepticism.

The personal narratives in the following chapters will be used, to a limited extent, for their empirical value. Conversely, the accounts will be examined more for the meanings and understandings they share about the past. As previously mentioned, when soldiers and medical personnel left their posts to assist at Bergen-Belsen, this was not always noted in official war diaries and reports. Thus, multiple personal accounts can help empirically verify when and why groups of men or women assisted at the camp at certain points in time. Nevertheless, the accounts will be relied upon, less for what they empirically demonstrate, than for the patterns of meaning they exhibit. The final section of this chapter will consider what the accounts can potentially offer the researcher.

Empirical and Moral Claims in Narrative

The experiences of British and Canadian military personnel at Bergen-Belsen are not empirically knowable. Facts, names, and dates can certainly be verified, and some of the sequence of events emplotted in the narratives can be checked and assessed. However, what happened on the ground can never be fully revealed and detailed in any narrative; moments will be forgotten, discarded, or purposefully ignored. Each individual who narrates his or her experience will select and reflect upon distinct parts, making connections to form patterns of meaning. Thus, we are left with parts empirical and parts representing a meaning or a moral. As Sissela Bok recognizes, "Autobiographical accounts constitute, in part, empirical and moral claims that individuals stake out about their lives and, in the process, about the lives of others they have known."[64] The men and women who shaped personal narratives in response to the situation at Bergen-Belsen did so for specific reasons. Some responded immediately, while others remained silent for decades until they were finally provoked to communicate. The following chapters investigate what these messages, these moral claims, are attempting to convey.

In the understanding of life, and therefore of lived experience, Wilhelm Dilthey emphasizes three categories of thought: value, purpose, and meaning. He associates meaning with the past, value with the present, and purpose with the future.[65] When we look back on the past through our memories, moments emerge and become identified as patterns from which we draw meaning. The present is experienced through feeling, which we then value positively or negatively in light of our subsequent realities. When confronting the future, our projective attitudes determine our purpose. Accordingly, since memory is a part of history and meaning relates to memory, then of Dilthey's three categories of thought, "meaning" is significant for the grasping of historical thought. Meaning embraces and arranges what we value and pursue in life.

These three categories of thought are certainly moral categories. Dilthey demonstrates how meaning could unite the different parts of life to its whole. He calls this the "connectedness of life."[66] Individuals grasp the meaning of past moments through their memory. The "connectedness of life," then, is equivalent to a life history. Accordingly, a life history is given its shape through narration. We survey and make judgments of events from our past through our narratives. Autobiography and autobiographical texts are thus communicative of one's historicity. In other words, the self grasps itself as it passes through history.

Narrative, as Paul Ricoeur puts forward, is the "first laboratory of moral judgment."[67] A narrative is always ethical or moral to some degree. Whenever a Canadian or British soldier sat down to write or speak to someone about his or her experiences at Bergen-Belsen, he did so from a particular point of view and for a specific reason. Accordingly, all narratives require some direction or motive for being given. The experiences at and observations about Bergen-Belsen were shared because the individual wanted the narrative to make a difference. The following chapters explore what differences the narrators were trying (are trying) to make through their first-hand accounts.

For many of the Allied military personnel working at Bergen-Belsen, the experience, in a variety of ways, changed them as individuals. Thus, the stories they told were not only about what happened, but also about what happened to them in the face of a momentous event. As Popkin notes, "Only narrative can resolve the paradox of how an individual or group can be seen as the same even as it changes over time."[68] As the following chapters will reveal, some personnel abandoned belief in god or religion, while others strove to become politically and socially active. Others delved into philosophy or returned to religious school searching for answers. For some the horror was incorporated, repeatedly, in future works of expression. Thus, Bergen-Belsen became a turning point in their lives. For a number of Allied personnel, memories of the war became organized as "before Bergen-Belsen" and "after Bergen-Belsen."

In *The Ethics of Memory* (2002), Avishai Margalit argues that acts of extreme evil can be defined as those that assault the very foundations of morality. Consequently, these assaults on morality should not be forgotten and ought to be documented.[69] In other words, crimes *against* humanity should be remembered *by* humanity. Thus, we are obliged to remember and, more importantly, to think in order to prevent deniers and revisionists from rewriting history with false accounts and to stop those from attempting to distort the collective memory. We see this responsibility from eyewitnesses to Bergen-Belsen in numerous examples. For example, Canadian airman Clifford Robb spoke to CFTO News in 1985 to confront the revisionism of Ernst Zündel. Moreover, in 1990 Lieutenant-Colonel Mervin Mirsky challenged Holocaust denier David Irving at a public lecture in Ottawa. For these two men, and for so many others, their stories (and photographs and films) serve to protect historical truth and counter revisionism.

It will also be important to remember that individuals often belong to more than one group. As Carr remarks, "it is clear that many of the moral conflicts and dilemmas facing individuals have their origin in the individual's sense of belonging to different groups at the same time."[70] Indeed, the moral claims in the personal narratives under investigation often emerge from a sense of belonging to multiple groups. For example, Jewish chaplain Leslie Hardman of the British Army recalls his commanding officer telling him that Bergen-Belsen held many of "his" people. He ultimately became an intermediary between the survivors and the British Army. He continuously felt the tensions, the demands, and the pulls from either side. His narrative speaks from being a member of the group of inmates, while at the same time – as a healthy, well-fed chaplain in the British Army – of not being one of them.

British and Canadian military personnel successfully carried out their assignments of crossing the Rhine River and descending on the Lüneburg Heath. However, dealing with the atrocities at the Bergen-Belsen concentration camp was never something for which they could have prepared. Any vision or plan of how the remainder of the war would progress was immediately thwarted. "In life ... we are always under certain constraints," writes Alasdair MacIntyre, "we enter upon a stage which we did not design and we find ourselves part of an action that was not of our making."[71] Passing through the gates of Bergen-Belsen was, for all who experienced it, to enter upon a "stage" of extreme violence and inhumanity. How could the scenes at Bergen-Belsen be described? How could they be explained?

Many Allied military personnel who attempted to describe or explain Bergen-Belsen felt overwhelmed by the horror. Even after months of intense fighting, and enduring all of war's brutalities, Allied forces could not be prepared for what they were to see at Bergen-Belsen. Entering the camp, they crossed into another realm and struggled with an assault on the senses. Countless witnesses repeated similar sentiments: Bergen-Belsen defied language and was simply beyond the mind's comprehension. Indeed, many encountered tremendous difficulties in finding fitting words to describe both the confusion they felt and the atrocities they witnessed. And yet, this does not necessarily mean that their narratives are empty and without value. While they struggled to adequately *detail* and *explain* what they saw, their responses do *mean* something. To find out what that something is, is the central aim of these chapters. Men and women took pen or pencil in hand, sat in front of typewriters or computers, retold stories to friends and family members, spoke in lecture halls or in front of television cameras, all because they had messages to share with audiences. Unearthing these messages illustrates the burden so many had in relating what they had seen, smelled, touched, and heard. "The representation of history as a constructed subject," explains Suzanne Langlois, "makes possible the integration of all the sources that contribute to sustaining a vision of the past."[72] In the weeks before and after the end of the war in Europe, the stories that news organizations and military personnel told to the world helped "sustain a vision" of the Holocaust. Their impressions aided in the shaping of public perception of the crimes.

"Where, in any account of reality," White remarks, "narrativity is present, we can be sure that morality or a moralizing impulse is present too."[73] Moral claims bestow meaning on both the past and the present, as well as help guide future directions. Personal narratives that recount real events are an attempt to bring a coherence and sense to the mind. Those who wrote to remember and warn of the tragedy at Bergen-Belsen did so in the face of pain and death. The author of the autobiographical, McCooey insists, "writes not only to relive, but to confront death: his own and other people's ... Fictional characters die fictionally, people die in actual fact."[74] It is to this confrontation at Bergen-Belsen that we now turn.

Chapter Two

The Rhine, the Heath, the Wire

It just happened in the course of our advance that we came across it. Nobody set out to liberate a concentration camp. So the word "liberator" is a misnomer, in a sense. Either we were all liberators or we were not liberators, but nobody specifically spent his or her time thinking, "How am I going to liberate a concentration camp?" First of all, we hardly knew that they existed. I didn't.[1]

      Alan Rose, 7th Armoured Division; former executive vice-president
             of the Canadian Jewish Congress

The deliverance of inmates from concentration and extermination camps in Europe was not an Allied military objective during the Second World War. The discovery of the camps was generally inconsequential from the perspective of securing military goals. Accordingly, the story of a concentration camp fits awkwardly within the context of military affairs. Indeed, the significance of the camps, and the Holocaust as a whole, relates more to morality, psychology, law, medical care, and politics than to military operations. And yet, those still clinging to life in the camps were released from their miseries because Allied armies liberated Europe and not because of any intentional aim to bring to an end Hitler's camp system. Thus, in order to grasp how British and Canadian forces descended upon the Bergen-Belsen concentration camp in April 1945 and in the months beyond, one must examine their military operations and formations.

 The beginning of the end of the war in Germany, and therefore in western Europe, commenced during the last week of March 1945 with the crossing of the Rhine River.[2] Operation Plunder, the name given to this final major military operation in northwest Europe, was unlike any other Allied assault on the continent. The aim of the Allied invasions of France, Belgium, and the Netherlands, for example, was to liberate; the objective of the Allied armies in Germany was not to emancipate, but to vanquish. Operation Plunder involved 21 Army Group, which comprised the Second British Army, the First Canadian Army, and the Ninth United States Army. Less than seven weeks after the commencement of Operation Plunder, the war in Europe was over. It was only a few short weeks after crossing the Rhine River that British and Canadian forces liberated the Bergen-Belsen concentration camp.

The topic of liberation, and, in particular, the issue of liberating units, can be both perplexing and contentious. As this chapter will demonstrate, there were a number of Allied divisions operating in northwest Germany in April 1945. Moreover, units often fell under different commands depending on both need and location. Indeed, several units often found themselves descending upon similar geographic areas and at times crossing divisional lines of battle. Thus, this could produce congestion in spots, and, for scholars, only adds to the confusion.

The method of formally identifying liberating units in the United States might be illustrative. In 1985 the US Army Center of Military History and the United States Holocaust Memorial Council began working together in order to properly identify and acknowledge American army divisions involved in the liberation of concentration camps during the Second World War. They established three main criteria for recognizing liberators in the United States. First, since many camps were liberated by smaller units, subordinate to a division, the numbers can be great. Thus, to simplify and avoid confusion, credit is assigned to the parent division of the respective lower-echelon unit.[3] As such, and due to the possible involvement of several smaller units, it is feasible for two or more divisions to be acknowledged as liberators of a camp. Second, recognition is assigned not only to the first division to reach a camp. It can also include any division that arrived at the same camp (or camp complex) within forty-eight hours of the initial division.[4] Finally, evidentiary basis for a liberating group must come from a primary source found in unit records or other contemporary documents.[5] Guidelines state that first-hand accounts and secondary sources alone are insufficient. Therefore, historical accuracy requires primary source evidence.

As this and other chapters demonstrate, several units encountered Bergen-Belsen within the first forty-eight hours, many of which came from different divisions. For example, a company from the 1st Canadian Parachute Battalion, which was part of the 6th Airborne Division, encountered Bergen-Belsen on 15 April 1945. Many other units, detachments, and personnel from a wide variety of divisions also became involved, including the 11th Armoured Division, the 7th Armoured Division, the 15th (Scottish) Division, as well as the Guards Armoured Division. While this book attempts to expand our knowledge of the Allied involvement at Bergen-Belsen, it does not try to make any final determination as to who is singularly deserving of the title of camp liberator. As Alan Rose suggests in the quote that opens this chapter, it is essential to consider that it was the collective Allied victory in Europe that made it possible for Hitler's brutal camp system to come to an end. It is also important to remember that there was never any overarching Allied plan to liberate concentration or extermination camps in Europe. While Bergen-Belsen was formally surrendered, other camps were regularly happened upon during the Allied advance across Europe.

The purpose of this chapter is to provide a general overview of British and Canadian military movements from the commencement of Operation Plunder, through to the takeover of Bergen-Belsen, as well as to indicate the locations of other military units that ultimately became involved at the camp in the ensuing weeks and months. Thousands of British personnel became involved at the camp. Moreover, well over a thousand Canadians encountered Bergen-Belsen, which has never before been detailed. The focus will be on the British and Canadian forces and not on the Americans, who were also involved in the Rhine crossing, and only on the divisions, units, battalions, squadrons, and wings that became involved at the camp. Thus, this is not a comprehensive account of Operation Plunder. After crossing the Rhine River, thousands of Allied military personnel descended upon Bergen-Belsen. Accordingly, the objective of this chapter is to discover how these men and women came to find themselves at this ghastly concentration camp, one that stood deep beyond the dark pinewoods surrounded by silver birches on the Lüneburg Heath in northwest Germany.

The Rhine: Operation Plunder

The Rhine River flows from the Swiss Alps and, 1,200 kilometres later, empties into the North Sea. It is a trade route, a natural border, and has been used as a defensive barrier in military battles. Hence, it is a symbolic boundary and one of the most vital rivers in Europe. During the late winter of 1944, the Rhine became Nazi Germany's last natural defence. For the Western Allies to gain access into central Germany and end the war in Europe, they had to cross the Rhine. It was only after crossing this mighty river that Allied military personnel, and subsequently, the general public in the West, became acutely aware of the horrors of the Third Reich.

Armies and units in 21 Army Group, commanded by British Field Marshal Bernard Montgomery, were to cross the Rhine during the last week of March 1945 at the towns of Rees and Wesel. In terms of its scale and complication, the operation rivalled the Normandy invasion. While Operation Plunder was the overall name given to the Rhine crossing, each major element had its own code word. Operation Varsity was the massive airborne operation; Operations Turnscrew and Torchlight were the assault river crossing; Operation Wigeon was the attack on Wesel, while Operation Flashlight referred to the American crossing. An additional operation, code-named Archway, was conducted by the Special Air Service (SAS) and was intended to provide supplementary support for the Rhine crossing. Men from 1 and 2SAS, referred to as "Frankforce," operating under Colonel Brian Franks, were to patrol in advance of ground forces after crossing the river at Wesel.[6]

Destined to be the last great battle of the war in northwest Europe, the British Second Army commanded the crossing. The Rhine River stretches 300 yards between Rees and Wesel, where the assault was to ultimately take place. A force of British, Canadian, and American military personnel was ordered to carry out the operation across the Rhine, north of the Ruhr. In terms of objectives, the Second Army was to assault the Rhine and establish a bridgehead between Rees and Wesel. Meanwhile, the First Canadian Army was to carry out feint attacks along the river.

Prior to the crossing on the night of 23 March 1945, the Royal Air Force (RAF) and the Royal Canadian Air Force (RCAF) commenced aggressive flying missions. The RAF's Bomber Command carried out devastating air raids on Wesel, overwhelming this small German garrison town.[7] Earlier that day, Spitfires from 126 Wing, RCAF, flew anti-flak missions, attacking German positions ahead of the river assault.[8] On the evening of 23 March 1945, troops from 1 Commando Brigade crossed the Rhine at Wesel.

As a result of the advances on the ground, paratroopers from Allied airborne divisions could now engage. The following morning, 24 March 1945, Operation Varsity began in earnest. The airborne assault involved the 6th British Airborne and the 17th US Airborne Divisions. The former comprised both British and Canadian battalions. The 6th Airborne's commitment to this operation was the 3rd and 5th Parachute

Brigades and the Airlanding Brigade. Indeed, it was to be the 3rd Parachute Brigade that was to lead the operation by dropping on the northwest corner of the Diersfordter Wald, a forest on the outskirts northeast of Wesel. The 3rd Parachute Brigade, commanded by Brigadier James Hill, comprised the 1st Canadian Parachute Battalion, as well as the 8th and 9th Parachute Battalions. It was a unique outfit in that it was the war's only mixed brigade of British and Canadian troops.[9]

As Allied airborne divisions made their preparations, the skies overlooking the Rhine River were being closely watched. On the morning of 24 March 1945, at an observation post near Xanten, Prime Minister Winston Churchill, along with Britain's Field Marshals Alan Brooke and Bernard Montgomery and Canada's General Henry Crerar, awaited the commencement of Operation Varsity, the single largest airborne lift operation in history.[10] At 0950 hours these four men watched as two Allied airborne divisions appeared overhead. Soon parachutists descended across the river. Operation Varsity was now underway.

The 6th Airborne Division dropped into an area only six miles long and five miles wide. Nearly 2,000 men from 3rd Parachute Brigade alone descended near the Diersfordter Wald. Their objectives were to move through the woodland, clearing and securing the area as they progressed. The brigades continued their assignments of taking hold of the commanding ground and hindering the arrival of any enemy reinforcements into the area. By the late morning of 24 March 1945, most of 6th Airborne Division's objectives had been met.[11]

Tactical responsibility for the entire area covered under Operation Plunder was given to 83 Group, consisting of both British and Canadian wings. It was 83 Group that was responsible for maintaining air superiority over the battlefield. Typhoons from 143 Wing, RCAF, for example, bombed gun positions near Bienen, allowing units to move towards Emmerich. Strong coverage and air superiority allowed Allied troops to continue to advance more rapidly and deeper into Germany.

During the second day of Operation Varsity, 25 March 1945, and all through the night, heavy Allied traffic, coming from the Rhine, began passing through the area secured by 3rd Parachute Brigade.[12] The 6th Airborne Division Headquarters was established in a farmhouse at Köpenhof, strategically located in the centre of the divisional area.[13] The initial tasks laid out for the brigades of the 6th Airborne Division were now fulfilled. Field Marshal Bernard Montgomery next gave orders for his 21 Army Group to move beyond Wesel and head both east and northeast. Allied forces were now pushing forward towards the Elbe River and the Baltic Sea.

Frankforce, comprising men from 1 and 2SAS, began crossing the Rhine at 1130 hours on 25 March 1945.[14] Consisting of men from A and D Squadrons, 1SAS was commanded by Major Harry Poat with the group then being subdivided into three large troops, led by Majors John Tonkin, Bill Fraser, and Alec Muirhead. After the crossing, 1SAS began reconnaissance patrols for the 6th Airborne Division. On 27 March 1945, near the town of Schermbeck, 1SAS provided assistance to the 1st Canadian Parachute Battalion, who met with resistance on their advance to Lembeck.

In the interim, while Operation Plunder was still underway, the British 11th Armoured Division, known as Black Bull, was being held in reserve. With the operational objectives ultimately being met, the division was placed under the command of VIII Corps along with the 6th Airborne Division.[15] On 28 March 1945, the 11th Armoured Division crossed the Rhine River and was soon northeast of Wesel. The division encountered hundreds and thousands of displaced persons (DPs) as it pushed further into Germany.[16] The 6th Airborne Division faced similar problems, and, in addition, it had to deal with thousands of German prisoners. The war diary of the 1st Canadian Parachute Battalion noted that they had captured almost as many prisoners as they had men in the entire battalion.[17] By the last day of March, the Black Bulls handed over Osnabrück to the 6th Airborne, who had kept remarkable pace with the division.[18]

During the last days of March and the first few days of April, wings from the Royal Canadian Air Force continued flying missions over Germany from bases outside of the country. Squadrons from 126 Wing, RCAF, continued with attack missions on the ground and accomplished significant victories in the air.[19] As ground and air successes continued, plans were being drawn up for both RAF and RCAF squadrons to move to air bases inside of Germany. Similar to the divisions moving ahead of them on the ground, the air personnel would face similar problems with a heavy traffic of prisoners of war (POWs) and refugees clogging the roads.

The first week of April saw the Allies making rapid advancement. By 3 April 1945, the 7th Armoured Division began clearing the northwest sector of the Teutoburger Wald, a range of forested mountains west of Osnabrück. Around the same time, the 29th Armoured Brigade captured the village of Birgte, while its 23rd Hussars entered the small town of Tecklenburg. On 8 April 1945, the 23rd Hussars crossed Petershagen and prepared for an attack on Leese.

In the intervening time, the 3rd Parachute Brigade was given the task of securing Minden. The Brigade's 1st Canadian Parachute Battalion arrived at Minden on 5 April 1945. After crossing the Weser River, embussed on the tanks of the 4th Battalion of the Grenadier Guards, the Canadians passed through Lahde and then quickly arrived at Wölpinghausen. On 8 April 1945, on the way to Wunstorf, the battalion cleared a small POW camp filled with French inmates.[20] Nearby, the 6th Airborne loaned a bridge at Bordenau to the 11th Armoured Division, while the 7th Armoured Division continued on the northern left flank. The Allies were now approaching the Lüneburg Heath and, within days, their engagement with the Bergen-Belsen concentration camp.

The Heath: Entering Lower Saxony

The Lüneburg Heath is a large woodland area in the northeastern part of the state of Lower Saxony in northern Germany. The area stretches between four rivers: the Elbe to the north, the Aller to the south, the Wümme to the west, and the Drawehn to the east. It is an expansive hinterland for the cities of Bremen, Lüneburg, Hamburg, and Hannover. This sprawling area features glacial valleys, moraines, heathland, moors, and wooded areas. Pine forests dotted by silver birch, sessile oak, and beech trees spread over the landscape.

Since the late nineteenth century, and due to the sparse population and unique landscape, the Lüneburg Heath had been used as a military training ground. In 1935 the Wehrmacht established the Bergen-Hohne Training Area, which became one of the most expansive military grounds in all of Europe. The Lüneburg Heath was also where Field Marshal Montgomery accepted the unconditional surrender on 4 May 1945 of German forces in northern Germany, Denmark, and the Netherlands, signalling the end of the Second World War in Europe.[21]

By 10 April 1945 many Allied forces were crossing through the Lüneburg Heath. The 11th Armoured Division prepared for a breakout around Grindau, Esperke, and Elze. The 1st Canadian Parachute Battalion rested in Luthe on 9 April 1945 and then marched to Brelingen the following day. The battalion spent three and a half days in Brelingen resting in billets. The 7th Armoured Division, meanwhile, had been given instructions to move towards Hamburg.

A few days earlier, on 8 April 1945, after leaving the village of Windheim, Major Tonkin's D Squadron, 1SAS, was heading northeast towards Neustadt, while A Squadron protected their left flank. Major

Bill Fraser's troops, now led by Lieutenant Ian Wellsted, became entangled with a German ambush near Nienburg.[22] Once the trouble was subdued and the area secured, Frankforce continued its advance east through the Lüneburg Heath.

On 12 April 1945, the VIII Corps' 15th Scottish Division arrived at Celle, an old ducal town approximately twenty kilometres southeast of Bergen-Belsen. Upon arrival, the soldiers discovered a terrible scene. Four days earlier, a train was stopped in a freight terminal in Celle carrying approximately 4,000 prisoners. It was struck as the Americans bombed the rail facility.[23] Half of the prisoners were killed by the bombs, while the other half fled. Along with some of the general public, members from the Schutzstaffel (SS), Wehrmacht, the Volkssturm militia, police, and army sought after the escapees. This became crudely known as the "Celler Hasenjad," the "Celle hare hunt," the tracking down of escaped inmates from the air raid.[24]

The "Celle hare hunt" lasted until 10 April 1945. Many escapees were shot dead or killed by other means. Approximately 1,100 prisoners, both men and women, were recaptured and taken to a nearby field. Thirty individuals were executed and around 500 were marched on foot to Bergen-Belsen. The remainder, many of whom were too exhausted, ill, or injured to walk, were imprisoned at Heidekaserne, a nearby infantry barracks. The inmates at Heidekaserne were left without food or medical attention. The prisoners were discovered by the 15th Scottish Division, many near death.[25]

Additional forces soon arrived in Celle. After leaving Esperke, 2SAS arrived in Celle on 12 April 1945. Men from 2SAS also witnessed the tragedy at Heidekaserne. The Coldstream and Scots Guards, having had to contend with blown bridges, also arrived in the area around the same time.[26] The 3rd Parachute Brigade war diary notes that its reconnaissance party left for Celle at 0830 hours on 14 April 1945.[27] The 1st Canadian Parachute Battalion left Brelingen and marched the forty kilometres to Celle, arriving in the town during the early evening of 14 April 1945. While in Celle, the battalion apprehended a number of suspected enemy "werewolves" (Nazi guerrillas) in the area.[28] By this time, many military personnel from various divisions and brigades had learned that there was a concentration camp in the area.

Before military personnel descended on Bergen-Belsen, British and Canadian air forces began establishing bases on the Lüneburg Heath and in the surrounding areas. On 11 April 1945, the air base in Celle, near Wietzenbruch, was turned over to the British and came under the command of the RAF. It became an RAF station, regimental headquarters, and military base. The RCAF also began using the air base in Celle; for example, its 414 Squadron was stationed there within a few short weeks.

Indeed, many RCAF wings now established their squadrons in northwest Germany. The RCAF's 126 Wing moved from Base (B.) 108 at Rheine to B.116 Wunstorf. The wing's move began on 13 April 1945 and was completed two days later, the same day Bergen-Belsen was formally surrendered. Two days later 39 Reconnaissance Wing joined 126 Wing at Wunstorf. On 14 April 1945, 127 Wing moved to B.114 Diepholz and a couple of weeks later to B.154 Soltau, where 39 Wing, once again on the move, joined them. On 12 April 1945, 143 Wing moved its base to B.110 Osnabrück, and after a couple of weeks, moved to B.150 Hustedt. Many of these air bases were on or near the Lüneburg Heath, some less than an hour away from Bergen-Belsen. While not part of the formal handover of the camp, scores of personnel from these RCAF wings either visited or became involved in the relief efforts at the Bergen-Belsen concentration camp.

The Wire: The Allies at Bergen-Belsen

While the negotiation and formal handover of Bergen-Belsen have been previously detailed and generally agreed upon, confusion still exists regarding which units initially entered the camp.[29] As Joanne Reilly notes in her history of the liberation of Bergen-Belsen, there are many "contenders in the quest for the credit" of having been the first to enter the camp.[30] Indeed, due to the sheer number of units operating in the area and the fact that small parties often broke away and went on reconnaissance missions, it is difficult to establish an accurate timeline. Moreover, Bergen-Belsen, like most camps in Hitler's system, was expansive. Its grounds covered approximately fifty-five hectares (or 136 acres). While the main gate, used for the transporting of inmates, was located on the east side of the camp, there was also a large gate on the west side of the camp, which was used to transport the bodies of POWs to a nearby cemetery. There were also some smaller gates used for special purposes.[31] Furthermore, the camp was organized into eight different sections which were strictly divided from one another.[32] Thus, it is conceivable that small groups or reconnaissance parties could have been in the camp at the same time without knowing that they had company.

Map 1 The establishment of new camp sections.

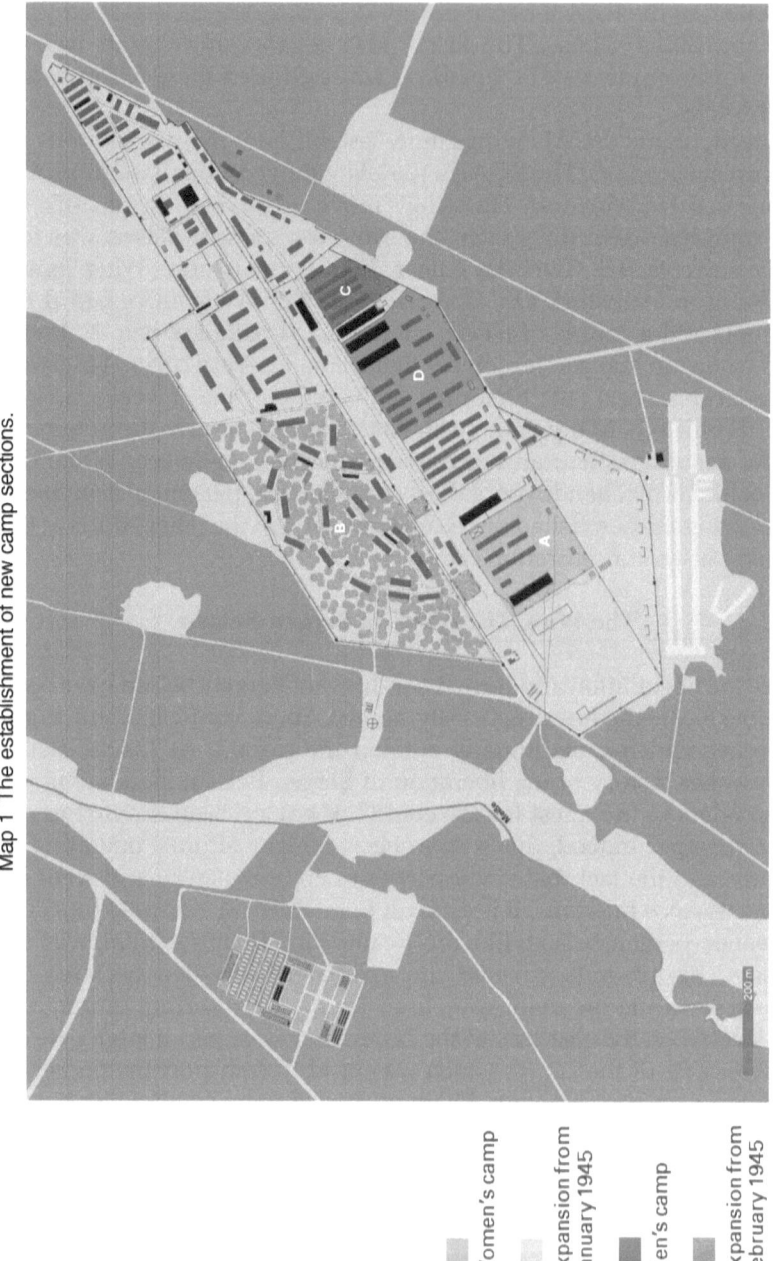

Bergen-Belsen concentration camp, 1945. Berthold Weidner, weidnerhaendle.de

While the formal agreement to surrender the camp was signed at 0100 hours on 13 April 1945, forces were delayed from entering for forty-eight hours due to fighting at the Aller River near Winsen and the village of Walle. It seems clear that the first military personnel to enter the camp did so on 15 April 1945. While instructions were to have the camp placed under the control of the commander of 63rd Anti-Tank Regiment, other British troops arrived earlier in the day. To complicate the matter further, the 1st Canadian Parachute Battalion, having left Celle on 15 April 1945, arrived at the gates of Bergen-Belsen the very same day.[33] The following section aims to provide a detailed overview of the surrender and to note which Allied groups entered the camp on both 15 and 16 April 1945, clearly two days of confusion and astonishment.

During the late evening of 12 April 1945, and under approval of Heinrich Himmler, Reichsführer of the SS, Colonel Hans Schmidt, an emissary from the 1st German Parachute Army, Lieutenant-Colonel Hans Bohnekamp, along with a medical officer and a translator, crossed British lines and declared that inmates in a nearby camp, Bergen-Belsen, were rife with typhus.[34] German representatives were then led to the VIII Corps' Headquarters at Winsen. Negotiations for the surrender of the camp began that evening between VIII Corps' Chief of Staff and the Chief of Staff of the 1st Parachute Army, Military Commandant Bergen. Signed in the early morning of 13 April 1945, the agreement set aside a neutral area of forty-eight square kilometres around the concentration camp and the military training grounds. This agreement, which was to last six days, subsequently led to instructions that the camp was to fall under the command of Lieutenant-Colonel Taylor, commander of the 63rd Anti-Tank Regiment.

Meanwhile, the negotiations and eventual agreement to surrender the camp impacted military movements in the area. The 3rd Parachute Brigade war diary states, "Difficulties in operation owing to BELSEN Concentration Camp negotiations."[35] Indeed, word quickly spread that a concentration camp was in the area and that its inmates were terribly ill. In addition, later in the day on 13 April 1945, the majority of the SS guards stationed at the camp fled. Camp Commandant Josef Kramer and nearly eighty warders, comprising both men and women, remained at Bergen-Belsen, along with approximately 2,000 armed Hungarian guards.[36]

In a 1995 essay, historian Paul Kemp states that the first British troops to arrive at Bergen-Belsen did so during the morning of Sunday 15 April

1945, when a small party from the 29th Armoured Brigade stopped at the camp.[37] Kemp cites a document written by Brigadier Robert B.T. Daniell confirming this detail.[38] And yet, elsewhere, Daniell has stated that he entered the camp much later. In his *Journal of a Horse Gunner: India to the Baltic via Alamein* (1998), Daniell claims that he arrived at Bergen-Belsen on 18 April 1945.[39] Furthermore, in a 1995 interview marking the fiftieth anniversary of the transfer of the camp, while Daniell indeed refers to himself as the first British soldier to enter, he also describes encountering gas chambers at Bergen-Belsen.[40] On the contrary, there were no gas chambers at Bergen-Belsen, although this continues to be a popular myth.[41] While some personnel from the 29th Armoured Brigade did enter the camp at some point, it is uncertain if it occurred during the morning of 15 April 1945.

What is clear, however, is that men from 1SAS entered Bergen-Belsen on the 15th and did so before the arrival of Lieutenant-Colonel Taylor and his assigned relief unit. The 1SAS was working with the 8th Parachute Battalion, providing a reconnaissance screen. As Paul Kemp correctly revises in a second article written six years later about the liberation of Bergen-Belsen, a detachment of 1SAS were patrolling the area for signs of any Allied POWs and members of the regiment who were possibly incarcerated at the camp.[42] The first of the SAS to enter Bergen-Belsen were part of Major John Tonkin's group, including Lieutenant John Randall and Sergeant Reginald Seekings.[43] Along with this group was Lieutenant Keith W. MacLellan, a Canadian from Aylmer, Quebec, also with the 1SAS.[44] As the first Canadian liberator to enter the camp, MacLellan has seen his efforts at Bergen-Belsen recognized by both the United States Holocaust Memorial Museum and the Canadian Jewish Congress.[45]

In a report on the liberation of Bergen-Belsen, Lieutenant-Colonel Taylor states that when he arrived at the camp, an SAS officer, most likely Major Tonkin, notified him that he had found a man from his regiment in one of the barracks and asked permission to remove him.[46] This was confirmed in a report filed the same day by Captain John W. Gray, General Headquarters (GHQ) Liaison Regiment, also known as Phantom.[47] Lieutenant-Colonel Taylor granted permission, and the individual was subsequently removed from the camp.

By the afternoon of 15 April 1945, Lieutenant-Colonel Taylor's 63rd Anti-Tank Regiment, Royal Artillery arrived in the neutral zone defined by the agreement. At shortly past 1500 hours, the leading party of Taylor's regiment, No. 249 (Oxfordshire Yeomanry) Battery, commanded by Major Benjamin Barnett, arrived at Bergen-Belsen. Meanwhile,

Map 2 The advances of British troops to Bergen-Belsen in April 1945.

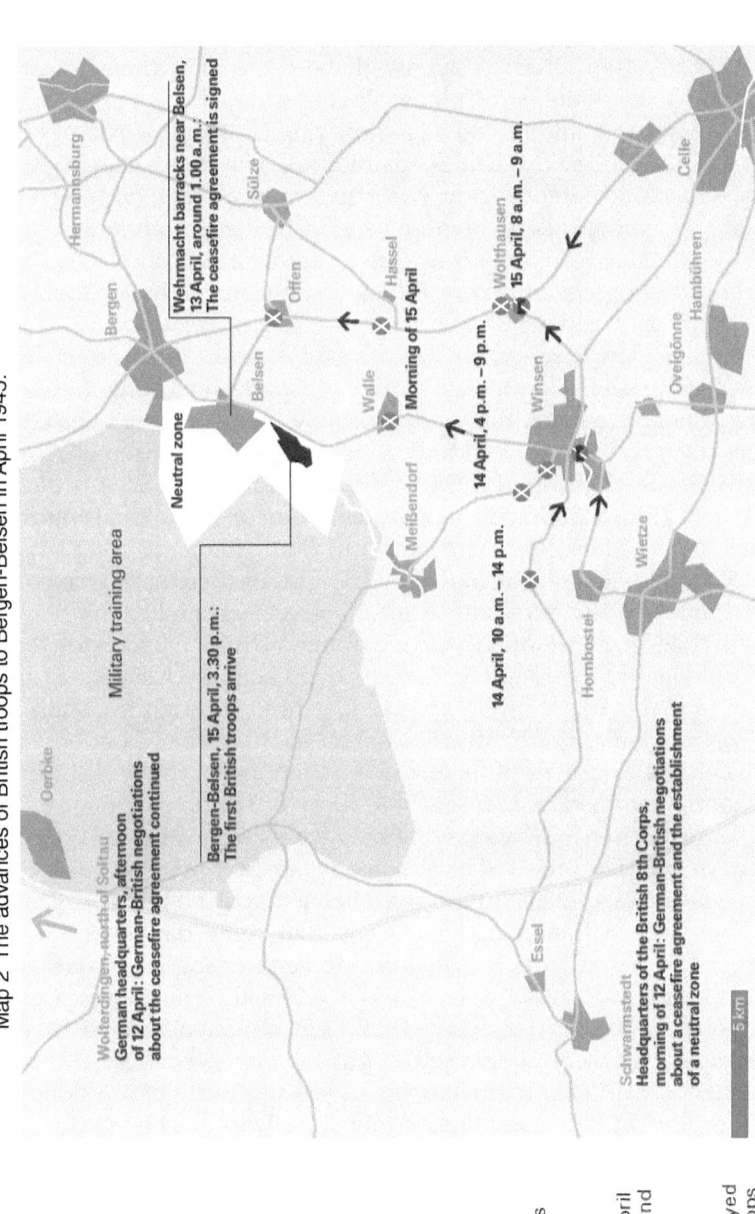

The Advances of British Troops. Berthold Weidner, weidnerhaendle.de

the 11th Armoured Division bypassed the camp and drove towards Ebstorf.[48] Next, Lieutenant-Colonel Taylor ordered Captain Derrick Sington, then commanding No. 14 Amplifying Unit and two other non-commissioned officers (NCOs), Sergeant Eric Clyne and Lance Corporal Sidney Roberts, to enter the camp with an armoured car equipped with a battery of loudspeakers. Sington was instructed to announce that while the inmates were now free, due to the typhus outbreak, no one was permitted to leave the camp. Lieutenant-Colonel Taylor then became camp commandant.[49]

Soon thereafter, Lieutenant-Colonel Taylor, and officers from VIII Corps Headquarters, conducted a partial inspection of Bergen-Belsen. Among other personnel, this group notably included Brigadier Glyn Hughes, Deputy Director of Medical Services (DDMS) Second Army, Brigadier J. Melvin, also of DDMS, and Captain W.R. Williams of the Supply and Transport Branch. Consequently, an urgent appeal was dispatched to both the Second Army and VIII Corps for medical aid, along with food and water. A patrol from GHQ Liaison Regiment arrived at approximately 1615 hours, shortly after personnel from DDMS.[50]

Meanwhile, by mid-April, the 7th Armoured Division had made their way from Diepholz through to Barnstorf, crossing the Aller River and stopping in Walsrode.[51] While prepared to move through to Soltau on their way to Hamburg, the division's 3rd/4th County of London Yeomanry entered the towns of Celle and Walle on the morning of 15 April 1945. Soon after, personnel from the County of London Yeomanry entered Bergen-Belsen.[52] While staying only for a short while, the men offered what supplies they had and radioed back for further support.[53]

While multiple appeals for aid were being dispatched, the 1st Canadian Parachute Battalion had left Celle that same day, en route to Eschede. The battalion had been coming across escaped POWs and refugees for the past couple of weeks. While travelling north from Celle, a company of the 1st Canadian Parachute Battalion arrived at the Bergen-Belsen concentration camp.[54] The convoy eventually stopped alongside the road next to the barbed wire fence, south of the camp. A section of the 224 Parachute Field Ambulance was attached to the battalion and a few of the men witnessed the appalling scenes at the camp.[55]

Moreover, some of the men from the 1st Canadian Parachute Battalion entered Bergen-Belsen to survey the scenes or to assist the prisoners, including Lieutenant-Colonel Fraser Eadie, the battalion's commanding officer, and Captain Patrick Gerald Costigan, a medical officer. Costigan was among the first doctors to provide medical aid to the inmates in the camp.[56] Costigan spent two days treating the ill in the camp before returning to his regular duties. This makes the men from the battalion the first group of Canadians to arrive at Bergen-Belsen.

The following day, 16 April 1945, a smattering of reinforcements arrived at Bergen-Belsen. The 11th Armoured Division made available a hygiene section. Thus, the Royal Army Medical Corps' 76 Field Hygiene Section soon arrived at the camp. In addition, Major A.L. Berney, a staff officer attached to VIII Corps, was sent to 817 Military Government Detachment, which had arrived the evening before, and was put in charge of general administration in Camp I.[57] According to 21 Army Group, the Military Government in Germany was responsible for the "issue of orders, obedience to which will be exacted … [it] is the instrument, so far as the civil population is concerned, by which these orders will be conveyed and enforced."[58] Major Berney then took steps to arrange for the organization and requisition of various supplies from surrounding villages and towns.

Aftermath: The Ensuing Days, Weeks, and Months

The first two days of British control of Bergen-Belsen saw a number of divisional units, detachments, battalions, and sections both enter and pass by the camp. It took nearly two days before substantial reinforcements arrived. On 17 April 1945, 224 Military Government Detachment, under command of Major W.H. Miles, arrived at 1400 hours and established its headquarters in Camp I.[59] Squadron Leader John Proskie of the RCAF, an agricultural expert from Edmonton, Alberta, was immediately sent to 224 Detachment's headquarters, arriving the same day.[60] Proskie was put in charge of planning the collection and employment of resources from the local area. The monumental task of organizing food for the inmates was left almost entirely to Proskie and his lone assistant, a sergeant in the British Army. Later, on 19 April 1945, 904 Military Government Detachment arrived, to work under 224 Detachment, and was put in charge of Camp II.[61] On 26 April 1945, 618 Military Government Detachment also arrived.[62]

Also reaching the camp on 17 April 1945 alongside 224 Detachment was 32 Casualty Clearing Station, commanded by Lieutenant-Colonel James Johnston and 11 Light Field Ambulance, led by Lieutenant-Colonel Mervin Gonin. On 18 April 1945, 10 Garrison assumed administrative control of Bergen-Belsen, with 113 Light Anti-Aircraft Regiment under its command, replacing the detachment of 63rd Anti-Tank

Regiment originally in charge of the camp.[63] That day also saw 30 Field Hygiene Section and 7 Mobile Bacteriological Laboratory arrive.

Allied photographic units arrived soon after the surrender of Bergen-Belsen. On 16 April 1945, Royal Canadian Air Force public relations officers arrived to document the scenes. The following day, 17 April 1945, the No. 5 British Army Film and Photographic Unit (AFPU) appeared, although some of the unit's photographers had already entered the camp earlier.[64] Members from the Canadian Film and Photo Unit (CFPU) also arrived around the same time. Visually documenting the dreadful situation at the camp became a preoccupation for many, even for personnel in non-photographic units. For example, numerous Canadian airmen took photographs while assisting at Bergen-Belsen. Moreover, in early May, personnel from the RCAF's No. 5 and No. 6 Mobile Field Photographic Sections, who went on a number of combined liberty runs to Bergen-Belsen, took a series of photographs of the terrible scenes at the camp.[65]

In addition to photographers, both countries saw war artists, official and not, enter the camp. Britain had two official war artists enter Bergen-Belsen, while three official war artists from Canada depicted scenes at the camp.[66] Likely the first artist to enter the camp was Sergeant Eric Taylor of the Royal Engineers shortly after liberation. British War Office artist Leslie Cole arrived not long after on 23 April 1945. Lieutenant Alexander Colville, who worked with 3rd Canadian Infantry Division, was sent to the camp and arrived on 29 April 1945.[67] Flight Officer Donald K. Anderson, of the RCAF's 127 Wing, arrived at the end of April or early May. Scottish-born Doris Zinkeisen, an artist for the St John Ambulance Brigade, likely arrived around the same time. Toronto-born Aba Bayefsky was with RCAF's 39 Wing when he arrived at Bergen-Belsen on 10 May 1945.[68] Finally, London-born Mary Kessell worked at the camp in August 1945, months after liberation, staying approximately six weeks.[69] These individuals are well known for having depicted the camp, although there were other artists from both countries who also documented the scenes at Bergen-Belsen.[70]

Within a week of the surrender of the camp, and after passing through the "human laundry," personnel began moving newly deloused survivors into an emergency "hospital" in buildings at the nearby Wehrmacht barracks.[71] Thousands of former inmates were treated at the emergency hospital. Later, once the numbers of patients subsided, the barracks were reverted into provisional housing for the survivors who no longer needed emergency medical care. Those still in need of treatment, and who could stand being moved, were eventually transferred to the German Military Hospital located a short distance from the main camp.[72]

By the end of April an advance party of the 9th British General Hospital arrived. They were soon joined by ninety-seven medical students from teaching hospitals in London, along with detachments from the British Red Cross Society. By the second week of May, 22 and 30 Field Transfusion Units, as well as 35 Casualty Clearing Station, moved into Bergen-Belsen.[73] On 16 May 1945 an advance party of the 29th British Hospital arrived. They were joined by the rest of the hospital staff a few days later.[74] At this time, the 29th British Hospital involved a number of Canadians, including Dr Charles Sutherland Rennie, Welfare Officer and St John Ambulance volunteer Elsie Deeks, and Doris Haines who worked with the Queen Alexandra's Imperial Nursing Service.

Furthermore, after the arrival of the 35 Casualty Clearing Station on 14 May 1945, the remainder of the sick were transferred to the recently cleared German Military Hospital.[75] Initially, this military hospital became known as Bergen-Hohne, or, more commonly, as Belsen Hospital. Later, it was renamed Glyn Hughes Hospital, after the humanitarian work of the well-known brigadier. It would soon become the largest hospital in Europe, housing over 13,000 patients.[76] The hospital was staffed by a mixed group including the medical students, Red Cross workers, and, controversially, German medical personnel – and yet, staff shortages continued.

Canadian Lyle Creelman, who in early June 1945 was appointed chief nurse for the British zone of occupied Germany, became aware of staff shortages at the hospital.[77] Staff were recruited from a variety of locations. Indeed, nurses from a range of countries worked at Belsen Hospital, including at least six Canadians.[78] Personnel in charge of administrative matters were constantly looking for ways to ease nursing shortages, as well as deal with the large number of patients. Ultimately, in August 1945 the United Nations Relief and Rehabilitation Administration (UNRRA) formally took over Glyn Hughes Hospital.

Thus, due to the number of inmates, military personnel continuously worked to ease the burden of the large number of inmates by transporting those who needed additional care out of the camp. Shortly after liberation, airmen from the RCAF's 437 Squadron, part of Transport Command, flew not only inmates out of Bergen-Belsen, but also high-ranking officials into the camp.[79] In addition, survivors from Bergen-Belsen, along with former prisoners from the POW camp at Sandbostel, were transferred to the No. 7 Canadian General Hospital, which had arrived at Bassum on 3 May 1945.[80]

On 4 May 1945 the RCAF's Nutrition Group, led by Wing Commander John F. McCreary, was sent from the Netherlands into Germany to examine the situation at Bergen-Belsen.[81] Accordingly, both of the RCAF Nutrition Group's Spearhead Survey Groups A and B arrived at the camp for inspection the following day. They surveyed the scene and completed a report. The groups were soon recalled, and on 7 May 1945 they proceeded in a convoy to Utrecht, establishing a base back at Bilthoven.

As mentioned above, numerous RCAF wings had air bases located on the Lüneburg Heath during the spring and summer of 1945. A number of the wings were visited by British padres, asking personnel to assist at Bergen-Belsen. During the last week of April, Padre Leslie Hardman visited a nearby RCAF base requesting food and medical supplies. The following day he received large lorry loads and jeeps carrying goods.[82] Reverend Louis Sanker, senior chaplain of the Second Tactical Air Force (TAF), also requested assistance and received numerous donations from RCAF's 126 Wing.[83] Most of the men from 39 Reconnaissance Wing visited Bergen-Belsen in early May, bringing along supplies, such as food, cigarettes, and medicine.[84] Likewise, 440 Squadron, 143 Wing, also sent loads of supplies to the camp.[85] Furthermore, a number of personnel from these wings spent days working in the camp, assisting the inmates, acting as translators, and contributing to the overall relief efforts.

As the weeks after Bergen-Belsen was surrendered turned into months, additional units, groups, and battalions continued to move into the area, and many came into contact with the camp and its former inmates. In June, companies in the 4th Battalion of the Wiltshire Regiment (Duke of Edinburgh's) moved to new locations in Celle District.[86] Battalion companies arrived in villages such as Bergen, Garßen, Bostel, and Winsen. Later that summer, the battalion headquarters was moved into the former SS barracks in Bergen-Belsen.[87] The 4 Wilts, as they were known, were unique in that the battalion featured a cross-section of Canadians who became members through the CANLOAN program, including Lieutenant Wilfred I. Smith, who was a platoon commander.[88]

In early 1945 British and Canadian officials agreed to work together in the disarmament of Germany. Shortly thereafter, within 84 Group, RAF, a disarmament staff and wings were established. By mid-May 1945, 84 Group Headquarters was located at Scheuen, near Celle.[89] The unit was fully established at the end of the month. By this time, thousands of survivors from Bergen-Belsen had been transferred to hospitals in Celle. Soon, a number of men from 8402 (RCAF) Disarmament Wing, one staffed entirely of Canadians, became intimately involved with the survivors, both in Celle and at Bergen-Belsen. Men such as Squadron Leaders Ted Aplin and John W. Thompson and Sergeant Stanley Winfield, along with many other personnel from 8402 Disarmament Wing, as well as British personnel from 84 Group, went to great lengths to assist the survivors during the spring and summer of 1945 and beyond.

Conclusion

During the late fall of 1944 and the early winter of 1945, the Soviet Union's Red Army came across a number of Hitler's camps in eastern Europe. Upon locating the sites of the camps at Bełżec, Sobibór, and Treblinka, the Soviets issued no major press releases, and the publicity of the discovery of Auschwitz was minimal. Accordingly, as the war in Europe was coming to a close and as Allied forces were spreading out across Germany, the horrors of the Third Reich came closer into view. The journey towards those horrors began, as this chapter attempted to depict, with the crossing of the Rhine River. Indeed, in the area surrounding the camp was an array of Allied forces. Some were instructed to remain at the camp, but even more continued on to other locations. Yet, even for those who spent only a few hours at the camp, the scenes were forever haunting. The war ended for many military personnel with the stark and unforgettable reality of humankind's vicious and brutal cruelty to their fellow beings. As those who entered the camps as part of the conquering Allied forces observed, there were realities of which they had never before conceived and human suffering beyond their imaginations.

Clearly, military personnel were completely unprepared for what they were to find at the camp. Liberating Bergen-Belsen was, as previously stated, not a military objective. When the camp was initially surrendered, the war, of course, still continued. Consequently, supplies were limited, personnel were largely unavailable, and many resources were occupied elsewhere. Those who remained to work at the camp were left with monumental tasks.

Between April 1943 and April 1945, the Bergen-Belsen concentration camp imprisoned, at various times, approximately 120,000 men, women, and children. Of that figure to date, only 50,000 prisoners are actually known by name. When British and Canadian forces arrived on 15 April 1945 there were approximately 60,000 prisoners in Bergen-Belsen. Thousands of corpses lay around the camp grounds. It is estimated that 35,000 people had died between January and March 1945.[90] In the months before the end of the war, the death rate increased rapidly. In the month of March 1945 alone, roughly 18,000 people died in the camp, including sisters Margot and Anne Frank.[91] In total, 50,000 people died in the Bergen-Belsen concentration camp before Allied forces arrived at the camp.[92]

Of the 60,000 prisoners still alive in Bergen-Belsen when the Allies arrived, the majority, approximately 60 per cent, were Jews.[93] The prisoners comprised a wide range of nationalities, although the majority appear to have been Polish and Russian. Women made up slightly more than half of the inmates. The death rate was extremely high at Bergen-Belsen. As Eberhard Kolb explains, "Belsen was a camp where terror was boastfully and openly perpetrated. Here, masses of people were not sent to the gallows. Here, there were no gas chambers. Here, they died slowly, but surely. Starvation, the wanton neglect of hygienic conditions, contagion, terribly overcrowded barracks, brutality, the feeling of total degeneration – all these ensured that the needs of the crematoria would massively and steadily be filled."[94] Starvation and disease were rampant in the camp and were the primary causes of death.

Tragically, large numbers of deaths continued even after the camp was surrendered and put under British control. Between 19 and 30 April 1945 approximately 9,000 people died of illness. The month of May saw around 4,500 deaths, while June saw just over 400 people die. Therefore, roughly 14,000 people died in the camp after its transfer.[95] In other words, nearly a quarter of the total number of prisoners still alive when the British and Canadians first arrived at the camp ultimately met their demise. Allied control of Bergen-Belsen did not mean an end to suffering and death. Certainly, these circumstances weighed heavily on everyone involved.

For the inmates of Bergen-Belsen, the surrender of the camp meant that they were largely free from the tyranny of the SS guards, but it did not mean that they were necessarily free. "For five-and-a-half years," explains Bergen-Belsen survivor Esther Brunstein,

> I had dreamt of one day being given the opportunity to eat and eat without the limit of time until I burst. I was robbed of that satisfaction for I was

too ill to swallow a crumb … I also feel cheated for not having the memory of experiencing the initial exhilarating moment of liberation. The first few days were joyous and yet sad, confusing and bewildering …

Looking out the window I could see German soldiers being made to clear the mountain of corpses – the fruit of their labour. The inmates had to be restrained from attacking them. There was murder in all of us and it scared me. I remember praying silently. I did not really know to whom to pray but I never prayed so fervently in all my life. I prayed not to be consumed by hatred and destroyed for the rest of my days.[96]

For Esther Brunstein and the survivors of Bergen-Belsen their internal and external struggles continued long after liberation. The ensuing days, weeks, and months were spent trying to survive, heal from illnesses, recuperate spiritually, and locate any surviving friends and family.

The British and Canadian military personnel who came into contact with these survivors became involved in a variety of ways. Likewise, their often emotional responses to these encounters touched upon a multitude of topics, such as religion, philosophy, morality, politics, history, and justice. In the following chapters we will examine the ways in which military personnel responded and the meanings they drew from their experiences at Bergen-Belsen.

Chapter Three

The Distance of Presence: Inside Seventy-Two Hours

On our way up to the Elbe River [we arrived] at a place called Bergen-Belsen just outside of Celle ... And it was a shambles I can tell you ... The prisoners in there were ... in absolutely dreadful shape.¹
Lieutenant-Colonel Fraser Eadie, Commanding Officer,
1st Canadian Parachute Battalion

What we saw was a nightmare which beggars description ... It's often assumed that liberation means people celebrating and coming to hug you, but they were too far gone. They would just sit and rock back and forth. As you watched, you saw one die in front of you.²
Lieutenant-Colonel J. Douglas Paybody, VIII Corps, British Second Army

The word "liberation" can summon images of liberty, elation, and camaraderie. The term perhaps even carries with it notions involving intent and purpose, strategy and preparation. However, first-hand accounts concerning the initial seventy-two hours after the formal surrender of Bergen-Belsen demonstrate that this was simply not the case. In fact, this merely distorts the stark reality that faced the utterly ill-equipped British and Canadian military personnel during the camp's capitulation by the German Army. The interpretations of the first few days are bursting with incredulity, grief, confusion, disgust, revulsion, and rage. Allied personnel thus drew from a broad breadth of negative emotions, and yet the responses demonstrate similar patterns of thought, language, imagery, and metaphors. While each man – as were nearly all personnel during those initial few days in the camp – presented his own particular perspective to the experience, there is a discernible intersection in what was documented.

This chapter surveys a wide variety of accounts offered in the days, weeks, months, years, and even decades after the liberation of Bergen-Belsen by military personnel who were present at some point between the afternoon of 15 April and 18 April 1945. The central focus will be on the language the British and the Canadians used to describe the camp, its internees, and its guards, with an additional emphasis on how personnel understood the situation they found themselves embroiled in. Before examining the responses, however, a brief overview of what was known about Nazi crimes prior to liberation in both Canada and Britain will be provided. Attention will be paid, first, on what British and Canadian officials knew; next, what was subsequently told to the general public via the media; and finally, what the average soldier could have been aware of prior to the spring of 1945. The remainder of the chapter will survey the responses from men who arrived around the time of the camp's surrender, which included detachments from such groups as the 1st Special Air Service, the 63rd Anti-Tank Regiment, the 1st Canadian Parachute Battalion, and personnel from VIII Corps.

Prior Knowledge of Nazi Crimes

Allied Governments

In October 1939, the British government's Foreign Office, concerned by the pre-war crimes of the Third Reich, published a White Paper on German Atrocities. Due to perceived public cynicism about reports concerning false atrocity stories published during the First World War, the government wanted to avoid having the information judged as propaganda.[3] The White Paper on German Atrocities documented the cruel treatment of political prisoners in that country. Nevertheless, the Foreign Office did not emphasize the widespread antisemitic incidents that were occurring in pre-war Germany. In particular, the Foreign Office wanted to avoid creating sympathy for the Jews in light of the situation in Palestine, as the government continued to curtail Jewish immigration. It also wanted to avoid linking the defence of the Jews to the British war effort.[4] However, it was evident that atrocities were being perpetrated on German soil.

Information concerning the brutal violence committed by Nazi Germany was gathered in a variety of ways. Indeed, the overall accomplishments of the Allied effort during the Second World War can be attributed to a number of different factors, and most certainly as a result of code breaking. As early as September 1939, the British began to regularly read German Order Police messages.[5] The interception of messages was conducted by the Government Code and Cipher School (GCCS) at Bletchley Park, Buckinghamshire, England. The high level of intelligence produced at Bletchley Park greatly aided the Allied war effort.

Accordingly, British analysts, by March 1940, had become aware of the involvement of German Order Police battalions in the murder and displacement of Jews and other "undesirables" in eastern Europe.[6] For example, in July 1941, Bletchley Park intercepted a message to Heinrich Himmler stating that 1,153 Jews were shot and killed by a Police Regiment Centre in Slonim (which was then part of German-occupied-Poland), as part of the day's "mopping up activities."[7] This was one of the first clear indications of the crimes being committed on the Eastern Front. As the killings of Jews and other groups increased, British intelligence continued to intercept messages documenting atrocities.

On 24 August 1941, as the war raged in eastern Europe, Prime Minister Winston Churchill broadcast a speech on the BBC. In his speech, Churchill declared that "scores of thousands – literally scores of thousands – of executions in cold blood are being perpetrated by the German police-troops ... there has never been methodical, merciless butchery on such a scale, or approaching such a scale. And this is but the beginning ... We are in the presence of a crime without a name."[8] In his announcement, while referring to mass executions in the east, Churchill did not refer to the killing of large numbers of Jews, which, it has been argued by a number of scholars, was likely due to the risk of revealing the code-breaking capacities of the British.[9]

In 1942 Jan Karski, then part of the Polish underground, was sent on a mission to London to report on the situation in German-occupied Poland. Before he left on this assignment, Karski was smuggled into the Warsaw Ghetto and, later, into the sorting and transit camp at Izbica Lubelska, which was located between the city of Lublin and the extermination camp at Bełżec.[10] Completely devastated by what he saw, Karski became one of the first eyewitnesses to report to the Allies about the fate of the Jews in German-occupied Poland.[11] He spoke directly to Foreign Secretary Anthony Eden and others from Britain's War Office. Prime Minister Winston Churchill later read a report by Karski in December 1942. Moreover, during the autumn of 1944, Karski travelled to Canada and spoke publicly about crimes being committed in German-occupied Poland while visiting both Ottawa and Montreal.[12]

Of all those who heard Karski speak and read his reports, few could grasp the sheer scale of violence, destruction, and suffering of European

Jewry. During the war Karski had also held meetings with US President Franklin D. Roosevelt and US Supreme Court Justice Felix Frankfurter, the latter later admitting he could not grasp the magnitude of what he was being told.[13] While most officials did not conclude that Karski was embellishing or being dishonest, the enormity of the situation was difficult to comprehend. As a consequence, Karski did not receive any notable assistance from Allied governments or Western organizations.

Therefore, by 1942, officials in Canada were aware of the plight of the Jews in Europe. The government of Canada had received graphic details through other Allied governments, by way of the Polish underground and other Jewish sources.[14] Furthermore, immigration to Canada for Jewish refugees and other east Europeans was virtually non-existent. Politicians and other officials in the country continually declined requests to aid the victims of Nazi Germany.

Along with reports of the crimes, the location of some camps was also known by the Allied governments relatively early into the war. Allied reconnaissance missions provided aerial views of several Nazi camps. For example, in 1942 and again in 1944, a number of photographs were taken of Bergen-Belsen during aerial reconnaissance.[15] Indeed, in September 1944 the Royal Air Force (RAF) took aerial photographs of the camp. Accordingly, its position, but not its specific function, was well known to Allied intelligence sources.

Despite basic knowledge of Nazi crimes, Allied governments were clearly not prepared to meet the challenges that they ultimately faced during the spring and summer of 1945. The Allies failed to comprehend fully the extremely desperate needs of the victims who had suffered at the hands of the Nazis. And for the small number of government officials who did know the specifics of the crimes, many either could not accept it or refused to act. Thus, the requirements needed by Allied military personnel to deal with the situation at Bergen-Belsen, as well as at other camps, were severely lacking. The spectrum of the anguish was simply not sufficiently appreciated.

The Media and the General Public

The coverage in both Britain and Canada of the crimes occurring in Nazi Europe, while scant, was still apparent and relatively accurate during the war years. As Walter Laqueur observes, there was a chasm between what was "known" and what was "believed."[16] Moreover, Laqueur explains, "the fact that some information has been mentioned once or even a hundred times in secret reports or in mass circulation newspapers does not necessarily mean that it has been accepted or understood. Big figures become statistics, and statistics have no psychological impact."[17] But what, exactly, did the media in Britain and Canada report to the public about Nazi crimes during the war? What warnings, if any, were published?

In the pre-war years, a number of individuals published documents condemning German crimes and cautioning against the creation of concentration camps. Born in Leipzig in 1896, Gerhart H. Seger was a former Social Democrat and a member of the German Reichstag. In 1933 he was arrested for opposing Hitler and sent to the Oranienburg concentration camp, located forty kilometres north of Berlin and one of the first detention facilities established by the Nazis. After escaping the camp, he fled the country and later emigrated to the United States. Published in English in 1935, Seger's *A Nation Terrorized* describes the author's ordeal in the camp.

Seger embarked on a number of speaking tours in the West, including both Canada and Britain. In 1934 he spoke in London to members of Parliament. It was also arranged for him to address the House of Commons.[18] Thus, as early as 1934, British politicians were aware of some crimes occurring in Nazi Germany. Moreover, Seger gave talks at the Canadian Club in Toronto in 1936, and again in 1943 and 1944, warning of the dangers of Hitler and Nazism. Also during the war, he spoke at events in Sarnia, Ontario, sponsored by the Rotary Club.[19]

In terms of the media, the London-based *Jewish Chronicle* obtained data on Jews in Polish ghettos as early as 1939–40, and it carried reports in 1940–1 about mass executions and overcrowding.[20] According to David Cesarani, news concerning the Final Solution emerged "gradually and haphazardly" in British media.[21] In June 1942, the *Daily Telegraph* reported that 700,000 Polish Jews had been killed in Chełmno, which was the first time a British newspaper reported the use of gas in killing large numbers of people.[22] Yet, as Tony Kushner has observed, by the summer of 1942, the general public in Britain was still largely unaware, in any specific way, of what was happening to European Jewry.[23]

Meanwhile, by early 1943, and while intermittent, large-scale murder in Nazi Europe was being reported in Canada. The first substantial report on mass killing published in Canada was in the US-based *Liberty*, one of the most widely read English magazines in the country.[24] The story was a feature on the massacre at Babi Yar, where over 30,000 Jews were killed by Einsatzgruppen detachments. However, by early 1944 media interest initially created by this story had declined.[25]

Likewise, by mid-1943, news relating the destruction of European Jewry also declined in Britain, with leading stories mostly dealing with domestic issues.[26] Of course, there were the exceptions. In a pamphlet distributed in 1943, titled *Let My People Go*, publisher Victor Gollancz reported on the potential annihilation of all of European Jewry. "Unless something effective is done," wrote Gollancz, "within a very few months these six million Jews will all be dead."[27] The article was dated "Christmas Day, 1942." In addition, the Gollancz pamphlet was quoted during a 1943 House of Commons debate in the Canadian Parliament.[28] Of course, this was not the first time Gollancz warned of the Nazi threat to Jews. As early as 1936, Gollancz had written and published *The Yellow Spot: The Extermination of the Jews of Germany*, with an introduction by Hensley Henson, Bishop of Durham.[29] Nevertheless, while the general public recognized that European Jews were experiencing incredible hardship, it is likely that only a smattering of individuals actually believed Jews were being systematically exterminated.

The capture of the Majdanek concentration camp on the outskirts of Lublin, Poland, in late July 1944 by the Red Army was the event that made significant headlines in both Canada and Britain. In the former, the *Globe and Mail*, the *Toronto Daily Star*, and the *Winnipeg Free Press* all carried major front-page articles.[30] Across the Atlantic, the *Jewish Chronicle*, the *Times*, and the *Illustrated London News* each published photos and commentary regarding the crimes.[31] However, once again, the public impact that the coverage made in both Canada and Britain was marginal.

According to David Goutor, from the fall of 1944 to March 1945, Canadian coverage of crimes in Nazi Europe was almost non-existent.[32] A rare feature was the September 1944 issue of *Maclean's* magazine. American reporter Anna Louise Strong's article, "Mass Murder!" was published in *Maclean's* and it documented crimes in eastern Europe, which she observed while travelling with the Red Army. "Jews of eastern Europe," she wrote, "have been slaughtered – destroyed by a plan pursued with German thoroughness – until almost none remain."[33] Nevertheless, articles such as Strong's were uncommon in the Canadian media.

The smattering of news accounts recording Nazi offences in occupied Europe did little to convince the British and Canadian public of the magnitude of the situation. In addition, during the fall of 1944 and the early winter of 1945, camps were being liberated by the Soviet Union's Red Army. Upon discovering the sites of camps at Bełżec, Sobibór, and

Treblinka, the Soviets issued no major press releases.[34] The publicity of the liberation of Auschwitz was minimal. Nonetheless, because these reports came from what was perceived as a less-than-trusted source, the news of camps liberated in eastern Europe made less of an impression on the public's imagination. Indeed, it would take the liberation of camps in western Europe by the apparently more reliable American, British, and Canadian forces before the horrors were believed and appreciated.

Military Personnel

Many of the British and Canadian military personnel who encountered the situation at Bergen-Belsen had been part of the war effort for years, either in battle or through training. While most men and women wrote and received letters from home, it was difficult for many to find the time to discuss the world news of the day. Most Allied personnel did not have regular access to their respective national and regional newspapers and magazines. Personnel typically kept up to date via BBC Radio or through army or air force newspapers.

It is difficult to gauge what the average soldier or airman was aware of regarding Nazi crimes prior to the spring of 1945. "I have racked my brain since then," recalls Maurice Victor of the Royal Canadian Army Medical Corps and a witness to Bergen-Belsen, "trying to recall what we did know about the horror in Europe, back in the warm safety of North America."[35] Victor, who later became a world-renowned neurologist, was born in Canora, Saskatchewan, and was raised in Winnipeg by Jewish immigrants from what is now Belarus and Lithuania. "We were certainly aware," he continued, "of what was happening to the Jews in Europe, but psychologically, few of us were prepared to accept the unprecedented scale and savagery of the annihilation."[36] As the son of immigrants, Victor was cognizant of the discrimination and hardship faced by Jews not only in Europe, but also in Canada.

Victor's father was a family physician and his mother was a schoolteacher, and both were politically active in Winnipeg. Victor remembers one incident, before he left for overseas with the Canadian Army. His father had returned home one day from a local meeting that featured a speaker who was a Jewish refugee from Germany. The speaker warned those at the meeting of the abhorrent crimes against the Jews occurring in Nazi-occupied Europe. When his father returned home, "the look on his face was indescribable ... he could only say now that what he had heard was unimaginable – and could not be doubted. People in general, I think, had no way of understanding just what was happening, not even people closely connected with Jewish life. We knew when we joined the army that Hitler had to be defeated, but we had to come face-to-face with Hitlerism before we understood."[37] For Maurice Victor and much of the Jewish community in Canada, knowledge of the crimes did not always fully coincide with a belief in the degree of those crimes. The Jewish community abroad was undoubtedly aware of the tremendous privations that existed in Nazi-occupied Europe, but time and further evidence were often required for one's consciousness to completely grasp the implication.

Likewise, the Jewish community in Britain had read in newspapers about the crimes of Nazi Germany, but, again, properly evaluating the scale was difficult. Alan Rose was born in Dundee, Scotland, and was a sergeant in the 7th Armoured Division when he and his men from 3rd/4th County of London Yeomanry entered Bergen-Belsen. In a 1982 interview Rose recalls that his decision to enlist was "prompted, first of all, because whilst nobody knew what Hitler was doing, we all knew what terrible things were happening in Europe."[38] Indubitably, news about the violence in Europe was being closely followed by Jewish communities in both Canada and Britain, although much was still to be learned.

After the war, Rose immigrated to Canada, where he became executive vice-president of the Canadian Jewish Congress. He notes that during the war military personnel steadily learned about the mass deportations and killings. "I had heard on the radio," Rose recalls, "on the BBC, that a concentration camp had been liberated in Eastern Europe ... One heard the horrors, but of course it was quite impossible to comprehend these horrors."[39] Rose was, unquestionably, preoccupied with heavy fighting and trying to survive the war. Furthermore, while news was being received, understanding the repercussions was also difficult. According to Rose,

> I mean, we had no idea in those days what deportation meant. I mean, it was inconceivable to us still in those days. And, you must remember, I lived in a very small world: I lived in a tank, and I heard the BBC news every night ... But, at that time, we had no knowledge of the gas chambers and the genocidal intention of the Nazis. At least, I didn't. I'm sure the Allied powers had. But, I'm the very lonely soldier sitting in a tank, with a very limited horizon.[40]

Thus, it should be clear that for most military personnel on the ground, news of Nazi crimes certainly existed, albeit in limited form. For the soldier in battle, ending the war as quickly as possible was paramount. Moreover, surviving combat and returning home safely were frequently on most soldiers' minds.

In regards to knowledge of Nazi crimes, much of the same can also be said of non-Jewish military personnel. Edinburgh-born John Gourlay Noble lied about his age as a sixteen-year-old in 1938 and enlisted in the Scots Greys.[41] In 1942 he joined the Special Air Service (SAS) as a driver. When the SAS came across Bergen-Belsen in April 1945, the then twenty-three-year-old driver recalls not knowing anything about the Nazi camp system.[42] He was young, and when not occupied with his duties, he was simply looking for a "good time."[43] Noble, who immigrated to Canada after the war and joined that country's army, claims that he also did not read much of the day's news while on leave. Grasping the enormity of the Final Solution came much later to him, years after the war.

The same is true for Ronald Ford "Andy" Anderson, a sergeant in the 1st Canadian Parachute Battalion. "We could not fathom the situation … we had no knowledge of the global situation," underscores the Toronto-born Anderson, who was twenty-two years old in the spring of 1945.[44] Much like Noble, he acknowledges that what was learned took place in the years and decades after the war. Moreover, many Allied military personnel did not stay in the camp long enough to develop a firm understanding of what inmates had to endure over the weeks, months, and years in Hitler's camps. "We had never heard of the word Holocaust or concentration camp," Anderson contends. Indeed, as Peter Novick reminds us, the term "Holocaust," as used today, is mainly a "retrospective construction," and in 1945 it would not have been employed or recognized by most people.[45] Furthermore, many military personnel conceived of "camps" as being used by the Germans for work, labour, or to perhaps to hold political criminals. The majority did not envision mass death in the camps.

It is therefore challenging to assess the average soldier's awareness of Nazi crimes prior to the spring of 1945. Certainly, news concerning the brutal suffering of civilians in eastern Europe existed. Moreover, most military personnel were aware that Jews and other "undesirables" were being harshly treated in Nazi-occupied Europe. However, it is also clear that the average man or woman in the British or Canadian forces had no prior comprehension of Nazi policies or procedures; they were unaware of the function of Hitler's camp system, and they were generally oblivious to the historical events that led to their formation. Consequently, military personnel, particularly those who entered Bergen-Belsen during those first few days, were not told what they could anticipate, nor were they instructed on how they should respond. The personnel who entered the Bergen-Belsen concentration camp were aghast at the scenes before them. Accordingly, their responses were raw because they were unprepared for what they were to experience. Often the words they chose were repeatedly harsh and unforgiving. As we will see, proximity to the brutal crimes did not necessarily bring affection for the suffering, but promoted a distance. It is this initial remoteness which will be examined in the subsequent section.

The Opening Encounter

The Camp

Some of the men from the 63rd Anti-Tank Regiment and 249 Battery, who were formally instructed to take control of Bergen-Belsen, were warned in advance that the concentration camp they were about to enter contained inmates suffering from typhus. German authorities had stated that the inmates were mostly "political criminals" and that there were approximately "1,500" typhus cases in the camp, although the actual figure was ten times that amount.[46] In other instances, some of the men who came across Bergen-Belsen during those first few days were completely unaware that there was even a camp located deep beyond the pine woods, until, that is, they actually came upon it. Either way, most personnel who initially encountered the camp were uninformed that it contained thousands of decomposing corpses and tens of thousands of extremely ill and starving inmates.

The camp proper and the area surrounding it provide a study in sharp contrast. Many of the men and women recall the general area's quiet, picturesque beauty. As the 1st Canadian Parachute Battalion pushed along the road towards Bergen-Belsen on 15 April 1945, Corporal Daniel Hartigan compared the scenery of the Lüneburg Heath to his native homeland. "The overtly pleasant pine tree forest," he writes, "was not unlike those in which nearly all of us had wandered during most of our young lives back in Canada, sung by every gentle sough of the springtime winds and evergreen foliage."[47] Likewise, O.G. Prosser, an officer with the Royal Army Medical Corps, who was posted to 10 Garrison Detachment, recalled that the surrounding area was "the

German counterpart of Salisbury plain ... The country around Belsen is well wooded and reminded me of parts of Deeside."[48] The splendour of the immediate region appears to have only heightened the dreadfulness of the camp itself. Personnel who were initially unaware that there was a camp in the area often found the space uncannily familiar to home.

The first sign that something was awry was the rancid smell wafting from the camp. Of the thousands of written and oral responses to the liberation and relief of Bergen-Belsen, the terrible smell, an offensive miasma, which could be detected kilometres away from the camp, was by far the most common observation.[49] "We'd been coming up through the forests," recalls Reginald Seekings of the 1SAS, "and for a day or so we'd had this horrible stink."[50] Initially, many of the men could not determine what the smell was or from where it was originating. Likewise, Staff Officer Mervin Mirsky of the First Canadian Army was on a reconnaissance patrol when he travelled off a main road and noticed something peculiar in the air. According to Mirsky, "The first signs were, we were on this side road ... and the terrible smell, we didn't realize it was the smell of death. We were half-a-mile away [from the camp]."[51] For the men who were uninformed about the presence of the camp, this was the first indication that something unusual was nearby. For those who were instructed to take over Bergen-Belsen, and were thus aware of its presence, the smell was the first warning that the camp was likely in a worse state than they had been originally told.

Years after an event takes place, an individual can recall the experience and associate it with a remarkable odour. According to Trygg Engen, an authority in the field of the chemosensory sciences, memory of odours can be impervious to the passing of time.[52] While auditory and visual memory can decline over a period, odour memory frequently remains unchanged. Correlating an odour to an event or an experience can form a "rigid bond" which rarely breaks once it is established.[53] Therefore, the terrible, enduring smell of the Bergen-Belsen concentration camp was for many personnel the first clear memory of that abysmal experience, one that haunted so many for the rest of their lives.

Indeed, John Randall was a twenty-four-year-old lieutenant in the SAS when he entered Bergen-Belsen. It took sixty years before he started to regularly speak about the camp. "The stench was horrific," he relates at the age of eighty-five. "It was a mixture of rotting flesh and excrement – a smell that I couldn't get rid of for weeks. I would wake in the night with this ghastly smell in my nose."[54] Describing the smell

A road sign at the entrance to the village of Bergen, Germany, which lies only a few kilometres from the Bergen-Belsen concentration camp. Image 77214, United States Holocaust Memorial Museum, courtesy of Jack and Iris Mitchell Bolton.

quickly returns the memory of the camp and makes Randall extremely emotional. Similarly, a then twenty-seven-year-old Lieutenant-Colonel Douglas Paybody has memories similar to those of Randall. He felt that the "stench got into your clothes, your hair, your ears and your mouth. You could empty water over yourselves, but it took ages to get rid of the smell."[55] For Randall, Paybody, and others, it was as though Bergen-Belsen was not only an appalling memory, but a physical, living thing that attached itself and of which they could not rid themselves.

Engen suggests that odour sensitivity is "situational, contextual and ecological."[56] An odour must be attributed to "something else," such as an event, a person, an object, or an environment. If this "something else" is noteworthy and distinguishable, its odour can be quite distinctive in one's memory.[57] "The smell inside these huts was indescribable," Lieutenant-Colonel James A.D. Johnston wrote days after the liberation, "When we started to work in them we found it difficult to do so for more than ten minutes or so at a time without being physically sick."[58] Associated odours can help recall entire episodes of even painful experiences. Thus, the unforgettable reek of Bergen-Belsen is closely linked with the haunting experience of working in the camp.

Furthermore, the impression of Bergen-Belsen as a constant, living entity which attached itself to those who entered the camp was something repeated by other personnel. Alan Rose felt that his experience in the camp was not simply a memory that remained, but something tangible. "It's something which is physical," he says, "I mean, not only mental in a sense … In fact, it's like the colour of your eyes: They never change. The haunting quality of Belsen has never left me. It's not just lingering; it's extremely strong."[59] For many, the manifestation of the camp endured long after the war. Its sights, sounds, and smells hovered and returned at different points in time. Individuals often had no control of when these thoughts of the camp would come back and make their impression felt.

By the time personnel started arriving at the gates of Bergen-Belsen, many began to surmise that the situation was to be highly unusual. Derrick Sington was a captain in the Intelligence Corps and was commanding No. 14 Amplifying Unit when he was instructed to enter the camp and make an announcement over a loudspeaker. In his 1946 offering, *Belsen Uncovered*, Sington describes his initial entrance into the camp:

> We swung through the almost deserted front compound of the camp … [and] we reached a high wooden gate with criss-cross wiring. It reminded me of the entrance to a zoo. Once through the gate this resemblance was strengthened. On the left of the thoroughfare stood row upon row of green wooden huts, and we came into a smell of ordure – like the smell of a monkey-house. A sad blue smoke floated like a ground mist between the low buildings. I had tried to visualize the interior of a concentration camp, but I had not imagined it like this.[60]

Sington's association of the camp with a "zoo" and its smell to a "monkey-house" is a typical pattern that will emerge as this study progresses. The evoking of language that one would use to describe farms, wildlife, and other animals was all too common. "I can give no adequate description of the Horror Camp in which my men and myself were to spend the next month of our lives," wrote Lieutenant-Colonel Mervyn Gonin of the 11th Light Field Ambulance.[61] Of the camp itself, Gonin said, "It was just barren wilderness, as bare and devoid of vegetation as a chicken run."[62] Men grasped at easily identifiable images. The fetid smells, the filthiness, and deterioration of the camp reminded many of rundown, decrepit farms. The dirt and grime of a farm are, accordingly, produced by the animals which occupy it. This association will continue in discussions of the camp inmates.

As the men entered Bergen-Belsen, they crossed into what survivor David Rousset has termed "l'univers concentrationnaire."[63] This was a world, military personnel soon discovered, where moral and philosophical norms were typically withdrawn. The soldier's perception of reality was seriously confronted, and frequently it was transformed forever. What was now present before their eyes was previously unthinkable. Maurice Victor explains: "There were no ovens at Bergen-Belsen, only places where people lived. Except you couldn't tell the barracks from the outhouses. The stench ... was overwhelming ... It had to be seen, it had to be smelled, for anyone really to grasp what the camps meant."[64] Many military personnel remarked continually that it was difficult to acknowledge what was in front of them. The campground and barracks that surrounded the men were littered with garbage, excreta, and urine. "We walked through the gate," recalls Royal Canadian Air Force public relations officer Fred Hopkinson, "and the first thing we saw was bodies of men, women and children."[65] While it was once challenging to believe the reports one read, for some it was equally difficult to – and yet impossible not to – accept as reality the terrifying scenes in their presence.

Brigadier Hugh Llewellyn Glyn Hughes, deputy director of medical services, VIII Corps of the British Second Army, took overall control of the relief operation. He was one of the first Allied personnel to complete a survey of the general condition of the camp. In remarks similar to Victor, Hughes notes that "no description nor photograph could really bring home the horrors that were there outside the huts."[66] For Hughes, being physically present was the only way one could truly

Royal Canadian Air Force public relations officer Fred Hopkinson and Sergeant Joe Stone of 39 Wing stand before the dead at the Bergen-Belsen concentration camp. Image PL-43511, Department of National Defence.

understand the brutality and inhumanity of Bergen-Belsen. What he discovered inside the barracks was even worse than what he saw around the campgrounds. "Conditions in the huts were indescribable," he explicitly wrote in a report, "and the appalling sanitary conditions in which excreta from those too weak to move or help themselves fouled the rooms or trickled through from upper bunks on to those below ... Latrines were practically non-existent and what there were consisted simply of a bare pole over a deep trench without any screening."[67] The description provided by Hughes demonstrates a world men felt totally unprepared and unequipped to grasp. For many, passing through the gates of the camp was much like stepping into another world, one with standards previously unthinkable.

The camp, its sights, and smells were frequently compared to farms and outhouses, and by others as some type of hell. "The scene in ... the days following our arrival," writes Sington, "resembled Dante's inferno."[68] Thus, in descriptions of the camp, the language could be obscure, severe, and distant. And it begs the question: if the camp was described as a soiled farm or a living hell, how were the sick and starving inmates described? The following section investigates the initial encounter between Allied personnel and the inmates at Bergen-Belsen.

The Inmates

The arrival of and the treatment provided by Allied military personnel undoubtedly saved thousands of lives. Allied soldiers and medics repeatedly gave up rations, searched for foodstuffs, and attempted to return the camp's water supply. They frequently put themselves at risk when working in close proximity – and at times without adequate protection – to inmates with a wide variety of diseases, and many showed tremendous empathy and compassion towards the dying. Indeed, Allied men and women should be commended for the life-saving work they provided to the inmates at Bergen-Belsen.

Many military personnel had tremendous difficulty relating to, as fellow human beings, the sick and starving inmates. The language offered to describe the inmates could betray the life-saving work they were providing. "Human reactions to the unthinkable," remind scholars George M. Kren and Leon Rappoport, "are inevitably primitive and visceral."[69] Those working in the camp could be appalled and even disgusted by the gaunt, half-naked inmates in ragged prison uniforms. Moreover, barriers such as language and cultural differences made it difficult for most personnel to interact and understand the inmates they were assisting. Nonetheless, even when those barriers were removed, the experience was still demanding for all involved.

Reverend Leslie Hardman was born in 1913 in Glynneath, Wales. His father had immigrated to Britain from Poland, while his mother was from Russia. After a series of attacks on Jewish families by mineworkers in South Wales, his family moved to Liverpool, which is where Hardman grew up. Arriving at Bergen-Belsen two days after its surrender, Hardman perhaps did as much as anyone to support the survivors.

In his 1958 offering, *The Survivors: The Story of the Belsen Remnant*, he recalls his first encounter with an inmate at the camp. He writes:

> I shall always remember the first person I met. It was a girl, and I thought she was a negress. Her face was dark brown, and I afterwards learnt that this was because her skin was in the process of healing, after being burnt. When she saw me she made as though to throw her arms around me; but with the instinct of self-preservation, I jumped back. Instantly, I felt ashamed ... I looked at her; fear, compassion and shame were struggling for mastery within me; but she was the more composed of the two. We walked into the compound, keeping our voluntary "no-man's-land" between us.[70]

For the survivors who had the strength, this might have been a moment to quietly rejoice and embrace their liberators. While inmates had typically suffered for long periods of time in the camps and had almost grown accustomed to viewing one another at their worst, this was simply not the case for Allied personnel. Many of the men had seen former inmates and refugees along the roads as they progressed deeper into Germany. However, few had seen so many distressed people in such an enclosed area, surrounded by rotting corpses. Hardman's initial act was an illustration of a natural defensive instinct. He spoke of the incident numerous times in interviews, always admitting embarrassment.

More specifically, we need to ask precisely what personnel did see among the inmates once inside the camp. Captain Patrick Gerald Costigan was a medical officer in the 1st Canadian Parachute Battalion. Born in 1917 in Stettler, Alberta, Costigan received a doctor of medicine in 1943 from the University of Alberta, where he was also an avid hockey player. After the war he settled in Banff as a general physician and surgeon. He was also a district coroner.

Captain Costigan arrived at Bergen-Belsen on 15 April 1945 with the 1st Canadian Parachute Battalion. He ultimately spent two days assisting inmates while working inside the camp.[71] In an interview during the summer of 1945, Costigan remarks, "There were traces of cannibalism ... I saw there the most terrible things I have ever seen."[72] The medics who entered the camp were completely understaffed and overwhelmed, not only by the sheer numbers of those in desperate need of treatment, but also by the severity of their illnesses and their sufferings. In another interview from July 1945, Costigan emphasizes: "Pictures don't show the worst part ... Typhus patients were the biggest problem."⁷³ The death rate remained extremely high as medics and other officers tended to the victims. Costigan also recalls that the water supply was damaged and there were even problems with the lights in the camp, making it difficult to work at night.⁷⁴

Typhus was certainly a major concern for personnel assisting in Bergen-Belsen. A louse-born disease, it is extremely dangerous and can be fatal, particularly for those who come from areas where it is not prevalent.⁷⁵ Of course, typhus was not the only disease present. British sculptor Jonah Jones served with the 224 Parachute Field Ambulance during the war. Jones was attached to the 1st Canadian Parachute Battalion when he arrived at Bergen-Belsen.⁷⁶ After the war, Jones became quite ill and eventually spent five years in sanatoria. He believes he contracted tuberculosis from the camp survivors to whom he had tended.⁷⁷

Accordingly, and if at all possible, personnel who initially arrived at the camp tried to keep a distance, either physically or psychologically, from the inmates. Many endeavoured to remain detached from what they were witnessing. For example, it was ensured that personnel from the British Army's Film and Photographic Unit (AFPU) did not work in too close proximity to the dead or to the survivors in the camp.⁷⁸ At times, however, this was difficult or even impossible. Consequently, there were men who worked closely and intimately with survivors.⁷⁹ Those who entered the camp during those first few days often had very specific tasks to perform. Many tried to silence their emotions, and some accomplished this better than others. But, when it came time to write or speak about the inmates, personnel often did so using comparable words and metaphors. The language, whether intentional or not, could often be degrading and dehumanizing to the very people they were attempting to help.

Metaphors symbolically transfer features or characteristics of one object or (living) thing to that of another. Accordingly, this transfer can offer a novel way of perceiving aspects of life. A metaphor can alter perceptions and offer a reflection on values and meanings. Moreover, what is reproduced in language is not reality but a construct. Therefore, our experiences are structured by conceptual systems, which are basically metaphorical.⁸⁰

Derrick Sington began writing his book about the liberation only months after the surrender of Bergen-Belsen. Upon entering the camp, Sington, whose father was Jewish, encountered a "strange simian throng," whom he then referred to as "clowns in their terrible motley."⁸¹

After observing camp Kapos (prisoner functionaries) striking other inmates, he describes the latter as "prancing zebras" who conducted "kangaroo jumps." He then notes that the Kapos pushed these "creatures" through what appeared to him as some sort of "cattle-drive."[82] Later, after discovering that some inmates had been shot dead by camp guards after raiding a potato patch, Sington writes, "It was pitiable to think of these men shot like rats on the very day of liberation."[83] On 17 April, upon coming across a pile of unburied bodies along a path, he states: "At close quarters they look inhuman ... It was like the overladen counter of a butcher's shop ... The emaciated, upturned face of another dead woman ... Her thin blue lips wore a pinched, unearthly expression ... She looked like a marionette."[84] Sington, like so many other Allied personnel, reached for language that, to them, was easily classifiable, but often unsuitable to the victims of Nazi atrocities.

Many of the words and metaphors selected from Sington's book demonstrate the employment of zoomorphic language. Simply put, zoomorphism is the attribution of animal characteristics to people or to their behaviour.[85] It is the opposite of anthropomorphism, which involves giving human characteristics to animals. Zoomorphism is a complex trope; as Wendy Doniger argues, "a human being is the explicit object, the bestial qualities imputed to the human ... teaches us simultaneously what sort of person it thinks that animal is like and what sort of animal it thinks that sort of person is like."[86] Like anthropomorphism, zoomorphism has been practised for centuries. Examining the uses of such language can reveal the complexity of a highly ambivalent situation whereby soldiers and medics want to help fellow human beings but are disturbed by their appearance and behaviour. Language contains our standards and conventions, and how we employ it to describe people also has an influence on how we later think about and even treat others.

In addition, we use metaphors to guide our observations about the world and the people in it. The substance of a metaphor is only meaningful to a particular group of people who share the same cultural conventions. Metaphors can influence our attitudes and beliefs, as well as the way we behave and act in the world. As James Greary recently put it, "The logic of metaphor is the logic of our lives. Metaphor impinges on everything, allowing us – poets and non-poets alike – to experience and think about the world in fluid, unusual ways. Metaphor is the bridge we fling between the utterly strange and the utterly familiar ... between I and the other."[87] The "bridge" that Sington hurled between the extraordinary other-worldliness of the camp and its inmates and the familiar image of farms and animals were also used by many Allied personnel.

And what did Sington's animal metaphors signify? "Simians" are primates such as apes and monkeys. According to Robert Palmatier in *Speaking of Animals: A Dictionary of Animal Metaphors* (1995), apes are awkward and unattractive animals, while monkeys are generally viewed as untidy creatures who are not directed by ethics or morals.[88] Inmates in striped camp uniforms are likened to "prancing zebras," an undomesticated, unpredictable animal. "Rats" are vermin who carry diseases and bite. A "cattle-drive" symbolizes the loss of independence for an animal that is observed as lacking judgment and choice. Sington initially viewed the behaviour of camp inmates as low-level animals, inferior to the rational, strong, and healthy Allied soldier. Doniger suggests that zoomorphism is an attempt to "reduce the otherness between humans and animals, to see the sameness beneath the difference."[89] Accordingly, the danger of this type of mental reduction is that, if left unchecked, it can lead to the cruel treatment of both humans and non-humans.[90]

Lieutenant-Colonel J.A.D. Johnston, commander of 32 Casualty Clearing Station, stated in a report, written three days after liberation, that the inmates were "a dense mass of emaciated, apathetic scarecrows."[91] A scarecrow is gaunt and ragged, used to scare away types of birds from harvests. In another report, Captain John W. Gray, GHQ Liaison Regiment, wrote, "A very large portion of inmates have lost all resemblance to human creatures, physically or mentally," and saw fighting over "a heap of raw turnips such as one would hesitate to give to cattle."[92] A cow is an animal of instinct often attributed with exhibiting limited intelligence. In addition, in a letter from 18 April 1945, Captain J. Grant of the 21 Light Field Ambulance commented that, for survivors, "self-respect and decency are gone ... They are reverting to animals."[93] While most of the inmates were too weak to rejoice, most military personnel were too horrified by the experience to attempt to make any sense of the survivor. Thus, many either hoped or were relieved to be posted elsewhere. This was an assignment for which no one could have expected to have been prepared. Employing terms such as scarecrows, prancing zebras, rats, cattle, marionettes, clowns, and the like all work to frame desperately ill survivors as less than the healthy soldier.

These types of metaphors were employed by myriad Allied personnel to sustain a division between themselves and the inmates. Referring to inmates as "animals" is to view them as reprehensible. As a metaphor, an animal is something "irrational, immoral, or uncivilized."[94] In this context, survivors were viewed as something repellent, uncivilized, and disagreeable. For some military personnel, this type of language was used as a defence mechanism. To view the survivors as something other than human was a way to protect the soldier against thinking that it was possible that this could also happen to them.

Clearly, military personnel had great difficulty viewing the inmates as normal fellow human beings. But were this difficulty and harsh language primarily the experience of non-Jewish personnel? Robert H. Abzug has surveyed large numbers of American responses to the "liberation" of a variety of camps. He notes that survivors were compared to animals or non-humans. However, he also explains that "the case was different for some Jewish-American soldiers."[95] Likewise, in her work examining Bergen-Belsen, Hagit Lavsky suggests, in regards to the responses made after liberation, that "the picture they painted was very much dependent upon whether they themselves were Jews or non-Jews, and even more so, whether or not they were British."[96] If the Jewish-Anglo or Canadian solider could also speak Yiddish or Polish, and some certainly did, then they could communicate better than the soldier who could not converse in the native language of the survivors.

However, closer inspection of the words and metaphors used by Jewish personnel demonstrates close similarities to their non-Jewish counterparts. Ben Shephard, examining the medical issues surrounding Bergen-Belsen, contends that "Leslie Hardman's version of Belsen, written in 1957 in collaboration with a journalist, is quite different from other British accounts … He could not distance himself or take refuge in euphemism."[97] Hardman worked determinedly for both the dead and the survivors at the camp. And he was frequently overwhelmed by his experiences. Joanne Reilly, in her comprehensive account of the liberation and relief of Bergen-Belsen, insists that Hardman did not demonstrate detachment and was able to overcome "feelings of horror and shock and view the survivors as human beings."[98] One should note that Hardman arrived at Bergen-Belsen on 17 April 1945 and spent a number of months working at the camp and getting to know the inmates.

Still, the evidence is far more complex. At the outset, Hardman, like most others, also struggled to relate to the inmates. As stated above, his initial reaction to the first survivor he encountered at the camp was to jump back in horror, to which he immediately felt shame, compassion, and fear. In his 1958 book he remarks that the survivors were "now reduced to hideous apparitions bearing no resemblance to man, but only witnessing to man's inhumanity."⁹⁹ Later, observing two British soldiers carrying sacks of potatoes near some survivors, he notes:

> And then, almost as though they had emerged from the ground itself, or had floated out from the retreating shadows of dark corners, a number of wraithlike creatures came tottering towards us ... Their skeleton arms and legs made jerky, grotesque movements as they forced themselves forward. Their bodies, from their heads to their feet, looked like matchsticks ... In an instant these human skeletons, whose appearance and approach were more hallucination than reality, fell upon the sacks and their contents almost like locusts descending upon a field of corn.¹⁰⁰

Hardman was taken aback and stunned by this episode and immediately sunk into a depression. He returned, shaken, to his quarters in Celle. The following morning, upon entering the camp, he was surrounded by an upset mob of female survivors, whose "sudden onslaught reminded me of a flock of cackling geese."¹⁰¹ In these examples, while the survivors' appearance is compared to the non-human or inanimate ("matchsticks"), their behaviours are related to animals ("emerged from the ground" and "like locusts descending upon a field of corn"). In the Bible, plagues of locusts have been considered accountable for epidemics of human illness.

Moreover, the British soldiers' Canadian counterpart made similar observations. Leo Heaps was born in 1922 in Winnipeg, the son of Abraham A. Heaps, a Jewish immigrant from Leeds who was a former member of Parliament and founder of the Co-operative Commonwealth Federation (CCF). Leo Heaps was a CANLOAN officer seconded to the British Army and spent time working with the 1st British Airborne Division and the Special Air Service. After surveying Bergen-Belsen shortly after the camp's surrender, he concedes, "The Nazis had succeeded. They had reduced the inmates to the state of beasts."¹⁰² Regarded as one of the lowest types of animals, "beasts" are detestable, deficient in intellect, decency, reason, and self-control. To Heaps, the dead were "as thin as dried leaves," and those clinging to life "stumbled along with the weariness of the living dead, plodding through hell."¹⁰³ Comparatively, the language the Winnipeg-born-Heaps used was similar, the images akin, to that of the British servicemen, both Christian and Jewish alike. Thus, the utter dreadfulness of the camp appears to have cut across nations, cultures, religions, and rank.

In Western culture, men and women often prefer to think they are in control of the environment and everything in it, including the plants and animals. As George Lakoff and Mark Johnson explain, along this line of thinking, our ability for reason places us above animals, or in other words, what is rational is above (human being) and that which is down, which lives closer to the ground, is irrational (animal). Thus, to "emerge from the ground" and to "fall upon the sacks" like an animal is something irrational, an act a supposedly rational individual would not perform. British personnel, Jewish, Christian or otherwise, simply could not grasp or accept the type of "irrational" behaviour that was on display during those first few days in the camp.

Furthermore, images, symbols, and metaphors that evoke animals certainly aim at something rather specific. The term can denote acts or behaviours one finds repugnant or disturbing. In general, not all associations to animals are negative. One can be as graceful as a swan, as innocent as a dove, or as brave as a lion. And yet, as demonstrated above, most animal metaphors (and similes) carry undesirable connotations. Associating animal behaviour with the actions of human beings is thus generally pejorative and demonstrates one's objection and aversion to that type of conduct.

Lakoff and Mark Turner highlight a hierarchy of concepts called "The Great Chain of Being" metaphors.[104] This system demonstrates how things in the world are related to one another. At the top of the basic chain are human beings, who maintain a high order of thoughts and behaviour. Next down the chain are animals, which are ascribed with instinctual attributes and behaviour. Third along the chain are plants (biological properties), followed by complex objects (structural attributes), and lastly, natural physical things (natural physical attributes). This theory can be traced back, in the Christian and Jewish traditions, to the Bible. Therefore, when one level of the chain is used to understand another level it becomes a metaphorical system.

And how does this correspond to the soldier's description of the survivors? Most of the inmates in Bergen-Belsen had been systematically starved, most to or near death. They typically had no access to medicine or therapeutic care. Few had the strength to fight for any small scrap of food that could be found. "They walk like dumb animals," wrote Reverend T.J. Stretch, "feeling nothing and thinking nothing."[105] In the final days of German control of the camp, there was no water or food. Sanitation facilities were non-existent. Disease and infection were rampant. Unquestionably, the suffering was tremendous, and by the time the

Allies arrived in April 1945, the appearance of most inmates was dreadful. Military personnel simply could not conceive the years of brutal suffering and degradation the inmates had faced.

To be sure, it was not only the appearance of most of the inmates that disturbed the men, but also their "abnormal" behaviour. John Proskie was born in 1906 in Edmonton, Alberta. Upon graduating university, he worked with the Department of Agriculture, Research and Economics at the University of Alberta. On 28 September 1942, Proskie joined the Royal Canadian Air Force and initially worked in the Education Branch.[106] After the war he accepted a position with the Department of Fisheries in Ottawa, where he worked until his retirement.

On 17 April 1945, Squadron Leader Proskie, a food and agricultural expert, was forwarded to the Military Government's 224 Detachment Headquarters. He immediately surveyed the camp and was put in charge of locating and collecting nearby resources for the inmates at Bergen-Belsen.[107] In a report dated 22 April 1945, Proskie notes the peculiar, surreal quality and conduct that existed in the camp, remarking: "The dead bodies and the living seem to be intermixed, for the living use the dead as pillows at night and in the daytime a place that is convenient to sit and eat their rations."[108] As corpses were scattered everywhere, in the huts and barracks and on the campgrounds, the survivors were constantly surrounded by death. Those who could muster the strength would walk around aimlessly in the vicinity of corpses, some partially clothed, and due to the lack of sanitation facilities, many were forced to relieve themselves out in the open. The scenes were incomprehensible and appalling to Allied military personnel. It could even be difficult to differentiate between the living and the dead. As Proskie later noted, "There apparently is little concern and no marked line between the living and the dead, for those who are alive today may be dead tomorrow. In fact, during the critical stage of the food in this camp, some of the inmates turned to cannibalism and thereby the dead helped to sustain life for the living until food was made available after liberation."[109] The prisoners spent years in the camp, were starved and beaten, and witnessed friends and family die in front of them. Death and anguish were commonplace.

Military personnel were therefore confronted with an experience nearly impossible to describe. Many were at a loss for words, and when they searched for images and metaphors, their responses were often detached and incongruous. As he reflected back on the events of April 1945 fifteen years later, Major Benjamin Barnett, commander of No. 249

Battery, offered a nuanced response, stating: "The things I saw completely defy description. There are no words in the English language which can give a true impression of the ghastly horror of this camp. I find it hard even now to get into focus all these horrors, my mind is really quite incapable of taking in all I saw because it was all so completely foreign to anything I had previously believed or thought possible."[110] Countless witnesses repeated similar sentiments: Bergen-Belsen defied language and was simply beyond the mind's comprehension. Many encountered tremendous difficulties in finding fitting words to describe both the confusion they felt and the atrocities they witnessed. Personnel struggled to locate suitable metaphors and images for what they wished to tell. And when they did endeavour to describe the internees and their conditions, words typically fell short in bringing any reasonable understanding to what they were witnessing.

At best, what the solider experienced in Bergen-Belsen was often used to bring a moral clarity, nearly after the fact, to fighting the war. After six years of hard battle, if anyone had doubts, it was now apparent to the men the importance of winning the war. While the vast majority did not enter the war to bring an end to Hitler's camps, nor to save the victims of Nazi Germany, the liberation seemed to justify the sacrifices they made by joining the war effort – albeit this was only learned at the end of the war. Recalling his fallen comrade, A.J. "Scotty" MacInnis, Corporal Daniel Hartigan of the 1st Canadian Parachute Battalion imagined what the lost paratrooper might have said had he survived long enough to witness the scenes at Bergen-Belsen. "Thank God we came over and fought this war, eh!" he envisions MacInnis saying, "The sight of these poor souls tells us ... we have fought for a just cause!"[111] Bringing an end to the suffering of so many survivors at the hands of the Nazis and their underlings helped to validate the sacrifices made in war. For the Allies, by the middle of April 1945, triumph over Germany was nearly complete. The following section will examine how the British and Canadians viewed the German and Hungarian military personnel who remained in Bergen-Belsen during and immediately following its surrender.

The Staff

Shortly after the truce agreement was signed between the Germans and the British, the majority of the SS personnel who worked in the camp departed. Soldiers from both the Wehrmacht and the Hungarian Army

– who were allies of Nazi Germany – remained on site to guard the outer perimeter of the camp. The commandant of Bergen-Belsen, Josef Kramer, and a group of seventy-seven SS men and women, who were considered either "Reichsdeutsche" (ethnic German citizens of the Reich) or "Volksdeutsche" (ethnic Germans typically from eastern Europe), stayed at the camp and worked in an administrative capacity, although this would not last long.[112] There were approximately 2,000 Hungarian guards working in the camp. The majority of the German and Hungarian personnel were still very much armed when British and Canadian forces arrived at the camp.

When men from the Special Air Service arrived, ahead of the 63rd Anti-Tank Regiment, they were unopposed by the guards and were permitted unfettered access to the camp. John Randall recalls seeing Commandant Kramer walking around the camp and notes that most of the guards remained silent and uninterested in their arrival. Upon seeing a guard beat a defenceless prisoner, Randall reveals that Reginald Seekings, a former amateur boxer, knocked out the antagonist with a couple of hard punches to the head.[113] Later, Seekings recollects the strangeness of watching some of the Germans leaving the area, unimpeded. "We were chatting to German soldiers," he remembers, "yelling out as they went past."[114] However, due to the truce agreement, nothing more could be done to exact any type of serious revenge.

The Germans and Hungarian military personnel continued to work in and around the camp, largely unrestricted and also armed, and this helped to make the situation all the more surreal for the Allies. Private Emmanuel Fisher, of the 32 Casualty Clearing Station, found the situation strangely comical. "Everywhere were Germans and Hungarians armed with rifles and hand grenades," he writes. "It was quite a common sight to see an armed Nazi walking out with his wife or best girl."[115] Camp staff typically had families living in the neighbouring area and they were able to visit them on a regular basis. The lack of sympathy and remorse on the part of the camp staff, and the fact that many still operated in the camp, only increased the anger of the Allies.

Major R.F. Waldon was amazed by the "luxurious quarters" set aside for the Germans and Hungarians. He noted the audacity of a German sergeant major who invited some of his men for a meal, telling Waldon that they "had plenty."[116] While the inmates were left without nourishment and had resorted to eating grass, the SS and the Hungarians, who had long been employed at the camp, had a surplus of food available to them. Major Barnett observed that Commandant Kramer was "not

A Hungarian sentry monitors the perimeter of the Bergen-Belsen concentration camp. Image 76491, United States Holocaust Memorial Museum, courtesy of Arnold Bauer Barach.

ashamed of all the horrors," and Sington reveals that the well-fed Kramer had twenty-five pigs housed behind Block 3 in a private stable.[117] Within a few days of the camp's surrender, the remaining SS would be under arrest.

And how did the Allies view the Germans in light of these terrible crimes? Canadian Leo Heaps had nothing but derision for the Germans. He encountered a number of SS and remarks, "I looked at these beasts, who had once been men ... No matter how degraded they had forced, by starvation and indignity, the people of the camp to become, the SS guards had reached by their own crimes untouchable depths of degradation. These men were the untouchables."[118] In each of them, Heaps saw individuals with no redeeming value and no moral fortitude. In fact, he refused to acknowledge any humanity within them. As he left the camp his driver, Stimpson, a twenty-four-year-old man from western Canada, repeated to Heaps, "You know, people who treat other people like that can't be human. They *can't* be human."[119] The degradation witnessed in the camp, combined with the lack of any compunction on behalf of the guards, provoked many to view the SS as inhuman beasts or monsters.

The Reverend T.J. Stretch was from Fishguard, Wales, and worked at the parish of the Holy Trinity Church in Aberystwyth prior to the war. He interpreted the male SS staff as loathsome and brutish figures. According to Stretch, "they loved their job and gloated over the sufferings they saw."[120] He emphasizes that the SS men were oblivious to the fact that they were working in a veritable hell of their own creation. For Allied personnel who often looked at the inmates through the lens of animal metaphors and imagery, in contrast, they viewed the SS as unearthly monsters, evil demons, or satanic devils.

Interestingly, it was usually the female SS guards who were viewed with the highest level of disparagement. Military personnel were generally surprised to find so many SS women working inside the camp. In his report from 15 April, Captain Gray of the GHQ Regiment refers to the female SS staff as a "nasty crew of Rhinemaidens."[121] In Richard Wagner's *Der Ring des Nibelungen* (*The Ring of the Nibelung*), Rhinemaidens are water-nymphs whose responsibility is to guard the powerful Rhine gold, which they ultimately fail to do. The Rhinemaidens, at the outset, appear harmless and innocent, but later display their needling, cruelty, and inhumanity. Likewise, Captain Costigan of the 1st Canadian Parachute Battalion said of all the Germans in the camp, the SS women were the "nastiest."[122] In a letter home, Reverend Stretch compares the SS men to the women, describing the latter as "stony-faced, hard and tough," who could be "more vicious and diabolical than the SS men."[123] He acknowledges that the SS women had been dubbed as the "Brides of Hell" and notes that this name was entirely fitting.[124] From the perspective of the Allied soldier, average men and women were incapable of such crimes; only malevolent creatures far more brutal and otherworldly could achieve such horrors.

The German staff received no sympathy or consideration from the British or the Canadians. Personnel from the Royal Engineers forced SS guards at gunpoint to transport and bury thousands of corpses that lay on the campground. Clearly, Allied military personnel described the SS

Former Bergen-Belsen camp personnel are lined up in front of a mass grave to hear a broadcast denouncing their treatment of prisoners. Image 74929, United States Holocaust Memorial Museum, courtesy of Hadassah Bimko Rosensaft.

harshly. Moreover, it was often the female SS guards who received much of the attention and scorn. Indeed, both soldiers and the media revealed a keen interest in the SS women at the camp. The woman who received much of the attention was Irma Grese, who held the positions of *arbeitsdienstführerin* (labour duty leader) and *rapportführerin* (report leader) in Bergen-Belsen. She worked in the women's section of the camp. Grese, who was from Wrechen, Mecklenburg-Strelitz, Germany, was young, blonde, and pretty. She was dubbed in the British press as

Schutzstaffel (SS) Irma Grese, left, and Josef Kramer, right, await trial before a British Military Tribunal. Image 78274, United States Holocaust Memorial Museum, courtesy of Hadassah Bimko Rosensaft.

the "Blonde Angel of Hell" or the "Beastess of Belsen."[125] Grese was frequently discussed and noted in the accounts of many Allied soldiers.

Accordingly, the brutality of Grese and many other female SS personnel, such as Hilde Lobauer – often referred to as the "S.S. woman without uniform" – an *arbeitsdienstführerin* who terrorized inmates, was often emphasized, described, and photographed.[126] Largely, the women were viewed as sadistic beasts and as evidence of the wickedness of Nazism. To know the real bestial nature of Nazi Germany and culture, argued a number of military personnel and journalists, one only had to view the female camp guards.[127]

Concluding Remarks

Much of this chapter has been dedicated to examining how military personnel responded to the camp, its internees, and its guards. Thus, the focus has been on what was said, written, and expressed. Some scholars have also studied what was *not* said or what was simply left out in official reports or media articles relating to the liberation and relief of Bergen-Belsen. It has been argued that while the majority of inmates were Jews, most reports and news items did not highlight this crucial fact.

In "The Memory of Belsen," Tony Kushner explains that most media reports were largely quiet on the essential point that the preponderance of inmates in Bergen-Belsen were Jewish; he states that this was intentional and it was not due to a lack of information.[128] Certainly, the majority of official images and media articles published in both Britain and Canada did not reveal that, at the time of the camp's surrender, inmates at Bergen-Belsen were unusually and predominately Jewish. Moreover, along with religion, the names, nationalities, and personal stories of internees were absent from newspaper reports during and immediately after the liberation. The identity of the victims was largely glossed over.

In her excellent study, *Belsen: The Liberation of a Concentration Camp* (1998), Joanne Reilly also suggests that for British military personnel, the tragedy of Bergen-Belsen was largely a human, rather than a Jewish one.[129] Like the media reports which remained silent, Reilly appears to propose that British liberators were also mum on the subject of the inmate's names, ethnicities, nationalities, and religion. Certainly, some Allied personnel admitted to being unaware of the identity of the internees. "And who are these people who have suffered so much?" Reverend Stretch confessed in a letter home. "We don't know; nobody knows. They have a number tattooed on their arms but it does not correspond to any name because all the records have been destroyed."[130] While language issues and the fact that camp records had been destroyed challenged Allied personnel, it did not take long for them to learn who was in the camp and for what reason.[131] In "The Filming of the Liberation of Bergen-Belsen and Its Impact on the Understanding of the Holocaust," Toby Haggith examines the daily "dope sheets" written by British cameramen. A "dope sheet" is a cameraman's list of shots, a description of what was captured on film. Haggith illustrates that many of the cameramen were well aware which survivors were Jewish, that they were in the majority, and what this signified.[132] In addition, Reverend Stretch later acknowledges that inmates "belonged to different races and creeds; they were Poles or Jews – that was their only crime."[133] While the larger historical implication was still largely unclear, men did know the religious and ethnic make-up of the internees.

Therefore, in a variety of documents from 1945 to 1946 – such as reports, letters, diary entries, and the like – both British and Canadian military personnel regularly highlighted the "identities" of the camp internees, ascertaining names, nationalities, and religion. In his report, written the day of the camp's surrender, Captain Gray notes that "Prisoners are of all nationalities, with a sizeable portion of Jews."[134] Likewise, in his report written only a few days later, his Canadian counterpart, Squadron Leader Proskie, stresses, "this camp contains the sweepings of Europe, including German criminals, in addition to political inmates and Jews who are here simply because they are Jews."[135] As an agricultural expert responsible for collecting food for the inmates, Proskie was well aware of the national diversity and religious make-up in the camp. As they gained their strength, Proskie received numerous requests for certain types of food, such as buckwheat to make kasha, while others asked for sauerkraut, potatoes, and the like. The dietary requests quickly revealed to Proskie and his colleagues the backgrounds of some of the inmates.

When he arrived in Celle, Reverend Hardman was told by his Colonel about the existence of Bergen-Belsen and explained that he would find "a lot of your people [there]."[136] In *Belsen Uncovered* (1946), Captain Sington states that "by the end of our second day in Belsen we had been able to find out the nationality groups in the camp ... They were a large part of the survivors of European Jewry."[137] In a letter from June 1945, Major Barnett notes that some of the dead were buried in separate cemeteries, one Jewish and one Christian.[138] Unfortunately, this only occurred during the later weeks and months. Initially, the bodies were mixed and buried together, regardless of nationality, ethnicity, or religion. The dead were left largely unidentified.

Nevertheless, it appears that Allied military personnel, both Canadian and British, both Jewish and non-Jewish, were aware of the identities of the dead and living in Bergen-Belsen. While it is clear that official government reports and the news media were generally silent on the point that the majority of inmates were Jews, this is not the case with military personnel on the ground. Soldiers and medics alike were conscious of the religious and ethnic make-up, despite the fact that many could not communicate verbally with the survivors and camp records were absent. And of course, while Jews were in the majority, they were not the only distinct group of people in the camp. Personnel also readily identified Roma, Polish, Russian, French, and Ukrainian inmates. The internees did indeed come from across the European continent.

When it came time to discuss the camp, the inmates, and the guards, there was a noticeable overlap in what was both written and spoken. The camp was usually viewed as a decaying farm, an outhouse, or a living hell. In recalling the camp proper, many personnel tended to focus on the rancid smell. Chemosensory scientists have shown that the way smell is processed in the brain makes odour memories particularly irrepressible and persistent. It was a powerful part of the experience and most men did not and could not forget it.

The inmates were typically described using animal or inanimate-object imagery and metaphor. The victims had been brutalized. In the words of Chaplain Ross K. Cameron of the RCAF, the treatment that the inmates received "was designed to reduce [them] ... to the indignity and squalor of animals ... There was a physical revulsion produced by such sights, which was beyond even the revulsion of the sights of a battlefield ... They were destined by the evil of National Socialism to be reduced physically, morally and spiritually to the level of animals."[139] Inmates had been starved and frequently beaten. They had been worn down by terrible abuse. To the eyes of the liberator, the conduct of the survivors was often abnormal and illogical. Their behaviour was likened to the seemingly "instinctual" and irrational actions of animals. They observed conduct that they could not fathom and actions they deemed as immoral or utterly bizarre. The words they used only distanced them from understanding the terrible reality of the situation. They employed language to reinforce the division between man and "animal."

The frightfulness of Bergen-Belsen had a levelling effect: virtually everyone who entered the camp experienced some sense of shock or distress. Indeed, the intense feelings of disgust and dismay cut across religious, ethnic, gender, and professional lines. As the following chapters will demonstrate, "time" had perhaps the greatest impact on an individual's response: either the point in time one entered Bergen-Belsen or the length of time one spent in the camp. In other words, the later one encountered Bergen-Belsen, the more humane were the descriptors employed in their narratives. Likewise, the longer one spent in the camp, particularly after the initial few weeks, and the greater the opportunity to bond and communicate, the more likely the liberator viewed the survivors as fellow beings.

But in those first few days, how could Allied personnel have understood the "concentrationary universe"? As Joanne Reilly aptly writes,

"The liberators were faced with a situation that mocks our vocabulary."[140] The men were not forewarned of the brutal circumstances that awaited them. And if they had been warned, they most likely would have still been overwhelmed by the horror. "What SHOULD you do when faced by 60,000 dead, sick and dying people?" asked Major A.L. Berney, a Staff Officer attached to VIII Corps. "We were in the army to fight a war and to beat the enemy. What we were suddenly thrust into was beyond anyone's comprehension, let alone a situation we could have been organized and effectively planned for."[141] The men worked with what they had at their disposal and searched for words they thought could help make sense of an ineffable situation.

While the inmates were often compared to animals and inanimate objects, the SS officers were likened to beasts, monsters, and demons. Women were predominantly focused upon. From a reference point as the softer, gentler, more humane sex, SS women at Bergen-Belsen were viewed as proof of the repugnant nature of Nazism and as a condemnation of German culture. Their "stony-faced, hard and tough" features were a symbol of all that was brutal in Nazism. Their ruthless acts were viewed as something not done by humans, but by maniacal beasts.

The Bergen-Belsen concentration camp was surrendered and handed over to the British Army. Its "liberation," the word most commonly used for its surrender, was not a moment of jubilation and celebration. Allied military personnel were initially overwhelmed, understaffed, and left without adequate supplies, equipment, and medicine. They were presented with an experience for which no one had been prepared or trained. As days turned into weeks, the situation at Bergen-Belsen slowly improved. It took time before Allied personnel could alter their gaze and their opinion of the survivors. In the following chapters, we will see how and why this gaze was transformed and, ultimately, rehabilitated.

Chapter Four

A Camp on Exhibit: Workers, Witnesses, Visitors Descend

The concentration camp at BELSEN is only a few miles from my present HQ. You have actually to see the camp to realize fully the things that went on ... The SS Commandant is a nice looking specimen![1]

Field Marshal Bernard Montgomery, 21 Army Group

As usual with any matter of interest, floods of visitors descended upon BELSEN, mostly without authority or clear purpose.[2]

21 Army Group, "Report on Relief Measures at Belsen"

And, near the town of Bergen, [I] came upon the Belsen concentration camp ... I had no business in the camp and I could be accused of voyeurism – a repellent thought. Yet I was there, I saw it and it is etched in my memory.[3]

Captain Jeffrey Williams, Calgary Highlanders

The initial period of Allied control of Bergen-Belsen saw a variety of British and Canadian divisional units, battalions, and sections both proceed into and bypass the camp. It took approximately three to four days before considerable reinforcements reached the camp and for larger-scale organized relief efforts to commence. Upon arrival, personnel accepted an assortment of tasks, such as providing inmates with medical aid and nourishment, securing the camp, and supervising mass burials. While some military personnel spent only a brief period of time assisting at Bergen-Belsen, others had their assignments extended from days to weeks and even from weeks to several months. The length of time spent in the camp made a significant impact on one's assessment of the situation. Accordingly, part of the focus of this chapter will be on the non-medical relief conducted at the camp by Britons and Canadians throughout the spring and summer of 1945.

Aside from those who performed approved, authorized roles at Bergen-Belsen, hundreds of other personnel descended upon the camp often without official permission from authorities. Thousands of British and Canadian soldiers, airmen, medics, and the like were working and fighting in and around the Lüneburg Heath. As news broke about Bergen-Belsen and military personnel became aware that this infamous concentration camp was located nearby, scores of individuals and small groups made their way to the site. Some came to bear witness to a significant crime in history, while others appeared out of a basic human curiosity. "Eventually the number of visitors became so large," a 21 Army Group report stated shortly after the camp's surrender, "that they impeded work."[4] Indeed, throughout the spring and summer of 1945, Allied personnel repeatedly made private, independent excursions to the camp, often in small groups while on leave or during time off. These journeys increased after the unconditional surrender of the armed forces of Nazi Germany. In addition, and not long after the camp's capitulation, large groups of military personnel from the surrounding areas were organized by authorities and brought by bus to take guided tours of Bergen-Belsen in an effort to have numerous eyewitnesses to the crimes.

The following chapter surveys the responses of British and Canadian military personnel in the weeks and months following the handover of the Bergen-Belsen concentration camp. The focus will be on the meanings mined by the Allies. In what ways did individuals respond? What did the crimes at Bergen-Belsen demonstrate to them? What stories did they emphasize and what does this ultimately signify? How and to whom did they assign blame? Finally, what prompted Allied personnel to discuss and describe the horrific crimes in the weeks, months, years, and even decades after the war? What did they hope to achieve by speaking out? These questions and others will be considered. The following chapter thus explores themes of shame and remorse, culpability and complicity, punishment and revenge.

As noted in chapter 1, the personal accounts examined in this study are employed, to a limited extent, for their empirical value. These narratives, instead, will be surveyed more for the meanings and understandings they share about the past. Each individual who narrates his or her experience will select and reflect upon different aspects, making associations to form patterns of meaning. Thus, for this study, one's interpretation of events is of primary concern rather than solely the veracity of an account. As scholar James E. Young emphasizes, "even if narrative cannot document events, or constitute perfect *fact*uality, it can document the *act*uality of writer and text."[5] In other words, how narrators have taken and related their experiences is of particular importance. Investigating multiple narratives about a specific subject can expose the narrative practices and meaning-making patterns of members from particular cultural groups.

This chapter is divided into two major sections. The first half will examine the responses of military personnel who performed formal, official, active roles at Bergen-Belsen. For example, individuals who were assigned by authorities to work in the camp will be considered alongside those who transported food, medicine, and supplies from the surrounding areas and spent time dividing and distributing those items in the camp to the inmates. The second half of this chapter will explore some of the hundreds of Britons and Canadians who entered Bergen-Belsen as witnesses and who did not provide any direct aid or assistance to the inmates or to the authorities working in the camp proper. Of particular importance will be to uncover the reasons why these individuals left their stations and made their way to a camp where they were not asked or required to work in any recognized, sanctioned capacity.

The Arrival of Reinforcements

Working in the Midst of Death

In the days following the camp's surrender word quickly spread about the gravity of the situation at Bergen-Belsen. As detailed in chapter 2, on 17 and 18 April 1945, a number of reinforcements arrived. For example, on 17 April, 224 Military Government Detachment, 32 Casualty Clearing Station and 11 Light Field Ambulance reached the camp, while the following day additional groups arrived, including 10 Garrison – which assumed formal administrative control of Bergen-Belsen – along with 113 Light Anti-Aircraft Regiment, 30 Field Hygiene Section, and 7 Mobile Bacteriological Laboratory. Personnel thus began the monumental tasks of restoring water and electricity, organizing food and transport, burying the dead, evacuating the inhabitable sections of the camp, as well as providing medical, hygiene, and sanitation services. In addition, men from a variety of Royal Canadian Air Force squadrons and wings, in and around the Lüneburg Heath, rushed food, medicine, and other supplies to the camp.

In many important ways, those who arrived in the days following the formal surrender of Bergen-Belsen had experiences similar to the Allied personnel who first entered the camp, both in terms of what they saw and in how they responded. The sense of shock and disturbance was much the same. The American psychiatrist and scholar of psychohistory Robert Jay Lifton reminds us that "anticipation is prior imagination, and the extent of one's capacity to imagine a profound event has important bearing upon the way in which one responds."[6] While warnings were issued to many who entered the camp in the days that followed, detailed reports, photographs, and moving images, by and large, had not yet been distributed and many found it difficult to conceive of or prepare themselves for such horrors until they were directly faced with them. Indeed, those who arrived between three to even seven days after the submission of the camp, viewed virtually the same conditions as those who, on the afternoon of 15 April 1945, first entered the camp. Improvement progressed slowly.

Major Alexander Smith Allan of the 113 Light Anti-Aircraft Regiment was in the area on 18 April 1945 but did not enter the camp until the following day. At the time he remembers that "the extent of the problem, and so on, had ... probably not been fully known, but we certainly were *not* told [what to expect]."[7] While Allan was aware of the existence of "camps" in Germany, he had never before imagined a site of such death, filthiness, and destitution. He was, quite frankly, overcome with feelings of horror and disgust. According to Smith, "it was incredible: the mass of bodies that didn't putrefy because they were so skeletal; there was so little flesh on them. Their arms and their legs were just like matchsticks really. But it was a gruesome, horrible sight that I will never forget, never."[8] The number of dead and dying was certainly a terrible sight to behold. However, the awfulness of the situation went beyond the sheer quantity of dead. There appears to have been something in the manner of death present at the camp that so profoundly disturbed the Allied soldier. In a way, Bergen-Belsen became a distressing "space of abjection."[9]

Put simply, the "abject" is that which is both part of and thoroughly rejected by the self. The writings of theorist and critic Julia Kristeva provide substantial insight on the complex notion of abjection. To operate as a social being, one must expel or do away with elements which the collective order considers contaminated or impure, such as waste, excrement, blood, vomit, bodily fluids, cadavers, and the like. In *Powers of Horror* (1980), Kristeva explains that "refuse and corpses show me what I permanently thrust aside in order to live. These body fluids, this defilement, this shit are what life withstands, hardly and with difficulty, on the part of death."[10] However, these elements, which we try to cast off, can never be completely disregarded. They linger and remain, haunting us – the subject, the self – in different ways, threatening with the suspension or interruption of our very being. As philosopher Giorgio Agamben acknowledges, "Whoever experiences disgust has in some way recognized himself in the object of his loathing and fears being recognized in turn."[11] The abject thus challenges the very boundaries and limits of the self.

Consequently, the abject exists somewhere between the subject and the object; it is situated outside the symbolic order. According to Kristeva, "It is thus not lack of cleanliness or health that causes abjection but what disturbs identity, system, order. What does not respect borders, positions, rules."[12] In other words, refuse, blood, and waste have a place, and when found where it does not belong, outside of its consigned domain, it sickens, disturbs, or repels. Accordingly, the "abject" was at one time a part of the self, something which one attempted to reject, yet cannot fully discard.

For Kristeva, the image of the corpse can be viewed as the extreme instance of abjection. She insists that a dead body, removed from its relegated realm, such as a mortuary or a hospital setting, is an example of "death infecting life."[13] To confront a corpse outside of its "proper context" can be an extremely traumatic experience. An individual recognizes the corpse as something, someone, who once lived, a reminder that we, now alive, will also die. "A decaying body," Kristeva submits, "lifeless, completely turned into dejection, blurred between the inanimate and the inorganic, a transitional swarming, inseparable lining of a human nature whose life is undistinguishable from the symbolic – the corpse represents fundamental pollution."[14] As a result, the corpse cannot and should not be left exposed and open, but removed, covered, buried, and placed out of sight. Otherwise, death begins to contaminate and upset life, and frequently, it remains long after the initial encounter.

Of course, for many Allied personnel, viewing death was not necessarily out of the ordinary, especially during times of war. In battle and conflict, as military lines moved forward, coming across an enemy or

Allied combatant killed by machine gun fire or bombing was something that occurred with some regularity; for most, it was to be anticipated. Perhaps less common and more difficult to accept were the civilian deaths due to Allied bombings. The extensive, strategic bombing of Germany by American, British, and Canadian air forces frequently led to mass death. Various Allied soldiers witnessed the effects of these bombing campaigns, later on and often in close proximity. Accordingly, and while still demanding on one's psyche, viewing death was and still is a part of war.

However, within the context of a concentration camp, for the vast majority of British and Canadian soldiers, airmen, and medics, large-scale death was not something expected or anticipated. Mass death in camps, such as in Bergen-Belsen, appears to completely defy any logic, order, or meaning. Indeed, Kristeva contends that the abject "draws me toward the place where meaning collapses."[15] The thousands of corpses scattered around the campgrounds, inside and outside of the decrepit barracks, along with the waste, excrement, and filth, functioned to greatly disturb, horrify, and even sicken military personnel.[16] And yet, there is also a component of fascination with the abject. One is both repelled from and pulled towards spaces of abjection, as well as to that which one might consider abject. Some military personnel were undeniably drawn to Bergen-Belsen, despite later warnings of the horrors that the camp contained. "There were stories of atrocities that the Germans had committed," recalls Louis Kochane of the 8th Royal Tank Regiment. "Then somebody said, 'Oh, [Bergen-Belsen's] near here.' I said, 'well, let's go and have a look at it.'"[17] For some, rumours and stark warnings only encouraged greater inquisitiveness.

And how can one's encounter with "spaces of abjection" manifest itself in oral and written communication? For Kristeva, language and writing are closely connected to the astonishment and antipathy spurred on by abjection. Responding to the abject through language is a method in which one attempts to defend against distress and anxiety in an effort to take control of a grim and demanding situation.[18] Rather than being dominated by the abject, one speaks out in order to master the revulsion and dread.

For example, the writer or speaker might adopt a specific style in order to fend off that which haunts. According to literary scholar Sylvia Mayer, irony and sarcasm can be implemented as rhetorical devices in responses to the abject. As a result, engaging these types of figures of speech indicates a need to situate oneself at a "distance from threats to bodily and psychic integrity ... [where] boundaries of [one's] identity are strongly challenged."[19] Language thus becomes a defensive wall against something which challenges one's own psychic barriers. Furthermore, narrative performances of the abject can simply offer a recounting of feelings of great disturbance – language thus becomes a conduit for the horror to call out.[20]

Indeed, there are numerous examples of Britons and Canadians employing the techniques of irony or sarcasm in their accounts. These rhetorical devices appear in brief snippets, as well as in longer narratives. For example, a number of photos of Bergen-Belsen feature bitter, sarcastic notes written on them. Corporal Gordon George Earle of the Royal Canadian Air Force (RCAF) took several photographs of Bergen-Belsen, including one featuring the camp's crematorium. On the back of that particular photo Earle offers a bitter comment, declaring that this is an illustration of "More Nazi Fun & Games."[21] In a photograph taken by Canadian Peter Gorst, an open pit is captioned as "Belsen graves awaiting customers."[22] Both men use bleak absurdity to label the unsettling scenes. Moreover, explicit sarcasm also appears in the extended stories told by other military personnel. In a lengthy narrative, Larry Mann – someone who will be discussed in greater detail in a subsequent section – recalls his childhood in Toronto during an interview with the Shoah Foundation Institute. Mann's maternal grandmother lived with the family in Toronto. As a child, his grandmother – a Polish émigré – cared for Mann and his brother while his parents worked. She communicated with the two brothers exclusively in Yiddish. By the time Mann entered primary school, he understood little English. Looking back on his first day of school, after being confounded by the language of instruction and upon grasping that he was being mocked for being Jewish, Mann ran home utterly distraught.[23] Later in the interview he discusses his encounter with Bergen-Belsen while serving with the RCAF's 39 Reconnaissance Wing. Upon listing the languages that he heard and understood while in the camp, he adds, rather sardonically, "I spoke Yiddish fluently, thanks to my grandmother, who, even though she didn't prepare me for school ... prepared me for Bergen-Belsen."[24] Mann's quip, of course, is meant to be bleak and sarcastic, but it is also revealing. He links his Polish-Jewish roots, and the antisemitism he experienced at home in Canada, to his experience in Bergen-Belsen. Moreover, Mann had relatives in Poland, and after losing contact with them during the war, he speculated whether any of these family members were ultimately sent to Bergen-Belsen. He wondered if it were possible that some of his – albeit distant – family was in the camp while he roamed the grounds as a free man. His encounter with the camp then was also deeply personal. Consequently, he repeatedly employs a dark, sarcastic tone throughout his interview to negotiate the horror, shock, and anger he felt while surveying the camp decades earlier.

Likewise, British personnel also adopted forms of dark humour to deal with a most dreadful experience. The longer one stayed in the camp, the more likely they were to adopt techniques to deal with the situation. While filming in Bergen-Belsen, Sergeant Richard Leatherbarrow of the Army Film and Photo Unit (AFPU) overheard such an example. As a bulldozer – which was used to move the dead into open pits – picked up one particular body and pushed it through the sand, Leatherbarrow heard his colleague Sergeant William Lawrie shout to fellow cameraman Sergeant Mike Lewis: "Look out Mike! Here comes a beauty."[25] Indeed, Lawrie admitted in another interview that in the rare instance when Bergen-Belsen was discussed at the end of the workday, after the men had returned to their billets, it was normally in the form of a wisecrack. In addition, he recalls Lewis making "horrible jokes," and admits that if one became too involved and caught up in negative emotions, one risked losing control of oneself.[26]

Therefore, irony and sarcasm became a way for some men to deal with a situation – an exasperating "space of abjection" – which greatly disturbed them. Indeed, the comments could be harsh, cruel, and untimely, and were frequently employed as a type of cognitive wall. Similar to the zoomorphic language and animal metaphors examined in chapter 3, rhetorical devices such as sarcasm, irony, and dark humour were adopted in order to keep a distance, either physically or psychologically, from a desperate situation. Moreover, many personnel endeavoured to keep themselves thoroughly detached from what they were witnessing in order to complete their assigned tasks. The language and comments they used helped separate themselves from the terrible reality of a stressful situation.

Searching for Explanations and Determining Guilt

While it was difficult for many military personnel to cope with the dead and, initially, to connect and relate to the still-living survivors, they had a much easier time passing judgment on the perpetrators, bystanders, and those they deemed complicit in the crimes. In a substantial number of responses, Allied personnel frequently attempted to explain why the crimes at Bergen-Belsen occurred and who was to blame. In chapter 3 we reviewed the ways in which the Britons and Canadians who first entered the camp regarded the SS: as monsters, demons, or satanic devils. Rational men, in the eyes of the Allied soldier, could not commit such crimes; rather, only wicked, evil creatures could achieve the depravity of such horrors. In the following section we will review how Allied personnel explained the crimes and whom exactly they blamed.

In *The Holocaust and the Crisis of Human Behaviour* (1980), historian George M. Kren and professor of psychology Leon Rappoport examine the psychological and socio-historical roots of the Holocaust. According to the authors, reflection on why Germany "created" the Holocaust typically leads to the consideration of three basic factors.[27] First, the corrupt cultural and social values of the German people are often highlighted by those searching for a cause for the crimes. Second, the defeat of Germany in the First World War and the punitive terms imposed on the country ushered in a virulent and militant fascist regime on a society in desperate need of direction and change. The third factor invariably considered is the extreme influence of Adolf Hitler.[28] The conditions in post–First World War Germany were ideal for a fanatical leader. In other words, causation is typically attributed to something corrupt in German culture and society, a lethal form of Nazism, and a zealous Adolf Hitler. These factors, report Kren and Rappoport, are generally offered as a basic schema explaining how Germany made the Holocaust possible. Accordingly, it is interesting to observe how closely these three broad features align to the conclusions drawn by a number of Allied military personnel immediately following the end of the war in Europe.

To begin with, an obedient adherence to a virulent National Socialism is something echoed by a number of Allied personnel. Perhaps no other Allied soldier, British or Canadian, discussed his encounter at Bergen-Belsen more than Toronto-born Matthew Nesbitt, a sergeant in the RCAF's 126 Wing.[29] After the war, Nesbitt, a former professional baseball player, emigrated to the United States and ultimately settled in the state of Georgia. Commencing sometime in the late 1970s, he began speaking regularly about Bergen-Belsen and the Holocaust for Dr Fred Roberts Crawford's Witness to the Holocaust Project at Emory University. Nesbitt worked determinedly in the field of Holocaust education, presenting his views at public lectures, granting television interviews, as well as speaking to high school and university students throughout the southeastern United States. He was also a member of the Georgia Commission on the Holocaust.

According to Nesbitt, he and about a dozen Canadians from his wing, after receiving permission from their Commanding Officer, left their station at Wunstorf and spent approximately four days assisting at Bergen-Belsen. In a number of his interviews, Nesbitt repeats a story about a remorseless German camp guard who followed him around, picking up the discarded cigarettes that he had tossed to the ground. Frustrated and concerned that he would end up assaulting him, Nesbitt barked at the German to get away from him and suggested that he, the guard, would be better off simply killing himself.[30] Shortly thereafter, Nesbitt claims that he and a colleague discovered that this same guard had indeed committed suicide; he was found hanging from the rafters in one of the barracks in Bergen-Belsen. Nesbitt proposes that the guard was merely, and obediently, following his "instructions."

While there is certainly evidence of SS personnel committing suicide in the camp, particularly after having been put to work collecting the dead, it is difficult to authenticate the veracity of Nesbitt's potentially hyperbolic story.[31] What is perhaps clearer is the reason why the story was repeated and what it signified. Nesbitt's story about the suicide of the camp guard seems to represent the alleged indoctrinated mentality of the adherents of Nazism, particularly those in official positions. Accordingly, when told to do something, no matter how extreme or unpleasant, the belief was that an SS or Wehrmacht was trained to follow through on the instructions. "And they had been brainwashed," advises Nesbitt, "to the extent that they obeyed every order, no matter what it was ... so that was the Nazi mind for you."[32] For Nesbitt, and others like him, indoctrination, a rudimentary obedience to authority, and a fear of discipline were the primary causes for the actions of the devotees of Nazism.

Undeniably, following orders and a concern for punishment have frequently been put forward as an explanation for the actions of perpetrators. Accordingly, under Nazi leadership, discipline and enforcement simply led to compliance with orders, thereby limiting an individual's choice. However, in *Ordinary Men: Reserve Police Battalion 101 and the Final Solution in Poland* (1992), historian Christopher Browning demonstrates how occasional punishment for lack of compliance was never proportionate to the severity of the crimes committed in the Holocaust.[33] While Browning's focus is on the case of the *Ordnungspolizei* (Order Police), who killed and rounded up Jews for deportation to the

Nazi extermination camps in Poland, he provides insight into the actions of perpetrators of the crimes of the Holocaust. According to Browning, while deference to authority certainly existed under Nazi authority, "obedience to orders out of fear of dire punishment is not a valid explanation."[34] Moreover, there are a number of examples of individuals refusing to participate in offences and not being punished for it. Nevertheless, for many British and Canadian officers, they concluded that orders came from the top down, and personnel from the SS or Wehrmacht had no other choice but to follow. British Major T.C.M. Winwood, in legal defence of Bergen-Belsen's camp commandant Josef Kramer, unsuccessfully argued: "National Socialism demanded two things: implicit obedience and trust on the part of the person carrying out the order."[35] On the contrary, Kramer was ultimately held responsible for his own abhorrent actions and decisions made at Bergen-Belsen.

Complicity in the crimes and attempts at judging the guilty also became subjects of some concern in the responses of Allied personnel. Likewise, this was a prevalent issue for many German academics, as it also was for its citizens. One scholar in particular offers a useful model in which to investigate the context of such judgments. A native of Oldenburg in northern Germany, Karl Jaspers was a psychiatrist and philosopher who published *The Question of German Guilt* (1947) not long after the end of the war. The work was based on lectures delivered in January and February 1946, less than a year after Nazi Germany surrendered to the Allies. In his study Jaspers scrutinizes the culpability of Germany as a whole for the crimes of the Third Reich. "In the summer of 1945," he recalls, "in all towns and villages the posters hung with the pictures and stories from Belsen and the crucial statement, 'You are the guilty!'"[36] Indeed, in the postwar period, Allied authorities marched citizens and local authorities through camps such as Bergen-Belsen. German citizens were also forced to watch camp atrocity films at local cinemas. Accordingly, Karl Jaspers wrote the book mainly for, and addressed it to, a German audience. It is important to remember that he composed his treatise for a population who lived through and mostly supported, albeit often submissively, the Nazi regime.

Jaspers's discussion of the question of German guilt revolves around a fourfold schema. The types of guilt presented are criminal, political, moral, and metaphysical.[37] The first, criminal guilt, includes offences that violate the law, and consequently, jurisdiction remains with the courts. The second type, political guilt, involves all citizens of a modern state. The citizens of the state are accountable for the conduct of their

Upon orders of Allied military authorities, citizens of Minden, Germany, gather to view a film about the Bergen-Belsen concentration camp. Image 55316, United States Holocaust Memorial Museum, courtesy of Joseph Eaton.

governments. Jurisdiction, in this instance, rests with the victorious powers. Moral guilt, the third type proposed by Jaspers, encompasses personal responsibility for one's actions. In this instance, jurisdiction involves one's own conscience. Morally, an individual can condemn only him or herself and no one else. Finally, the fourth type, metaphysical guilt, involves everyone's responsibility for the crimes and injustices in the world. This is especially true for offences of which one has knowledge or that were committed in one's presence. According to Jaspers, jurisdiction for metaphysical guilt remains with "God alone."[38] Of the four types, Jaspers considered himself culpable for the last three categories he distinguishes: politically, morally, and metaphysically guilty. He was at fault politically because he was a citizen of Hitler's Germany, a "criminal state"; he was morally guilty, as he acknowledges, because he did not act against the policies and practices of the Third Reich; and he was certainly metaphysically guilty, as this category suited anyone who permitted the crimes of Nazi Germany to transpire.

While Jaspers was a German citizen and lived in the country throughout the war, the victorious powers from abroad were also quick to assign guilt. Initially, the determination of "guilt" occurred outside of the court system, frequently on the grounds of the newly opened camps, such as Bergen-Belsen. British and Canadian military personnel, in their letters, articles, and interviews, felt compelled to pass personal judgment on the crimes they witnessed in the camp and the stories they heard directly from the survivors. Furthermore, the Allies passed judgment not only on the agents in the camp proper, such as the SS, Wehrmacht, and Hungarians – most of the latter were gendarmes assigned to guard the camp – but also on the local population and the German public at large.[39]

Cyril J. Charters was a projectionist with 37 Kinema Section, Royal Army Ordnance Corps (RAOC) of the British Army. He spent weeks working in the camp, presenting films for the survivors, as well as for the servicemen and women. In a letter to his wife he writes, "I wish that every possible German could be conducted around the camp to see with his own eyes what his blind faith and idolatry of the Nazi creed made possible, or what his fear allowed to continue."[40] Political guilt was what occupied his mind. For Charters, it was also adulation and an unquestioning belief in Nazism that created camps such as Bergen-Belsen. He suggests that if the general population of Germany had not sustained, or been afraid to confront, National Socialism, then the crimes might not have occurred. Therefore, they are also, as Jaspers classifies and Charters seems to suggest, metaphysically guilty. Charters connects the offences not only to the Nazi party, but also to a passive German population. Thus, it was steadfast belief and reverence that were the essential problems.

Meanwhile, others were in disagreement with Charters about the complicity of the German public. The 113 Light Anti-Aircraft Regiment's Alexander Smith Allan certainly did not blame the average German citizen. On the contrary, Allan notes that when the citizens of nearby Celle were brought in to view the crimes, they were horrified and wept openly.[41] He concludes that as the camp itself was a considerable distance from the nearest town, and thus not well known, the average

German was likely unaware of the extent of such offences. Unlike Charters, Allan focuses on criminal and not political guilt. Consequently, he insists that the burden of criminal guilt remains with those directly involved with National Socialism.

Likewise, Wolfville, Nova Scotia native Glen Hancock also feels blame should be focused on the Nazi party and not on the German citizenry. Like Allan, his concern is for criminal guilt. Hancock was a pilot with the RCAF's 408 "Goose" Squadron. In April 1945 he was put on special assignment where he was asked to transport high-ranking British officials to Bergen-Belsen. In his memoir, *Charley Goes to War* (2004), Hancock contends that German civilians who lived near the camps "always claimed they knew nothing of the goings-on there ... it is difficult to see what they would have done to stop what was happening."[42] Hancock also discusses, in his view, the significance of the long history of antisemitism in Germany, tracing it back to the sixteenth century and the writings of Martin Luther. According to Hancock, when the local citizenry were brought in to view the crimes, they "would never again deny the crimes of their fellow men."[43] While he is uncertain as to what the average local citizen knew, he suggests that responsibility ultimately lay with the representatives of National Socialism.

Indeed, many individuals were divided on whether or not the average German citizen had prior knowledge about the crimes and debated if they should be held accountable. Thus, the attention again is on criminal and not political guilt. "I am convinced," Patrick Gordon Walker, BBC commentator and chief editor of Radio Luxembourg noted in his diary, "that very many Germans did not know about the exact details and the exact location of these camps."[44] And yet, later, Gordon Walker admits that he is certain that Germans had at least a cursory knowledge of the camps. Likewise, Stanley Winfield, a Canadian airman from Calgary who served with 84 Group Disarmament, suggests that while civilians from the surrounding areas claimed to have been unaware of the specific crimes occurring at Bergen-Belsen, he always suspected they knew more than they admitted.[45]

Remarkably, a study into the knowledge and reactions of German citizens to Nazi atrocities that was commissioned immediately following the end of the war drew similar conclusions. The study was directed by American sociologist Morris Janowitz, who served with the United States Army's Research and Analysis Branch of the Office of Strategic Studies.[46] According to Janowitz, while the majority of Germans interviewed were cognizant of the presence and purpose of concentration camps, they were unaware of any specifics and the magnitude of the crimes.⁴⁷

Regardless of whether or not one believed that the average citizen was familiar with what was occurring in Hitler's camps, most British and Canadian soldiers felt it necessary for all Germans, at the very least, to view the crimes first-hand. Citizens and local authorities were paraded through a number of camps by Allied authorities, including Bergen-Belsen. Still, how could one explain such crimes? What was the cause of such a deliberate disregard for human life? And once one had decided upon the cause, how did this affect one's assessment of responsibility? A cross-section of Britons and Canadians considered these crucial questions.

"I can't believe how there could be such a fanatic race as the bloody German people," wrote an exasperated Saul Stein to his family in April 1945. Stein was a Canadian airman who, along with other men from the RCAF's 126 Wing, brought food and other supplies to the camp.⁴⁸ Many personnel simply did not distinguish between the German people and the Nazi regime. In addition, the stereotypical terms used to label the perpetrators of these crimes included fanatics, madmen, and lunatics. As previously examined, Allied personnel frequently referred to the SS as beasts and monsters. Yet, as philosopher Tzvetan Todorov warns, "if the concept of monstrousness is of limited utility in helping us understand evil, positing some reversion to bestial or primitive instincts takes us no further."⁴⁹ There were, however, military personnel who moved beyond fantastic and surreal terminologies and metaphors, and looked elsewhere for answers.

In 1930 Edwin Miller "Ted" Aplin emigrated from England to Canada, settling first in Toronto and later taking up permanent residence in neighbouring Scarborough. A staunch socialist, he was involved in various peace movements after the war. In 1942 he enlisted in the Royal Canadian Air Force. He was sent overseas in late 1944, and by the spring of 1945 he was stationed in Germany with the Royal Air Force's 84 Group H.Q. Disarmament Staff. While in Germany, Squadron Leader Aplin worked closely with 8402 (RCAF) Disarmament Wing, a group made up entirely of Canadians. Their assigned task was to disarm the Luftwaffe in northwest Germany. The headquarters for 84 Group was located at Scheuen near Celle. However, the work for which they had been trained was limited. As a report written at the end of the war indicated, "it became quite apparent that no major Luftwaffe Headquarters organization existed in the 84 Group Area."⁵⁰

Canadian servicemen and Bergen-Belsen child survivors at an outing organized by Royal Canadian Air Force Squadron Leader Ted Aplin, 1945. Accession 2010-5/15, item 28, Ontario Jewish Archives.

While there were unquestionably Luftwaffe personnel lurking in the area, many men found that their formal duties had become futile.[51] Consequently, a number of individuals, like Aplin, became restless and searched for ways to occupy their time.[52]

In early June 1945 Squadron Leader Aplin made his first visit to nearby Bergen-Belsen. "I have just seen Belsen and am ashamed," he wrote in June 1945 in a now frequently published letter to family friend and lawyer Lillian Sandler in Toronto. "Ashamed that Gentiles all over the world have not risen in one vast crusade to erase forever this evil mark on their record."[53] Aplin expands culpability beyond Nazi Germany to encompass all nations, to countries that did not act sooner to prevent the crimes from occurring. In other words, he found the world "metaphysically guilty," to borrow Karl Jaspers's concept.[54] For Aplin, the moral burden could not belong exclusively to the agents of Hitler's

Third Reich; rather the responsibility must be shared by all. Moreover, Aplin was also quick to connect the crimes to antisemitism, arguing that the prejudice against the Jews has now been "carried to its final extreme."[55] It is interesting to note that Aplin, who normally wrote letters to his wife and family back in Canada, specifically addressed this letter to Sandler, a Jewish lawyer in Toronto who had fought to establish a successful practice in what was a most "inhospitable climate for women and Jews in the profession."[56] Moreover, when he returned to his headquarters near Celle, Aplin insisted that his colleague, Stanley Winfield, a Jewish airman from Calgary, visit the camp as soon as possible. While initially reluctant, Winfield ultimately toured the camp and later became closely involved in helping the survivors.[57]

Indeed, in the ensuing weeks and months, Aplin, Winfield, and many other men from 84 Group, notably Edgar Jamieson, Bernard Yale, and John W. Thompson, worked industriously for the survivors of Bergen-Belsen.[58] In his letter to Sandler, Aplin went to great lengths to further link the murder of European Jewry, not to German character, but to fascism. He was aware that Allied propaganda had depicted the entire German race as wicked fiends. Contending that all Germans should be made acutely aware of the crimes of the Third Reich, Aplin argues:

> Bombard the German people with this story ... Make them accept their share of responsibility for their leader's degeneration. But let us not fail to identify all this with Fascism itself. Our own people must also learn that Anti-Semitism leads to Belsen ... In this war against Fascism, the Jews have paid in blood the biggest price of all. This the Gentile people can never repay.[59]

According to Aplin, it was fascism, rampant antisemitism, and a corrupt and debased Nazi leadership that are the primary sources of such crimes, and yet we all must be held accountable and learn from the offences. Aplin frequently emphasized the innumerable lessons that could be taken away from Bergen-Belsen. More recently, sociologist and philosopher Jürgen Habermas has drawn attention to "learning from catastrophes," meaning that societies both acknowledge and confront past tragedies, striving to comprehend, in a critical fashion, what has transpired and for what reason.[60] Hence, while deeply disturbed by what he saw at Bergen-Belsen, Aplin separated the acts committed under fascism from the any inherent trait of the German people.

Similar to Aplin's arguments, the 7th Armoured Division's Alan Rose – who was discussed in greater length in the preceding chapter – also proposes that while the crimes committed in Bergen-Belsen and in other camps must be attributed to Nazi Germany, the rest of the world should also be implicated. According to Rose, "it is terribly important to point out ... that if you look back at the period, the great politicians of the democracies are as much to blame for what happened by their cowardice, and the German people are as much to blame."[61] As reviewed in chapter 2, Western governments were cognizant of many of the crimes of the Third Reich in the years before the end of the war. Moreover, mass killings were published in select media outlets, and eyewitnesses such as Jan Karski and Gerhart H. Seger went on public speaking tours of both Canada and Britain. "Thus, the quality of democracy," emphasizes Rose, "is made up of resistance to racism of all kinds. That's a very strong lesson which people have got to learn."[62] What Rose and Aplin are promoting is a type of integrated, international response to injustices throughout the world. They endorse an absolute solidarity with their fellow human beings, in this instance, the Jews of Europe and others who suffered at the hands of Hitler's Third Reich.

Quarrels relating to the accountabilities of Allied governments, as well as the burden owed to Western societies, have long been explored by scholars over the years in works such as Michael R. Marrus's *Bystanders to the Holocaust* (1987), Raul Hilberg's *Perpetrators, Victims, Bystanders* (1992), and, more recently, David Cesarani and Paul Levine's *'Bystanders' to the Holocaust: A Re-evaluation* (2002). As the authors of the latter work observe, the twenty-first century has continued to see a "proliferation" of studies regarding the activities of neutral and Allied governments during the Holocaust.[63] Indeed, the issue of transnational duty has long been debated by Western scholars. For Rose, Aplin, and others who have drawn from their personal experiences at Bergen-Belsen, the weight of the crimes must be the concern of all people.

Furthermore, these men felt compelled not only to share their thoughts and concerns with family and friends, but to express them publicly.[64] In *Narrating Evil: A Postmetaphysical Theory of Reflective Judgment* (2007), María Pía Lara stresses the importance of debates generated by the reflexive relationship between historical atrocities and their subsequent stories and retellings.[65] While a variety of Britons and Canadians merely concluded that the primary cause for the crimes was a corrupt or debased German character, a select few underlined the significance of fascism and antisemitism as primary reasons, as well as stressing the responsibility for all mankind to atone for the sins of Nazi Germany.

Crime and Punishment: Revenge and Retribution

"I am now convinced that the Nazis are not human beings," wrote a seething Sergeant Norman Midgley of the Army Film and Photographic Unit, "but vermin that must be exterminated." As we have reviewed, Britons and Canadians often swiftly drew conclusions as to who should be deemed guilty and for what reasons. Consequently, Allied personnel felt that reprisals for the inmates must be obtained. For some it was agreed that justice should be decided through the courts and military tribunals. However, those voices tended to be in the minority. Most felt that due process either would take too long or was pointless. How could any form of punishment, exacted by trial, suffice for all the suffering and mass death in the camps? Thus, many felt it necessary to seek a kind of personal vengeance for the crimes.

According to philosopher Berel Lang, in the context of the Holocaust, "the phenomenon of revenge and the serious issues it raises have been largely avoided (at least 'on the record') in practice as well as in reflection."[66] Nevertheless, random, violent acts of retaliation by both inmates and military personnel did occur and some have been documented. Revenge took on a variety of forms in Bergen-Belsen. In some instances survivors attacked Kapos and the local German citizenry; in other cases inmates assaulted each other.[67] As noted in chapter 3, upon initial entrance to the camp, a member of the Special Air Service (SAS), a former amateur boxer, knocked out a camp guard. In addition, during interviews with other members of the SAS, several men confess to having observed violent attacks being exacted on the SS and camp guards.[68] However, reprisals were not always physical confrontations; revenge occasionally took the form of a psychological attack.

W.J. Barclay was a sergeant in 649 Company of the Royal Army Services Corps, 11th Armoured Division. Approximately one week after the surrender of Bergen-Belsen, Barclay and his transport team brought supplies to the camp. Stunned by the suffering endured by the internees, he was satisfied to see that, under British authority, members of the SS were being forced to carry the dead to the open pits. According to Barclay, "The S.S. have to do the dirty work each under armed guard

Survivors attack a former guard at the Bergen-Belsen concentration camp.
Image 30428, United States Holocaust Memorial Museum,
courtesy of Lev Sviridov.

who make sure that the job is done at the double and done properly. Women S.S. have the same treatment as the men. A bayonet jab is a useful spur to energy."[69] While the length of time spent removing the dead by SS and other camp staff was brief, most Britons and Canadians felt this type of work was more than justified. "The greatest pleasure I had in the camp," concurred Canadian Saul Stein, "was to see German [SS who are now] prisoners load the dead and believe me the army is working the ass off them."[70] To be sure, some individuals relished the suffering camp staff now had to endure. Nonetheless, and as Lang contends, payback, in whatever form, can be problematic because it can be both unpredictable and excessive, which the rule of law attempts to

Former camp guards and military personnel dig a mass grave where some of the dead of Bergen-Belsen concentration camp will be buried. Image 74945, United States Holocaust Memorial Museum, courtesy of Hadassah Bimko Rosensaft.

circumvent.⁷¹ Barclay later tells the addressee of his letter: "You will probably be pleased to hear that ... typhus has started on [the SS and] that combined with overwork has started to reduce their numbers."⁷² Either convinced that he was incapable of doing enough to help the dying or was unable to deal with their suffering, Barclay appears to have felt more in control of the situation by witnessing that the SS were also suffering at the hands of the liberating forces.

In addition to removing the dead, the SS and other staff were forced to subsist on stale bread and unpalatable scraps of beef. Typically, this inedible food was tossed to the ground as the guards were generally not provided with plates and mess tins.⁷³ Moreover, the SS were not afforded washroom facilities, thus being forced, both men and women, to relieve themselves in the open.⁷⁴ Indeed, punishing, embarrassing, and humiliating the SS was the primary intention.

The responses about punishment varied greatly among those who saw Bergen-Belsen. Two men, both with ties to the military, to radio broadcasting, and to psychological warfare groups were Canada's King Whyte and England's Patrick Gordon Walker. The former served with the First Canadian Army's Department of Psychological Warfare as a public relations officer. In addition, Whyte worked at the recently acquired Radio Luxembourg, which served as the voice of the Supreme Headquarters Allied Expeditionary Force (SHAEF). Likewise, Gordon Walker, who presented daily broadcasts from Germany for the British Broadcasting Corporation (BBC), also began working from Radio Luxembourg in 1944, while following the British Army. And similarly, both men entered Bergen-Belsen in April 1945, shortly after the camp's surrender.

In a series of letters and photographs to his wife, Canadian singer Dorothy Alt, Whyte expresses his anger and revulsion at being in Bergen-Belsen, the "most horrible festering scab there has ever been on the face of humanity."⁷⁵ In his first letter concerning the camp, dated 24 April 1945, Whyte exclaims, "I want to weep and go out in the streets and kill every Nazi I see when I think of what they have done to those countless thousands of people."⁷⁶ While it is quite unlikely that Whyte would have ever acted on these threats, his anger was palpable. Later, he notes that an SS man who was loading the dead onto a flatbed collapsed and was promptly beaten up and thrown into the truck on top of the corpses; he remained there until he woke up.⁷⁷ Like Sergeant Barclay before him, Whyte suggests that the terrible situation was being suitably dealt with by the Allies, noting the harsh treatment experienced by the perpetrators.

In contrast, while just as irate, Gordon Walker continually emphasizes the importance of lawful impartiality in dealing with the crimes. He also warned against threats or engaging in acts of personal revenge against those regarded as "guilty." According to Walker,

> I do not think in all history the world has ever been menaced by such naked evil, by evil so unabashed. What are we to do about it? … We must root these things out. The vengeance of the world must be relentless. There must be no mercy. But our vengeance must discriminate. If we wreak our wrath on guilty and innocent we shall undo our ends. Our aim must be to restore respect for each individual human life – German lives too. And respect for human life means that there must be order, formality and proven guilt before any life is taken away. We must not kill indiscriminately[78]

This diary entry was written sometime in late April 1945 and it is remarkable for its prudence and forethought. Indeed, less than five months later a British military court held proper trials.[79] Accordingly, the Bergen-Belsen hearings, formerly known as the "Trial of Josef Kramer and 44 others," and commencing on 17 September 1945, were held in Lüneburg. On trial were forty-five SS men, women, and other camp staff.[80] As a non-combat participant in the Second World War, Gordon Walker perhaps held a broader perspective on the war as he worked behind the scenes and witnessed, from a distance, how his countrymen and other Allies battled a six-year-long war. He understood the rage of the British and Canadian military personnel and he urged restraint. "The only way back now," he professed, "is that the German people admits and recognizes … that these 12 years have been the blackest in the whole of Europe's history."[81] Gordon Walker deemed this Germany's "national guilt." In many ways he anticipated some of the arguments of Karl Jaspers. Gordon Walker states that those who were directly responsible – those who were "criminally guilty" – should have their day in court. And for the actions of the Third Reich, he holds that Germans must be considered, to use Jaspers's concept, "politically guilty."[82] Moreover, while suggesting that the general public did not know the exact details of the camps, Gordon Walker was confident that the citizenry still "had a very good general idea" about the purpose of Hitler's camps, thus implying that they too are – to use Jaspers's term – "metaphysically guilty" for the genocide of European Jews.[83] Like

Jaspers, he left "moral guilt" to each individual. For Gordon Walker, only one's conscience could determine that level of culpability.

Alas, the types of arguments proposed by Gordon Walker, especially at the time they were made, were exceptional. The majority of military personnel, however, desired immediate "justice" for the inmates of Bergen-Belsen and wanted it to be conducted outside of any courtroom. Many felt that no court of law was capable of providing the appropriate type of justice for the dead and for those who survived. Undeniably, many had their way: some SS were shot and fell ill, while a number of Kapos were beaten immediately following liberation. The written responses concerning the German population were, time and again, unequivocal and vitriolic in their tone. While most men never acted on these words – these threats – some certainly did. Meanwhile, military authorities eventually arrested the remaining SS and other staff, although the majority had already fled the camp. Ultimately, these small few would have their day in court. Many were convicted, and some, like Commandant Josef Kramer and ten other staff, were sentenced to death and executed.[84]

Camp Tours: Witnesses, Spectators, and Voyeurs

"While we were stopped in Celle for a while," recalls Louis Kochane, a Jewish soldier in the 8th Royal Tank Regiment, "there was a rumour going around that there was a camp nearby where lots of people were incarcerated in deplorable conditions ... mainly Jews as well ... So we got a truck, took the truck, and went there, and drove in."[85] Like Buchenwald before it, news of Bergen-Belsen quickly spread, capturing the attention and piquing the curiosity of countless military personnel. As a result, many felt the need to go beyond reading newspaper reports, which even at the time, as we will examine, some were suggesting was Allied propaganda.[86] "No doubt you have seen the newspapers lately," Toronto airman Alex Pancer wrote to his mother. "Well, a bunch of us fellas visited ... the Belsen concentration camp & until this day I still can't believe what I saw there."[87] During the spring and summer of 1945, for Allied soldiers, airmen, medics, and the like, going to visit the concentration camps, particularly those in Germany, occurred with some regularity. Either as part of organized excursions or in small, unofficial groups, British and Canadian personnel – not to mention a smattering of Russians, Poles, Australians, among others – descended upon Bergen-Belsen in substantial numbers. As historian Robert H.

Abzug confirms, the touring of recently opened concentration camps was a "ritual of exorcism and revelation" for Allied personnel in occupied Germany.[88] In the camps, Britons and Canadians alike were able to find a reason or confirmation as to why the war needed to be undertaken and, for the Allies, had to be won.

The following section will explore the responses of military personnel who arrived at Bergen-Belsen to view the crimes first-hand and who either did not have official permission or did not provide any formal assistance to the inmates and staff. Put simply, this section surveys those who arrived at the camp to witness and to do so exclusively. To begin with, attention will be paid to the reasons why these individuals made their way to the camp. Next, the types of stories told and what they ultimately signified will be scrutinized. Finally, the employment of what Northrop Frye calls "associative clusters" will be examined. In other words, what symbols or images recur in the telling?

Reasons for Visiting the Camp

The majority of British and Canadian military personnel in northwest Germany became aware of Bergen-Belsen not long after the first troops entered the camp. And while the media throughout Canada, Britain, and the United States either downplayed or neglected the fact that the majority of inmates were Jews, this was something of which many Allied personnel in the area were aware. In fact, this became a primary reason for some of the visitors to travel to the camp, particularly when it came to British and Canadian personnel of Jewish descent.

In the previous section, we briefly reviewed the dark humour and sarcasm employed in a lengthy interview by Toronto-born Larry Mann. Well-known to North American audiences, Larry D. Mann was a disc jockey, actor, and animated voice personality.[89] Serving as a mechanic and instrument technician, Mann was assigned to 39 Reconnaissance Wing of the Royal Canadian Air Force.

According to Mann, by mid-April 1945 he was at an airfield near the town of Celle. The Wing's chaplain was Father Norman Gallagher, who later became the first padre ever to be consecrated a Roman Catholic Bishop in Canada (Thunder Bay). Mann explains that once Father Gallagher learned about Bergen-Belsen from an intelligence report, he "rounded up a bunch of the guys that he thought would be interested, which turns out to be all the Jewish kids who were on the squadron, plus others."[90] Mann, as noted above, was of Polish descent and had a personal interest in the camps. In addition to Mann, some of the other Jewish personnel included Leo Velleman, who later wrote an article about the experience in the Wing's *Flap* magazine (1945); Henry S. Abramson, who painted the corresponding picture; and the aforementioned Alex Pancer.[91] The fact that these servicemen were Jews appears to have played an important role in their visiting this particular concentration camp.

Likewise, the 126 Wing's (RCAF) Monty Berger has revealed that he was compelled by his Jewish identity to travel to Bergen-Belsen.[92] He made his way to the camp on 1 May 1945 and brought along his colleagues and fellow airmen Gordon Panchuk, Bob Francis, and Carl Reinke. Berger knew the importance of enlistment and fighting fascism, as did many Jewish Canadians: approximately 17,000 Jews enlisted in the Canadian armed forces. Proportionally, Canadian Jews enlisted in the Royal Canadian Air Force in numbers higher than the national population.[93] According to Berger, "As the son of a rabbi ... I knew well enough! ... And, not unlike other Jews in Canada, I had heard of cousins and relatives who had disappeared, or were killed ... my identity as a Jew ran deep."[94] Thus, his Jewish faith was certainly part of his reason for visiting the camp. Similarly, while not Jewish, for his colleague Gordon (Bohdan) Panchuk, religious and cultural roots played a role in his travelling to Bergen-Belsen. A Canadian of Ukrainian descent and born in the village of Meacham, Saskatchewan, Panchuk was an intelligence officer in 126 Wing. In addition to his service in the air force he was the president of the Ukrainian-Canadian Servicemen's Association (Active Service Overseas), and after the war he became the director of the Central Ukrainian Relief Bureau (CURB) in London.[95] According to Panchuk, "Our mission was to go into Bergen-Belsen ... I was the only Ukrainian and interested in Ukrainians primarily."[96] While speaking to members of the Canadian Senate, he noted his astonishment regarding the significant numbers of Ukrainians who had been held prisoner in Bergen-Belsen.[97] Accordingly, Panchuk made repeated visits to the camp, which was largely due to his mounting concern for the hardships faced by the Ukrainian inmates.

An experience concerning another Jewish serviceman was related by Max Dickson, who worked with No. 3 (X) Troop, a formation of the No. 10 (Inter-Allied) Commando unit of the British Army. This particular troop comprised mainly German-speaking Jewish refugees. Born Max Dobriner in 1926, Dickson was from a market town in eastern Germany. Leaving his family as part of the kindertransport (also known as the "Refugee Children's Movement") at the age of thirteen, he was billeted at Barham House in Claydon, near Ipswich. In 1944 he enlisted in the British Army. According to Dickson, while working in interrogation as part of the British Army of the Rhine (BAOR), he asked for and received compassionate leave to search for his family and relatives with whom he had lost touch.[98] Upon hearing about Bergen-Belsen, he quickly made his way to the camp. "I went there," he writes, "in the hope of finding someone alive."[99] He was stunned by the scenes and was unable to locate any family members. His need to visit the camp was primarily familial and deeply personal.

Nevertheless, the huge numbers of visitors who descended on Bergen-Belsen did not typically do so for religious, ethnic, or even cultural reasons. In fact, it appears that a significant number of Britons and Canadians travelled to the camp to see first-hand what the newspapers and radio broadcasts had been reporting. Perhaps more than any other camp, Bergen-Belsen was a major news story as it made international headlines and was presented in numerous forms of media.

Squadron Leader F.J. Lyons served with 8501 Air Disarmament Wing of the Royal Air Force. He was well acquainted with the news reports concerning both Bergen-Belsen and Buchenwald. He became rather concerned about stories he had heard about the British public back home suggesting that the atrocities were merely inflated propaganda.[100] Certainly, there is evidence demonstrating that the British public was still sceptical, even after the opening of concentration camps by the Allies in western Germany.[101] Consequently, Lyons was eager to make his way to nearby Bergen-Belsen and to see for himself. In a letter about his visit to the camp on 17 June 1945 he writes: "I'm sorry if I upset you by writing about this, but I feel sure you will endorse my reason for going. If, in five years' time, I hear people saying that Belsen, etc., were so much propaganda, I shall be in a position to argue with conviction. Please keep this letter for me."[102] Addressed to "Darling," Lyons's letter makes it clear that he will forever be a witness to the crimes at Bergen-Belsen and that his letter will help serve as confirmation. Back home in Britain, the people who knew him may not have trusted the media or the government, but they would have to believe him because he was there in person and saw for himself: together with his letter, he had concrete, individual, and independent evidence.

Of course, some military personnel visited the camp purely out of curiosity. The news, the rumours, and the images made a significant impact, particularly on the British and Canadian airmen stationed nearby on the Lüneburg Heath. Clifford Denzel "Denny" Wilson, from Hamilton, Ontario, was a Spitfire pilot in the RCAF's 411 Squadron. While Bergen-Belsen became a life-altering experience for him – which is something that will be discussed later on in the chapter – he admits that it was curiosity that first brought him to the camp. "We were stationed just south of Hamburg, Germany," Wilson remembers. "Somebody came to us one day and said, 'Boy, you've got to see what I've just seen.' A bunch of us jumped into a jeep and went to the Bergen-Belsen concentration camp, and when I walked through the gate, I was staggered."[103] Wilson's trip was strictly unofficial and he went on an impulse. The reports and the gossip had many of the servicemen intrigued, and most simply submitted to their visceral curiosities.

Finally, there were those military personnel who were formally organized and brought to the camp by authorities. An example would be the RCAF's 402 Squadron. While stationed at a nearby airfield in Wunstorf, men from the squadron were taken by bus to view the crimes at Bergen-Belsen. According to the squadron's Brian MacConnell, "we were taken there to tell people what we had seen."[104] The men were shown around the camp by a British army officer not long after the camp's surrender, becoming witnesses to the aftermath of the crimes. Decades later, in his discussions with high school students, MacConnell makes a point to reveal what he witnessed in Bergen-Belsen that day in April, countering any revisionism and deniers.[105]

Military personnel visited the Bergen-Belsen concentration camp during the spring and summer of 1945 for a variety of reasons. Some travelled to the camp because news quickly spread about the large number of European Jews in the camp. Some Jewish personnel had family still living in Europe and felt the urgency to view the camp firsthand and to offer their support. Meanwhile, there were personnel who were aware of or anticipated those who would later deny the veracity of the crimes. They felt the need to view the offences and become witnesses themselves. Finally, some personnel journeyed to the camp unofficially because they had heard about the attrocities and wanted to see them for themselves; others were part of organized groups who were granted authorized guided tours.

Stories Told, "Clusters" Offered

After viewing the crimes at Bergen-Belsen, many personnel went back to their airfields or stations and wrote letters to family and friends or jotted notes in diaries; some waited until they returned home before sharing their stories. While a variety of accounts were told, a number of subjects were repeated time and again. Frequently, Britons and Canadians told similar stories and evoked analogous images and comparisons. The following section reflects on the stories told and the archetypes offered.

In *The Soldiers' Tale: Bearing Witness to Modern War* (1995), literary scholar Samuel Hynes suggests that, with the opening of the concentration camps, the end of the war in Europe had revealed that "a greater evil had been done than we had imagined possible in our world … [this] had not been imagined before – had not had to be imagined, because [it] had not been possible."[106] What is interesting to note is that while the camp system and what occurred inside had not been properly conceived by the Allies *prior* to liberation, the fact remains that even *after* leaving the camp, many personnel still had difficulty measuring and registering what they had just witnessed. "We couldn't believe," remembers Toronto's Matthew Nesbitt, "that what we saw was actually what we saw … Did we actually see what we saw? We saw such inhumane things … We didn't believe it for a while. I know it to be true, but still sometimes I think back when I'm talking: did it really happen? Of course it did, I have the pictures and the documents. But, how could one person do this to another?"[107] Indeed, countless visitors to the camp repeated a similar sentiment: the scale of the horror was almost too overwhelming to adequately catalogue. "They say memory works like a film," adds Ron Laidlaw, a public relations photographer with the RCAF. "I didn't have much film and my damnable memory is full of editing splices! I think we must have been shocked out of our minds. In fact, I know we were!"[108] The experience became an incredible challenge to effectively chronicle. This acknowledgment was made repeatedly in the weeks and months after Bergen-Belsen's surrender to the British Army.

While personnel had difficulty registering the horror, most were dedicated to ensuring that the crimes would be believed and not forgotten. As discussed in the previous section, the letters of Cyril Charters illustrate the urgency of convincing those back home of the veracity of the crimes. Charters willingly admits that if he was still a civilian back in England he might be the first to claim that stories of Bergen-Belsen were selected propaganda.[109] However, after he had viewed the crimes first-hand, his concern became to substantiate the news reports. "I wish," he wrote in a letter to his wife, "I could put this letter in the

'Western Independent' [so] that Westcountry folk could have a Westcountryman's testimony form [the] truth of what they have read and seen in papers and on films."[110] The First World War's "atrocity stories," propaganda about an enemy's crimes, were typically a reason for doubt. Charters's aim is, at the very least, to convince his local community that the stories are true and were being confirmed by a known, reliable source.

Larry Mann was also concerned about not being believed when he returned home to Toronto. "And I do remember saying," he concedes, "'nobody is ever going to believe this in a million years, I better take some pictures.' And I did."[111] Mann searched for ways to better authenticate his claims when he arrived home from overseas. Like many of the men, he thought that visual aids, typically photographs, were the best way to convince people of his stories. While he claims that he later donated some of his photographs to an archive, he retained copies in order to continue to have personal evidence on hand.

While personnel openly discussed their concerns about not being believed by the public when they returned home, many attempted – either consciously or unconsciously – to focus their stories on specific individuals. Rather than continually referring to the mass of dead and still living, Canadians and Britons found ways to discuss specific individuals they either spoke to or saw in the camp. Discussing particular individuals rather than generalizing was a method to humanize a terribly dehumanized situation. At times, figures remained unidentified, while some recalled not only names, but countries of origin, family members, and so forth.[112]

Much like Larry D. Mann, Dirk Bogarde was a well-known actor who also served with the RCAF's 39 Reconnaissance Wing. Bogarde's encounter with Bergen-Belsen has been questioned by some critics over the years, although it seems certain that he did visit the camp not long after it was taken over by the Allies.[113] Throughout his life Bogarde frequently referred to Bergen-Belsen in his own writings, as well as in numerous interviews. In his 1978 autobiography, *Snakes and Ladders*, he recalls an ill woman he met in the camp, her "shorn head covered in scabs, face cracked with running sores from which she carelessly waved away the April flies."[114] Bogarde attempts to illustrate the complexity and tragedy of the situation in the camp even after its liberation – a state of affairs where inmates were no longer prisoners of Nazi Germany, yet were still not permitted their total freedom by the Allies. According to Bogarde, the woman, grabbed my hand and stumbled with me along the sandy tracks amongst the filth, talking, crying, singing all at the same time, pointing me out proudly as we went, her filthy striped skirt flapping, breasts swinging like empty pockets against her rib-lined chest. A Corporal, red-faced and gentle, took her from me and pulled us apart, thrusting her away. She stood appalled for a moment, and then with cascading tears pressed both hands to her lips and threw me kisses until I had gone from her sight.[115]

The inmate was sick with a contagious ailment, and the corporal was concerned about the disease spreading and infecting Allied personnel who were still on active duty. The range of emotion was typical of many survivors. "For the great part of the liberated Jews of Bergen-Belsen," recalled camp survivor Dr Hadassah Rosensaft, "there was no ecstasy, no joy at our liberation. We had lost our families, our homes. We had no place to go, nobody to hug, nobody who was waiting for us, anywhere. We had been liberated from death and from the fear of death, but we were not free from the fear of life."[116] Although they were no longer prisoners of Bergen-Belsen, the years of abuse, and the loss of family and home, made it difficult and often impossible to revel in their liberation.

Flight Lieutenant Victor Le Gear, who served with the RCAF's 439 Squadron, was troubled decades later by the memory of a Roma survivor and her mother. Le Gear, from Barrie, Ontario, visited the camp in May 1945 with members from his squadron. "A small gypsy girl in a very threadbare cotton dress," he recalls. "Her eyes had a vacant look, her frame so small and fragile … The home for her and her mother was a shallow whole in the ground, covered by a ragged sheet. It was a graphic illustration of how low in the social scale the gypsies were when they could not get shelter in the long shabby barracks."[117] Of the thousands in the camp, Le Gear focused part of his retelling on these two Roma inmates. He suspected that the daughter was going to die, and perhaps in that very same pit, exposed to the elements huddled with only her mother beside her. This image, distilled and kept alive decades later, was one Le Gear hearkened back to and recounted: the vulnerability and isolation of two individuals in a camp where thousands suffered; the lonely, haunting eyes stood out for Le Gear and was an image he could not shake or forget.

Larry Mann also centred part of his narrative on a single individual with unforgettable eyes. But, unlike Le Gear's memory, the lone individual in Mann's narrative reappeared decades later. While in the camp, according to Mann, "I saw a man; I guess he was a man: he was short, gaunt, his eyes were sunk. But, those eyes were piercing. And I looked into that man's eyes, and I think I looked right through his eyes, right through his head and out the other side; he just penetrated. And then I was off into something else."[118] Mann continued to look around the camp and left shortly thereafter. He later returned to Bergen-Belsen, but did not see the man with the penetrating eyes. Before long the war was over. He was demobilized and returned to Toronto. Decades later, in the early 1990s, Mann explained that he was in Palm Springs with his wife and friends at a function for the survivors of the Holocaust. While he walked alone in the lobby of the theatre, Mann broke down during the interview and revealed simply, "And I saw a man." He paused and then added, "And our eyes locked and we approached each other."[119] The man in Palm Springs was, according to the Toronto-born actor, the same survivor with the piercing eyes he saw in Bergen-Belsen. The survivor's name was Bert Linder, author of *Condemned without Judgment: The Three Lives of a Holocaust Survivor* (1995). Linder and Mann remained friends until the former passed away years later.

In Mann's story the eyes of the survivor are paramount. The image of the eyes, compounded by Mann's moments of silence and the subtle emotion apparent during his retelling, offers far more than could words. The story of the eyes of the survivor appears to give Mann some unspoken, painful truth, a bond which traverses both time and space. And through his recounting, on the grounds of Bergen-Belsen, Linder's eyes spoke to Mann in that moment. "Those eyes," author and Holocaust survivor Elie Wiesel writes, "remind you of your childhood, your orphan state, cause you to lose all faith in the power of language. Those eyes negate the value of words; they dispose the need for speech."[120] A survivor of Hitler's camp system, Linder lived through more than Mann could likely have ever imagined or understood. His eyes, a barometer of emotions, reflected his years of hardship and loss.

Eyes are one of many items focused upon in the narratives of Allied military personnel's encounters in Bergen-Belsen. In an individual's search for meaning a paradigm can be employed to better demonstrate a point. Indeed, patterns can be identified in numerous accounts concerning Bergen-Belsen. By drawing from both history and literature, Britons and Canadians employed a variety of associations with which they – and their respective cultural communities – were familiar. In *Anatomy of Criticism* (1957), Canadian literary critic and theorist Northrop Frye draws attention to what he terms "associative clusters." A type of learned cultural standard, associative clusters are deeply rooted associations that are familiar for a given number of people in a social community.[121] For example, in an effort to illustrate what they experienced in the camps, Holocaust survivors frequently evoke archetypes such as galley convicts, the types of torture used in the Middle Ages, and the Catholic Inquisition in their personal testimonies.[122] Associative clusters then, are multifaceted, allowing experiences and feelings to be made intelligible to others.

A number of clusters are repeated continuously in the accounts of Allied military personnel. These patterns have the capacity to communicate sentiments, values, beliefs, experiences, and outlooks. Studying these types of strongly entrenched cultural associations can offer insight into how an individual employs language to make sense of or come to terms with an experience.

One of the most prominent "associative clusters" offered in narratives by Allied military personnel is that of the "Inferno" (Hell) from the first part of Dante Alighieri's fourteenth-century epic poem the *Divina Commedia* (*Divine Comedy*). A work well known throughout the Western world, including in Britain and Canada, Dante's poem and its description of the suffering and torture in Hell is used in countless Allied responses concerning Bergen-Belsen. "I can't really describe it very well and I don't really want to," Dirk Bogarde said in an interview. "The gates were open and then I realized that I was looking at Dante's Inferno ... I still haven't seen anything as dreadful and I never will."[123] The sight of such sorrow and death challenged his ability to portray it to the extent that he even admits wanting to avoid trying ("I don't really want to"). For Bogarde, Dante's description of Hell would have to suffice. To his eyes, Bergen-Belsen was a frightful place, one of suffering and agony, a veritable Hell. However, in his epic poem, Dante's inferno is the place where sinners are punished, and linking Holocaust victims to sinners is deeply problematic. Inmates, of course, did nothing to deserve being cast away in Hitler's camp system.

However, many personnel evoked similar imagery. Lieutenant-Colonel Hugh Stewart commanded No. 5 Army Film and Photographic Unit (AFPU) during the spring and summer of 1945. Born in Falmouth, Cornwall, and the son of a clergyman, he felt uncomfortable verbalizing the scenes. In an interview later in his life he remarks, "I'll never forget it. You're asking me to describe Dante's vision of hell ... Death pits, piles of bodies, people wandering around mad."[124] In this instance, Stewart is attempting to illustrate the sense of hopelessness he feels in adequately describing such things. In their journey through Hell, Dante and his guide, the Roman poet Virgil, hear the cries and moans of the damned souls. Clearly, many Allied personnel viewed the terrible scenes in Bergen-Belsen from their own particular perspective, and not from the standpoint of the inmates. For many of the Allies, the misery appeared hellish, an inferno, but most understood that the inmates were in no way deserving of such a fate.

Other "associative clusters" include references to a phrase from Scottish poet and lyricist Robert Burns's "Man Was Made to Mourn: A Dirge" (1784): "Many and sharp the num'rous ills / Inwoven with our frame! / More pointed still we make ourselves / Regret, remorse, and shame! / And man, whose heav'n-erected face / The smiles of love adorn, / *Man's inhumanity to man* / Makes countless thousands mourn!"[125] A familiar refrain employed over the centuries, it has been used to describe various lessons drawn from wars, the treatment of indigenous peoples, the slave trade, and any other acts of extreme violence. Although decades of overuse have turned the phrase banal, it was a common descriptor of Bergen-Belsen.

Harold Morden was a leading aircraftman serving with the Casualty Air Evacuation Unit, RCAF. A mortician by trade, Morden was asked by his commanding officer to visit the camp and to bring his camera. "I don't think we realized," he recalls in the documentary *Portraits of War* (2007), "the hate that the German army had against the Jews ... It was unbelievable. We used to say: man's inhumanity to man."[126] While identifying the fact that Jews were in the majority, Morden also appears to recognize the generalized trope of "man's inhumanity" and its common usage at the time ("We used to say"). Indeed, the phrase was employed by several military personnel, including Canadians Larry Mann and Brian McConnell, and Britons George Rodger and Leslie Hardman, to name only a few.[127]

Of course, there is a hazard in using such a sweeping phrase to respond to the Holocaust: it can encourage abstraction, disort meaning, or lead to a universalizing of the event. John K. Roth, American professor of philosophy of religion, suggests that universalizing the Holocaust "leads to the banalizing blur found in clichés about 'man's inhumanity to man.' Such banality overlooks differences that make all the difference in the world."[128] While many Allied military personnel were aware of some of these differences, Burns's phrase was well known, something easy to hold onto in an effort to describe an experience so unique, shocking, and disturbing.

The Britons and Canadians who visited the Bergen-Belsen concentration camp did so for a variety of reasons. While religion and ethnicity certainly played a role, most went to confirm the details read in newspaper articles or out of simple human curiosity. Those who went to the camp told stories they feared would not be believed back home. Some took photographs as evidence, others wrote detailed letters to loved ones. At times stories focused on specific individuals, perhaps as a method of making their stories more believable. The personnel who visited the camp often made associations with historical events and literary works known to friends and family in Britain and Canada. Many searched desperately for ways to make a frightful experience intelligible.

Concluding Remarks

This chapter has examined the accounts of British and Canadian military personnel in the weeks and months following the handover of the Bergen-Belsen concentration camp. Those assigned to work at Bergen-Belsen, along with those who visited the camp, grappled with a variety of issues in their responses. While many told their stories in the days, weeks, and months after the surrender, some waited decades before commenting on what they witnessed. "We tell stories," Ricoeur explains, "because in the last analysis human lives need and merit being narrated. This remark takes on its full force when we refer to the necessity to save the history of the defeated and the lost. The whole history of suffering cries out for vengeance and calls for narrative."[129] For most, the impulse to narrate could never be permanently silenced. Before we conclude this chapter, let us examine what prompted these later responses and discern any sustained or lingering effects of the experience on Allied military personnel.

"I don't think," Reverend Leslie Hardman underlined in 1962, "sufficient tribute has been paid to the Canadian troops who helped out at the concentration camp at Belsen."[130] Hardman, the British padre who himself did so much for the inmates at the camp, searched for the Canadian airmen who assisted him at Bergen-Belsen while visiting that country nearly twenty years after the war. With the help of the local media, he tracked down Gordon McGregor, the former commanding officer of 126 Wing, RCAF, and the then president of Trans-Canada Air Lines (later renamed Air Canada).[131] Indeed, most of the personnel who became involved at Bergen-Belsen generally did not seek or receive any form of recognition for their work. However, those who were prompted to speak about what they witnessed after decades of silence often did so because of something stirring in the media. However, it usually was not those, like Reverend Hardman, looking to thank them for their work; rather, it was often in response to the work of revisionists and deniers that military personnel decided to speak openly and publicly about the experience.

"Why did you want to tell your story today?" asked Rona Arato to Canadian airman Bernard Yale in an interview fifty-three years after the camp's surrender. "For several reasons," he replied. "To contribute towards the memory of what actually did occur and to counteract anyone who tries to deny that it happened."[132] In various interviews and articles, Allied military personnel revealed that their years of silence had been broken by those who attempted to refute the crimes at Bergen-Belsen or the Holocaust as a whole. For example, in some of his accounts, Matthew Nesbitt directly references war criminal John Demjanjuk and the rise of the neo-Nazi movement in the United States as reasons for his testimony; Yale and airman Clifford Robb worked to counteract the revisionism of Ernst Zündel; Mervin Mirsky, meanwhile, spoke out against Holocaust denier David Irving.[133]

For some, motivations about whether or not to speak publicly had more to do with the climate of the times. Immediately following the end of the war, James Ernest Thompson discovered that it was rare for people to believe the stories he relayed.[134] He was a Flying Officer in the RCAF's 437 Transport Squadron. Between 25 and 29 April 1945 Thompson flew high-ranking Allied authorities to and from Bergen-Belsen, and evacuated a select number of inmates to Lille, France.[135] Due to a less than receptive audience back home in Canada, he acknowledges with regret, "I don't tell [about] it very often."[136] It usually took the prompting of others, as well as the negative reactions or actions of some, for men and women to tell of their experiences.

The effect of the experience of working at or visiting Bergen-Belsen varied considerably among the men and women who saw it. "It was a real horror camp," acknowledges Harold Morden, "but, it's never affected me mentally. I know fellas that it did ... I don't think you get hardened to anything, it's just that you're able to cope with it."[137] Hearing this response, artist Alex Colville, who will be discussed in the next chapter, agreed with Morden: "Am I an exceptionally callous person?" he asks. "Of course you feel badly about it, but you're not ruined by it."[138] And yet, as we will see in chapter 5, there are lingering effects in the work of Colville, which, as some suggest, stem from his encounter with the camp.

Others have admitted to having their direction in life transformed because of the experience. John Doerksen was a medical technician in the RCAF when he entered the Bergen-Belsen concentration camp.

During a symposium on the Holocaust at the University of British Columbia, Doerksen revealed that the impact of the camp prompted him to enrol in a Bible college after the war in search of answers. "I'm a Christian guy," he explains, "and I believe in God and I have a lot of faith. I'm a human guy – I get emotional. I could not understand why God would permit something like this."[139] For Doerksen, the experience inevitably led to a crisis of meaning, which made him question his faith. And yet, while some, like Doerksen, grappled both spiritually and intellectually with the experience, other individuals took partisan action and became involved in activities they might never have otherwise taken up.

"It is time this nonsense was ended," Ted Aplin wrote in an article soon after the war. "Let us raise our voices and call for the opening of the doors of Palestine."[140] Indeed, for many Allied servicemen and women, the situation in Palestine became even more urgent. While some, like Aplin, expressed their strong opinions in print and in public debates, others offered their support through funding or helping Jews illegally migrate to Palestine. In addition, there were those who were willing to continue serving as soldiers and airmen, under a different flag, by taking the fight from Europe to Palestine.

After the war, Canadian airman Denny Wilson became a "Machalnik," taken from the Hebrew acronym "Machal" (Mitnadvei Chutz L'Aretz) meaning "volunteer from abroad." He joined the understaffed Jews in British Palestine in the 1948 Arab-Israeli War. As a Machalnik and a non-Jew, Wilson served with 101 Squadron of the Israeli Air Force (IAF), fighting alongside men such as Ezer Weizman, future president of Israel. "I am often asked why I went," Wilson explains. "I had seen the Bergen-Belsen concentration camp and it seemed to me that the [future] State of Israel was the underdog."[141] Like Wilson, other Canadians who encountered Bergen-Belsen and later fought alongside Jews in Palestine in the Arab-Israeli War included Montreal's Howard Cossman (7th Brigade, 72nd Battalion), Winnipeg's Leo Heaps (9th Brigade), and Whitby's Abraham "Abe" Levine (7th Brigade, 79th Battalion), to name a few. For these men, both Jews and non-Jews, the impact of what they saw at Bergen-Belsen encouraged them to leave Canada and fight for Israeli independence.

The situation was often much more forbidding for those in the British forces. Due to the British Mandate, numerous veterans of the Second World War found themselves serving under a directive preventing Jewish migration to Palestine. And for those who encountered the remnants of Hitler's camps, this assignment could be all the more painful. Born in 1928 in Biggleswade, Bedfordshire, John Burrows joined the British Army towards the end of the Second World War and was "on hand" for the liberation of Bergen-Belsen.[142] After the war, Burrows volunteered and was posted to the 6th British Airborne Division near Netanya, Palestine. It was not long after being ordered to search illegal ships full of Jewish refugees from Europe that Burrows deserted, joined the Haganah, and became a Machalnik. According to his son, after witnessing Bergen-Belsen, his father could no longer stand to watch the suffering of Europe's surviving Jews.[143] Upon his return to England, John Burrows was court-martialled and sentenced to two years in prison.

Likewise, Irishmen Michael Flanagan and Thomas O'Sullivan served in the British Army during the Second World War and were also on hand for the liberation of Bergen-Belsen. After the war both men were stationed in Mandatory Palestine. Flanagan was assigned as a technician in the armoured forces, while O'Sullivan, like John Burrows, served with the 6th Airborne Division. Flanagan and O'Sullivan were frustrated by British involvement in Palestine and supported Israeli independence. Soon they came into contact with the Haganah. In 1948 Flanagan and O'Sullivan were involved in the theft of three British Cromwell tanks, which were then turned over to the Israeli military. Both men became deserters and participated as Machalniks in the Arab-Israeli War. During their service in Palestine, they met their future wives; Flanagan even converted to Judaism in order to marry fellow soldier Ruth Levy. After their encounters at Bergen-Belsen and their experiences during the Arab-Israeli War, Flanagan and O'Sullivan remained staunch supporters of the state of Israel throughout their lives.

It is clear that for all those who witnessed the crimes in Bergen-Belsen, the experience made an indelible imprint. Some Britons and Canadians could never forgive Germany for its actions during the war and especially for the Holocaust. Some exacted justice in the camps, while others urged that criminal acts be punished in the courts. Some built up psychic barriers to deal with their emotions, while others were able to adjust themselves accordingly. Some Allied military personnel blamed the German people as a whole, while most attributed the crimes exclusively to the agents of Nazism. In their responses, individuals searched history, literature, and religion for connections to make their thoughts and feelings intelligible. In the end, they felt something change within them. "We … followed the black and yellow signs to Bergen-Belsen," Dirk Bogarde observes, "where we lost our boyish laughter forever."[144] Indeed, the world somehow looked different now, and not for the better.

Chapter Five

The Impossible Real: Bergen-Belsen in Art and Photography

There is not an artist in all the world who can mix colors bold enough ... to portray the horror and the tragedy of death ... or of the living under the regime of the planners and builders of the crematorium world.[1]

Josef Rosensaft, former president of the
World Federation of Bergen-Belsen Survivors

My painting of ... Belsen ... I think was a failure. It's inadequate. This is not my kind of material. Some people have got some kind of sense of what was happening from the stuff I did in Belsen. But, basically, I think I was the wrong guy for the job in a way.[2]

Lieutenant D.A. Colville, Official Canadian War Artist

This had to be recorded somehow.[3]

Sergeant William Lawrie, British Army Film and Photographic Unit

Visually documenting the scenes in Bergen-Belsen, through the use of photography and other forms of artistic interpretation, such as painting, drawing, and sketching, was a substantial historical undertaking and a considerable stylistic, moral, and aesthetic challenge. War artists and photographers alike sought to depict the anguish they witnessed in the camp, while being sensitive to not exploit the dead and the ailing survivors. Individuals who felt compelled or who were formally assigned to portray the Nazi offences in Bergen-Belsen were confronted with serious moral and ethical demands. When photographers directed their cameras and artists opened their sketchbooks they did so among sights, sounds, and smells that they had never before experienced.

Many felt the weight of appropriately and accurately representing the brutal conditions of the inmates inside the camp.

Photographers and war artists were thus faced with a situation that assailed the senses and to which they felt duty-bound to record. Many recognized that their assignment was an important one, but some felt strained working in their respective mediums. The experience in Bergen-Belsen was momentous for all involved. It impacted their personal lives and often transformed the way they viewed their modes of representation in the future.

As they toiled away in the camp, neither artists nor photographers were neutral as they decided upon how and on what scenes to capture. Moreover, their efforts were not always mutually exclusive. War artists often used photographs to focus and ground their work, while photographers were indubitably influenced by artistic expression as some sought to evoke specific imagery within their pictures. Indeed, both groups were swayed by each other.

The following chapter surveys the accounts of British and Canadian war artists and photographers who attempted to depict and interpret Bergen-Belsen. The central focus will not be simply on how artists and photographers responded to the situation at the camp, but also on how they understood their responsibilities and how they struggled with their respective modes of representation. In addition, while the actual work of the artists and photographers will certainly be considered, and keeping with the theme of this book, the emphasis will be more on the oral and written responses to that work. For the instructive purposes of this chapter, a number of individuals who were not formally part of – but often worked closely with – the military, such as British photographer George Rodger, who worked for *Life* magazine, are also included.

Accordingly, this chapter is divided into four sections. The first section will provide a brief overview of the theoretical issues facing those attempting to visually depict the Holocaust. The second section offers a basic background to the British and Canadian war arts programs, along with the expectations of the two countries' war photographers. The third section is devoted to the work of the war artists, both official and not, while the fourth and final section inspects the efforts of various war photographers and photojournalists. Together this chapter explores how two modes of representation – art and photography – offer both analogous and diverse cultural codes, and it also examines how their makers endeavoured to capture a momentous and dreadful period in history.

Surveying Debates on Holocaust Representation

The Holocaust and artistic expression, such as painting and photography, appear as distinct counterparts. Each seems to belong to entirely different realms. The Holocaust was the ruthless, bureaucratic, state-sponsored, systematic destruction of six million European Jews and hundreds of thousands of others such as Roma and the mentally and physically disabled. Art concerns itself with the act of creation and often grapples with aesthetics and various types of expression. Thus, there can be a great tension, an uncomfortable correlation between the Holocaust and artistic production. As Lawrence Langer stresses, "There is something disagreeable, almost dishonorable, in the conversion of the suffering of the victims into works of art."[4] And yet, for art and representation to disregard the crimes would also be disagreeable and dishonourable.

Scholars, theorists, and artists have long debated the challenges and difficulties of Holocaust representation. Commencing with German-born Jewish sociologist and philosopher Theodor Adorno's well-known, frequently cited, and often misunderstood 1949 claim – which he later revised – that "to write poetry after Auschwitz is barbaric," artists and writers have been cautious of the ethical implications in rendering the Holocaust.[5] Appearing in "Cultural Criticism and Society," the essay had little to do with the topic of the Nazi genocide. Indeed, the phrase is often quoted as a single line, removed from its proper context. Adorno's entire passage from which the quote is taken is as follows:

> The more total society becomes, the greater the reification of the mind and the more paradoxical its effort to escape reification on its own. Even the most extreme consciousness of doom threatens to degenerate into idle chatter. Cultural criticism finds itself faced with the final stage of the dialectic of culture and barbarism. To write poetry after Auschwitz is barbaric. And this corrodes even the knowledge of why it has become impossible to write poetry today. Absolute reification, which presupposed intellectual progress as one of its elements, is now preparing to absorb the mind entirely. Critical intelligence cannot be equal to this challenge as long as it confines itself to self-satisfied contemplation.[6]

The phrase "to write poetry after Auschwitz is barbaric" was pounced on by critics as it made an immediate impact in Germany and soon throughout the Western world. Indeed, Adorno's argument questions the entire enterprise of historical and artistic representation. His warning had much to do with his immense sense of guilt in finding any type of pleasure in Holocaust reproduction. Furthermore, Adorno was also deeply concerned with insensitive manipulation of the Holocaust. As we will soon review, while Adorno would later revise his claim, his dictum has left a substantial impression on artists, scholars, and theorists around the world.

In response, Adorno's contemporary, German author and poet Hans Magnus Enzensberger, argues in a 1959 essay for the importance of cultural expression to endure after the Holocaust.[7] Writing in honour of poet and playwright Nelly Sachs, as well as to counter Adorno's familiar statement, Enzensberger stresses that literature, poetry, and – one might add – artistic expression as a whole, must struggle against silence in the shadow of the Holocaust. Still, both Enzensberger and Adorno recognized and continuously emphasized the great difficulty in grasping and depicting the enormity of the Holocaust.

Recently, literary scholar Michael Rothberg has reflected on the debates relating to creative production after the Holocaust. He situates the divergent approaches to Holocaust knowledge and representation into two camps: "realist" and "antirealist." According to Rothberg, "realists" tend to view the Holocaust as something that is tangible, epistemologically, and as a consequence it is thus possible for this knowledge to be illustrated in representational forms.[8] "Realists" are typically scholars such as historians and social scientists who, by employing rigorous methodology, strive to both grasp and understand the Nazi genocide.[9]

The "antirealists," as Rothberg has labelled, view the Holocaust as either unknowable or as something that could only be grasped or represented under "radically new regimes of knowledge" or by experimental or unconventional modes of representation.[10] "Antirealists" normally consist of artists, philosophers, literary critics, and psychoanalysts, who stress the impossibility of ever fully comprehending the Holocaust, as well as recognizing its sheer incommensurability.[11] Thus, the gulf between the "realists" and "antirealists" is immense.

According to Rothberg, part of the problem lies in the fact that Holocaust studies regularly exhibits a multidisciplinary structure. The field brings together scholars from various disciplines, many who frequently read and cite one another. However, much of their own work remains within the boundaries of a particular, traditional discipline.[12] In an effort to bridge this great divide, Rothberg underscores three fundamental demands to comprehending and representing the Holocaust. As such, he offers that there is a "demand for documentation, a demand for reflection on the formal limits of representation, and a demand for the risky public circulation of discourses on the events."[13] In other words, there is an expectation that Holocaust art will be grounded in documentary evidence and offer an unembellished, factual reality, that it will be self-reflexive, and that it will be conscious of communal reception and transmission. In the work of various war artists and photographers, these three claims are frequently reflected upon during production. But then, how does one wrestle with the idea of visually representing the terrible crimes of the Holocaust? One which could then be described as a work of art?

Brett Ashley Kaplan examines the aestheticization of suffering in relation to Holocaust representation. She refers to this as "unwanted beauty." Rather than as something simply attractive or nice-looking, Kaplan defines "beauty" in works of art as that which offers "ambiguous, diverse, complicated, open-ended reflections on the Holocaust."[14] She readily acknowledges the ongoing debates that suggest the Holocaust is either so traumatic that it is indescribable and cannot be represented in images or that it can be depicted and symbolized like any other historical moment in time. Kaplan advises that "unwanted" or disturbing "beauty" in Holocaust art and reproduction can both complicate and extend our understanding of the crimes.[15]

According to Kaplan, there are three main reasons "beauty" has been rebuked and shunned in Holocaust art. First, "beauty" was exploited by Nazism and has thus been contaminated. Second, Adorno's maxim regarding the barbarity of poetry after Auschwitz has exerted an abnormally significant influence on the topic of Holocaust representation. Third, Kaplan proposes that because the Holocaust is viewed as incomparable, artists have searched for distinct representational approaches, which are often bereft of beauty.[16] In opposition to these reasons, Kaplan argues that "the unwanted beauty of such depictions encourages us to see the complexity of the Shoah in ways that conventional works fail to achieve."[17] Therefore, art that is striking and which depicts the Holocaust directly is not necessarily or inherently profane, but rather a way to unearth unexpected and disturbing revelations of a horrifying past.

Indeed, years after making his bold claim, Adorno began to reconsider it. He was aware of the controversy and debates that stemmed from his famous maxim. In 1962 he admitted:

I have no wish to soften the saying that to write lyric poetry after Auschwitz is barbaric; it expresses in negative form the impulse which inspires committed literature ... But Enzensberger's retort also remains true, that literature must resist this verdict; in other words, be such that its mere existence after Auschwitz is not a surrender to cynicism. Its own situation is one of paradox, not merely the problem of how to react to it. The abundance of real suffering tolerates no forgetting.[18]

While Adorno acknowledges the need for art to remain faithful to suffering, he remained ill at ease with the possibility of extracting any enjoyment from Holocaust art. It was not until four years later that Adorno carefully revised his familiar claim by stating, "Perennial suffering has as much right to expression as a tortured man has to scream, hence it may have been wrong to say that after Auschwitz you could no longer write poems."[19] Here Adorno recognizes the emotional necessity and right to give voice to suffering and pain through artistic expression. Of course, he was referring to the expression of the survivors who agonized in the Nazi camp system. How do we reconcile the work of Allied war artists and photographers who entered the camps as witnesses, years after so much of the pain, suffering, and death had already taken place?

In general, artists often attempt to reflect on or transform reality in their work. Some will strive for individual expression, while others employ traditional motifs and forms of expression. The Canadian and British war artists and cameramen who arrived at the Bergen-Belsen concentration camp did so with the prevailing intention of documenting and detailing the crimes. Characteristically, Allied personnel attempted to put the "facts" ahead of "art," at least in the immediate aftermath. According to art historian Ziva Amishai-Maisels, liberators tended to focus more on documentation and factual representation rather than on grand, inflated artistic expressions.[20] Through their contact with the camp and its inmates, Allied personnel and journalists frequently articulated "their own feelings of sympathy, identity or revulsion by means of their treatment of the corpses."[21] As Rothberg notes in the above, the focus was on realism, the specifics, and the facts, instead of embellishment and aggrandizement.

Thus, war artists and photographers, while certainly not devoid of any creative use of symbolism and the like, maintained a restraint and pragmatism in their work. War artists regularly strove to produce their works as any recording journalist would, while a number of photographers documented the scenes knowing their pictures could possibly be used as evidence in a future war crimes trial. Indeed, both groups often worked as though they were objective "crime reporters." And yet, as will be demonstrated, both war artists and photographers alike could also display fairly inventive and personalized perspectives on the crimes in the camp.

As the horror was so extreme, war artists and photographers also struggled with striking a measured balance in their depictions of the dreadfulness. Amishai-Maisels comments that non-inmate artists, "in order to communicate their messages, had to ensure that the spectators would look at their works and not turn away in rejection … These artists had to devise tactics that would capture the attention of the spectator, force him or her to examine the work of art and thus confront the subject of the Holocaust."[22] Certainly, the suffering, stench, and gloom in the camp were extreme, and to amplify the horror would lead only to distortion. The war artists and photographers thus regularly used space and a sense of limits in much of their framing and expressions. Israeli author and child survivor Aharon Appelfeld perhaps put it most convincingly when he stated:

> By its very nature, when it comes to describing reality, art always demands a certain intensification, for many and various reasons. However, that is not the case with the Holocaust. Everything in it already seems so thoroughly unreal, as if it no longer belonged to the experience of our generation, but to mythology. Thence comes the need to bring it down to the human realm. This is not a mechanical problem, but an essential one. When I say, "to bring it down," I do not mean to simplify, to attenuate, or even to sweeten the horror, but to attempt to make the events speak through the individual and in his language, to rescue the suffering from huge numbers, from dreadful anonymity, and to restore the person's given and family name, to give the tortured person back his human form, which was snatched away from him.[23]

The sheer size and scope of death and disease in Bergen-Belsen were overwhelming for most military personnel and journalists. Allied artists and photographers often reached back to traditional and familiar motifs in their attempts to comprehend what they were seeing. The thousands of dead, the lack of knowledge regarding the names and life stories of the vast majority, made it difficult for personnel to bond on a personal level. Consequently, many searched for that connection through art by focusing on smaller groups or the lone individual.

As we have seen in previous chapters, Allied military personnel frequently suggest that the awfulness of Bergen-Belsen was beyond language. And yet, they frequently employ that very language to describe and make sense of the disaster. The often-repeated "there are no words" phrase was used more as a trope, a motif, or as an overstatement than it was in actual practice. If the Holocaust was planned and carried out by – albeit exceedingly evil – individuals, then the language of humankind should be adequate to describe its reverberations. Thus, it makes sense that the actions of human beings can therefore be described by the very words they have created. As scholar Berel Lang declares, "I propose ... to claim ... that the Holocaust is speakable, that it has been, will be ... and, most of all, ought to be spoken."[24] And what can be said for language can also be said for art. The work of survivors, military personnel, and journalists has been and continues to be accomplished. How war artists and photographers have grappled with their different modes of representation offers a perspective on the way individuals both think and act when confronted with incredible anguish. But, before we examine how the work was done, we must review the system that allowed artists and war photographers to operate and the instructions they ultimately received to carry out such work.

War Arts Programs and the Role of Photography and Photojournalism

During the First World War, artists from both Britain and Canada created significant war art. Of particular importance was the Canadian War Records Office (CWRO), established in 1916 by Maple, Ontario–born Sir Max Aitken (later Lord Beaverbrook). Its role was to film, photograph, and print a detailed record of the war from the Canadian perspective. Shortly thereafter Aitken added the Canadian War Memorials Fund (CWMF), to be administered by the CWRO, becoming Canada's first official war art program. As art historian Laura Brandon notes, the CWMF – with most of its art actually created by British-born artists and British subjects – became the prototype for the British and Australian schemes in the two world wars.[25]

Indeed, soon after the Second World War began, London-born Sir Kenneth Clark looked favourably upon the model of the CWMF when he helped establish Britain's War Artists' Advisory Committee (WAAC) within the Ministry of Information. Clark, who was then director of England's National Gallery, argued – in perhaps an overstatement –

that artists were unlike photographers in that they could unite personal style and interpretation alongside historical documentation.[26] Clark aimed to create both a historical record and to discreetly lift the British public's confidence in the war effort through this arts program.

Between 1939 and 1945, the WAAC commissioned and purchased approximately 6,000 pieces from over 400 artists.[27] Each of the three armed services agreed to take on war artists, and thus artwork covered a wide variety of subjects, both civilian and military. Artists were employed by contract, and the WAAC also encouraged submission for possible purchase from non-contracted war artists, often individuals who were in active service.

According to the Imperial War Museum's Roger Tolson, the WAAC's contracted war artists were given a great degree of latitude in terms of the amount of work they were required to produce, as well as the subjects they covered within defined limits.[28] And yet, since the vast majority of artists supported the battle against Nazi Germany, most paintings were rarely disapproving or condemning of the Allied war effort.

Back in Canada, it was not until 1943 that the country's Second World War arts program was re-established and directed by the country's War Artists' Committee (WAC). Accordingly, the Canadian War Records (CWR), as it was called, was formed in January 1943 under the influence of H.O. McCurry, then director of the National Gallery of Canada, and Vincent Massey, the country's high commissioner to Britain. Canadian war artists worked within all three branches of the military. To be sure, the WAC wanted artists to take part in active operations and to see the war first-hand.

In total there were thirty-two official war artists hired to produce work for the CWR. According to Brandon, all were anglophone except one officer who was born in the United States. Of course, francophone war artists also produced important work, but they were not part of Canada's thirty-two official war artists, despite being encouraged to apply.[29] Of the thirty-two artists, the only female was Molly Lamb, a one-time private in the Canadian Women's Army Corps. By war's end, the CWR had produced approximately 5,000 works of art.[30]

Unlike their British counterparts, Canada's official war artists were given little flexibility in terms of subject matter and in overall expectations. They were expected to create two 40 × 49 inch canvases, two 24 × 30 inch canvases, and ten 22 × 30 inch watercolours.[31] Artists were also encouraged to sketch in the field. When it came time for artists to complete their paintings at the end of the war, supplementary factors undoubtedly influenced the final product. Artists reported to and were counselled by official historians; they were also encouraged to consult war diaries and photographs to aid in providing a "more 'accurate' reflection of what had happened, even though the artist's field sketch gave evidence to the contrary."[32] Much of the art was completed in studios back in Canada after the end of the war in Europe.

In terms of war photography, in late 1939 the Canadian Government Motion Picture Bureau's commissioner, Frank C. Badgley, recommended that the Canadian Army establish a film and photographic unit. Its role, among other items, would be to "record in motion pictures and photographs the day by day activities and achievements of ... units actively engaged in the combat zones."[33] Its objectives would be to contribute to the historical record, to bolster public morale, and to provide material for worldwide distribution.[34] As a result, in September 1941 the Canadian Army Film and Photo Unit (CFPU) was formed. Many of those employed were former commercial or press photographers, while others learned the trade after they enlisted.

For the first two years of its existence, the CFPU mainly documented the army's training program.[35] Most photographers employed the Speed Graphic 4 × 5 press camera or the smaller 2¼ × 2¼ Rolleiflex camera, which was easier to handle in active combat situations. By early 1944, the CFPU had expanded to involve three distinct groups, with Number 3, under the direction of Major Jack McDougall, operating in western Europe.[36] Each group worked closely with military personnel on the ground and suffered some of the same hardships.

The Royal Canadian Air Force (RCAF) also had its own, albeit quite dissimilar, photographic units. Much like the Canadian Army and the Royal Canadian Navy, the RCAF established publicity services during the war. Former journalists were frequently recruited as public relations officers (PROs). Accordingly, PROs both liaised with the press and relied upon newspaper reports and radio broadcasts in their work.[37]

In stark contrast, but also dealing in film, was the RCAF's 39 Reconnaissance Wing, which was responsible for high-level and low-level oblique photography, as well as visual, artillery, and contact reconnaissance. During the war, 39 Wing was seconded to the British Second Army and operated as a part of it.[38] They were denoted the "eyes" of Montgomery's 21 Army Group. Like many of those in the CFPU, a number of the men had photographic training before the war, and, consequently, several personnel frequently took high-quality photographs of sites, events, and people on the ground, which were not necessarily related to reconnaissance.

Exposed film was normally processed by Mobile Field Photographic Sections (MFPS), which were attached to 39 Wing. The MFPS worked in conjunction with the Army Photographic Interpretation Section (APIS). The MFPS of 39 Wing consisted of Numbers 5 and 6 and worked to process huge numbers of films and photographs like an assembly line.[39] And like some of the men involved in reconnaissance section of the Wing, a number of men from 5 and 6 MFPS frequently took their own photographs while on the ground.

The British, meanwhile, formally established the Army Film and Photographic Unit (AFPU) in October 1941, under the control of the Directorate of Public Relations at the War Office. Based at Pinewood Studios in Buckinghamshire, England, the men trained to work in the AFPU were taught the fundamental principles of photography through a combination of theory and applied practice.[40] After the demoralizing evacuation of Dunkirk, officials believed that the employment of film and photography could successfully restore the army's image in the mind of the British public.[41] In addition, the AFPU's intention was to offer a visual historical record of the army's military manoeuvres and to provide footage to commercial newsreels.

According to Toby Haggith, the training for AFPU cameramen was intended to provide a rudimentary knowledge of war photography.[42] While personnel were expected to capture scenes that could be suitable for public viewing, the main objective for members of the AFPU was to contribute to the historical record of the army. Unlike the American Field Photographic Branch (FPB) and Special Coverage Unit (SPECOU), the AFPU had no formal guidelines on how to film military or civilian deaths. Instead, cameramen instituted their own personal set of guidelines.[43] Typically, the men used one of four cameras, the more popular being the British made Vinten Normandy and the US-manufactured DeVry.

Furthermore, film and photography professionals in the Royal Air Force also trained at Pinewood Studios.[44] Recruits were educated to comply with war requirements, much like members of the APFU. In addition, those employed in the RAF for film and photography work were instructed in techniques relating to air reconnaissance and fighting and bombing missions. The number of personnel working in film and photography for the RAF was much higher than with the AFPU.

War artists and cameramen, in both the British and Canadian forces, were not given direction, instructions, or advice regarding how and what to cover in Nazi concentration camps. As one would expect, and like everyone else who entered the camp, artists and cameramen were professionally and psychologically unprepared for what they encountered in Bergen-Belsen. Any guidelines observed often related more to a particular individual's own set of judgments, principles, and moral compass. And it is to these individuals to whom we must now focus.

The War Artists

Discussions of the artists who depicted the scene at Bergen-Belsen typically revolve around the same four men and two women: Alexander Colville and Aba Bayefsky from Canada, and Leslie Cole, Doris Zinkeisen, Mervyn Peake, and Mary Kessell from Britain. Their works have been displayed prominently in art galleries and museums in both countries. However, a number of additional artists – official and non-official – from both countries also encountered and depicted Bergen-Belsen.[45]

Other individuals of note include Toronto-born Flying Officer Donald Kenneth Anderson, an official war artist with the RCAF's 127 Wing. A commercial artist before the war, he enlisted in the RCAF in April 1941. According to Anderson, he completed numerous sketches of Bergen-Belsen and its inmates.[46] He ultimately completed only one watercolour of the camp, which is held by the Canadian War Museum.[47] Montreal's Henry S. Abramson, a leading aircraftman (LAC) with the RCAF's 39 Reconnaissance Wing, visited the camp in early May 1945 and made several attempts at depicting the scenes he witnessed in Bergen-Belsen. One of his pieces, a full-colour painting of the dead in one of the large open pits, was published in the Wing's *Flap* magazine from August 1945.[48] Canada's first and only female official war artist sent overseas during the Second World War, Molly Lamb (later Bobak), visited Bergen-Belsen with her driver during the late summer of 1945 but opted not to sketch or paint it.[49] Overall, the above-noted Canadian artists completed significant works that are of historical importance and certainly deserve a larger audience.[50]

Other notable British artists include Sergeant Eric Taylor of the Royal Engineers. An established painter and printmaker before the war, Taylor was likely the first Allied war artist to enter Bergen-Belsen. He completed five watercolour works relating to the camp and its inmates.

An untitled painting depicting the dead in one of the pits at the Bergen-Belsen concentration camp by Leading Aircraftman Henry S. Abramson of 39 Wing, RCAF. Used by permission of Ronney Abramson for the estate of H.S. Abramson.

Edgar Ainsworth was the art editor for *Picture Post* magazine. He made three separate visits to Bergen-Belsen during the spring and summer of 1945. He completed a number of highly detailed works, some of which are now held at the Imperial War Museum. Bryan de Grineau worked for the *Illustrated London News* and was a well-known motoring artist before the war. His sketches of Bergen-Belsen were published in the *Illustrated London News* in early May 1945. His watercolours have been obtained by the Imperial War Museum. Like their lesser-known Canadian counterparts, these are works of great historical value.

Consequently, how and why did these artists make their way to the Bergen-Belsen concentration camp during the spring and summer of 1945? To begin with, we must distinguish between official commissions, personal motivation, and artists on assignments. Artists who received official commissions were formally instructed by authorities to record the scenes at Bergen-Belsen. Second, and contrary to what many have written, when the camp was surrendered to the British it was not difficult for outside military personnel and journalists – at least initially – to enter and witness. Thus, a number of artists felt personally motivated to both observe and comment on the crimes. They were not given formal instruction but felt compelled to make their way to the camp and record the experience. This group would also include soldiers who were part of the liberating forces. Finally, there were also artists, often working as journalists, who were requested by newspapers and magazines to enter Bergen-Belsen on assignment.

Of the Canadian artists, Lieutenant Alex Colville was the only one to receive formal instruction from authorities to depict the camp. According to Colville, when Vincent Massey learned that Bergen-Belsen had been overrun, he requested that the Canadian Army send a war artist to deliver a visual record of the scenes. As a result, Colville received instructions on 26 April from Major A.T. Sesia to travel to the camp and complete some sketches.[51] He initially felt that it would be another "kind of chore" to which he was being assigned.[52] After spending three days at the camp, Colville made his way to Wismar, where the 1st Canadian Parachute Battalion – who had encountered the camp two weeks prior – had been resting in billets. Of the other three Canadian war artists to visit and record Bergen-Belsen, none were given official commission to work at the camp. Flight Lieutenant Aba Bayefsky was attached to 39 Reconnaissance Wing in Lüneburg when he first learned of the camp. With Bergen-Belsen about an hour's drive away, Bayefsky recalls, "When I heard what was there, I went immediately [on 10 May 1945] and it has clearly affected my thinking."[53] Also with 39 Wing, LAC Henry Abramson visited the camp around the same time when he decided to paint what he saw. In contrast, Flying Officer Donald K. Anderson was with 127 Wing, one of many RCAF groups who drove trucks of supplies into the camp.[54] According to Anderson, sometime in April he was told to help bring food to Bergen-Belsen with a few of his colleagues. When he arrived at the camp and saw the conditions of the inmates, he began sketching the scenes.[55]

Belsen by Flight Officer Donald K. Anderson, Official Canadian War Artist. Image 19710261-1309, Beaverbrook Collection of War Art, Canadian War Museum.

Of the British war artists, only Captain Leslie Cole and Mary Kessell received formal commissions from WAAC to produce works of Bergen-Belsen. According to art historian Brian Foss, Cole was a logical choice for WAAC because he had experience portraying the consequences of extreme violence.[56] Kessell was one of only three female British official artists to work on the Continent during the war.[57] She spent six weeks working at the displaced-persons camp at Bergen-Belsen, arriving in August 1945, long after its surrender. Sergeant Eric Taylor was serving with the Royal Engineers when he arrived at the camp in mid-April. After assisting in the relief efforts, Taylor rarely spoke about his experiences; instead he offered five watercolours of the camp, which were purchased by WAAC and are now held at the Imperial War Museum. Doris Zinkeisen was commissioned by the British Red Cross and the St John War Organisation to document the work of doctors and nurses in northwest Europe. She arrived not long after the camp's surrender, towards the end of April. Zinkeisen ultimately produced three oil paintings relating to Bergen-Belsen.[58] Edgar Ainsworth, working for *Picture Post* magazine, made three separate trips to the camp. Initially, he requested a commission from WAAC to depict atrocities in Europe, but instead he was asked to submit works after completing them.[59] He published some sketches in *Picture Post* in September 1945, and WAAC later purchased two drawings of Bergen-Belsen. Finally, Mervyn Peake, whose requests to become an official war artist had been declined, served as a Ministry of Information Artist in 1943, a position he held for a number of months. When he arrived at Bergen-Belsen on 20 June – dropped off by journalist Tom Pocock – he was working for *Leader* magazine. He was commissioned by Charles Fenby, editor of *Leader*, to record his impressions of western Europe at the end of the war. He produced numerous sketches and a poem – of which a number of versions exist.

The artists' verbal responses to the camp at times echo those of other military personnel, primarily in their inability to find suitable words to describe the suffering of the inmates. Donald Anderson remembers the experience as being too overwhelming to even be absorbed, calling it something "right off the emotional scale."[60] Bayefsky reiterates Anderson's comments, likewise noting that Bergen-Belsen "was shocking to the point you can't really explain it."[61] Difficulties in absorbing the experience, frustration at locating appropriate words for the situation, were again all too common among the men and women of all ranks and positions. Colville expanded on these thoughts when he confessed, quite candidly, that once inside the camp, "the extremity of the situation ... it's just unbelievable. And the fact is that, you know, you're not capable of registering what you feel when you see one person and you can't manufacture that by seven thousand or thirty-five thousand times. So the reaction is not proportional to the scale of what has happened."[62] For Colville and the others, processing the pain of a single individual seemed entirely plausible, the agony of thousands quite impossible. Proportion, scale, capability, and appropriateness of a response immediately came to the forefront in the artist's mind. In a letter to her husband, Zinkeisen confesses, "I've just got back from Belsen and feel far too hurt and sore inside, too full of emotion to really write anything sensible ... I cannot describe how awful it was. Quite, quite awful."[63] Unable to speak clearly of their feelings, many artists turned to their formal training in art, whether it was through sketching, painting, or drawing. Feeling utterly incapable of "proportionally" registering the situation through language, how did artists wrestle with expressing, visually, the agony of others? And what right did one have to do so?

These questions forever haunted Mervyn Peake, artist, poet, writer, husband, and father. Peake was born in China to British parents and spent most of his first decade in that country. It was less than a month before his thirty-fourth birthday when Peake entered Bergen-Belsen. As he made his way through the camp he visited the makeshift hospital, located not far from the main camp. There he focused upon a sickly and dying young girl. As he sat before her, he began to observe, not only as a man and a father, but also as an artist. The subsequent ink and wash painting features the nameless girl with her short cropped hair and large black eyes peering over a blanket. He told his wife, Maeve, that he also wrote a poem about her.[64]

The poem, which became "The Consumptive: Belsen, 1945," is an admission of remorse concerning his intrusion on the dying girl.[65] "Then where is mercy?" he penned, "And what / Is this my traffic? for my schooled eyes see / The ghost of a great painting, line and hue / In this doomed girl of tallow?"[66] Peake asks how the image of the dying girl, like tallow – an animal fat that is moulded into a candle – can be turned into something else, in this case art. He worries if he will one day commit an injustice of memory by forgetting the girl and her suffering: "Her agony slides through me: am I glass / That grief can find no grip," but he later promises, "Though I be glass, it shall not be betrayed / That last weak cough of her small, trembling head."[67] There is a deep sense

Dying Girl at Belsen by Mervyn Peake for *Leader* magazine. Reprinted by permission of Peters Fraser and Dunlop on behalf of The Mervyn Peake Estate.

of shame Peake feels about his act of painting the dying girl. He questions his own sense of pity and probes the value of his apparent duty to record the suffering and pain he beheld. Peake's biographer, Malcolm Yorke, contends that the girl was "a stranger who had given this foreigner no permission to sit by her bed and make art from her last moments of glory."[68] Her name unknown, her identity thus obscured, what remains is Peake's painting: a young, frail child, her black, bulging eyes gazing over a blanket.

Although Peake was forever disturbed by and felt guilty for turning suffering into art, this was not always a central issue for other artists. While the enormity of the situation certainly overwhelmed him, Alex Colville looked at his task somewhat differently than did Peake. When asked how he kept himself composed depicting mass death he insists: "I suppose it would be the equivalent of being a police reporter, you know, someone who works for a big city newspaper and covers the courts and the whole business of crime and violence."[69] He claims to have taken the position of the "detached observer," closing himself off in order to complete his work. Whereas Peake felt overcome with emotion, Colville saw it as an assigned task. His was a more pragmatic approach to depicting violence and suffering. "If you're a writer or a painter," he confesses, "your material is life as you see it being lived and that's it, you get to work and do it."[70] He admits that he felt bad for not feeling worse. This is not to say that Colville lacked feelings of sympathy or empathy for the inmates and the dead; rather, he remained steadfast, focusing on documenting what he saw and completing his "assignment." The effect of this resolute intention appears in the work that he submitted of the camp. His pictures are unswerving in their presentation of the dead, but never grotesque. His best-known image of the camp, *Bodies in a Grave, Belsen*, is an oil painting on canvas. Four emaciated corpses lie horizontally, one on top of the other. The bodies appear faint, phantasmagorical, as if they were about to fade into the muted landscape.

American psychiatrist Robert Jay Lifton has conducted numerous studies of the psychological causes and effects of war and violence. When surrounded by overpowering death and horror, individuals can unconsciously restrain their emotions, despite being fully aware of their environment. Lifton terms this "psychic closing-off," a partial numbing of the senses amid pain and suffering.[71] Through restrained emotion, artists like Colville were able to accomplish their tasks of recording the scenes in the camp. But was this always the case?

Bodies in a Grave, Belsen, by Lieutenant Alex Colville,
official Canadian war artist. Image 19710261-2033,
Beaverbrook Collection of War Art, Canadian War Museum.

While reviewing his initial, shaky sketches of Bergen-Belsen with interviewer and art historian Joan Murray, Donald Anderson admits, "You can see the initial shock ... that's just pure shock. You'd think I was drunk or something."[72] While he was able to make a number of quick – albeit unsteady – sketches over a few days, Anderson found it problematic to work in the camp. Lifton reminds us that any level of "psychic closing-off" cannot fully protect the individual from the negative experience.[73] Doris Zinkeisen, who, according to her son, suffered from terrible nightmares of Bergen-Belsen after the war, was also able to complete a few sketches while in the camp, but by the time she returned to headquarters, she collapsed, overcome by the experience.[74] Even Colville, who completed a handful of sketches while in the camp, admitted in a report that "The subjects were not of a sort which can be executed expressively at the time, on the spot."[75] While some artists could maintain focus in order to complete some of their works in the camp, most were only capable of quick sketches, completing their art at a later date, usually after the war's end and far away from Bergen-Belsen.

And when it came time to turn sketches into larger paintings, upon what images did the artist focus and why? Many artists selected scenes that exposed the surreal and disturbing disparities present in the camp. In one of her better known pieces, *Human Laundry, Belsen: April 1945*, Zinkeisen depicts the German nurses who were instructed to wash down and disinfect the inmates to help curb the spread of typhus. The blatant contrast between nurses and inmates is startling in her painting: the former, standing well-fed and plump in white smocks; the latter, naked and emaciated, most lying prostrate on hard wooden tables. In a letter to her husband, Zinkeisen underscores that after being brought into the hospital the inmates "were then laid on these tables and washed down by fat German nurses quite irrespective of age and sex. The contrast between the German fat and these bones is quite ridiculous."[76] The fact that many of the healthy and robust doctors and nurses were from Germany – from the "enemy" country – and were being forced to tend to the victims of that very country's regime, only adds to the oddity of the scene.

In an ink painting titled, *One of the Death Pits, Belsen: SS Guards Collecting the Bodies*, Leslie Cole notes that the SS were carelessly throwing the dead into a large open grave. The painting offers an unbroken view of the pit and the bodies, with the camp in the background. "[They] were made to go into the pit and create some semblance of order," he writes about the scene, "if the pit was not being neatly filled."[77] The painting features SS guards carrying bodies to the open grave, being supervised by British soldiers. One can see, in small scale, an SS guard standing deep in the pit, surrounded by bodies which he appears to be rearranging. The picture of a lone individual in a pit filled with hundreds of corpses, arranging the bodies is both bizarre and disturbing. The distinction between the large number of dead and the few living is glaring.

Indeed, disparity was ubiquitous as the artist took in the frightening scenes at the camp. Colville remembers that upon arriving he began surveying the relief efforts. Looking between rows of huts he saw "two medical guys carrying out a beautiful, naked young woman. She was in or on a grey blanket – I don't know if she was dead; she was

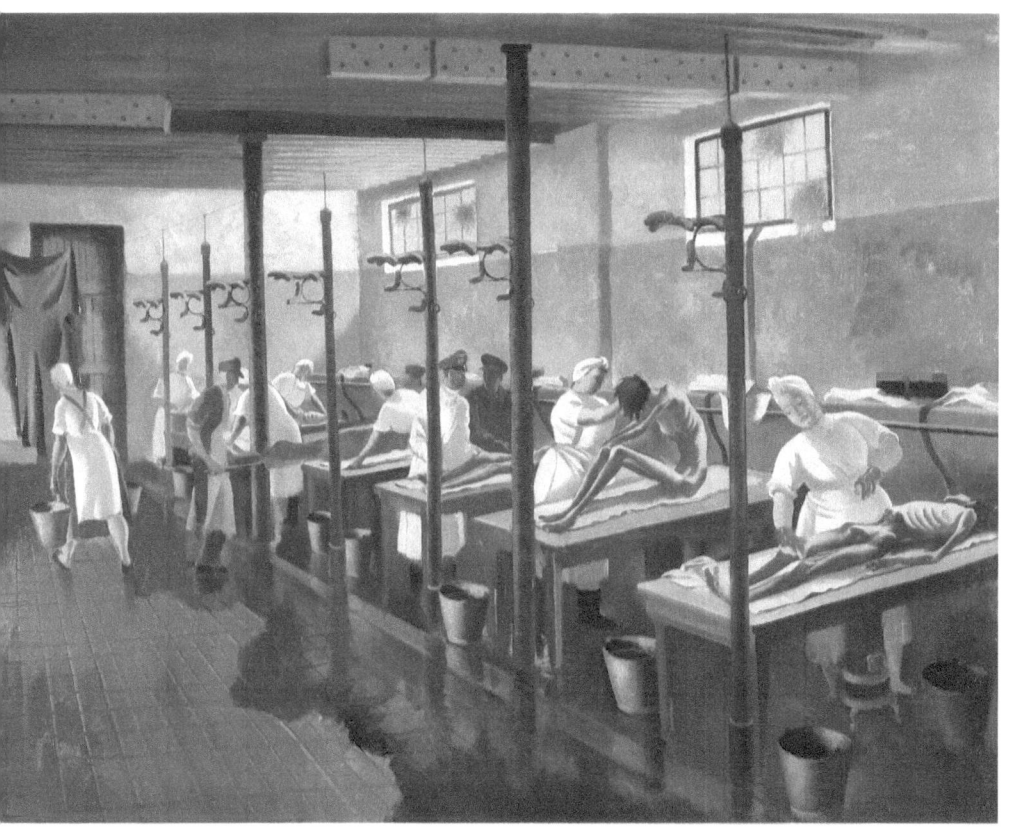

Human Laundry, Belsen: April 1945, by Doris Zinkeisen of the St John Ambulance Brigade. Image ART LD 5468, Imperial War Museum.

probably alive. But the incongruity of this was just bizarre."[78] The naked body of a beautiful young woman appeared entirely out of context for Colville. If only for a moment in that rotten camp, somehow death and beauty seemed to coexist. While he ultimately did not submit a painting of the woman, the imprint of this memory remained with Colville for decades.

According to Ziva Amishai-Maisels, portraying the piles of emaciated corpses scattered on the campgrounds became a dominant theme, if not a symbol, of the Holocaust.[79] Indeed, Canadian artists Abramson, Bayefsky, and Colville all produced similar types of work evoking this

One of the Death Pits, Belsen: SS Guards Collecting Bodies by Captain Leslie Cole, official British war artist. Image ART LD 5105, Imperial War Museum.

particular image, as did British artists Ainsworth, Cole, Taylor, and Zinkeisen. "I saw pits with thousands of dead bodies piled in them," Bayefsky remembers. "[It] had a profound impact on me ... It was a major experience of my life."[80] The sheer magnitude of bodies lying around the campgrounds and in open pits was the most common image reproduced by the war artists.

We must now ask, how did the artists view their own work and what meanings did they draw from their experiences? For Aba Bayefsky, the impact was undeniable. As a Jewish Canadian, he had long been personally affected by antisemitism. Growing up in Dufferin Grove, a non-Jewish neighbourhood of Toronto, Bayefsky and his brother experienced antisemitism as a part of daily life. As children they frequently had to

In the foreground, Fritz Klein, a former SS doctor in Auschwitz and Bergen-Belsen, makes an announcement for British newsreels while behind him SS guards bury corpses in a mass grave. Image 69245, United States Holocaust Memorial Museum, courtesy of Hadassah Bimko Rosensaft.

fend off attacks to and from Brock Junior Public School, which they both attended.[81] When he enlisted in the air force, Bayefsky remembers encountering numerous antisemites, suggesting that it was likely the first time many of the enlisting men had ever met a Jew.[82] As a result, Bayefsky believes that his encounter with Bergen-Belsen, and its thousands of Jewish inmates, had a tremendous effect on him because of his religious upbringing and the biases he faced throughout his life.[83]

Many official Canadian war artists were landscape painters. They tended to focus on the environment or on the machines of war. While Bayefsky was mostly a figurative painter, he could and did paint landscapes and other objects. After Bergen-Belsen, he no longer saw the point of depicting airplanes.[84] His focus was now even more resolutely on the human side of life. And in light of the crimes he witnessed, he emphasizes that art must make bold statements. "In the work that I did at Belsen," he observes, "I want to be clear in what I'm saying ... art that doesn't say anything is just meaningless to me." There appears to be no "psychic closing-off" for Bayefsky. During one of his visits, he became ill near one of the pits.[85] His anger and emotion are entirely evident in both his words and in his art. The Holocaust, antisemitism, and Bergen-Belsen recur throughout his life's work. Indeed, politics and social commentary became more focused and apparent in his postwar art.

Sergeant Eric Taylor, in contrast, rarely spoke of his experiences with the Royal Engineers at Bergen-Belsen. He readily admits that any complexity and strength found in his personal style stem from his life experience, particularly from his years as a soldier.[86] Reflecting on his time assisting in Bergen-Belsen, and the subsequent art he produced, he stresses, "To me, any attempt to explain in words the overall influence of this experience [in Bergen-Belsen] on my work appears to weaken what I endeavor to say in my painting ... It means so very much."[87] Accordingly, the overwhelming intensity of the experience was, for Taylor, better expressed through painting than through words. Most of his art pertaining to the concentration camp focuses on the lone individual, either sitting on a chair or a bench, drained, staring off into the distance or lying prostrate, too ill to move, on an army blanket or stretcher. He adheres to Appefeld's notion of refusing to intensify or amplify the event and by rescuing the individual's suffering from the anonymity of the group.

Mary Kessell was stationed at Bergen-Belsen longer than any other Allied artist.[88] She arrived months after its surrender, and conditions in the camp had improved dramatically, although there was still much

Belsen Concentration Camp, Malnutrition Wards by Flight Lieutenant Aba Bayefsky, official Canadian war artist. Image 19710261-1393, Beaverbrook Collection of War Art, Canadian War Museum.

work to be done and grief to witness. She was also afforded the opportunity to spend time with and get to know many of the survivors from the camp, particularly the children. When she arrived in August 1945, upon touring the camp, she notes in her diary, "It's vast and quite wonderful. What drawings and paintings ... They are all beginning to live again ... I was amazed by all I saw, it was exciting and most moving."[89] It is important to note that Kessell's diary and art depict not the Bergen-Belsen concentration camp, but the Bergen-Belsen – or what in June 1945 the British unsuccessfully renamed Höhne – Displaced Persons' Centre.[90]

However, despite the "excitement," Kessell was deeply saddened by the suffering that still lingered in the camp, months after its surrender.[91] From her war diary she did not appear to feel guilty for drawing and painting those in the camp. Kessell did, however, feel remorseful for other reasons. "Who am I to have escaped all this?" she asks. "There are people in this camp who can never go home, because they have

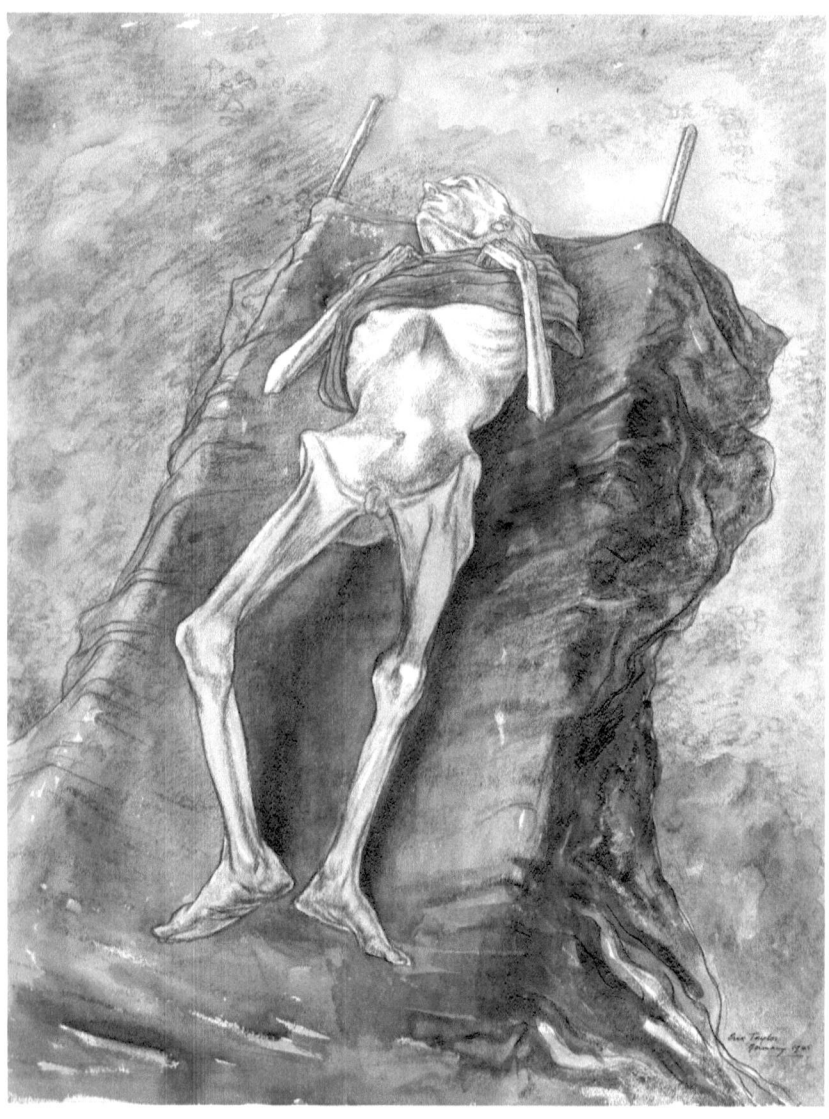

A Living Skeleton at Belsen Concentration Camp, 1945, by Sergeant Eric Taylor of the Royal Engineers. Image ART LD 5587, Imperial War Museum.

nowhere to go. Children who will never know what it is like to have a mother and a father, sisters and brothers, and who will never have an opportunity to do the work they love."[92] Her entries are frequently focused on and worried about the future of the displaced people in the camp. She appears to have tried to help many find even the smallest form of happiness and she often displayed her work to them. "They love my drawings," she says, "and say they are beautiful. They have seen so little, for so long."[93] Her preoccupation was often with the women and children, and much of her artwork focused on both groups. She even had plans to write a special article on the children of Bergen-Belsen.[94]

It is clear that for many of the war artists the impression of Bergen-Belsen endured. For some it reappeared in their work, for others it manifested itself in other ways. Art curator Ulrike Smalley has suggested that, at least for the British war artists who depicted Bergen-Belsen, they did not continue to address the camp or the Holocaust in their later work.[95] However, as we will soon see, there are exceptions. For the Canadian war artists, meanwhile, this is certainly not the case. Regarding his encounter with Bergen-Belsen, Bayefsky declares, "It was the determining factor in everything I have done since."[96] Indeed, the camp and the Holocaust have been a source for much of his future oeuvre, particularly his set of works titled *Epilogue*, a forty-one-piece collection.[97] In a study examining Colville's life work, art historian Tom Smart posits that Bergen-Belsen "haunts" much of Colville's postwar art.[98] While it is not addressed directly, a number of art historians have observed that subsequent Colville pieces reference his Bergen-Belsen work.[99]

A number of other artists did indeed address the camp in later work. Polish-born Feliks Topolski settled in England in 1935, securing British citizenship in 1947. Topolski was a war artist for both the British government and the Polish government-in-exile when he entered Bergen-Belsen in April 1945. He returned to the image of the camp and the Holocaust in his massive installation *The Memoir of the Century*. Started in 1975, it is a 600-foot-long panoramic painting, standing from 12 to 20 feet high; it was created in railway arches of Hungerford Bridge on London's South Bank. A panel of this installation evokes one of the mass graves he saw decades earlier at Bergen-Belsen. This panel stretches across the ground, under a mirrored ceiling. Looking up one sees their reflection in the pit. Upon his first encounter with the camp and the dead, Topolski writes, "*This* could be me, *that* somebody close

Remembering the Holocaust by Aba Bayefsky. Image 19970112-001, Beaverbrook Collection of War Art, Canadian War Museum.

to me: thus I try to inject myself with responses. The piles of corpses, the multitude *in extremis* ... Indeed, one is hard pressed to believe one's senses – immersed in stench, stumbling over bodies pulled by the legs into the open, passing among living ghosts, molesting one or doubled up in excrement."[100] As a memory, the imprint of Bergen-Belsen was indelible. Accordingly, the experience continued to appear in Topolski's art, decades after the initial meeting.

Other British war artists, while not addressing the topic directly in their later artwork, do, like Colville, make reference to or conjure their monumental encounter at the camp. For example, the sick girl in the hospital that Mervyn Peake both painted and featured in a poem became the inspiration for the character of Black Rose, a dying woman, in his novel *Titus Alone* (1959). The work is an attempt at reconciling human goodness with human evil. In a future poem titled "The Victims," Peake, without naming it, arouses the terrible scenes from the camp's makeshift hospital. Even Peake's son, Sebastian, was affected by his father's work at Bergen-Belsen. Acknowledging that the camp remained in his father's consciousness and subconsciousness throughout his life, Sebastian confesses to an "emotional kind of voyeurism," claiming to have personally read everything he could on the subject, speaking to former inmates, visiting the site of a number of camps, and writing his own poems about Bergen-Belsen.[101]

It is clear that for the Canadian war artists, as well as for some of the British, Bergen-Belsen remained a preoccupation and an influence in their subsequent work. While photographers were perhaps better equipped for straightforward documentation, artists were able to emphasize other features. Indeed, a number of artists focused on the stark and distressing incongruences present in the camp. And yet, nearly all who worked at Bergen-Belsen maintained a conservative, documentary style in their art. While some artists were sent in an official capacity, most went to the camp unofficially, driven by personal motivation and a need to comment on the atrocities. Finally, while some certainly felt guilty about working and "creating" in the camp, most war artists managed to complete moving, captivating art.

War Photographers and Photojournalists

"I do hope eventually," Doris Zinkeisen put forward in a letter to her husband, "that I can satisfy myself that I have produced something that will give a semblance of the utter frightfulness, which no photography in the world can ever hope to penetrate."[102] According to Zinkeisen, there was a limitation to the photographers' medium, preventing them from capturing the sheer horror of the camp. And where Zinkeisen saw a limitation, Donald Anderson saw impropriety. When he went to the camp, Anderson brought along two cameras with him, but he refused to take any photographs. "It was like infringing on other people's privacy," he insists. "It was like, going up to a coffin and taking a photograph. There are just some things you do and some things you don't do. That's the way it affected me."[103] For Anderson, taking a photograph of the sick, starving, dying, or dead was an ethical matter. While he apparently had no issues drawing in his sketchbook, he had a problem with the photographic image. And yet British and Canadian photographers took countless pictures at Bergen-Belsen.[104] This section examines how the cameramen coped with their assignments, with the images they captured, and their personal responses concerning their encounter with the camp.

War photographers who entered Bergen-Belsen had a number of issues to deal with that were comparable to those the war artists faced. They struggled with the intrusion of their tools into the lives of those who had suffered terribly. Should they be assisting in the relief efforts or taking pictures of the dead and dying? Some had serious concerns about making artistic renderings of such horror. How should they frame those who had died? Should it be a close-up shot or ought they to keep a distance? Moreover, they wrestled with accurately documenting the horror, but without magnifying it and forcing future audiences to look away and ignore it. How could they thus objectively document the scenes so that they would be believed as evidence of the crimes?

While only a few members of the Canadian Army Film and Photo Unit (CFPU) entered Bergen-Belsen, a significant number from the British Army Film and Photographic Unit (AFPU) did. The first men from the AFPU arrived on 15 April 1945 as they accompanied personnel from the 11th Armoured Division. These men included Sergeants Peter Norris and Ian Grant, and, later, Lieutenant Martin Wilson and Captain E.G. Malindine, along with Sergeants Harry Oakes, Mike Lewis, Bill Lawrie, A.N. Midgley, and Bert Hardy. Their Canadian counterparts in the CFPU included Sergeant A.H. Calder, Lieutenant Charles H. Richer, and Sergeant Mike Lattion, all of whom were with the 1st Canadian Parachute Battalion.[105] RCAF public relations officers Ron Laidlaw and Fred Hopkinson, along with Sergeant Joe Stone of 39 Wing, arrived at Bergen-Belsen on 16 April 1945 and recorded the terrible scenes.[106] In fact, a large number of Canadians with 39 Wing and the Mobile Field Photographic Sections (MFPS) took scores of photographs while at Bergen-Belsen. Some of these men included Flight Lieutenant Allan Ironside and Leading Aircraftmen Lloyd E. Thompson, James Arthur Stubbs, and Lloyd H. Bloom. Photographing the atrocities was a preoccupation for many military personnel. Countless men, even those not serving in photographic sections or units, took pictures of Bergen-Belsen.

For many of the men who took photographs of the camp, their reasons were largely evidentiary. Upon arriving at the camp many personnel worried that their stories would not be believed. "I'm going to enclose a couple of pictures of [Bergen-Belsen]," Flight Lieutenant Ironside wrote in a letter home, "so that you will know it first hand what sort of things have been going on in Germany. The papers are full of atrocity stories and one never knows what to believe and what may just be propaganda."[107] Ironside, who served as Officer Commanding a Mobile Field Photographic Section, sent letters and photographs about Bergen-Belsen back to Canada, not only to counter any doubt that the crimes occurred, but also as a reminder as to why the war was worth fighting. Ironside accurately states that the crimes he witnessed were a "systematic brutal plan to exterminate Jews and other enemies of the Glorious Reich."[108] While most military personnel did not enter the war to save the Jews or to end Hitler's camp system, seeing the camps firsthand and documenting the crimes helped them appreciate the sacrifices they made while serving their respective countries.

The photographer's camera was thus used in an attempt to provide an objective account of the scenes at the camp. And yet, according to art historian and cultural theorist Andrea Liss, to view the photographs of Nazi crimes exclusively as "documentary" is a "misnomer of catastrophic proportions."[109] For Liss these types of photographs are not solely documentary, but also function on a more profound emotional level. There is an unequal, uneasy relationship between the subject and photographer, thereby challenging the boundaries of any "documentary" aspect.

Still, Sergeant William Lawrie certainly saw the evidentiary benefits of taking pictures. As he worked he believed that the photographs he took might one day be used at a war crimes trial.[110] Indeed, months later, film shot by Sergeant Harold Haywood, Lawrie, and Lewis was viewed at the war crimes trial of Josef Kramer and forty-four other defendants. For Sergeant A.N. Midgley – in direct contrast to Zinkeisen's belief of its limitation – photography was the only way to possibly conceive of the camp. "I have read about such camps as this," he writes, "but never realized what it was really like. It must be seen to be believed."[111] Nonetheless, while primarily focused on recording the crimes, some cameramen also confronted the ethical dimensions of aestheticizing the images they were capturing.

George Rodger was born in 1908 in Hale, Cheshire, England, and was of Scottish descent. He was a photojournalist and one of the most influential photographers of the twentieth century. After the war he founded Magnum Photos, an international photographic cooperative, along with some of the most skilled photographers of the century, including Robert Capa, David Seymour, Henri Cartier-Bresson, and William Vandivert. During the Second World War, Rodger worked as a war correspondent for *Life* magazine. He saw the war from a variety of perspectives and took well-known pictures of the Blitz, the British in Burma, and the liberations of France, Belgium, and the Netherlands. He arrived at Bergen-Belsen five days after the camp's formal surrender.

Rodger had seen considerable violence, suffering, and death during the war. Yet his initial shock at the camp was overwhelming; his driver has stated that it was the only time he had seen Rodger visibly upset.[112] But before long, Rodger acknowledged the importance of his assignment, attempting what Lifton called "psychic closing-off," and started to take a series of potent pictures.[113] As his experience and training had taught him, he began considering lighting and exposure, framing and composition. He found himself stimulated by the scenes around him as he "subconsciously arrang[ed] groups and bodies on the ground into artistic compositions in the viewfinder … treating this pitiful human flotsam as if it were some gigantic still life."[114] He worked not only to document, but also to stir emotion in the viewer. Thus, art and documentation coincided. Years later Rodger acknowledges:

> The natural instinct of the photographer is always to take good pictures, at the right exposure, with a good composition. But it shocked me that I was still trying to do this when my subjects were dead bodies. I realized there must be something wrong with me. Otherwise I would have recoiled from taking them at all. I recoiled from photographing the so-called "hospital" which was so horrific that pictures were not justified.[115]

Rodger refers to an internal conflict, a terrible culpability he felt by making creative configurations from the horrors of the camp. His images are undoubtedly the labours of an experienced photographer. It is clear that the pictures were not taken haphazardly: lighting, scale, composition, effect, and image selection were all carefully considered by the skilled cameraman.

Rodger's biographer Carole Naggar suggests his guilt ran much deeper than simply taking imaginatively framed photographs of Bergen-Belsen. Upon examining his essays, diaries, and letters from this time period, Naggar suggests Rodger's guilt was perhaps due more to previous antisemitic remarks as "he describes Belsen's systematic destruction repeatedly in general terms – as 'atrocities,' not *genocide*; and again, not once in his black notebook, not once in his *Time-Life* report, does he use the word 'Jew.'"[116] Naggar's first charge is of course anachronistic, as the term "genocide" was not coined until 1944 by Polish lawyer Raphael Lemkin in his *Axis Rule in Occupied Europe*, and it was not until December 1948 that the United Nations approved the Convention on the Prevention and Punishment of Genocide. Thus, the term would have been unfamiliar to Rodger at the end of the war. As for never uttering the word "Jew," Naggar appears to contradict herself. She quotes from Rodger's 1945 war diary, where he discusses camp commandant Josef Kramer, calling him a "brutish hulk of a man with close-set piggish eyes ... His mind is very alert and he gives quick and clever replies except when asked what he thinks of the *Jews*. He hesitates and answers that he has been taught to hate them since he joined the Nazi party."[117] Also adding to the confusion is that Rodger's lifelong friends and partners at Magnum, in particular Robert Capa (born Endre Ernö Friedmann) and David "Chim" Seymour (born Dawid Szymin), were Jewish. While Naggar makes a case in revealing Rodger's latent antisemitism, it is clear that he was utterly distraught and horrified at the site of the crimes and worked tirelessly to document what he witnessed.

One of Rodger's better-known photographs from the camp is a near panoramic shot of a Dutch Jewish boy walking down a long path. An extended row of corpses are lined up along the grass. The boy's head is turned away from the bodies, his face strained and tensed. Two women, off in the distance, follow behind. According to Rodger's son, Peter, the boy is Sieg Maandag, and the photograph, one shown around the world, was noticed by his shocked aunt and uncle, who had fled to New York before the war.[118] The child, who had thought his family had already been killed, was later reunited with his mother in Amsterdam. Rodger's photograph inadvertently helped the boy reunite with his family.[119] Moreover, Susan Sontag reminds us that photography can exhibit both an objective moment in time and an interpretation of that moment.[120] In this chilling photograph, Rodger frames the innocence of a child caught in a world in which no adolescent – or anyone else for that matter – should ever find themselves.

Many of Rodger's photographs of the dead, as well as of the survivors, are taken from a noticeable distance. It is rare to find a macrophotographic image of the dead in his body of work of the camp. In sharp contrast, nearly all of his pictures of the camp staff and of Commandant Kramer offer an extreme close-up. The shots are taken from unusual angles, distorting the physical appearance of the perpetrator. And due to the sharp focus of the lens, the camera thus acts as judge and jury before facial expressions laid bare. This series of stark images comes across as if Rodger were somehow attempting a type of forensic analysis through his camera lens. Furthermore, many of these photographs are of the female camp guards; we see mostly only their faces: they often appear tough, hard, nasty, and, at times, even bewildered or without expression. One imagines a photographer filled with rage and revulsion.

Bergen-Belsen was the beginning of the end of George Rodger, war photographer. Aside from the last few weeks of the war, Rodger would never again photograph extreme violence. "I was not proud of my pictures," he wrote in his essay for *Time*, "and I vowed never to cover another war or to profit by others' suffering."[121] Immediately following the war, Rodger was ready to leave continental Europe behind, along with its death and violence. He longed to travel to Africa. A few years later his aspiration came true. In 1948 George Rodger began his journey through Africa in search of a people who had not contributed to the slaughter of the recent war.

While Rodger strove for personal expression and documentation in his efforts at the camp, other cameramen struggled to offer anything coherent in their work. Historian Cornelia Brink suggests that photographs, and thereby the photographers, frequently came into conflict between the "objectivity" of the medium and the "unreal" character of the events being captured.[122] Canadian cameraman Al Calder of the CFPU felt his medium was unable to convey the awfulness of the camp. While he was overwhelmed by the experience, so too was his mechanism for documentation and representation. Calder observes that Bergen-Belsen was "one I hate to even think about; something that you could never put into a picture hit us ... The sounds that came from these people, whimpering sounds, utter misery, unbelievable conditions."[123] He recorded what he could, but was left discontented with the

Young boy walks by corpses, a photograph taken in Bergen-Belsen by George Rodger, war correspondent for *Life* magazine. Image 50605938, George Rodger, The LIFE Picture Collection, Getty Images.

results. Calder felt his photographs lacked a precision and were unable to unlock the potency of the actual event. And like so many other military personnel, it was more than just the visual that disturbed him. "The other thing that you can't record is the unbelievable stench ... Those are the things I can never forget, never."[124] Calder's focus was on accurate documentation, and in this task he felt he was unable to adequately accomplish it. Pilot Officer Ron Laidlaw, who worked with the RCAF in public relations, offered a similar sentiment about his encounter. "A thousands rolls," he mused, "would not have captured the horrors of Belsen."[125] Still, others attempted something more than simply photographing the scenes accurately and plainly. A number of photographers sought to evoke the symbolic in their pictures.

Indeed, a number of photographs taken at Bergen-Belsen conjure religious imagery, icons, and symbols. And while a majority of the inmates in the camp were Jews, the photographs – largely taken by non-Jewish cameramen – intermittently offer Christian frames of reference. Art historian Carol Zemel insists that despite their documentation of the Jewish genocide, the photographs of the camps are often "discursively wrapped in Christological symbols and iconographies."[126] A number of cameramen opted for sacred or religious representational images in their work, adding further complexity to the pictures. Of course, the employment of Christian imagery to symbolize the Jewish experience in the Holocaust is profoundly offensive to many Jews. A long history of condemnation and suspicion by practitioners of Christianity, accusations of blood libel, and being falsely blamed for the killing of Christ make this a particularly sensitive issue. In addition, during the rule of the Third Reich, the Nazis employed propaganda against the Jews that incorporated Christian symbols, such as the crucifix and other religious imagery.

Mike Lewis was a cameraman with the AFPU. Entering the camp soon after its formal surrender, and to keep his mind from dwelling too closely on the horror, he immediately occupied himself with filming the camp. He worked not only to record but to induce symbolic imagery. In one memorable sequence Lewis shot, Father Michael Morrison and Father Stanislaus Kadziolka are standing before a mass grave. The men appear to be reciting a prayer or a blessing over a pit of dead men and women.[127] Lewis was able to frame the image of the two priests in the background, with a long spade, appearing like a cross, captured in the foreground near the grave. The shot was knowingly framed in this manner. According to Lewis, "I remember one scene in this mass of bodies which comes back to me: there was a spade there with a crosspiece in it. It was just on the part of the earth where corpses were buried. It was a grey, dreary, depressing scene, and it suddenly came to me that this spade looked like the cross. And I put it in the foreground of my pictures. I believe it was used like that."[128] Lewis thus evokes the icon of the cross, a well-known symbol of Christianity and of the Western world. It is the sign most commonly used to represent the crucifixion of Jesus Christ. For many Christians, suffering and death are fundamental aspects of the faith.

It is important to note that cameraman Mike Lewis was Jewish – he spoke Yiddish and interacted with the Jewish survivors. Why then evoke an image that is frequently associated with Christianity? Of course, the photographer's intention does not necessarily govern how the image will be perceived by an audience. The viewer may read into an image something its creator had not intended.[129] And yet, it is clear that some photographs, such as the one of Father Morrison and Father Kadziolka, go beyond straightforward documentation. Does Lewis's image somehow signify the suffering or martyrdom of the dead or does it attempt to highlight the lack of intervention and silence of non-Jews in Europe during the war? Due to the fact that Lewis captured the image in April 1945, it seems more likely that the framing of this scene emphasizes the responsibility of non-Jews to atone for and mourn the crimes. Or perhaps it is recognition that at Bergen-Belsen non-Jews also suffered and were killed. Carol Zemel underscores that "if suffering and death are central icons of Christian culture, if they encourage and abet visual mediation on these themes, then photographs like these ... may supplement that iconography of suffering and install a Christological frame for Holocaust history and remembrance."[130] Adding to the complexity of the photograph is that Father Stanislaus Kadziolka was a survivor of Bergen-Belsen who spent years suffering in Hitler's camp system.

In addition, a number of photographs taken in Bergen-Belsen by both British and Canadian cameramen focus on corpses, typically male, arms spread across the ground appearing like the image of Jesus Christ on the cross. For example, whether deliberate or not, the APFU's Lieutenant Martin H. Wilson's regularly reprinted image – which has been titled "Ecce Homo" in various publications – features two men, heads resting next to each other with arms spread horizontally away from their bodies.[131] The image and the motif of "Ecce Homo" are used to portray the anguish and deprivation of the inmates. Before the war,

A frame of film shot by Lieutenant Mike Lewis of the Army Film and Photo Unit. Image FLM 3719, Imperial War Museum.

Glasgow-born Wilson worked for three years with Scottish Films Limited and later with Realist Films in England; he was an accomplished tactician of the visual image. Another group of photographs, much less known, were taken by the RCAF's Lloyd H. Bloom and Lloyd E. Thompson and feature a number of partially nude male bodies appearing in and around the camp and wrapped only in a ragged "loincloth."[132] The Hamilton-born Bloom, an ethical vegetarian since childhood, was a professional photojournalist and operator of Lloyd Bloom Photography before and after the war. Belleville-born Thompson, meanwhile, was a photographic artist who would become known across the country after the war for his portraits of well-known Canadians. In this collection, the Bloom and Thompson photos seem to evoke the Man of Sorrows, an iconic devotional image.

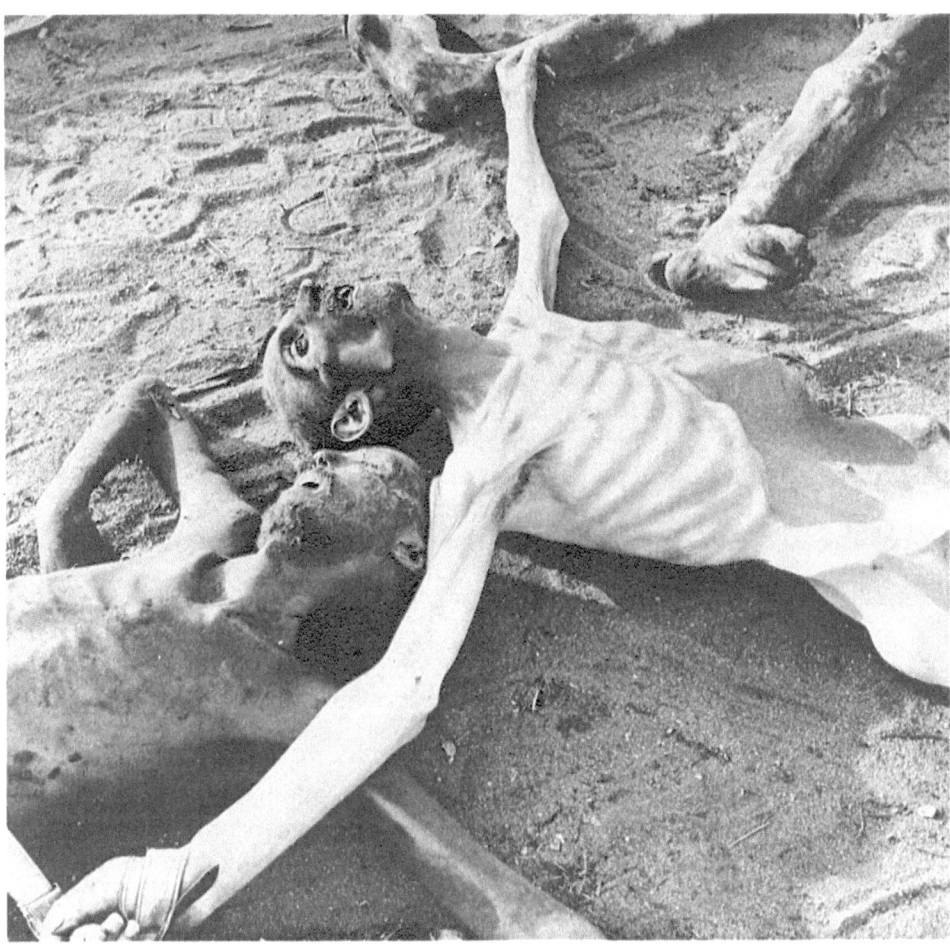

The bodies of former prisoners lie on the ground in the Bergen-Belsen concentration camp. Image 23032, United States Holocaust Memorial Museum, courtesy of courtesy of Solomon Bogard.

These recreations may have been unintentional, but the photographs certainly lend themselves to these interpretations. As a result, the images evoked lead to important questions about Christianity, Judaism, the Holocaust, and representation. According to Ziva Amishai-Maisels, "the relationship between Christ and the Holocaust was reinforced towards the end of the war by the parallels found between the camp corpses and traditional depictions of Christ … the message both Jewish and Christian artists tried to get across was that in killing Jews or other innocent victims, Christians were not only betraying Christ's ideas, but killing Christ himself."[133] Whether or not this was premeditated in the work of these photographers, it is, nevertheless, clearly one of the many possible readings of it.

Therefore, the work of various war photographers illustrates a twofold purpose: to document the crimes and to offer a personal reflection on those crimes. Some photographers attempted to frame the dead and the suffering from a distance while, conversely, taking close-up shots of the perpetrators as if to shine a light on their guilt. A number of photographers, such as George Rodger, felt conflicted for having made artistic compositions of certain moments in the camp. And yet, these types of images, as Brett Ashley Kaplan has theorized, can complicate and deepen our understanding of the crimes, prompting multifaceted and diverse discussions. Indeed, the work of photographers like Lewis, Bloom, and Thompson stimulate uneasy, yet important considerations of the role of religion and antisemitism in the crimes. However, those who offered some sort of personal reflection in their images were in the minority. Most saw the purpose of their work as the documentation of a terrible offence. It is evident that many cameramen took pictures in a basic and unadorned fashion in an effort to leave a lasting record and to counter any possible future denial of the crimes.

Concluding Remarks

This chapter has examined the production of artists and photographers who worked at the Bergen-Belsen concentration camp. The men and women from these two groups saw first-hand the terrible crimes that occurred at the camp. And yet, during the war, they were not the only military personnel to encounter these images. While not directly involved in the efforts at Bergen-Belsen, a number of individuals assisted in the construction of these pictures, helping to process the visual fabrication. Before this chapter concludes, the impact that this work had on other Allied personnel is worth examining.

Jack Shadbolt was born in the Essex County village of Shoeburyness, England. In 1912, when Shadbolt was three years old, his family emigrated to the province of British Columbia, Canada, moving first to Nelson and then, two years later, settling in Victoria. He studied art at Victoria College and soon became an art teacher, all the while still producing his own artwork. Molly Lamb, who later entered Bergen-Belsen, became one of his students shortly before the outbreak of the war. Shadbolt enlisted in the Canadian Army on 23 November 1942 and had hopes of being named an official war artist. Instead, he undertook a number of assignments, typically away from the frontline. In February 1945, Shadbolt was transferred overseas to be an administrative officer at the Canadian Military Headquarters, where he also became involved with the war artists' program.[134] While still not an official artist, he continued to sketch and paint the war.

While he was in London, part of Shadbolt's job was to file and catalogue the photographs that were coming from the army in Germany and in other parts of Europe. In April and May he began processing the photographs taken at Bergen-Belsen. According to Shadbolt, he also "had the privilege of having copies made, as war artists, as reference material."[135] And as was the practice of a number of official Canadian war artists, Shadbolt also used the photographs to ground his own artwork. While he had still not encountered the camp directly, the as yet unpublished photographs profoundly moved the young artist.

"I found the experience devastating," he later recalled. "For some time after this I had the need for a violent image of pathos to relieve my feelings, in my work, of this traumatic revulsion and to express my outrage."[136] The influence of viewing the photographs of the dead and dying, of the pits of hundreds of corpses, began to dominate his art – not directly, as in the work of Aba Bayefsky, but indirectly, as is evidenced in the art of Alex Colville. Shadbolt's work became darker, bleaker, and more menacing, such as 1946's *Aftermath* and *Terror of a Street*, as well as two violent pieces from 1947 titled *The Dogs* and *Victim*. Viewing numerous photographs of emaciated human beings in Bergen-Belsen thus led Shadbolt to question realism in painting. Subsequently, he became disillusioned with realist art and began to embrace abstraction. By war's end, according to the artist himself, "I found it totally impossible to say anything direct with the figure. It is such a treacherous image, you are either into realism or you're into graphic melodramatic things or you're into high drama or you're into sensuous anatomy … I wanted to say something about the human condition, I had that very much in mind, but … I couldn't find it in a direct way."[137]

Consequently, Shadbolt began evoking the "figure" of the human in his work symbolically or through abstraction. In *Sketch for "The Yellow Dogs"* (1947), four canines hover, growling over skeletal remains. The work symbolizes the primitive, the uncivilized, and the debasement of living beings. It is clear that many of Shadbolt's paintings from this period are a response to or a reflection on the images of Bergen-Belsen which he filed and catalogued during the war.

Like Shadbolt, Patricia Mary Holden also saw a fair bit of the infamous Bergen-Belsen photographs during the war. Born in Wallasey, Merseyside, she was sixteen years old when she was evacuated to Canada with her younger brother during the war. Holden settled in Winnipeg and in 1942 enlisted at a recruiting centre. She served in the RCAF Women's Division.[138] Despite a lack of experience, she volunteered as a photographer and was soon sent overseas to London, where she worked in the RCAF's Public Relations Department at Lincoln's Inn Fields. She functioned as a senior photographer in and around London, where her assignments were typically weddings, funerals, and medal presentations. She also spent much time in the darkroom, processing film.[139]

It was during this task that Holden began developing the large number of film rolls taken at Bergen-Belsen, one of the most photographed camps in all of Europe. Little did she know that around the same time her future husband, Peterborough, Ontario–born Arthur Stewart Collins, a man she had yet to meet, also came across the camp while with the RCAF's 400 Squadron.[140] For Holden, the experience was jarring. "Well, the thing is," she remembers decades later, "when you're developing a picture, you have to know what you're developing, what the picture's about. And I was turning it upside down and around, and I thought, what the hell is this? And it was just mounds and mounds of bodies on top of each other that had been photographed in open graves … [it] was just mind boggling."[141] For Holden the terrible tales she had heard over the years were now confirmed.

While we have seen examples of photographers making personal choices in their framing of shots, by and large the focus was on rigid documentation. On the receiving end, for Holden and the general public in the West, this was to be the beginning of formal and widespread recognition of what occurred in the camps. While these frightful images took place at the last stages of the war, they did not show gas chambers or other extermination equipment – for these types of death camps did not exist in Germany proper – nor did they depict the train systems used to deport Hitler's victims or the killing sites set away from the camps. Thus, the photos of Bergen-Belsen do not give a clear and full picture of the Holocaust, and yet they did begin a dialogue and aroused extensive awareness of some of the crimes of the Third Reich. "I didn't take the pictures," Holden acknowledges. "I only developed them ... It was earth shattering to everybody when they saw the pictures ... And, of course, it was our introduction to the camps."[142] Indeed, while the photographs did not assist the public in fully understanding or making sense of the crimes, they did demonstrate the capacity of humankind to commit large-scale evil on their fellow beings.

In conclusion, the British and Canadian war artists and photographers who worked in Bergen-Belsen were challenged with sober moral and ethical burdens. It is clear from their work that they operated in a largely conservative, documentary style and avoided embellishment and aggrandizement. When they did exert their personal interpretations, many sought religious imagery, icons, or symbols. In addition, a number of artists and cameramen focused on scenes that uncovered the surreal and distressing disparities present in the camp. Most felt their work was important, yet felt guilty for operating in their respective mediums. The experience at Bergen-Belsen often forced those who operated in visual media to reassess how they went about their work. For some it meant a change in the way they painted or filmed; for others it created a deeper awareness of the limits of their respective forms of representation.

In *The Writing of the Disaster* (1980), the French philosopher and literary theorist Maurice Blanchot meditates on the helplessness of one's meeting with calamity. "Write," he stresses, and to which he could have also added paint and photograph, "in order not simply to destroy, in order not simply to conserve, in order not to transmit; write in the thrall of the impossible real, that share of disaster wherein every reality, safe and sound, sinks."[143] Here the encounter with death – the disaster – and its consequences remains uncertain, difficult to hold, demanding to be captured, intolerable to even re-imagine. One then becomes estranged from the experience of the terrible encounter. The shock of Bergen-Belsen devastates the senses. "It was the worst thing I saw in the war," confesses artist Donald Anderson. "I don't relate to it ... it was just too great to be absorbed."[144] The horror camp was an affront: to the artists' medium, to the craft, to imagination, to tolerance, to ethics, and to humanity. And yet the works were rendered, the canvases and sketchbooks filled, the film taken, and the words written. They framed and signified what was not thought possible, now all too real.

Chapter Six

Padres, Patients, and Pathologies: Medical and Spiritual Relief

I am working with the people liberated from a concentration camp at Belsen. Can you imagine what that means? ... Typhus, starvation, despair. Oh God! God! Give me strength to carry on. I work among them from seven in the morning until far, far into the night ... I feel encouraged but then I turn and see thousands of others and I need to call on every nerve of courage to continue.[1]
                      Dr John W. Thompson, RCAF, 84 Disarmament Group

If all the sky was paper and all the trees in the world were turned into pens, and all the waters in the oceans were ink, we would still have insufficient materials in which to describe all the horrors and sufferings these people here underwent at the hands of those foul, bestial and inhuman beings called the SS ... May the final redemption come to these people with whom I am now living.[2]
                      Leslie Hardman, Jewish Chaplain, VIII Corps, Second Army

The monumental task of tending to the physical, mental, emotional, and spiritual needs of the inmates at the Bergen-Belsen concentration camp was mainly hoisted upon the Allied armies' medical corps and chaplains of various denominations. The roles assigned to and accepted by padres, doctors, nurses, and other medical staff generally went far beyond their typical military responsibilities. Personnel found themselves thrust into situations they had not anticipated, for which they had not prepared, and for which they had not been trained. Consequently, chaplains often became involved in non-religious activities, such as collecting various supplies for the camp from the surrounding area, while medical personnel adopted tasks outside their usual obligations, such as sanitation duties and the distribution of food and water.

Assessments began almost immediately in the camp. Indeed, while systematized medical relief attempts commenced several days after the camp's formal surrender, initial surveys of Bergen-Belsen occurred earlier, consisting of small groups of medical and religious authorities, such as the VIII Corps' Brigadier Glyn Hughes, deputy director medical services; Lieutenant Colonel A.M. Michie, assistant director of hygiene; Reverend H.H. Welchman, senior chaplain (Roman Catholic); and Reverend Leslie Hardman, chaplain (Jewish), to name a few.[3] These various groups both evaluated the situation and advised in the organization of personnel required to assist the inmates in the camp.

Accordingly, the following chapter examines the medical and spiritual relief efforts at Bergen-Belsen during the spring and summer of 1945. British and Canadian padres, doctors, nurses, and other medical personnel arrived at the camp at various points in time to partake in vital therapeutic work. As noted in chapter 2, approximately 14,000 people died in the camp *after* it was formally surrendered to the British. Understandably, serious questions and concerns have been directed at the British Army as a result of this significantly high death rate.[4] However, this chapter does not delve into those particularly complex issues.

Instead, the primary focus of this chapter is on the British and Canadian personnel in both the medical corps and the chaplaincy services, and more specifically, their responses to their respective assignments and to the situation at Bergen-Belsen.[5] How did these men and women deal with their enormous responsibilities? What medical, moral, and theological dilemmas were confronted? In the case of the padres, how did they negotiate their religious and military obligations while working in the camp, especially when the two invariably came into conflict? Similarly, and challenged with so many thousands of inmates barely clinging to life, how did medical personnel continue their work when faced with such an apparently hopeless situation? These questions and more will be examined in this chapter.

In terms of its structure, this chapter is divided into two main sections. The first part will survey the responses of the medical personnel who worked at the camp. And while the main focus will be on the medical relief offered by those serving in the British and Canadian forces, an examination of those operating under and alongside military authority will also be considered. For example, the work of the British Red Cross and the Order of St John, which joined together to form the Joint War Organisation, will be carefully observed, as will those working with the United Nations Relief and Rehabilitation Administration (UNRRA).

Likewise, the efforts of some of the medical students from London teaching hospitals will also be scrutinized.

The second part of this chapter will explore the military chaplains who encountered Bergen-Belsen during the same time period. A significant number of British and Canadian chaplains of various denominations – including Roman Catholic, Protestant, and Jewish – arrived at Bergen-Belsen; some came to assist the military and the inmates, while others travelled to the camp to bear witness, pay their respects, or offer prayer. Indeed, military chaplains struggled to make sense of the tragedy and as a result looked to their respective faiths to find guidance. What they discovered will be inspected in this second and final section.

Medical Relief

Critical Treatments: The Who and the How

During the Second World War, the Royal Army Medical Corps (RAMC) and its counterpart, the Royal Canadian Army Medical Corps (RCAMC) were responsible for providing medical attention to their respective military personnel on the field of battle. These two medical organizations maintained field ambulances, casualty clearing stations, general hospitals, and the like. In addition, both British and Canadian medical corps were fully equipped to offer specialized and sophisticated surgical procedures when and where called upon.

The RAMC was established in 1898 from officers and staff of the Army Medical Department. Along with the Queen Alexandra's Imperial Military Nursing Service (QAIMNS), it operated under the authority of the Army Medical Services (AMS).[6] And as it did during the First World War, the RAMC continued to employ supplementary nursing assistants in the form of Voluntary Aid Detachments (VADs). The British Red Cross and the Order of St John, together as the Joint War Organisation (JWO), recruited and prepared VADs for the war. Working under the direction of military authorities, VADs typically functioned as nursing assistants, but they were sometimes used as ambulance drivers and clerical staff.

Meanwhile, the Canadian Army Medical Corps (CAMC) was formed in 1904, receiving its royal title in 1919 and thereby being redesignated as the Royal Canadian Army Medical Corps (RCAMC).[7] Thousands of Canadian nursing sisters served in the RCAMC. In addition, an unknown number of Canadian nurses – who were often left on waiting lists for the RCAMC or other branches of the military – enlisted, as an alternative, in the QAIMNS.[8] Similar to their counterparts in Britain, Canada both trained and employed VADs, mainly for domestic duties, but some also saw overseas work. These VADs not only served in Canada and Britain, but, as we will see, found themselves working at camps like Bergen-Belsen.[9]

Furthermore, as the British and Canadians operated as part of 21 Army Group in northwest Europe under Field Marshal Bernard Montgomery, there were inevitably intersections and overlap. While Canadian elements who fought with the British Second Army had their own medical units, the two sides remained closely integrated with each other. Indeed, one-half of the I British Corps of the Second Army was a force consisting of both Britons and Canadians, and as a result, they frequently employed the same medical units.[10]

When the British and Canadians arrived at the camp on 15 April 1945 it became quite clear that vital and timely assessments and surveys of a desperate situation were required. At the outset, the Allies were grossly ill-prepared to handle the huge number of inmates who needed urgent attention. As the war in Europe continued, medical teams at Bergen-Belsen were initially lacking personnel, supplies, equipment, facilities, and medications.[11] Plans were soon established to bury the dead in mass graves and to evacuate the living to the nearby Panzer Training School. Despite these early efforts, headway was slow. Evacuation of the filthy barracks was further complicated as healthier survivors intermingled with the ill and near dead.[12] Distressing decisions regarding prioritization of the inmates had to be made.

Undeniably, ethical dilemmas were forced upon military authorities almost immediately, particularly on the broad shoulders of Brigadier Glyn Hughes, deputy director of medical services. Born in 1892 in Ventersburg, South Africa, and raised in Swansea, Wales, Hugh Llewellyn Glyn Hughes, a veteran of the First World War, ran a small medical practice in London. During the interwar period he rejoined the service and by early 1945 had been made chief doctor to the British Second Army. He arrived at Bergen-Belsen shortly after the first Allied personnel entered the camp. Concerning which inmates would receive priority treatment Brigadier Hughes adopted a type of utilitarian perspective and approach. According to Hughes,

> Under the conditions which existed it was obvious that thorough diagnosis and elaborate treatment of individual patients ... would take up so

Former camp staff throw corpses into a mass grave at the Bergen-Belsen concentration camp. Image 25001, United States Holocaust Memorial Museum, courtesy of Hadassah Bimko Rosensaft.

much time that only a small fraction of them could be dealt with and that to the exclusion of the elementary care of the remainder. The principle adopted was that the greatest number of lives would be saved by placing those who had a *reasonable chance* of survival under conditions in which *their own tendency to recover* could be aided by *simple nursing and suitable feeding*, and in which further infection could be prevented.[13]

Clearly, Hughes made the decision to offer a highly focused and concentrated type of aid that would ensure the greatest number of people were saved. It was essentially a plan of triage. Inmates were divided into three categories: the first two comprised those who would likely survive and those who would likely die, regardless of the care they received; the third consisted of those for whom immediate care could mean the difference between life and death. Thus, for medical personnel it was not simply an instance of selecting whoever needed the most urgent attention; on the contrary, it was a calculated decision to select for evacuation those who stood a better chance of surviving with only basic care. As a consequence, those who had suffered the most, and who were *less likely* to survive the next few hours or days, were not necessarily given special priority.

This grim decision was made for a number of reasons. By mid-April 1945, although the war was coming to a close in Europe, Germany had yet to surrender, and as a result, British and Canadian forces were still engaged in battle. Thus, soldiers, doctors, nurses, and other medical personnel were being deployed in other areas of Germany. Along with these individuals were their supplies, equipment, and medicine. Thus, military personnel who were employed at Bergen-Belsen had to work with what they had on site and from the surrounding areas. As we will soon see, Allied authorities had to improvise and, like Brigadier Hughes, had to repeatedly make challenging and unpleasant decisions.

In addition, soon stretcher bearers were needed to remove inmates from the barracks to the nearby Panzer Training School. Again, deciding which inmates would be removed from the barracks for treatment created yet another dilemma. In his account, Lieutenant-Colonel Mervin Willett Gonin, the officer commanding the 11th Light Field Ambulance revealed:

> The MO went into each hut and marked on the forehead of each patient a cross to indicate to the bearers that this patient would be moved. The MO made no attempt to fix a diagnosis – all he did was decide whether the patient had any chance of living if he or she were moved or what the chance of survival might be if the patient were left in the camp for another week. It was a heart-rending job and amounted to telling hundreds of poor wretches that they were being left to die. But, as I have said, the individual did not count.[14]

Lieutenant-Colonel Gonin, like Brigadier Hughes, recognized the difficult decision of prioritizing the ill based on which inmate had a reasonable chance of surviving the ordeal. Indeed, it appears that the individual did indeed become a number, and saving the highest figure was given precedence. Those still barely clinging to life were thus passed over.

The inmates who had the strength would cry out, desperate to be removed from the decrepit barracks and from their miseries. It became an unbelievably dreadful situation for those making the judgments.

Myrtle Beardwell, a relief worker with the British Red Cross, witnessed some of these painstaking choices. "This was almost an impossible proposition," she remarks about one particular doctor who had to make a number of these judgments. "Those whom he knew had only a few hours to live he had to leave."[15] Undoubtedly, it became a nightmarish experience for all involved. Inmates begged and clamoured to get out in hopes of receiving proper medical attention. According to Beardwell, the situation became so difficult that "they had to have decoy stretchers at one door of the hut whilst the doctor went in at the other and quickly grabbed a sick person."[16] As these terrible scenes continued, the short-staffed Allied medical teams searched for alternatives in caring for and evacuating the thousands of inmates in desperate need of attention.

In chapter 4 it was noted that the SS were initially used to help bring the dead to the open pits or to load corpses onto flatbed trucks. According to historian Joanne Reilly, and employing a ratio of one nurse for every ten patients, Bergen-Belsen would have required 5,000 nurses at the time of the camp's surrender.[17] Of course, there was nowhere near that number of Allied medical personnel available. Consequently, Germans were employed in these other areas of necessity. To alleviate the overwhelming need for additional personnel, local German military doctors and nurses were used in the camp as part of the Allied medical staff.[18] While a number of accounts note that these German military personnel worked diligently, the psychological effect on the surviving inmates was deeply upsetting. "We were obliged to take in German military doctors and nurses," recalls Dr Hadassah (Bimko) Rosensaft, a former internee of Bergen-Belsen who provided remarkable care to the inmates before and after liberation. "They were in Wehrmacht uniforms, not SS, but the psychological effect was bad enough on me – imagine what it was like on the severely ill."[19] Soon more and more German personnel were received: some were simply local civilians, while others again came from the military and some were even former prisoners of war. As an inevitable consequence, there were a number of reports that some of these temporary personnel were also being attacked by some of the stronger inmates.[20] And yet, while the death rate ultimately began to drop, and as days turned into weeks, German personnel continued to be employed in the camp, as well as in

Belsen hospital (later renamed Glyn Hughes Hospital). And with their continued use came unrelenting criticism, which flooded in during the weeks and months that followed.

Deeply involved in this tense situation was Canadian Lyle Creelman. Born in Upper Stewiacke, Nova Scotia, Creelman was educated at both the University of British Columbia and Columbia University.[21] Prior to the outbreak of the war she was the director of public health nursing for the city of Vancouver and president of the Registered Nurses Association of British Columbia. Towards the end of the war, and due to her expertise, she was named chief nurse of the British zone of occupied Germany with the United Nations Relief and Rehabilitation Administration (UNRRA). Accordingly, Creelman was responsible for the supervision of nurses throughout the British zone and, in particular, at Belsen hospital. Muriel Knox Doherty, principal matron at said hospital, frequently came into conflict with Creelman, and it was often over the employment of German nurses, particularly in regards to their care of Jewish patients.[22]

According to Creelman, as a result of the service of German nurses, Belsen hospital had a higher ratio of patients to nurses than any other hospital she had visited in Germany.[23] The work was what mattered, despite the psychological effect. While acknowledging that these decisions caused significant condemnation, Creelman insisted that "the care given the patients was of good quality ... [And yet] there was much criticism from many sources of the continued use of German personnel but ... it was not possible to obtain a sufficient number of qualified DP personnel in spite of the many statements made claiming that 'hundreds of qualified nurses were available.'"[24] Rather than consider the perspective of the long-suffering patients, particularly the Jews under the care of German nurses, Creelman viewed the situation with a distant pragmatism. Thus, the employment of German doctors and nurses continued unabated. Nevertheless, and perhaps as a result of the heavy criticism, Creelman went on to pioneer specialized nurses' training programs in the British zone, assisting and teaching young women in displaced-persons camps so that they could provide their own medical care to those in need.[25]

This idea that the work was all that mattered was echoed by a number of other Allied medical staff. One of four professionally qualified nurses in a group of Red Cross personnel which arrived at the camp on 20 April 1945, Beatrice Mary (Molly) Silva Jones was in her early forties and had years of training from which to draw when she began working at Bergen-Belsen. Jones was in the camp early on when the decision was initially made to employ German staff. Psychologically, she calls it a "detrimental move, but a practical necessity."[26] It appears that one had to look past the psychological impact and focus primarily on the physical recovery of the inmates. How the task was accomplished was not as important as simply getting the work done. It was the ends and not the means that counted. "It was the job that mattered every time," offers Jones, "not the person, [nor] the position – for the time one lived in an atmosphere of a task that was bigger than the individual, in which first things came first."[27] In a terribly sad twist of fate, the inmates, who had been generally treated as a worthless mass at the hands of Nazi Germany, were again being regarded in terms of quantity rather than as individuals, as the Allies attempted to save as many human beings as possible.

Day-to-Day Obstacles: Languages, Conflicts, and Illnesses

There were a number of issues that Britons and Canadians had to contend with on a daily basis while providing medical attention in the camp. The most obvious was working with former internees, now patients, who represented a cross-section of the European continent. Medical personnel confronted a multitude of people with diverse languages, religions, and cultural backgrounds, most of whom had endured years of abuse and neglect. This made working and communicating with patients both trying and time-consuming.

One of the more common issues noted in the responses of Allied medical personnel had to do with language. In most instances, at least early on, a number of British and Canadian nurses had great trouble explaining to their new patients what tasks they were performing and precisely how they were trying to help; likewise, internees struggled to make themselves understood, while some even feared what was being done to them. Katherine J. Elvidge, a nursing sister with the Queen Alexandra's Imperial Military Nursing Service (QAIMNS), was attached to the 29th British General Hospital and emphasized this particular complication in her account. "I could not attempt to explain the difficulties," she contends. "The chief one is that of languages. The majority of the patients have some Jewish origin, but are from all countries under the sun. Russia, Poland, Hungary, Czechoslovakia, Belgium, Holland and France, and only about four of them have a smattering of

English."[28] Accordingly, medical personnel often felt isolated as staff had to be spread out, working in different sections over a large area in order to treat as many people as possible. In addition, not only was it problematic to communicate with one's patients, difficulties also developed when additional assistants were allotted to the Allied doctors and the nurses. In a letter home Elvidge notes that, aside from the one English VAD with whom she worked, she was given Polish and Russian nurses who functioned alongside Hungarian soldiers, who did the cleaning, and German nurses, who worked the night shift; of that group only one Polish nurse spoke a modicum of English.[29] Time and again nurses had to put aside usual approaches and experiences to find ways to accomplish their tasks.

However, not all nursing staff viewed the lack of communication as a negative while operating in the camp. There were those who felt that verbally interacting with patients who had been through so much mistreatment would have merely added to the stresses and worries of the job. Indeed, Welsh-born Ada Evelyn (Lyn) Brown was a St John Ambulance nurse who admitted to feeling this way. In her autobiography she discloses: "Perhaps it was a mercy that there was language difficulty for if all had been understood it would have been impossible for some [nurses] to have carried on."[30] Undeniably, for the nurses to have heard detailed descriptions of years of abuse, the loss of families, and the patients' numerous fears for the future – compounded with the physical pain that they could so clearly see in front of them on a daily basis – might have proved overwhelming for many.

Likewise, the Allied doctors and medical students had their own challenges with the assistants they were allotted in the camp. A colleague of Katherine Elvidge's in the 29th General Hospital was Canadian Dr Charles Sutherland Rennie. Born on a farm near Truax, Saskatchewan, and raised in Saskatoon, Dr Rennie joined the Royal Canadian Army Medical Corps in April 1941 and was later seconded to the 29th General Hospital. In his memoir he notes that some of the the work at the camp was being done by German doctors and nurses who had been former prisoners of Bergen-Belsen, along with a smattering of French, Belgian, and Russian personnel.[31] Dr Rennie, who communicated to his patients via an interpreter, reveals that his newly extended staff frequently squabbled with one another, particularly when it came to the Russian personnel.[32] A definite problem in the camp was inmates who had a strong dislike for one another and who were often forced to live side by side in close quarters. As Dr Rennie observes, quarrels also occurred in the hospital sections, where former internees – at least those who were healthy enough – aided British and Canadian personnel.

Even in the weeks following the camp's surrender the situation was still stifling and grim. Medical student Thomas Gibson admits to his great frustration at attempting to care for inmates while lacking medicine and adequate nursing aids. While he toiled with two other medical students from England, and like his other colleagues at Bergen-Belsen, he was afforded additional helpers gathered from the camp and the local area. Not only was it vexing, but it was also potentially dangerous. "To explain to a Pole who speaks little French," he illustrates, "to give a course of sulphonamide to a Russian with erysipelas who only speaks Russian is no easy matter, and we had no means of ensuring the course was correctly given."[33] Gibson notes that during the month of May the medical students' only reprieve was being "adopted" by some Canadian airmen who brought his team cigarettes, chocolates, and other domestic articles.[34]

Aside from the language troubles and conflicts between assistants, medical personnel also had to be concerned about catching the various illnesses present in Bergen-Belsen.[35] While precautions were certainly taken to inoculate against the infectious diseases rampant in the camp, it is perhaps unsurprising that Allied medical personnel inevitably became ill. According to Lieutenant-Colonel F.M. Lipscombe, who was attached to the 32 Casualty Clearing Station, at least ten Royal Army Medical Corps personnel contracted typhus while working at the camp. In addition, another twenty-three German nurses contracted the disease while assisting inmates. And while none of the RAMC staff died, two of the German nurses ultimately succumbed to their illnesses.[36]

Likewise, Dr D.T. Prescott, who served with the 11th Light Field Ambulance, also reveals the consequences of working in such disease-ridden quarters. Each night personnel from the 11th Light Field Ambulance visited the makeshift hospital to assist in the removal of the dead. Consequently, Prescott reveals that typhus "took a toll, of our Unit 10% contracted the disease ... they were all seriously ill for about a week and then recovered only slowly after several debilitating weeks."[37] Indeed, at least twenty men from his unit became sick, although all, quite fortunately, survived.

Moreover, infectious disease was not the only manner in which Allied personnel struggled. Elsie May Deeks of Winnipeg was a VAD and a welfare officer with the St John Ambulance Brigade. One of a number of

Canadians who served with the 29th British General Hospital, Deeks notes that many of the haunting images in the camp could not simply be forgotten, including emaciated inmates, the worn-out crematoria, and the mass graves.[38] According to Deeks, who suffered a bout of bronchitis while working at Bergen-Belsen, living conditions for some Allied personnel were also dismal. Since so much of the camp was decrepit and unliveable, personnel from the 29th General Hospital were forced to sleep outside in tents. The medical team and other personnel lay atop sleeping bags and mattresses on the cold, damp spring ground since there was no room for cots. Years later, the experiences and the images continued to disturb, sometimes in unexpected ways. "It was a long, long time," Deeks acknowledges in an interview, "before I could look at a pair of blue-and-white striped pajamas again [which the prisoners wore]."[39] And while memories returned, some doctors and nurses found ways to dull or mute the dreadfulness.

As historians Ben Shephard and Joanne Reilly have observed, alcohol was available in large supply and played a significant role in Bergen-Belsen.[40] While some personnel abstained from drinking, many, like Joy Traverner, witnessed the effects on others. Raised in west London, Traverner (later Trindle) was just twenty-three years old when she arrived at Bergen-Belsen as a QA nurse with the 29th General Hospital. She was troubled by her memories and suffered from nightmares. Moreover, Traverner acknowledges that alcohol was a factor with nurses in the camp. "We had no one to talk to," she admits. "We just had to keep going. Two of our sisters started drinking heavily and were sent home ... we all supported each other and cried every night with our arms around each other."[41] In a letter home, Traverner's colleague Elsie Deeks made note of a party she attended with some Canadian airmen stationed nearby in Celle, where "the refreshments were grand and ... [the] fruit Punch Had a whisky base but quite nice."[42] Indeed, personnel found a variety of ways to deal with their situations. But, more often than not, nurses had only each other on which to rely. In a letter to her parents Deeks confesses that "at present we are trying to keep up the morale of the sisters more than the patients."[43] The long hours of exhausting work far away from home took its toll on many personnel. Left to their own devices, doctors, nurses, and other staff found different ways to negotiate their feelings of isolation and despair.[44] Some, as we saw in chapter 4, turned to dark humour, while others found solace by busying themselves with their work or by drinking or smoking heavily to dull the senses.

Assessments and Opportunities?

"The whole epidemic and the condition of mass starvation," observed Brigadier Hughes not long after he first entered the camp, "provided a wonderful opportunity for research."[45] Despite the difficulties of their tasks, many personnel felt that the experience at Bergen-Belsen would be of value in terms of studying rare and complex medical conditions. Indeed, for some personnel, patients became living models from which to learn and study. Medical student Alan MacAuslan acknowledges this aspect. "One of the parts of Anatomy which I found difficult to learn for my exams," he declares in his memoir, "was the structure of the back of the throat and top of the gullet." His work in the camp afforded him a rare opportunity. Regarding a woman who was missing the lower half of her jaw due to infection, he continues in unsettling detail:

> In the Anatomy museum there were wax models of various bits of the body, the artificial muscles in striated brown, bone and cartilage white, arteries bright red, veins bright blue, the rest of the body cut away to show the throat. In this poor woman, we could see the model in real life; the parts moved when she moaned ... It was one of the times when our scientific detachment was eroded, the more especially as there was nothing we could do to help her.[46]

For some, Bergen-Belsen became a chance to view, first-hand, rare diseases and conditions many had only read about or viewed though illustrations in medical journals. For others, a focus on uncommon illness was simply another way to keep one's mind off extremely difficult tasks.[47]

While a few medical personnel saw Bergen-Belsen as an occasion for important research, most agreed that the time, place, and circumstances made any serious, scientific inquiry problematic. A group that was called upon to carry out research in the camp was the No. 1 Vascular Injuries Research Section, RAMC. The section's Captain P.L. Mollison, in a report to 21 Army Group, acknowledges the "difficulties of carrying out any work of scientific value under such conditions."[48] Mollison went on to list as reasons: the lack of inmate records, language limitations, busy orderlies who did not have the time to properly collect and record specimens, personnel shortages, and so on. His colleague, Lieutenant-Colonel Lipscombe, was more frank. He argued that any effective outcome was often more as a result of the particular doctor and nurse on duty than the type of medical treatment being delivered.[49] Accordingly, he suggests that any of their findings had "little real scientific worth."[50] Due to this inability to control variables, the conclusions drawn by physicians, surgeons, and the like were frequently anecdotal.

Nevertheless, as Allied medical personnel toiled away in Bergen-Belsen, and like others employed in a variety of other positions in the camp, they made subjective, independent determinations and assessments of the inmates. One of the more common complaints, comments, or observations by British and Canadian medical personnel concerned the moral standard and social behaviour of the survivors. It appears that the majority of those who worked closely with the inmates, in the capacity of patient welfare, made similar assessments concerning their conduct.

Indeed, suffering and starvation were influential factors in the actions of most internees. Scholar Elaine Scarry, author of *The Body in Pain* (1985), suggests that pain not only resists but actively destroys language. Moreover, pain results in "an immediate reversion to a state anterior to language, to the sounds and cries a human being makes before language is learned."[51] Lacking in "referential content," pain is often marked through its "unsharability," thus making it demanding for those not experiencing the same sensation to fully grasp it.[52] Consequently, accurately describing pain is as problematic as it is for an "outsider" to fully understand it.

According to Scarry, while pain and physical suffering abolish language, morally acceptable acts typically align with articulate communication.[53] Thus, for those in anguish, language becomes less important than basic reaction or instinct. The movements and behaviours of someone who is under severe duress can appear, at least outwardly, to defy all reason and logic. Likewise, the same can also be said of individuals suffering from starvation. The conduct of someone undergoing extreme malnourishment is often governed by instinct and not by societal norms. Hunger changes perceptions and alters one's relationship with both time and space. In this instance, biological need generally supersedes all else.

While the crimes in Bergen-Belsen and other concentration camps were being publicized throughout the Western world, a clinical study was taking place at the University of Minnesota under lead investigator and American scientist Dr Ancel Keys.[54] Beginning in 1944, in what was known as the "Minnesota Starvation Experiment," Keys and his team scrutinized the physiological and psychological effects of severe and prolonged malnourishment in healthy men. The findings of the project were intended to later guide the Allied powers in their dealings with the victims of famine in Europe and Asia at the end of the Second World War.

Formally published in 1950, the conclusions from the experiment appeared as *The Biology of Human Starvation*, a two-volume, 1385-page work that was instantly regarded as a landmark treatise on the subject of starvation.[55] Appearing almost five years after the end of the war, the study did not make the impact Dr Keys and his team had initially hoped. As biochemist Sir Jack Drummond – scientific adviser to the Ministry of Food and later a nutrition consultant to the Supreme Headquarters Allied Expeditionary Force (SHAEF) and the Allied Control Commissions (ACC) – acknowledges in the book's foreword, "My admiration was tinted with only one regret, that the investigation had not begun three years earlier."[56] Still, the findings in the book provide valuable insight on the assessments made at Bergen-Belsen by British and Canadian medical personnel.

According to Dr Keys and his team, physical changes due to starvation consist of a decrease in body size, slower movements, and cold extremities. There is an increase in apathy and melancholy, a decrease in mental capacity, a narrowing of interests, an increase in neurosis and hysteria, and sensitivity to noise. In addition, subjects become obsessed by and possessive of food, while aversion to certain fare vanishes. Finally, those suffering from starvation are often found to isolate themselves, becoming self-centred and egotistical; social interaction becomes stilted; politeness appears artificial; and subjects are frequently unable to control their emotions.[57]

In light of these findings, it is interesting to observe the overlap when reviewing the candid accounts of Allied medical personnel. Born in Eganville, but raised in both Arnprior and Sudbury, Ontario, Dr John F. McCreary served with the RCAF Nutrition Group during the war. His team consisted of Squadron Leader Dr Hugh Branion and Warrant Officer J.R.F. Sauve. In 1944, McCreary and his team were seconded to SHAEF to conduct clinical surveys of children in various concentration camps across northwest Europe.[58] Along with the rest of his team, he travelled to Bergen-Belsen in early May 1945 to survey the conditions of the inmates.[59] They made a number of observations, and McCreary took photographs of the situation at the camp.[60]

Upon his return to Canada, McCreary gave an address at the Empire Club of Canada in Toronto.[61] According to McCreary, the internees could be divided into three main groups: the first cluster included recent arrivals that, because of their brief time in the camp, remained relatively fit. The third and final group involved those too ill to digest any type of food, and as a result, had the highest death rate. In regards to the second group of inmates, McCreary describes them as those who had deteriorated physically but, with a proper diet, could once again regain their bodily strength. However, their mental recovery would take additional time. In McCreary's point of view, this group

> had been so disturbed mentally by so long a period in the camp that their mental return was far from as rapid as their physical return. When we saw the people in the camp [some] … had lost their ability to see. They had of course no idea what their names were. They had no idea where they came from. They didn't know how long they had been there. They were simply mute. They were people whose only noise was a high pitched cry. There were thousands of these people and they represented the most disturbing sight to be seen in the Belsen Concentration Camp.[62]

McCreary's words seem to echo Scarry's comments concerning the way pain and physical suffering abolish language. Like other nutritional experts in the camp, McCreary was aware of some of the psychological and physiological effects of starvation. And being cognizant of the effects, he and others doubted that anything could be done for many of the inmates. "It looked for a long time," he offers, "as if there was absolutely no hope of any return to normal of this group."[63] As we will discuss in the concluding section however, in time many inmates were indeed able to regain some "normalcy" and function without the assistance of others.

Despite all this information and knowledge of the effects of starvation, abuse, and neglect, many medical personnel were still generally shocked and dismayed by the behaviour of the inmates. Turning to biology, medical student Alan MacAuslan evoked the theory of recapitulation (also known as the biogenetic law or embryological parallelism) in his writings. Simply put, this theory, promulgated by German biologist Ernst Haeckel in the nineteenth century, posits that during its course of embryonic development, an organism passes through a sequence of stages representing our fully grown ancestors (i.e., ontogeny recapitulates phylogeny). While most biologists abandoned this concept in the early twentieth century, the theory points to a primitive or animal-like behaviour at one end of the spectrum, and higher-level, sophisticated civilization at the other.⁶⁴ While the theory of recapitulation was meant to be taken in an absolutely factual sense, it has also found use as a metaphor.

According to MacAuslan, while physical illnesses astonished, psychiatric conditions greatly unnerved the British medical students. Referring to a specific group of internees, and recalling his early medical training, he states:

> What were we taught "ontology recapitulates phylogeny"? The development of the individual mirrors the development of the species. The human foetus goes through all the historical stages from single cell to tadpole, via fish with gills to mammal, climbing in the womb from primordial slime to human being. These bemused people seemed to have reversed the process, slipping down below herd consciousness, abandoning family and personal ties, to become more primitive than reptiles, more primitive than gastropods. They were exiled from civilisation, stunned into bare existence ... Perhaps this is what starvation does to you, would do to us.⁶⁵

As reviewed in chapter 3, depicting or associating the behaviour of inmates as something animal-like, overly instinctual, or as something irrational, immoral, or uncivilized, was all too common. However, rather than looking only externally at the inmates, MacAuslan also searched his inner psyche, asking himself if he would have acted in a similar fashion. "Of course not," he replies with some doubt. "We had been brought up to act otherwise, codes of ethics, self sacrifice for others and all that."⁶⁶ But then again, uncertainties lingered, questions remained for MacAuslan. "How do you know what you would do?" he continued asking himself rhetorically. "Liberal toleration struggled with frank disgust, not of the people we tended but of mankind overall. We were perhaps card board cut outs of civilisation, all of us. Better to drink more and not think about such things."⁶⁷ Indeed, morality and civilization now appeared in disarray, perhaps in utter ruins. Despair replaced hope; the decency of the individual seemed more and more like a charade. For many, an existential crisis was now fully underway.

For the British and Canadian medical personnel who entered the Bergen-Belsen concentration camp during the spring and summer of 1945 the experience was enormously trying, and one that ushered in a variety of medical and moral dilemmas. Initially lacking staff, supplies, equipment, facilities, and medications, personnel frequently had to improvise and adopt roles they never before had to perform. And while the physical deterioration of inmates shocked them, it was often the moral and social collapse that so disturbed many of the doctors and nurses. Struggling with issues of language limitations and isolation, medical staff treated rare and complex illnesses under trying circumstances. At times, medical care seemed to offer little optimism. And when science struggled to offer sufficient hope, some turned to faith and religion.

Spiritual Relief

Whose People? Services, Prayers, and Burials

"Keep a stiff upper lip, Padre," the commanding officer (CO) told Chaplain Leslie Hardman. "We've just been into Belsen concentration camp, and it's horrible; but you have got to go there; you'll find a lot of your people."[68] From the start, the Allies were aware that the preponderance of inmates in Bergen-Belsen were Jews. And since the religious and ethnic make-up of many of the internees was known, it appeared – at least to this CO – that the inmates, "his" people, would be the concern of the regiment's Jewish chaplain. "Many of your people are there," Hardman later repeated to himself. "My people? – anyone's people – everyone's people."[69] Indeed, with the camp now formally surrendered, the inmates, each and every one, were the responsibility of the British Army – with the assistance of the Canadians, as well as other Allies and volunteers.

While Jews made up the bulk of the inmates, there were also thousands of Catholics, Protestants, and other groups held prisoner in the camp. In the intervening time, chaplains of various denominations continued to arrive at Bergen-Belsen, some to offer acts of worship for the living, others to contribute a prayer for the dead. In addition, military chaplains assisted in a variety of other ways, such as gathering food, medicine, and supplies, as well as attempting to help inmates locate friends and family members. Accordingly, the final section of this chapter explores the responses of British and Canadian military chaplains to their experiences and various assignments at the Bergen-Belsen concentration camp.

In Britain, military chaplaincy has a long tradition. Formed in 1796, the Army Chaplains' Department (AChD) received its "Royal" designation following the end of the First World War. During the Second World War, padres with the Royal Army Chaplains' Department

(RAChD) were classified as either Jewish or as a member of a Christian denominational group.[70] The Royal Air Force Chaplains' Branch, meanwhile, was formed in 1919, and its members, like the chaplains in the RAChD, were commissioned officers and wore military uniform.

The Canadian Chaplain Service (CCS), meanwhile, was formed in 1915 only to cease operation five years later following the end of the First World War. During the Second World War, Canadian military chaplaincy was revitalized.[71] Furthermore, in early 1940, Ottawa officially recognized the creation of the Chaplain Services for the Royal Canadian Air Force.[72] By the end of the war, the Canadian Chaplain Services was formally re-established. Similar to their British counterparts, Canadian army and air force chaplains were classified as either Jewish or one of the Christian denominations.

In terms of address, military chaplains in the British and Canadian forces were generally referred to as "padre." The term originates from the Latin word *pater* ("father") and was typically used by Roman Catholics to identify priests. British and Canadian military personnel, however, employed the term to refer to Catholic and non-Catholic chaplains alike.[73] The adoption of the informal term "padre" is now looked upon as a time-honoured tradition.

The enlistment of padres into military service occurred for a variety of reasons. Certainly, wherever the military goes, chaplains tend to follow. Chaplains were and are seen to be contributing to the war effort by supporting and bolstering morale among military personnel. However, there were additional factors that influenced enlistment during the Second World War. For example, historian Michael Snape suggests that, after the fall of France, the increase in Jewish refugees led to the expansion of the Jewish chaplaincy in England.[74] The enlistment of chaplains was encouraged in the Jewish community. Indeed, religious figures registered into the chaplaincy services for a multitude of reasons.

The role performed by a military chaplain, according to historian Alan Robinson, was often determined by a variety of factors including context, denomination, character, attitude of the men they served, and military policy.[75] While roles could be wide-ranging, expectations were often alike. Padres were expected to encourage the welfare and confidence of those they served. In addition, chaplains helped strengthen regimental unity, provided spiritual guidance, tended to the sick and injured, and boosted morale. And yet, as historian Doris Bergen acknowledges, chaplains often find themselves in complex situations, pressed between two entities: one religious, the other military.[76] While under the spiritual direction of their respective religious institutions, chaplains are also under the command of military leaders. As we will see, this caused some clashes between padres and their military superiors.

The first military chaplains to enter Bergen-Belsen were part of VIII Corps and included Senior Chaplain (Roman Catholic) Herbert H. Welchman, Deputy Assistant Chaplin (Baptist) O.D. Wiles, and Chaplain (Jewish) Leslie Hardman. These men were later followed by several other chaplains serving in the British forces, including Michael Morrison, Edmund Swift, George Galbraith, T.J. Stretch, and Isaac Levy, to name a few. In addition, a number of Canadian military chaplains also became involved at Bergen-Belsen, such as Norman J. Gallagher, Edwin S. Light, Ross K. Cameron, Wilfred H. Dunphy, J.P.E.M. Sylvestre, Norman Jack Crees, and Samuel Cass.[77] All of these chaplains, and others, offered their time and effort in a variety of capacities.

During the initial period of the surrender of Bergen-Belsen, military chaplains spent most of their time offering last rites and blessings or reciting the Mourner's Kaddish. Many found that there was not much time to complete additional tasks. According to Father Welchman, "At first so high was the death rate that the greater part of the day was spent administering the last Rite."[78] In addition, and due to the thousands of dead and the lack of an adequate labour force, *how* the dead were being buried became a serious point of controversy and disgust.

Isaac "Harry" Levy was born and raised in Paddington, west London. He studied at University College London and the Yeshiva Etz Chaim, a prestigious Talmudical academy. After serving in the Middle East, Reverend Levy was named the senior Jewish chaplain of the British Second Army. He arrived at Bergen-Belsen shortly after the camp was submitted to the British. As the bodies were being relocated from the campgrounds and removed from the huts, Levy became greatly disturbed by the method of "burial."

As previously noted, mass graves had been dug by bulldozers provided by the Royal Engineers. Initially, the dead were dragged to these large, open pits by the remaining male and female SS personnel. The bulldozers that had been used in the digging were later employed to shovel the dead into the graves. Thus, the bodies were pushed into the pits, unidentified, with a single marker noting the approximate number of dead. Levy, along with his colleague Reverend Hardman, conducted short burial services at the pits. According to Levy,

A photograph of burials by Corporal A.P. (Pete) Holborne, a public relations officer with 39 Wing, RCAF. Peter Holborne / Brian Musson Collection.

Both of us were profoundly affected by this most inadequate form of religious ministration. To recite the Kaddish over such a heap of emaciated bodies cast helter-skelter into pits ... seemed to negate the concept of man created in the divine image. Their humanity had been denied them by the Nazis, and now their place of disposal set the seal on that denial. They had not been buried as we would understand the meaning of burial, they were cast into pits without any personal identification, an anonymous mass of skeletons whose flesh had been destroyed by disease and the privations of hunger.[79]

The burials of the Jewish dead were not carried out according to religious tradition. The *Taharah*, the ritual of preparing the body for burial, did not occur as there was no washing (*rechitzah*), ritual purification (*taharah*), or dressing (*halbashah*).

As Levy notes, Hardman was intensely distressed by the use of the bulldozers to dispose of the dead. Watching the large machine pushing numerous corpses towards the pit with its steel blade, while also observing the SS throwing bodies haphazardly, became too much. In his memoir Hardman remarks, "As I looked down on those pitiful bodies, a great sadness came over me. Man returns to dust, but must he return like refuse thrown into a bin? I turned to the officer in charge. 'Is it not possible to show some reverence to the dead?'"[80] Alas, due to the threat of infectious disease, the officer in charge told him, regretfully, this was simply not possible. The risk to the living – the survivors, the Allies, the local civilians – appeared too great. The work continued, in the same manner, to the dismay of Hardman and others.

Years later, reflecting on his initial encounter with the crimes at Bergen-Belsen, Hardman admits that he could be "neither Aaron nor a David" while in the camp.[81] After his sons, Nadab and Abihu, were consumed by fire for disobeying God's instructions, the Torah records "*Vayidom Aharon*" ("Aaron remained silent").[82] Aaron did not protest, nor did he cry out in anger or grief at the tragic death of his sons. His response, instead, was absolute silence. In contrast, when faced with his own suffering, King David was "not silent" ("*V'lo Yidum*"), continuing to sing praise to God.[83] For many, Aaron's silence is surpassed only by King David's transcendence and virtue in the midst of sorrow. According to the nineteenth-century Hasidic Rabbi Menachem Mendel Morgensztern of Kotzk (also known as Kotzker Rebbe), "three ways are open to a man who is in sorrow. He who stands on a normal rung weeps, he who stands higher is silent, but he who stands on the topmost rung converts his sorrow into song."[84] For Kotzker Rebbe, the latter is the preferable response. Nonetheless, upon entering and surveying the camp, Hardman could not remain steadfast; nor could he be in admiration of a higher power. "I could not accept," he explains, "with perfect faith and equanimity as Aaron did, nor could I sing praises to God."[85] Therefore, at least initially, when face to face with overwhelming misery, he could not transcend the "rungs" of his grief. "Keep a stiff upper lip, Padre." This recommendation indeed seemed utterly impossible at first. In those early days of liberation, Hardman became ill with dysentery, was depressed, and openly wept. But, as we will soon review, he also worked determinedly and industriously to improve as best he could the situation for the survivors.[86]

How did the chaplains feel they were received by the survivors? Father Welchman highlights that, for the inmates who were Roman Catholic, they were "overjoyed" when they heard a military chaplain would be permanently placed at the camp.[87] One week after the camp's surrender, Father Michael Morrison, an Irish Jesuit priest, gave the first Mass for some of the Catholic inmates. It rained all day, and Father Morrison considered cancelling the service. When he arrived at the improvised altar arranged in the camp, to his amazement a large crowd of people were waiting for him to begin. "They were drenched through," he said, "but that did not diminish the fervor and enthusiasm of their singing."[88] Father Morrison called the day one of the greatest of his life.[89]

Arrangements and Regulations

Born in Toronto in 1908, Samuel Cass studied at City College and later earned a master's degree and a doctorate in Hebrew literature at the Jewish Theological Seminary in New York.[90] In 1933 he was ordained and became a rabbi at the Beth Israel Congregation in Vancouver. In 1942 he was appointed as a military chaplain and served as senior Jewish chaplain for the Canadian Amy. While overseas he was stationed with the First Canadian Army and at the Canadian Military Headquarters.

Cass first came into contact with survivors of Bergen-Belsen in May 1945. He recognized that while they were now free from Nazi tyranny, their struggles remained. He sent letters back to Canada asking various organizations and individuals for donations of clothing and other supplies.[91] Cass later distributed these contributions to the inmates in the camp. Months later, in a letter published in the *Canadian Jewish*

Chronicle, he stressed how the donations not only helped the survivors of Bergen-Belsen recover their well-being and strength, but, recognizing the support from abroad, provided the former inmates with hope.[92] Cass, however, was not alone in his attempts to bring in food and supplies from outside areas, through uncharacteristic channels. A number of padres took it upon themselves to collect from the surrounding areas.

Indeed, Squadron Leader and Senior Jewish Chaplain Louis M. Sanker, Second Tactical Air Force, contacted the Royal Canadian Air Force's 126 Wing, located nearby, for assistance.[93] Multiple trucks of food, medicine, cigarettes, and clothing were collected and delivered on behalf of the inmates at Bergen-Belsen. It was Sanker who told Hardman that there were RCAF squadrons stationed in the surrounding area.[94] Likewise, Hardman paid the Canadians a visit and was also able to procure a significant amount of food, medicine, and other supplies.[95] He returned to Bergen-Belsen "heartened and grateful" and was further moved when Canadian airmen returned the following day with additional supplies, along with recently killed deer carcasses strapped to their jeeps.[96]

Feeling that any progress made in the camp was far too slow, Hardman admits to working more like an independent operator and, with the help of Canadian airmen, claims to have brought in more supplies in two days than the army had collected in an entire week.[97] Consequently, Hardman came into some conflict with military authority. He felt the strain of functioning as a moral, religious individual while still fulfilling his duty to the military. According to his colleague in the chaplaincy, Isaac Levy, "whilst according to army regulations our first duty was to our own military flock, our religious loyalty demanded that we devote time and energy to our fellow Jews who were in such dire straits."[98] The consequences were sporadic moments of tension between some padres and their authorities in the army and air force. A number of the chaplains urged authorities to look at things from the perspective of the survivors. Often, their points of view were ignored.

Indeed, something that greatly bothered Chaplain Samuel Cass was the separation – or lack thereof – of the inmates in the camp. After liberation, internees were classified as displaced persons and, as a result, were separated by nationality, rather than ethnicity, race, or religion. Thus, Jews were not separated as a distinct group, even though it was clear that they were in the majority and that their suffering was immense.[99] In his war diary Cass makes note of the conflicts between

Polish gentiles and Jews in the camp. In particular, upon his arrival at Bergen-Belsen, he draws attention to the looting of a small, makeshift synagogue located in the camp by a group of Poles.[100] Moreover, he emphasizes that the Jews in Bergen-Belsen and in places like Celle did not want to be repatriated back to Poland. According to Cass, Palestine was the only destination suitable for most of the survivors.[101]

Someone who became intimately involved in the plight of the Jews at Bergen-Belsen was Toronto-born Shalome Michael Gelber.[102] Educated at Upper Canada College, Columbia University, New York University, and Union College, Gelber was an education officer with the Royal Canadian Air Force when he first encountered Bergen-Belsen during the spring of 1945. Following his discharge from the air force he hastily became a field representative to United Nations Relief and Rehabilitation Administration (UNRRA) and worked with the Joint Distribution Committee Bergen-Belsen.[103] While he had not yet been ordained as a rabbi when he worked at the camp, the focus of much of his writing and work was religious.

In an article titled "Wherein Is This Night Different? A Report from Bergen-Belsen, Germany" (1947), Gelber argues that the persecution of Jews during the Second World War is unlike anything previously experienced, bringing with it unparalleled consequences.[104] And now – with Jews still suffering in cramped conditions in Bergen-Belsen and elsewhere – liberation, he suggests, has lost its "grace and beauty."[105] He evokes Isaiah 21:11, which asks, "Watchman, what of the night?" Awaiting a message of hope, the Israelites are initially confused by the ensuing response: "Morning is coming, but also the night." It soon becomes clear that Israel is responsible for its own situation.[106] Gelber thus stresses that the future for the remaining Jews of Europe must be in Palestine. For the survivors, he writes, "it is as though the very word 'Belsen' is continually jostling them to be mindful of their faith that Palestine, if not the best answer, is the only answer."[107] While assisting survivors in Bergen-Belsen, Gelber admits to coming into contact with the Bricha, an underground organization that helped Jewish Holocaust survivors escape from Europe. In addition, Gelber acknowledges actively participating in assisting Bergen-Belsen survivors to illegally emigrate to Palestine, often using his authority as a Canadian officer to open the channels of communication.[108]

Chaplains and other religious figures, therefore, often found themselves in clashes with military authorities. Some, like Gelber and Hardman, used their influence as enlisted men to assist the survivors at

Bergen-Belsen. And yet, as Levy demonstrates, disobeying military authority was sometimes necessary in order to assist their "flock" in so desperate of need. The situation was difficult for all. As Gelber later remarked, "originally the situation was absolutely impossible, and later on it was just impossible. The difference was from absolute impossibility to just impossibility."[109] And yet, despite the impossibilities, in the midst of bereavement, suffering, and fear, there was often a search for meaning.

Deductions: Inadequacy, Identity, and Faith

Due to the extreme nature of the conditions in the camp, military chaplains – like the soldiers, artists, doctors, and nurses whom they worked alongside – felt overcome by the situation. Padres acknowledged feelings of inadequacy when faced with the growing physical, spiritual, and emotional needs of the inmates around them. According to Hardman, "when I considered the thousands who needed urgent treatment ... I felt that my puny efforts were of no avail, and my cup of hopelessness brimmed over."[110] Exhausted, depressed, and shocked, padres began to question themselves, the condition of man, and even their respective faiths.

Ross Ketchen Cameron was born in 1904 in Stratford, Ontario. He grew up in nearby Georgetown. In 1929 he received a bachelor of arts from University College at the University of Toronto. He earned a master's degree in philosophy from the same institution, and in 1932 he graduated in theology from Knox College. Prior to the war he worked at the Dovercourt Road Presbyterian Church in Toronto. As the Second World War commenced, Reverend Cameron left his position at Dovercourt to serve as a chaplain in the Royal Canadian Air Force.[111]

In late April 1945, as a padre with 39 Wing, Reverend Cameron and his colleague, Chaplain Wilfred H. Dunphy, left their station at Soltau and travelled to Bergen-Belsen.[112] Disgusted by the scenes, Cameron turned his attention to the people of Germany. Morality and the principles of Christianity, he said, had clearly been abandoned. Aware that Germany was a predominantly Christian country and observing how National Socialism had attacked race and religion, he states plainly that "the liberty and happiness of mankind demand, as one the first requirements, racial tolerance. The brotherhood of man was one of the two cardinal principles of Jesus' faith and teaching."[113] This, he charges, was what Germany had forsaken. Accordingly, any solution for the people of

Germany could not come solely through education. Reverend Cameron felt that something more than basic edification would be necessary.

A spiritual awakening, he advises, was the remedy needed for what ailed a broken Germany. "Christian missionaries," he preached, "are needed to carry the gospel in its truth and power to complete the liberation of men who, without it, will continue in spiritual darkness."[114] He went on to add that the gifts God has granted humankind must be shared among all of his creatures, including those who wronged, and it must be done in peaceful and in tolerant ways. "This God requires of us," he urges, "who have been given so much."[115] For Cameron, Germany's complete redemption could be found through a return to spirituality and the tenets of Christianity. It was a country enveloped in darkness, and without redemption its future was in peril. Reverend Cameron was not alone in his concerns about Germany's condition.

Edwin "Ted" Light was born in 1914 on a homestead in northern Saskatchewan. He grew up in the village of Leask. In 1933 he enrolled in theology at Emmanuel College, University of Saskatchewan. He was ordained a deacon in 1938 and in 1941 he enlisted in the Royal Canadian Air Force. In 1944 he was posted overseas to the RCAF's No. 6 Group, Bomber Command, where he served as a chaplain to 420 and 425 Bomber Squadrons. He later worked with the occupation forces until October 1945, when he returned to Canada. While he was serving with the occupation forces in Germany, his faith was repeatedly tested. "It was terrible," he recalls. "We were located close to Camp Belsen. There was destruction everywhere and refugees all over."[116] Years of arduous experiences during the war, compounded with the horrors of Bergen-Belsen, led to serious spiritual questions. "I must say that for a time I was really depressed and wondered whether the whole teaching of the Christian church – brotherhood, charity, love, forgiveness, compassion – really had a place in the world."[117] With a newborn son back in Canada, his concerns for the future were amplified. If the crimes that occurred in Bergen-Belsen could happen in a country as cultured, religious, and civilized as Germany – or at least as it had once appeared – what did this say about human nature? "The result of the whole thing," Light continued, "was it shook one's faith in whether humanity could ever establish itself again – whether kindness and generosity were really viable."[118] For years Light had provided religious guidance to others, and now he became the one who looked to be guided.

While Germany shook his faith in humankind, it was also where he was able to restore it. A story Light told repeatedly in his life involved the generosity of a young German girl after the war in Europe had ended, and following his encounter at Bergen-Belsen. According to Light,

> One afternoon, my faith in people was restored – and it took a little girl to do it. I was having an internal debate as we were going through a village, trying to locate the graves of Canadian airmen. Suddenly, a little girl of six or seven came up to me, and smiled and said, "Guten tag." I gave her some Lifesavers or gum, and she thanked me in German and ran off. About a half an hour later I saw her talking to her mother. She came back with a parcel wrapped up in newspaper and gave it to me. I opened it and saw a couple of plums from their garden. After all that had happened, that little girl still had the instincts to accept a gift and give one in an honest and natural way.[119]

It took the simple gesture of a child to help give Light a renewed sense of a hope for the future. The young German girl, with limited possessions, became a symbol that there was still some good to be found. While the adult world had immersed itself in mass violence and destruction, for Light this child became a sign of the possibility of humanity "reestablishing itself again."

Clearly, for some military chaplains, their beliefs and identities were challenged. However, for others, Bergen-Belsen only strengthened their resolve. As historian Michael Snape illustrates, Jewish soldiers and chaplains often had their belief and religious identity actually sustained by their encounters at the camp.[120] According to Chaplain Isaac Levy, in Bergen-Belsen Jewish military personnel found their spiritual brethren and were inspired by those who had endured; certainly, one had the belief that, through their survival, "Israel lives."[121] The inmates in turn, were pleased to find many Jewish personnel in the British and Canadian forces. Thus, an even greater sense of unity and purpose was formed between some of the Jewish personnel and the survivors of Bergen-Belsen.

In the end, because of his experiences, Leslie Hardman would emphasize the agency of the individual as the true representation of God on earth. He concluded that humankind's dependence on the intervention of God alone is simply inadequate. "I do not believe," he would later stress, "we are entitled just to ask God to save us without doing something for ourselves ... I agree with the Jewish preacher who says: 'It is not God alone who saves, but human beings who are his moral agents on earth' ... In other words, God's reputation rises or falls in relation to our own deeds."[122] The present, and therefore the future, rests in the hands of the individual. And like Chaplain Light, who found courage in a considerate child in a village somewhere in Germany, so too did Hardman know where his faith could be found. "We are the children of prophets," he advises, "creating conditions for a better future. Our faith is not in what has happened but in what yet will be."[123] Indeed, Hardman held onto his faith, like most of the chaplains who encountered Bergen-Belsen, and despite what he and they had seen and experienced. Hardman demonstrated that the foundation of one's actions belongs to the sovereignty of the individual and that one must strive to assist others for the betterment of the collective whole.

Concluding Remarks

Under regular wartime circumstances, medical personnel and chaplains cared primarily for their colleagues battling on the front lines. Upon arrival at Bergen-Belsen, however, their attention shifted to the internees who were in so desperate need. "It's hard to believe," Padre Norman Crees of the RCAF's 126 Wing observed, "that those people were still alive."[124] And while staff was, at least initially, in short supply, there does not appear to have been much complication between tending to the needs of Allied personnel and those of the survivors of the camp. On the medical side of things, this was likely due to the war's winding down. While injuries and death still befell men on the front lines, the numbers had lessened by the spring of 1945 with Germany's defeat fast approaching. There are examples of chaplains tending to military personnel who were troubled by the scenes in the camp, although this was not a major preoccupation. Hardman, for example, regularly encouraged his colleagues in the army, asking them for their patience and understanding when dealing with the inmates.[125] Likewise, he too received encouragement from his fellow officers.[126]

In chapter 5 it was noted that the British war artist Mary Kessell, while aware of the sufferings that occurred in Bergen-Belsen, was also surprised and enthused upon her arrival by some of the goings-on in the camp. Of course, Kessell arrived at the camp just shy of four months after its initial surrender to the British Army. But, it is important to consider that by the late summer of 1945, although conditions in the camp were far from ideal, headway had been made and was noticeable. Moreover, the condition, appearance, and attitude of many of the inmates had vastly improved. While not – and maybe never – fully recovered, countless former internees were now beginning to look for a better future for themselves and for their friends and family that survived. Consequently, the accounts of Allied personnel from the months of July, August, and beyond show a discernible difference than the responses that emerged from the first few hours, days, weeks, and months after the camp's submission. Before concluding, let us consider some of these accounts.

Working under the general supervision of Lyle Creelman at the hospital at Bergen-Belsen were Canadian nurses Janet Vanderwell, Louise C. Bartsch, Jean Lazecko, and Edna Osborne, to name a few.[127] When these UNRRA nurses arrived at Bergen-Belsen in the summer of 1945, they were surprised by the situation they found. For Vanderwell, who was from Toronto and had prior experience working in the displaced-persons camps at Wesel and Dusseldorf, Bergen-Belsen was not at all what she had anticipated. "I expected Belsen to be a depressing place," she revealed a month after first arriving at the camp, "and was glad to find it rather cheerful. Few of my Polish patients know where to go from here, as they may not be able to return to Poland, but somehow they all feel confident that there will be a place for them to settle down after they leave hospital."[128] The images of the thousands of unburied dead, burned-out crematoria, and emaciated survivors which were splashed across newspapers throughout the Western world in April and May 1945 were still fresh in everyone's minds. And yet, by the summer and fall of 1945, the situation had changed dramatically. The main camp and its decrepit barracks had been burned down, the dead had been buried in mass graves, and the surviving inmates were receiving adequate treatment. Vanderwell also notes the rich culture that was re-emerging among the inmates in the camp – arts and crafts were now common. According to Vanderwell, "They do that to get the nightmare out of their system."[129] Haunted by their experiences, the survivors looked for ways to express themselves and frequently did so through art. Ottawa-born Edna Osborne, who had worked at Western Hospital in Montreal, found the survivors' ingenuity and optimism for the future inspiring. "Their hopes are very genuine ... We must keep that spark of hope alive."[130] Gone it seems, among the doctors, nurses, and other military personnel who worked alongside the recuperating survivors, were the harsh words, the animal metaphors, and cynicism: pessimism was slowly and gradually being replaced by hope.

Shortly before he left the camp, and while not discounting the pain of the past, Hardman found confidence that the future would somehow be better for the surviving inmates. "My last days as a Padre at Belsen," he wrote, "were filled with many activities ... Mostly we spoke of what the future held for them [the survivors], and of their belief that the world would not turn its back on them, but would help them individually as human beings, and collectively as Jews. I was of the same belief, and it did my heart good to put their faith into words, and to talk about it with them."[131] The day he left Bergen-Belsen he took with him the vivid memories of the people he had met, the experiences he had had, and the stories he had heard. Upon his return to London, Hardman was appointed minister at Hendon United Synagogue. He became chaplain to the psychiatric unit at Edgware Hospital and a supporter of Holocaust Educational Trust (HET), a British charity. Throughout his life, Hardman occupied himself in Holocaust education work, ensuring that the future would remember this terrible past.

In conclusion, the British and Canadian padres, doctors, nurses, and additional medical personnel performed a variety of roles in Bergen-Belsen. They all arrived at the camp unprepared and faced situations they had never before encountered. Their tasks were difficult, and some individuals suffered greatly because of the work: dysentery, isolation, depression, and feelings of inadequacy were common. And yet, most accepted their assignments willingly, working with the resources they had around them.

Medical personnel had to deal with language limitations, unfamiliar cultures, untrained staff, and rare illnesses. Consequently, difficult decisions had to be made. Initially, not everyone was given adequate care. Patients were selected for treatment, and not all of those who needed it received attention. Thousands of inmates died, and this weighed heavily on all involved. German military personnel were employed, much to the great dismay of the survivors. The work of Allied medical personnel was vital, and while thousands died, many more thousands were saved.

Meanwhile, military chaplains were called upon to offer religious services in front of open graves filled with thousands of dead: men, women, and children who were often left unidentified. The padres also did more than the typical military duties asked of them. Almost always acting on their own initiative, chaplains tended to the sick, gathered food, listened to the stories of the inmates, and encouraged their fellow military colleagues, all the while maintaining their religious beliefs. And yet, those beliefs were frequently tested by their trying experiences at Bergen-Belsen. In the end, and despite the horrors, the questions, and the doubts, British and Canadian military chaplains held onto their respective faiths.

Conclusion

A Past Intensity

At a press conference in April 1996, over half a century after Bergen-Belsen was surrendered to the British Army, the Imperial War Museum in London announced its decision to mount a major, permanent Holocaust exhibition. As scholars Suzanne Bardgett, Donald Bloxham, and Tony Kushner have discussed, however, there were subsequent criticisms regarding the plan and there were those who argued that the exhibit had no place in a national museum in Britain.[1] Despite a smattering of concerns and uncertainties, in June 2000 the Holocaust exhibition at the Imperial War Museum was opened to the public, receiving acclaim in both the press and academia.[2]

In 1997, while work on the London exhibit was underway, plans were released for an expansive Holocaust memorial gallery to be included in the new Canadian War Museum in Ottawa. Once the idea became public knowledge – but before it had received formal approval – a heated controversy erupted.[3] Accordingly, in February 1998, the Senate Subcommittee of Veteran Affairs held hearings to debate the issue. Upon conclusion of the hearings, the plan for a Holocaust memorial gallery was promptly abandoned. In the view of many who testified, the Holocaust, while considered an important part of history, either had no place in the country's war museum or held no direct connection to Canada or to its military.[4] Consequently, in May 2005, the new Canadian War Museum opened without the proposed Holocaust gallery.[5]

These accounts involve two countries, two national war museums, and demonstrate two vastly different outcomes. The Holocaust and the liberation of Nazi concentration camps have become a part of Britain's remembrance of the war. The same cannot be said of Canada. While major moments of the Second World War – Dieppe Raid, D-Day,

Operation Plunder – are a part of Canada's remembrance of the war, the liberation of the camps has largely been ignored.

As these two examples demonstrate, history and the ways in which it is remembered frequently come into conflict. During the Canadian Senate Subcommittee hearings, for example, veterans' groups, historians, museum management, and government officials squared off in lengthy and, at times, impassioned debates. None of the participants were against a Holocaust memorial per se; rather, many argued that a Canadian war museum was simply not an appropriate place to house one. History and memory then can be at distinct odds in the retelling of the past.

Whereas museologists are often faced with difficult decisions regarding what to include and what to evoke in their respective institutions, history must not be fused together with memory – for the two are not the same. Memory is personal, and while it vows to be faithful to the past, it is susceptible to the vagaries of time. History is more durable, a scholarly reconstruction of the past which demands to be substantiated. And yet, as we have seen, history and memory can come to the aid of each other. When documentary sources, such as reports, war diaries, and personnel lists are deficient, a researcher must then rely on memory by way of first-hand accounts or eyewitness testimonies.

Indeed, while the British encounter at Bergen-Belsen is largely well documented, the record of the Canadian involvement is sorely lacking. There are certainly documentary traces indicating, for example, that Lieutenant Keith W. MacLellan was one of the first Allied military personnel to enter Bergen-Belsen or that the 1st Canadian Parachute Battalion came across the camp on the day of its surrender and its Captain Patrick Costigan provided initial medical care to the inmates. And formal records do show that Squadron Leader John Proskie was put in charge of planning the collection and employment of local resources for the camp's inmates and that Lyle Creelman, chief nurse for the British zone of occupied Germany, was forced to deal with staff shortages at the Belsen hospital. Nevertheless, it is the memories and stories of their work that have offered a more meaningful perspective.

One of the themes of this book is that Bergen-Belsen, and thus the Holocaust, are unquestionably a part of both British and Canadian history. Though the crimes of the Third Reich are – or at least should be – the concern of all humanity, there were those who became directly involved in assisting the victims of some of those brutal offences. The experience made a tremendous impression on individuals from both nations. And yet one must also be cognizant of what has been termed the "nativization" of the Holocaust.[6] This makes reference to the reality that depictions of the Holocaust take specific form depending upon their national context. Thus, the representation of the Holocaust can vary from country to country. Left unchecked, the "nativization" of the Holocaust can distort the event.

Nevertheless, it should be recognized that both Britain and Canada sent personnel and volunteers to aid the victims of Bergen-Belsen. Allied military personnel arrived to provide food, medicine, and treatment to the sick and dying inmates. Moreover, many of these individuals left behind detailed and moving accounts of their efforts.

And what about these stories, the plethora of narratives offered by and concerning British and Canadian military personnel? This brings us to the second theme of this book: distance. While often working in close proximity to the dead and the critically ill, many military personnel found ways of separating themselves, psychologically, from the frightful scenes – at least in the dreadful days and weeks following the camp's surrender. At liberation there was no rejoicing by the British and Canadians, nor, typically, by the inmates. Initially, these two groups, the Allies and the survivors, rarely bonded. As we have reviewed, for military personnel, the experience was an amalgam of shock, sorrow, and shame. Whether it was harsh language used to keep a division between themselves and the inmates, or the intake of alcohol, cigarettes, or other distractions, Britons and Canadians employed various techniques to complete their assignments, all the while preventing themselves from breaking down emotionally or psychologically. The war photographers and photojournalists used their cameras as buffers and artists busied themselves with their craft via painting and sketching.

A third theme of this study has to do with change or transformation. For many of the Allied men and women who worked in or ventured to Bergen-Belsen, the experience brought an immense change in their life – whether it be one of direction, attitude, or belief. For example, a firm belief in pacifism was sorely tested for Welshman Jonah Jones, a medic with the 224 Parachute Field Ambulance attached to the 1st Canadian Parachute Battalion. A former conscientious objector – as were many in the 224 – after his experience at Bergen-Belsen, Jones concluded that his pacifism was an "untenable" position.[7] For other personnel, it was their course in life that was radically altered by the experience. As we saw in chapter 4, there were those who fought alongside Jews in Palestine in the 1948 Arab-Israeli War. The 7th Armoured Division's Alan Rose, later of the Canadian Jewish Congress, for example, served as a volunteer in the Haganah, a Jewish paramilitary organization, only a few short years after being a witness at Bergen-Belsen.[8] His encounter at the camp only strengthened his identity as a Jew. "I intended to be an architect," he confesses, "but I decided then [at Bergen-Belsen] to spend my time doing what I could to restore the remnants of Jewish life."[9] Finally, for others, a change in attitude or an approach to life and work was the unexpected result of the experience. Some of these individuals were like the Royal Canadian Air Force's Dr John W. Thompson, who found his outlook forever altered by his encounter. As his biographer Paul J. Weindling explains, Thompson's sensibilities and impulses were utterly transformed by his time spent with the survivors at Bergen-Belsen.[10] After the war, Thompson's scientific research was based more squarely on moral and philosophical grounds.[11] Change occurred in a myriad of ways for many of those who witnessed and worked at the camp.

In 2007, Simone Veil, a French survivor of Bergen-Belsen who later became a renowned lawyer and politician, addressed the United Nations in New York during the International Day of Commemoration in Memory of the Victims of the Holocaust. "I can still see the horrified faces of the soldiers," she said of the troops who entered Bergen-Belsen on 15 April 1945, adding solemnly that there were "no cries of joy on our part – only silence and tears."[12] There were no plans to liberate this or any other concentration camp during the war. The British and Canadian troops who entered Bergen-Belsen on that Sunday afternoon simply happened to be in the area. Accordingly, for all involved, the encounter at Bergen-Belsen would become their brief window into some of the intended consequences of Hitler's Third Reich. In the years that followed, military personnel explored ways to estimate their distance from the Belsen heap.

Notes

Preface

1 Fania Fénelon, *Playing for Time*, trans. Judith Landry (New York: Atheneum, 1976; 1977), 255.
2 ITS Digitized Collections, USHMM, 2.2.2.2., "Official Certificates (marriages and deaths), western zones, general," Alfred Roe, 76849722_0_1-76849722_0_2. A special thank-you to Ms Jo-Ellyn Decker of the United States Holocaust Memorial Museum for sharing her expertise on the International Tracing Service database. The Commonwealth War Graves Commission dates Roe's death as 9 April 1945 (aged thirty-nine).
3 Concerning Mayor, see the depositions of Rolf Klink and Max Markowicz in *Trial of Josef Kramer and Forty-Four Others: The Belsen Trial*, edited by Raymond Phillips (London: W. Hodge, 1949), 671–2 and 677–8. The Commonwealth War Graves Commission dates Mayor's death as 7 April 1945 (aged twenty-two).
4 In addition to Mayor, Roe, and Le Druillenec, there are reports that an SAS officer with the surname "Jenkinson" had been found in one of the barracks and removed ("Jenkinson" is discussed in further detail in chapter 2). According to ITS, records list a foreign national named Robert Jenkinson being held in custody. See ITS Digitized Collections, USHMM, 2.1.1.1, "Lists of all persons of United Nations and other foreigners, German Jews, and stateless persons; American Zone; Bavaria, Hesse," Robert Jenkinson, 70263290 and 70263696. In addition, it is possible that some Canadians – or those with links to the country – had been held as inmates. According to Derrick Sington – a British Army captain who was commanding No. 14 Amplifying Unit when he entered Bergen-Belsen – he was asked by Brigadier Glyn Hughes on 17 April 1945 to locate

Madame Chassaigne, a "niece of Lord Bennett, the former Canadian Prime Minister." Sington notes that she was married to a Frenchman and living in Tours when she was arrested and sent to Bergen-Belsen. She was quickly located and evacuated. According to records held at Gedenkstätte Bergen-Belsen, a woman named Violette de Chassaigne is documented in a list made four days after liberation by a group of French survivors. Violette de Chassaigne died shortly thereafter. See Derrick Sington, *Belsen Uncovered* (London: Duckworth, 1946), 56–7. My thanks to Bernd Horstmann at Gedenkstätte Bergen-Belsen for supplementary information. For additional information on Ms. Chassaigne see: ITS Digitized Collections, USHMM, 0.1, "Central Names Index," Violette de Chassaigne, 17090520-17090523. Lastly, historian and Belgian air force officer Peter Celis recounts the fascinating story of a Royal Canadian Air Force Squadron Leader named Teddy Blenkinsop. Celis posits that Blenkinsop spent time at Bergen-Belsen and suggests it is likely that this is where, in January 1945, he ultimately died and was cremated. See Peter Celis, *One Who Almost Made It Back: The Remarkable Story of One of World War Two's Unsung Heroes, Sqn Ldr Edward 'Teddy' Blenkinsop, DFC, CdeG (Belge), RCAF* (London: Grub Street, 2008). However, according to ITS records, Blenkinsop died at the Neuengamme concentration camp. International Tracing Service (ITS) Digitized Collections, USHMM, 0.1, "Central Names Index," Edward Blenkinsop, 14704159–14704167.

5 While Bernstein and Hitchcock did not complete the film, in 1984 a five-reel rough cut was put together under the title *Memory of the Camps*. It was broadcast on *Frontline*, part of the WGBH Boston PBS network. In 2014, a documentary titled *Night Will Fall* directed by André Singer about the making of the Bernstein and Hitchcock film premiered. In April 2015, marking the seventieth anniversary of the liberation of Bergen-Belsen, the Imperial War Museum released the completed and restored *German Concentration Camps Factual Survey*.

6 Jon Savage, *England's Dreaming: Anarchy, Sex Pistols, Punk Rock and Beyond* (New York: St Martin's Griffin, 1991; 2011), 458. The Sex Pistols are not the only British musicians to reference Bergen-Belsen in song. For example, English composer Adrian Snell's "Kaddish for Bergen Belsen" was inspired after taking part in a tour of the former campgrounds. The track appears on his 1985 album *Alpha and Omega*. In addition, film and television composer Debbie Wiseman evokes the name "Bergen-Belsen" in a track of the same name on her 2011 album, *The Promise*. Likewise, Canadian composer Oskar Morawetz's piece *From the Diary of Anne Frank* (1970) was inspired by Frank's experience during the Holocaust and her

death at Bergen-Belsen. Canadian mezzo-soprano Judith Forst has performed Morawetz's composition several times. In 2001, she recorded the piece with the CBC Orchestra. It received a Juno Award for "Best Classical Composition" in 2001. Canadian rock band Rush recorded "Red Sector A" for their 1984 album *Grace under Pressure*. The song was influenced by Manya Rubenstein and her liberation at Bergen-Belsen. Her son, Rush lead singer Geddy Lee, also wrote about his mother and her survival on the track "Grace to Grace," which appeared on his solo album *My Favorite Headache* (2000). That song was co-written with fellow Canadian Ben Mink, a multi-instrumentalist and another child of Holocaust survivors. In 1995, Lee, along with his brother and sister, accompanied his mother back to Germany to take part in the fiftieth anniversary of the liberation of Bergen-Belsen. See Scott R. Benarde, "How the Holocaust rocked Rush Front Man Geddy Lee," *Jweekly*, 25 June 2004.

7 The opening lines are: "Belsen was a gas, I heard the other day / In the open graves where the Jews all lay / 'Life is fun and I wish you were here' / They wrote on postcards to those held dear." The song appears on their 1979 album *The Great Rock 'n' Roll Swindle*. In addition, the Sex Pistols also refer to Bergen-Belsen on their track "Holidays in the Sun." For this song, the opening lines are: "I don't want a holiday in the sun / I want to go to the new Belsen / I want to see some history / Cause now I got a reasonable economy." The track appears on the band's 1977 album *Never Mind the Bollocks, Here's the Sex Pistols*.

8 Nigel Parry, "British Graffiti Artist, Banksy, Hacks the Wall," *Thresholds*, 1 October 2006.

9 Part of the original Gonin quote in question is as follows: "It was shortly after the [British Red Cross Society] teams arrived, though it may have no connection, that a very large quantity of lipstick arrived. This was not at all what we men wanted, we were screaming for hundreds and thousands of other things and I don't know who asked for lipstick. I wish so much that I could discover who did it, it was the action of genius, sheer unadulterated brilliance. I believe nothing did more for those internees than the lipstick. Women lay in bed with no sheets and no nightie but with scarlet lips, you saw them wandering about with nothing but a blanket over their shoulders, but with scarlet lips. I saw a woman dead on the post mortem table and clutched in her hand was a piece of lipstick. Do you see what I mean? At last someone had done something to make them individuals again, they were someone, no longer merely the number tattooed on the arm. At last they could take an interest in their appearance. That lipstick started to give them back their humanity. Perhaps it was the most pathetic

thing that happened at Belsen, perhaps the most pathetic thing that's ever happened, I don't know. But that is why the sight of a piece of lipstick today makes my eyes feel just a little uncomfortable." Imperial War Museum Department of Documents, 3713: Private Papers of Lieutenant Colonel M W Gonin DSO TD. There appear to be small alterations to the Gonin quote Banksy used on his website. For further discussion see James Brassett, "British Irony, Global Justice: A Pragmatic Reading of Chris Brown, Banksy and Ricky Gervais," *Review of International Studies* 35, no. 1 (2009): 234–5.

10 The exhibition, *A Prayer for the Dead*, featured paintings and drawings referencing the Holocaust by Herzl Kashetsky. The exhibit was organized by the New Brunswick Museum and the Beaverbrook Art Gallery.

11 *Prayer for the Dead: Herzl Kashetsky*. Produced and directed by Lisa Lamb. New Brunswick Museum, Saint John Jewish Historical Museum and Fundy Community Television, 1997. DVD.

12 For example, see "At the Belsen Memorial" in Irving Layton, *Fortunate Exile* (Toronto: McClelland and Stewart, 1987), 84–5. Also see Cohen's "Lines from My Grandfather's Journal," part of which reads as follows: "It is painful to recall a past intensity, to estimate your distance from the Belsen heap, to make your peace with numbers. Just to get up each morning is to make a kind of peace." See Leonard Cohen, *The Spice-Box of Earth* (Toronto: McClelland Stewart, 1961). Cohen also evokes the Holocaust and references Bergen-Belsen in his 1966 novel *Beautiful Losers* (Toronto: McClelland and Stewart, 1966; 2003), 203. For a general discussion of this particular reference, see Linda Hutcheon, *Leonard Cohen and His Works* (Toronto: ECW Press, 1992).

13 "Holocaust Song Has Cellular Firm Squirming," Reuters UK, 15 September 2007.

14 Debra Black, "Bell Pulls 'Death Camp' Ads," *Toronto Star*, 15 September 2007. Moreover, in comparing conditions at the Wandsworth Prison in London, John Taylor, Baron Taylor of Warwick, also evokes the image of Bergen-Belsen. "Wandsworth Prison is not a holiday camp," he explains and later adds, "And I looked around and it was surreal. This is Belsen, this is Victorian. I thought, 'Is this 2011'?" See Robert Winnett, "Lord Taylor of Warwick: 'I Have a Role to Play in House of Lords,'" *Telegraph*, 8 November 2011. Of course, eliciting the image of Bergen-Belsen is certainly not limited to Canada and Britain. In 2007, Dr Peter Phelps, an Australian politician, sparked controversy when he employed the term as a metaphor against a Labour Party candidate. At a public meeting Dr Phelps accused Colonel Mike Kelly, an Australian soldier who served in Iraq, of using the Nuremberg defence, "like the guards at Belsen."

For a more detailed discussion, see Stuart Glover, "Viral Words: Belsen." *New Matilda* 5 (5 October 2007): 2.
15 It should be noted that both British and Canadian forces were involved in the surrender and relief of additional Nazi camps in northwest Europe. For example, the British liberated other camps in Germany such as Sandbostel, Fallingbostel, and, although it had been emptied of prisoners only days earlier, Neuengamme. The Canadians, meanwhile, were involved in the liberation of the Herzogenbusch (Vught) concentration camp, the Amersfoort concentration camp, and the Westerbork transit camp, all of which were located in the Netherlands. The aforementioned liberations have not received much scholarly attention. For information on Westerbork see Cecil Law, *Kamp Westerbork, Transit Camp to Eternity: The Liberation Story* (Clementsport: Canadian Peacekeeping Press, 2000).
16 Weiner Library, 15323: Addresses and Speeches, Commemorative Ceremony of the 50th Anniversary of the Liberation of Concentration Camps, held in the memorial of Bergen-Belsen (27 April 1995).

1 Experience, Narrative, and Meaning

1 Hayden White, *The Content of the Form* (Baltimore: Johns Hopkins University Press, 1987), 1.
2 Joan W. Scott, "The Evidence of Experience," *Critical Inquiry* 17, no. 4 (Summer, 1991): 797.
3 Laidlaw Family, Private Collection: Memoir of Ron Laidlaw, RCAF, Public Relations Officer, 27–8.
4 Dan Stone, *History, Memory and Mass Atrocity: Essays on the Holocaust and Genocide* (London: Vallentine Mitchell, 2006), 107.
5 For a discussion on the effect of the Holocaust on the Canadian Jewish community see Franklin Bialystok, *Delayed Impact: The Holocaust and the Canadian Jewish Community* (Montreal and Kingston: McGill-Queen's University Press, 2000).
6 For example see: Christopher Browning, *Ordinary Men: Reserve Police Battalion 101 and the Final Solution in Poland* (New York: HarperCollins, 1992), and *Remembering Survival: Inside a Nazi Slave-Labor Camp* (New York: Norton, 2010). For a primarily theoretical discussion, see Christopher Browning, "German Memory, Judicial Interrogation, and Historical Reconstruction: Writing Perpetrator History from Postwar Testimony," in *Probing the Limits of Representation*, ed. Saul Friedländer (Cambridge: Harvard University Press, 1992), 22–36.
7 Browning, *Remembering Survival*, 9.

8 Christopher Browning, *Collected Memories: Holocaust History and Postwar Testimony* (Madison: University of Wisconsin Press, 2003), 39.
9 Yehuda Bauer, "On Oral and Video Testimony," *Past Forward* (Autumn 2010): 22.
10 Paul Ricoeur, *Temps et récit* (Paris: Seuil, 1985), 3:204. Translation mine (unless otherwise noted): "what was and is no more."
11 Walter Laqueur, *Thursday's Child Has Far to Go: A Memoir of the Journeying Years* (Toronto: Maxwell MacMillian, 1992), 401.
12 Hayden White, *Content of the Form*, 1.
13 Maurice Halbwachs, *On Collective Memory*, ed. and trans. Lewis A. Coser (Chicago: University of Chicago Press, 1992), 38.
14 Marianne Hirsch, "Editor's Column: What's Wrong with These Terms? A Conversation with Barbara Kirshenblatt-Gimblett and Diana Taylor," *PMLA* 120, no. 4 (October 2005): 1500.
15 Scott, "Evidence of Experience," 779.
16 Edward Sapir, *Culture, Language and Personality* (Berkeley: University of California Press, 1962), 69.
17 Sidonie Smith and Julia Watson, *Reading Autobiography: A Guide for Interpreting Life Narratives* (Minnesota: University of Minnesota Press, 2001), 25–6.
18 White, *Content of the Form*, 48.
19 Hayden White, *Tropics of Discourse* (Baltimore: Johns Hopkins University Press, 1978), 82.
20 Ibid., 24.
21 Saul Friedländer, "Introduction," in *Probing the Limits of Representation*, 9.
22 Hayden White, "Historical Emplotment and the Problem of Truth," in *Probing the Limits of Representation*, 38.
23 Ibid.
24 David Carr, *Time, Narrative, and History* (Bloomington: Indiana University Press, 1986), 16.
25 David Carr, "The Reality of History," in *Meaning and Representation in History*, ed. Jörn Rüsen (New York: Berghahn, 2006), 126.
26 Carr, *Time, Narrative, History*, 16.
27 Ibid., 61.
28 Carr, "The Reality of History," 126.
29 Paul Ricoeur et al., "Discussion: Ricoeur on Narrative," in *On Paul Ricoeur: Narrative and Interpretation*, ed. D. Wood (New York: Routledge, 1991), 186. As a prisoner of war Ricoeur witnessed first-hand some of the crimes of the Third Reich. On approximately 22 April 1945 he was liberated by a group of Canadians while marching away from a prison camp near Hannover. Ricoeur explains: "We witnessed the brutality inflicted on the

Russian prisoners near our camp in Pomerania. But we had not discovered the horror of the deportation and extermination camps until the day we were liberated, because we found ourselves next to Bergen-Belsen. The English had emptied the village of Belsen as a reprisal, and we interrogated Germans who claimed not to know what was happening in the camp seven kilometres away. I saw the survivors coming out so haggard, many of them dying after taking their first steps, after eating jam or something. It was dreadful. All of a sudden, we had the feeling we had been incredibly spared." See Paul Ricoeur, *Critique and Conviction: Conversations with François Azouvi and Marc de Launay*, trans. Kathleen Blarney (New York: Columbia University Press, 1995; 1998), 19. For further details regarding his imprisonment and liberation see Charles E. Reagan, *Paul Ricoeur* (Chicago: University of Chicago Press, 1996), 7–14.
30 Paul Ricoeur, *Time and Narrative* trans. K. McLaughlin and D. Pellauer (Chicago: University of Chicago Press, 1983; 1984), 1:3.
31 Richard Kearney, "Parsing Narrative – Story, History, Life," *Human Studies Journal* 29, no. 4 (December 2006): 485–6.
32 Ibid., 486.
33 Ibid., 487.
34 Ibid.
35 Ibid., 488.
36 Sara R. Horowitz, *Voicing the Void: Muteness and Memory in Holocaust Fiction* (Albany: State University of New York Press, 1997), 44.
37 Marlene Kadar, *Essays on Life Writing: From Genre to Critical Practice* (Toronto: University of Toronto Press, 1992), 10.
38 Wilhelm Dilthey, *Selected Writings*, ed. and trans. H.P. Rickman (Cambridge: Cambridge University Press, 1976), 213.
39 Ibid., 215.
40 Ibid., 218.
41 James Olney, *Metaphors of Self: The Meaning of Autobiography* (Princeton, NJ: Princeton University Press, 1972), xi.
42 Ibid., 37.
43 David McCooey, *Artful Histories: Modern Australian Autobiography* (Cambridge: Cambridge University Press, 1996), 164.
44 Ibid., 189.
45 Jeremy D. Popkin, *History, Historians, and Autobiography* (Chicago: University of Chicago Press, 2005), 279.
46 Ibid.
47 Smith and Watson, *Reading Autobiography*, 4.
48 Ibid., 14.

49 Ibid., 193.
50 Sandrine Arons, "Self-Therapy through Personal Writing: A Study of Holocaust Victims' Diaries and Memoirs," in *The Psychological Impact of War Trauma on Civilians*, ed. S. Krippner (Westport, CT: Praeger, 2003), 124.
51 Karl J. Weintraub, "Autobiography and Historical Consciousness," *Critical Inquiry* 1, no. 4 (June 1975): 827.
52 James Young, *Writing and Rewriting the Holocaust* (Bloomington: Indiana University Press, 1988), 29.
53 Robert McGill, "The Life You Write May Be Your Own," *Southern Literary Journal* 36, no. 2 (Spring 2004): 38.
54 Janet Malcolm, *The Silent Woman: Sylvia Plath and Ted Hughes* (London: Picador, 1994), 110.
55 McGill, "The Life You Write," 38.
56 Mary Jean Corbett, "Literary Domesticity and Women Writers' Subjectivities," in *Women, Autobiography, Theory: A Reader*, ed. Smith and Watson (Madison: University of Wisconsin Press, 1998), 262.
57 Weintraub, "Autobiography and Historical Consciousness," 826.
58 Browning, *Collected Memories*, 40.
59 Ibid., 84.
60 Henry Greenspan, "Survivors' Accounts," in *The Oxford Handbook of Holocaust Studies*, ed. Peter Hayes and John K. Roth (Oxford: Oxford University Press, 2011), 415.
61 Julia Creet, "On the Sidewalk: Testimony and the Gesture," in *Memory, Haunting, Discourse*, ed. Maria Holmgren, Troy and Elisabeth Wennö (Karlstad: Karlstad University Press, 2005), 139.
62 Bauer, "On Oral and Video Testimony," 20. For further discussion of Eichmann's revelations concerning the Wannsee Protocol, see David Cesarani, *Eichmann: His Life and Crimes* (London: W. Heinemann, 2004), 112–16.
63 Jacques Derrida, "The Law of Genre," trans. Avital Ronell, *Critical Inquiry* 7, no. 1 (Autumn 1980): 65.
64 Sissela Bok, "Autobiography as Moral Battleground," in *Memory, Brain and Belief*, ed. Daniel L. Schacter and Elaine Scarry (Cambridge: Cambridge University Press, 2000), 308.
65 Wilhelm Dilthey, *The Formation of the Historical World in the Human Sciences*, ed. Makkreel and Rodi (Princeton, NJ: Princeton University Press, 2002), 222.
66 Ibid., 253.
67 Paul Ricoeur, *Oneself as Another*, trans. Kathleen Blamey (Chicago: University of Chicago Press, 1992), 140.

68 Popkin, *History, Historians, and Autobiography*, 43.
69 Avishai Margalit, *The Ethics of Memory* (Cambridge: Harvard University Press, 2002), 79.
70 Carr, *Time, Narrative, and History*, 155.
71 Alasdair MacIntyre, *After Virtue: A Study in Moral Theory* (London: Duckworth, 1981), 199.
72 Suzanne Langlois, "Making Ideal Histories," in *Secret Spaces, Forbidden Places*, ed. F. Lloyd and C. O'Brien (New York: Berghahn, 2000), 117.
73 White, *Content of the Form*, 24.
74 McCooey, *Artful Histories*, 190.

2 The Rhine, the Heath, the Wire

1 Alan Rose, "Transcript of Interview with the Holocaust Documentation Project," SV257–SV259, 17 March 1982, Canadian Jewish Congress Records, CJCCC National Archives, p. XX.
2 During the Vistula-Oder Offensive, which began in January 1945 and ended less than a month later, the Red Army crossed the borders of the Third Reich from the east.
3 Edward J. Drea, "Recognizing the Liberators: U.S. Army Divisions Enter the Concentration Camps." *Army History* (Fall/Winter 1992–3): 4–5. My thanks to Mr Ron Coleman at the United States Holocaust Memorial Museum for bringing this article to my attention.
4 Ibid., 2.
5 Ibid., 5.
6 Anthony Kemp, *The SAS at War, 1941–1945* (London: Penguin, 1991), 213.
7 Lloyd Clark, *Crossing the Rhine* (New York: Atlantic Monthly, 2008), 294–5.
8 Donald Nijboer, *No 126 Wing RCAF* (Oxford: Osprey, 2010), 104.
9 Brian Nolan, *Airborne* (Toronto: Lester, 1995), 48.
10 Clark, *Crossing the Rhine*, 299.
11 Tim Saunders, *Operation Varsity: The British and Canadian Airborne Assault* (Barnsley: Pen and Sword, 2008), 179.
12 Stephen L. Wright, *The Last Drop: Operation Varsity, March 24–25, 1945* (Mechanicsburg: Stackpole, 2008), 273.
13 Peter Harclerode, *Go to It! The Illustrated History of the 6th Airborne Division* (London: Bloomsbury, 1990), 141.
14 Gavin Mortimer, *Stirling's Men: The Inside History of the SAS in World War II* (London: Cassell, 2004), 310.
15 Patrick Delaforce, *The Black Bull* (Dover: Alan Sutton, 1993), 205–6.
16 Ibid., 209.

17 *War Diary of the 1st Canadian Parachute Battalion*, compiled and edited by Walter Romanow, Morris Romanow, Helene MacLean, Rosalie Hartigan, and Bill Dickson (Calgary: Bunker to Bunker, 2006), 211.
18 Delaforce, *Black Bull*, 218.
19 Nijboer, *No 126 Wing RCAF*, 105.
20 Bernd Horn and Michel Wyczynski, *Paras versus the Reich: Canada's Paratroopers at War, 1942–45* (Toronto: Dundurn, 2003), 219.
21 Martin Gilbert, *The Second World War: A Complete History* (New York: Henry Holt and Company, 1989), 684.
22 Anthony Kemp, *SAS at War*, 219.
23 Klaus Neumann, *Shifting Memories: The Nazi Past in the New Germany* (Ann Arbor: University of Michigan Press, 2000), 41.
24 Ibid., 42.
25 Ibid.
26 Patrick Forbes, *6th Guards Tank Brigade: The Story of Guardsmen in Churchill Tanks* (London: S. Low, Marston, 1946), 158–62.
27 WO 171/4306: War Diary, 3rd Parachute Brigade
28 *War Diary of the 1st Canadian Parachute Battalion*, 216. While the Nazis' "Werwolf" plan made little impact militarily, it was successful as a propaganda tool.
29 Indeed, several scholars have come to vastly different conclusions regarding who should be considered as *the* "liberator" of Bergen-Belsen. For example, in a 1991 article Paul Kemp denotes Lieutenant-Colonel Robert Daniell, 13 Regiment, Honourable Artillery Company, Royal Horse Artillery, as the "first British soldier to enter the camp." Upon revision six years later, Kemp suggests that the "first British soldiers to arrive at Belsen" were men from the Special Air Service. In contrast, while acknowledging the confusion regarding who was the first to enter the camp, in her 1998 offering Joanne Reilly states that the 63rd Anti-Tank Regiment should be considered as the "official 'liberators'" of Bergen-Belsen. In 2005, Ben Flanagan and Donald Bloxham argue that the 29th Armoured Brigade were the "first British troops to come across the Belsen camp." On its website, and in accordance with its guidelines of designating divisions, the United States Holocaust Memorial Museum lists the 11th Armoured Division as the liberators of Bergen-Belsen. Meanwhile, Ben Shephard writes that on the day the camp was liberated, the "11th Armoured [Division] fought its way to Belsen. The main body of tanks paused only briefly to approach the wire and then swept on." As this chapter demonstrates, all of the above groups, and more, became involved at various points in time at Bergen-Belsen. It remains to be seen as to whether or not

one of the above groups can be considered as *the* "first" to enter the camp. For further reference see the following works: Paul Kemp, "The Liberation of Bergen-Belsen Concentration Camp in April 1945: The Testimony of Those Involved," *Imperial War Museum Review* 5 (1991): 28–41; Paul Kemp, "The British Army and the Liberation of Bergen-Belsen, April 1945," in *Belsen in History and Memory*, ed. Jo Reilly et al. (London: Frank Cass, 1997); Joanne Reilly, *Belsen: The Liberation of a Concentration Camp* (London: Routledge, 1998); *Remembering Belsen: Eyewitnesses Record the Liberation*, ed. Ben Flanagan and Donald Bloxham (London: Vallentine Mitchell, 2005); United States Holocaust Memorial Museum, "The 11th Armoured Division (Great Britain)," http://www.ushmm.org/wlc/en/article.php?ModuleId=10006188 (accessed 3 March 2013); Ben Shephard, *After Daybreak: The Liberation of Bergen-Belsen, 1945* (New York: Schocken, 2005).
30 Reilly, *Belsen*, 23.
31 My thanks to Klaus Tätzler, Department of Research and Documentation, Gedenkstätte Bergen-Belsen, for this information.
32 Monika Gödecke, Rolf Keller, Thomas Rahe, and Wilfried Wiedemann, *Bergen-Belsen: Explanatory Notes on the Exhibition* (Hannover: Niedersächsische Landeszentrale für Politische Bildung, 1991), 53.
33 This has not been noted in any study on Bergen-Belsen of which I am aware. Indeed, men from the 1st Canadian Parachute Battalion entered the camp on 15 April 1945, providing medical assistance and food to the inmates. "Canadians are never mentioned at all," recalls a frustrated Ronald Ford Anderson of the battalion's encounter with the camp. "[This was] the first entry into Bergen Belsen and it was done by ... the First Canadian Paratroop Battalion ... we were a lone battalion enveloped in the second British Army and there's never been any mention of it." See Historica Dominion Institute, Ronald Andy Anderson interview (1 November 2011).
34 Kemp, "The Liberation of Bergen-Belsen Concentration Camp in April 1945: The Testimony of Those Involved," 30–1.
35 WO 171/4306, War Diary, 3rd Parachute Brigade.
36 Ben Shephard, *After Daybreak: The Liberation of Bergen-Belsen, 1945* (New York: Schocken, 2005), 32. For additional information on the Hungarians who worked at Bergen-Belsen, see Cecil D. Eby, *Hungary at War: Civilians and Soldiers in World War II* (University Park: Pennsylvania State University Press, 1998).
37 Kemp, "The Liberation of Bergen-Belsen Concentration Camp in April 1945: The Testimony of Those Involved," 31.
38 Ibid., 41. See Imperial War Museum (hereafter IWM), Department of Documents, 85/9/1.

39 Robert B.T. Daniell, *Journal of a Horse Gunner: India to the Baltic via Alamein*, IWM, 67/429/1
40 Tony Kushner, David Cesarani, Jo Reilly, and Colin Richmond, "Approaching Belsen: An Introduction," in *Belsen in History and Memory*, ed. Jo Reilly, David Cesarani, Tony Kushner, and Colin Richmond (London: Frank Cass, 1997), 7–8.
41 "Bergen-Belsen Death Camp Did Not Have Gas Chambers," *Toronto Star*, 20 September 2007.
42 Paul Kemp, "The British Army and the Liberation of Bergen-Belsen, April 1945," 135.
43 IWM, 29966, interview with John Randall (March 2002).
44 "Introducing the 'Cookie Pusher' of the Montreal St. Andrew Society," *Journal of the St. Andrew's Society of Montreal* (Fall 1993): 2.
45 For MacLellan's recognition in Washington at the 1981 International Liberators Conference, see *The Liberation of the Nazi Concentration Camps 1945: Eyewitness Accounts of the Liberators*, ed. Brewster Chamberlin, Marcia Feldman, and Robert Abzug (Washington: United States Holocaust Memorial Council, 1987); for his acknowledgement by the Canadian Jewish Congress, see "Keith MacLellan Honored for Wartime Services," *Suburban*, 2 November 1988, A.26. It is possible that Alan Rose, executive vice-president of the Canadian Jewish Congress, who entered Bergen-Belsen shortly after MacLellan with the 7th Armoured Division, made sure that the ever-modest MacLellan was recognized for his wartime contributions. A special thank-you to Dr Keith MacLellan, as well as to Anne-Marie and Andrew MacLellan for additional details.
46 WO 171/4773, Report on Belsen Camp by Lt-Col. R.I.G. Taylor, 2.
47 National Army Museum, 1994-06-201: Report on Conc. Camp, Belsen (15 April 1945). Captain Gray writes that "[Major] Tonkin, Patrol [Officer] and four members [of the] SAS entered the camp, and with some difficulty found their man who is Jenkinson, naturalised Frenchman … captured while in French Army 1940, escaped [in] 1941 and reached England … joined Special-or Auxiliary-Forces, landed in France by Lysander, captured by Gestapo, 11 Nov. 43, the day before he was due to return to England and has since spent 15 months in various [concentration] camps … Bona fides checked by [Major] Tonkin who dropped in [the] same area and vouches for his knowledge of local places and FFI personalities … Patrol [Officer] left area, with Jenkinson, [approximately] 2000 hrs." For an additional description of the removal of Jenkinson by the SAS see F.R. Waldron, "An M.O.H. with Second Army," *Public Health* (May 1947): 158.
48 RAMC 1103, *An Account of the Operations of Second Army in Europe, 1944–1945*, compiled by Headquarters Second Army (Volume II), 376.

49 Derrick Sington, *Belsen Uncovered* (London: Duckworth, 1946), 7–11.
50 National Army Museum, 1994-06-201, Report on Conc. Camp, Belsen (15 April 1945).
51 F.A.E. Crew, *The Army Medical Services: Northwest Europe* (London: Her Majesty's Stationary Office, 1962), 4:484.
52 *Bitburg and Beyond: Encounters in American, German and Jewish History*, ed. Ilya Levkov (New York: Shapolsky, 1987), 686.
53 United States Holocaust Memorial Museum, RG-50.234*0024, oral history interview with Alan Rose.
54 For general descriptions see: Daniel R. Hartigan, *A Rising Courage* (Calgary: Drop Zone, 2000), 1; and *Victory from Above: The 1st Canadian Parachute Battalion* (Koch International, 2002), 88 minutes, DVD.
55 WO 177/360, War Diary, A.D.M.S. 6 Airborne Division (also see Appendix A and D). In addition, the 224 Field Ambulance was later instructed to send a surgeon, Major H. Daintree-Johnson, to Bergen-Belsen. See Howard N. Cole, *On Wings of Healing: The Story of the Airborne Medical Services, 1940–1960* (Edinburgh: William Blackwood and Sons, 1963), 177. My thanks to David Johnson for additional details about H. Daintree-Johnson.
56 "Paratrooper Remembered on Banff Avenue," *Banff Crag and Canyon*, 10 November 2009, 7.
57 Reilly, *Belsen*, 27.
58 As quoted in Major L.F. Ellis, *Victory in the West: The Defeat of Germany* (London: Her Majesty's Stationary Office, 1968), 2:421.
59 WO 171/7950, War Diary, 224 Military Government Detachment.
60 WO 219/3944A, Report on visit to Belsen Concentration Camp, 12A. I have discussed Proskie's involvement at Bergen-Belsen in greater detail in an interview with CBC Radio. See Mark Celinscak, "John Proskie's Story," an interview with Kim Trynacity, Radio Active, CBC Edmonton (26 October 2011). My thanks to the University of Alberta's Donna McKinnon and the CBC's Kevin Wilson for arranging the interview.
61 WO 171/8095, War Diary, 904 Military Government Detachment.
62 WO 171/8035, War Diary, 618 Military Government Detachment.
63 RAMC 1103, *An Account of the Operations of Second Army in Europe, 1944–1945*, 418.
64 *Holocaust and the Moving Image: Representations in Film and Television since 1933*, ed. Toby Haggith and Joanna Newman (London: Wallflower, 2005), 33.
65 Operations Record Book, No. 5 Mobile Field Photographic Section, RCAF, 3–4 May 1945.
66 The two official war artists from Britain were Leslie Cole and Mary Kessell. Eric Taylor sold some of his work to the War Artists' Advisory Committee (WAAC), while Doris Zinkeisen was commissioned by the Red Cross and

St John War Organisation. My thanks to Ulrike Smalley, former curator at the Imperial War Museum's Department of Art, for these details regarding the British war artists. The three official war artists from Canada were Alex Colville, Donald Anderson, and Aba Bayefsky. Of the three, only Colville was given official permission to enter the camp. Bayefsky and Anderson went along with groups of RCAF airmen who assisted at the camp.

67 Library and Archives Canada, R2111–0-5-E, MG 30, D292, Progress Report by LT D.A. Colville.
68 Laura Brandon, "Reflections on the Holocaust: The Holocaust Art of Aba Bayefsky," *Canadian Military History* 6, no. 2 (Autumn 1997): 67.
69 Mary Kessell, "German Diary, August-October 1945," IWM, Department of Documents.
70 Additional artists also entered the camp. From Britain were Mervyn Peake, who entered on 20 June, as well as Edgar Ainsworth, Polish-born Feliks Topolski, and Bryan de Grineau. From Canada was H.S. Abramson from the 39 Reconnaissance Wing, RCAF. In addition, Canada's first female official war artist and the only one to be sent overseas, Molly Lamb (later Bobak), visited Bergen-Belsen in the months after the camp's surrender but did not depict it.
71 Shephard, *After Daybreak*, 87.
72 WO 222/201, Account given to the Royal Society of Medicine by Lieut-Colonel J.A.D. Johnston, R.A.M.C.
73 RAMC 1103, *An Account of the Operations of Second Army in Europe, 1944–1945*, 421.
74 WO 177/1257, War Diary, 29 (Br.) General Hospital.
75 J.A.D. Johnston, "The Relief of Belsen Concentration Camp. Recollections and Reflections of a British Army Doctor," Rosenstaft Papers, United States Holocaust Memorial Museum, 12.
76 As noted in Shephard, *After Daybreak*, 115.
77 Susan Armstrong-Reid and David Murray, *Armies of Peace: Canada and the UNRRA Years* (Toronto: University of Toronto Press, 2008), 275.
78 Ibid., 278.
79 Operations Record Book, 437 Squadron, RCAF, April 1945.
80 *Official History of the Canadian Medical Services, 1939–1945: Organization and Campaigns*, ed. W.R. Feasby (Ottawa: Queen's Printer and Controller of Stationary, 1956), 1:293.
81 "Report of Activities of R.C.A.F. Nutrition Group Detached to S.H.A.E.F." (25 June 1945), John McCreary fonds, University of British Columbia, p. 2.
82 Leslie Hardman and Cecily Goodman, *The Survivors: The Story of the Belsen Remnant* (London: Valentine Mitchell, 1958; 2009), 46–7.
83 Operations Record Book, no. 126 Wing, RCAF, April-May 1945.

84 Leo Velleman, "Belsen," in *Flap: 39 Reconnaissance Wing* (Hamburg: Vollmer and Bentlin KG, 1945), n.p.
85 Operations Record Book, no. 440 Squadron, May 1945.
86 WO 171/5290, War Diary, 4th Battalion, Wiltshire Regiment, June 1945.
87 *The Maroon Square: A History of the 4th Battalion, The Wiltshire Regiment*, comp. A.D. Parsons, D.I.M. Robbins, and D.C. Gilson (London: Franley, 1955), 198.
88 Wilfred I. Smith, *Experiences of a CANLOAN Officer, 1944–1945* (Ottawa: Public Archives, 1977), 6. Born in Port La Tour, Nova Scotia in 1919, Wilfred I. Smith obtained a PhD (History) from the University of Minnesota after the war. From 1970 to 1984 he was Dominion Archivist at the Public Archives of Canada (now Library and Archives Canada). He is also the author of *Code Word CANLOAN* (Toronto: Dundurn, 1992), a history of Canadian officers who served in the British Army during the Second World War. Regarding Bergen-Belsen, Smith quotes from some of his own wartime letters to his parents. However, the letters are not accurately quoted in the book. A number of revisions and omissions are evident. In particular, see the letter dated 29 July 1945. Library and Archives Canada, MG 31, E 96, Wilfred I. Smith Fonds, volume 24.
89 Air Ministry (AIR) 55/169, Historical Record of Disarmament 84 Group, p. 8.
90 Paul Weindling, "Belsenitis: Liberating Belsen, Its Hospitals, UNRRA, and Selection for Re-emigration, 1945–1948," *Science in Context* 19, no. 3 (2006): 403.
91 Ulf Zander, "To Rescue or Be Rescued: The Liberation of Bergen-Belsen and the White Buses in British and Swedish Historical Cultures," in *The Holocaust on Post-war Battlefields: Genocide as Historical Culture*, ed. Klas-Göran Karlsson and Ulf Zander (Malmö: Sekel, 2006), 345.
92 Ibid.
93 David Cesarani, "A Brief History of Bergen-Belsen," in *Belsen 1945: New Historical Perspectives*, ed. Suzanne Bardgett and David Cesarani (Edgware: Vallentine Mitchell, 2006), 6.
94 Eberhard Kolb,. *Bergen-Belsen: From "Detention Camp" to Concentration Camp, 1943–1945* (Göttingen: Vandenhoeck and Ruprecht, 1986), 136.
95 Shephard, *After Daybreak*, 201–2.
96 The testimony of survivor Esther Brunstein, as quoted from *Belsen in History and Memory*, 214.

3 The Distance of Presence

1 *Victory from Above: The 1st Canadian Parachute Battalion* (Koch International, 2002), 88 minutes, DVD.
2 Douglas Paybody, "The Liberator," *Observer*, 9 January 2005.

3 Tony Kushner, "Different Worlds: British Perceptions of the Final Solution during the Second World War," in *The Final Solution: Origins and Implementations*, ed. David Cesarani (London: Routledge, 1996), 249.
4 David Cesarani, "Great Britain," in *The World Reacts to the Holocaust*, ed. David S. Wyman (Baltimore: Johns Hopkins University Press, 1996), 605.
5 Richard Breitman, *Official Secrets: What the Nazis Planned, What the British and Americans Knew* (New York: Hill and Wang, 1998), 89.
6 Ibid., 91.
7 Michael Smith, "Bletchley Park and the Holocaust," in *Understanding Intelligence in the Twenty-First Century*, ed. L.V. Scott and P.D. Jackson (London: Routledge, 2004), 112.
8 As quoted in Martin Gilbert, *The Holocaust: The Jewish Tragedy* (London: Collins, 1986), 186.
9 Martin Gilbert, *Churchill and the Jews* (Toronto: McClelland and Stewart, 2007), 186; and Michael Smith, "Bletchley Park and the Holocaust," 118.
10 For many years it was believed that Karski had been smuggled into the Bełżec extermination camp. As scholars and even Karski himself came to realize, this is unlikely. His descriptions more closely match the brutal Izbica Lubelska transit camp, which was situated relatively close to the Bełżec extermination camp. For further details see E. Thomas Wood and Stanisław M. Jankowski, *Karski: How One Man Tried to Stop the Holocaust* (New York: J. Wiley and Sons, 1994), 128–32.
11 Doris L. Bergen, *War and Genocide: A Concise History of the Holocaust* (Lanham, MD: Rowman and Littlefield, 2003), 195.
12 See "Jan Karski to Speak," *Montreal Gazette*, 5 December 1944, 4; "Nazi Underground Seen Future Evil," *Montreal Gazette* (18 November 1944), 19; and "Nazi Underground to Be Best of All," *Regina Leader-Post*, 18 November 1944, 16.
13 Bergen, *War and Genocide*, 195.
14 Irving Abella and Franklin Bialystok, "Canada," in *The World Reacts to the Holocaust*, ed. David S. Wyman (Baltimore: Johns Hopkins University Press, 1996), 757.
15 *The Topography of the Bergen-Belsen Camp: Six Maps*, ed. Monica Gödeck (Stuttgart: Druck and Design, 2008), 3.
16 Walter Laqueur, *The Terrible Secret: An Investigation into the Suppression of Information about Hitler's Final Solution* (New York: Henry Holt, 1998), 204.
17 Ibid., 99.
18 James J. Barnes and Patience P. Barnes, *Nazi Refugee Turned Gestapo Spy: The Life of Hans Wesemann, 1895–1971* (Westport, CT: Praeger, 2001), 33–5.

19 "German Appeals for Germany," *Windsor Daily Star*, 3 February 1943, 2.
20 Cesarani, "Great Britain," 606.
21 Ibid.
22 Ibid.
23 Kushner, "Different Worlds," 253.
24 Irving Abella and Harold Troper, *None Is Too Many* (Toronto: Lester and Orpen Dennys, 1982), 164.
25 David Goutor, "The Canadian Media and the 'Discovery' of the Holocaust, 1944–1945," *Canadian Jewish Studies* 4–5 (1996–7): 92.
26 Cesarani, "Great Britain," 608.
27 Victor Gollancz, *Let My People Go* (London: Victor Gollancz, 1943), 1.
28 *Debates: Official Reports*, Canada, Parliament, House of Commons, vol. 5 (Ottawa: Queen's Printer, 1944), 4606.
29 Victor Gollancz, *The Yellow Spot: The Extermination of the Jews of Germany* (London: Victor Gollancz, 1936).
30 Goutor, "Canadian Media," 93.
31 Cesarani, "Great Britain," 609.
32 Goutor, "Canadian Media," 95.
33 Anna Louise Strong, "Mass Murder!" *Maclean's*, 1 September 1944, 11.
34 Barbie Zelizer, *Remembering to Forget: Holocaust Memory through the Camera's Eye* (Chicago: University of Chicago Press, 1998), 50.
35 As quoted in Harry Gutkin, *The Worst of Times, The Best of Times* (Markham, ON: Fitzhenry and Whiteside, 1987), 74–5. In April 1945, Maurice Victor was attached to the 1st Headquarters Army Group, Corps of the Royal Canadian Engineers. He was later posted to the No. 12 Field Dressing Station. My thanks to Dr Benjamin Victor, University of Montreal, for additional information.
36 Ibid., 75.
37 Ibid.
38 Alan Rose, "Transcript of Interview with the Holocaust Documentation Project," SV257-SV259, 17 March 1982, Canadian Jewish Congress Records, CJCCC National Archives, 2.
39 Ibid., 5.
40 Ibid., 5–6.
41 Gavin Mortimer, *Stirling's Men* (London: Cassell, 2004), 101.
42 Imperial War Museum, 18175, interview with John Gourlay Noble (1987-03-07).
43 Ibid.
44 As quoted in Frances Kraft, "Survivors Pass 'Torch of Remembrance,'" *Canadian Jewish News*, 6 May 2005.

45 Peter Novick, *The Holocaust and the Collective Memory: The American Experience* (London: Bloomsbury, 2001), 20.
46 Weiner Library, 01623, Belsen Concentration Camp Report, Appendix B, by Glyn Hughes.
47 Daniel R. Hartigan, *A Rising Courage: Canada's Paratroopers in the Liberation of Normandy* (Calgary: Dropzone, 2000), 1.
48 IWM, 13408, Private Papers of O.G. Prosser (05/2/1), 1.
49 I have shared correspondence, via letter, telephone, and email, with numerous men who served with the 1st Canadian Parachute Battalion. Every single man I communicated with remembered the putrid smell, and described it quite vividly, despite the fact that more than seventy years had passed.
50 As quoted in Gordon Stevens, *The Originals: The Secret History of the Birth of the SAS* (London: Ebury, 2005), 297.
51 USC Shoah Foundation Institute, 39023, interview with Mervin Mirsky (22 February 1998).
52 Trygg Engen, *Odor Sensation and Memory* (New York: Praeger, 1991), 81.
53 Ibid., 82.
54 As quoted in Alexander van Straubenzee, "The Stench of Death," *Spectator*, 9 April 2005.
55 Douglas Paybody, "The Liberator," *Observer*, 9 January 2005.
56 Engen, *Odor Sensation*, 86.
57 Ibid., 87.
58 J.A.D. Johnston, "The Relief of Belsen Concentration Camp. Recollections and Reflections of a British Army Doctor," Rosenstaft Papers, United States Holocaust Memorial Museum, p. 5.
59 Alan Rose, "Transcript of Interview with the Holocaust Documentation Project," SV257–SV259, 17 March 1982, Canadian Jewish Congress Records, CJCCC National Archives, p. 16.
60 Derrick Sington, *Belsen Uncovered* (London: Duckworth, 1946), 15–16.
61 IWM, 3713, Private Papers of M.W. Gonin (85/38/1), 5.
62 Ibid.
63 David Rousset, *L'univers concentrationnaire* (Paris: Éditions de Pavois, 1946). Trans.: "The concentrationary universe."
64 As quoted in Gutkin, *The Worst of Times*, 76–7.
65 Hopkinson letter as quoted in Laidlaw Family, Private Collection, Memoir of Ron Laidlaw, RCAF, Public Relations Office, 29. My thanks to Fred Hopkinson Jr for his assistance. A special thank-you to Major Mathias Joost and Mr Warren Sinclair of the Department of National Defence for their guidance regarding the images of Bergen-Belsen taken by Ron Laidlaw, RCAF.

66 As quoted in *Trial of Josef Kramer and Forty-Four Others*, ed. Raymond Phillips (London: William Hodge, 1949), 31.
67 Weiner Library, 01623, Belsen Concentration Camp Report, Appendix B, by Glyn Hughes.
68 Sington, *Belsen Uncovered*, 46.
69 George M. Kren Leon Rappoport, *The Holocaust and the Crisis of Human Behavior* (New York: Holmes and Meier, 1980), 125.
70 Leslie H. Hardman and Cecily Goodman, *The Survivors: The Story of the Belsen Remnant* (London: Vallentine Mitchell, 1958; 2009), 2.
71 The late Patrick Costigan was honoured by his family when they dedicated a building in his name in Banff, Alberta. The building, at 94 Banff Avenue, is where Costigan ran his medical practice after the war. A plaque has been installed on a pillar outside the building that notes his war service, including his time spent working in Bergen-Belsen. See "Paratrooper Remembered on Banff Avenue," *Banff Crag & Canyon*, 10 November 2009, 7.
72 "Even Parachutists Lacking Limbs 'Full of Fight.'" This article is from the family's personal collection and it is missing a date and the name of the newspaper (definitely from July 1945 and likely an Alberta paper).
73 "Stettler Doctor Returns to Describe Crossing of Rhine with Paratroopers," *Edmonton Journal*, 4 July 1945, 5.
74 Ibid.
75 Paul Weindling, "Belsenitis: Liberating Belsen, Its Hospitals, UNRRA, and Selection for Re-emigration, 1945–1948," *Science in Context* 19, no. 3 (2006): 403.
76 Jonah Jones, *The Gallipoli Diary* (Bridgend: Seren, 1989), 38.
77 Ibid.
78 Toby Haggith, "Filming the Liberation of Bergen-Belsen" in *Holocaust and the Moving Image*, ed. Toby Haggith and Joanna Newman (London: Wallflower, 2005), 38.
79 As he was providing much-needed medical aid, Captain Costigan worked closely with numerous survivors. While assisting one particular individual, Costigan presented his soda crackers. His offer was initially refused. The survivor insisted on exchanging the crackers for a ring featuring a black hematite gemstone that had been smuggled into the camp. Recognizing that this was an act to uphold dignity, Costigan made the trade. The ring was kept in memory of both that terrible day and that remarkable act. It remains with Costigan's children. My sincere thanks to the Costigan family for sharing this story with me.
80 George Lakoff and Mark Johnson, *Metaphors We Live By* (Chicago: University of Chicago Press, 1980), 4.

81 Sington, *Belsen Uncovered*, 16.
82 Ibid., 17.
83 Ibid., 23.
84 Ibid., 49–50.
85 *Anthropomorphism, Anecdotes, and Animals*, ed. Robert W. Mitchell, Nicholas S. Thompson, and H. Lyn Miles (Albany: State University of New York Press, 1997), 57.
86 Wendy Doniger, "Zoomorphism in Ancient India: Humans More Bestial Than the Beasts," in *Thinking with Animals: New Perspectives on Anthropomorphism*, ed. Lorraine Datson and Greg Mitman (New York: Columbia University Press, 2005), 17.
87 James Greary, *I Is an Other: The Secret Life of Metaphor and How It Shapes the Way We See the World* (New York: HarperCollins, 2011), 224–5.
88 Robert Palmatier, *Speaking of Animals: A Dictionary of Animal Metaphors* (Westport, CT: Greenwood, 1995), 7 and 257.
89 Wendy Doniger, "Epilogue: Making Animals Vanish," in *Animals and the Human Imagination: A Companion to Animal Studies*, ed. Aaron Gross and Anne Vallely (New York: Columbia University Press, 2012), 351.
90 Ibid.
91 Johnston, "Relief of Belsen Concentration Camp," 4.
92 National Army Museum, 1994-06-201, Report on Conc. Camp, Belsen (15 April 1945), pp. 4–5.
93 IWM, 9161, Private Papers of J. Grant (99/82/1).
94 Palmatier, *Speaking of Animals*, 5.
95 Robert H. Abzug, "The Liberation of the Concentration Camps," in *Liberation 1945*, ed. Susan D. Bachrach (New York: United States Holocaust Memorial Council, 1995), 41.
96 Hagit Lavsky, *New Beginnings: Holocaust Survivors in Bergen-Belsen and the British Zone in Germany, 1945–1950* (Detroit: Wayne State University Press, 2002), 56.
97 Ben Shephard, *After Daybreak: The Liberation of Bergen-Belsen, 1945* (New York: Schocken, 2005), 68.
98 Joanne Reilly, *Belsen: The Liberation of a Concentration Camp* (London: Routledge, 1998), 45 and 185.
99 Hardman and Goodman, *The Survivors*, 10.
100 Ibid., 14.
101 Ibid., 17.
102 Leo Heaps, *Escape from Arnhem: A Canadian among the Lost Paratroops* (Toronto: Macmillan, 1945), 157.
103 Ibid., 153–4.

104 George Lakoff and Mark Turner, *More Than Cool Reason: A Field Guide to Poetic Metaphor* (Chicago: University of Chicago Press, 1989). For their discussion on the Great Chain of Being metaphor see ch. 4, 160–213.
105 IWM 11561, Private Papers of TJ Stretch (01/30/1)
106 "23,000 Hungry at Belsen Fed by Canadian Expert," *Toronto Daily Star*, 18 July 1945, 24. After the war, in 1946, Proskie was given a contract with the British Foreign Office, where he helped organize and administer the supply and distribution of food for the Berlin Airlift. After Proskie passed away in 1993, his sister, Rosalie Rector, established the John Proskie Memorial Scholarship in 1994 at the University of Alberta and the University of Ottawa. The scholarship provides financial assistance and encouragement to graduate students studying in the area of agricultural economics. It continues to be offered to students at both schools. My thanks to Donna McKinnon and Ken Crocker at the University of Alberta for this information.
107 WO 219/3944A, Report on visit to Belsen Camp by ADMG Sups, 22 April 1945.
108 WO 219/3944A, "Belsen Concentration Camp" by J. Proskie, 22 April 1945.
109 Ibid.
110 Liddell Hart Centre for Military Archives, GB 0099 KCLMA, Barnett Papers.
111 Hartigan, *A Rising Courage*, 259.
112 My thanks to Klaus Tätzler, Department of Research and Documentation, Gedenkstätte Bergen-Belsen, for this information.
113 As noted in van Straubenzee, "The Stench of Death." This incident was also recounted in Mortimer's *Stirling's Men*, 324.
114 As quoted in Stevens, *The Originals*, 297.
115 IWM 3056, Private Papers of E. Fisher (95/2/1).
116 Army Medical Services Museum: Belsen Concentration Camp Report by Major R.F. Waldon (1 May 1945).
117 Liddell Hart Centre for Military Archives, GB 0099 KCLMA: Barnett Papers and Sington, 32.
118 Heaps, *Escape from Arnhem*, 155–6.
119 Ibid., 158.
120 IWM 11561.
121 National Army Museum, 1994-06-201, Report on Conc. Camp, Belsen (15 April 1945).
122 "Stettler Doctor Returns to Describe Crossing of Rhine with Paratroopers," *Edmonton Journal*, 4 July 1945, 5.

216 Notes to pages 71–8

123 IWM 11561.
124 Ibid.
125 Shaaron Cosner and Victoria Cosner, *Women under the Third Reich: A Biographical Dictionary* (Westport, CT: Greenwood, 1998), 62.
126 See "The End of Belsen?" *Time*, 11 June 1945, 36. Also see "Study in Evil: The SS Women of Belsen," *Daily Mail*, 23 April 1945, 3.
127 For example, see Heaps, *Escape from Arnhem*, 158; WO 171/4773, Lt-Col. Taylor, DSO, MC, Report, April 1945. Also see "Mass Murderess: Woman Leader of Nazi Guards at Belsen Camp Sets Record for Evil," *Life*, 8 October 1945, 40.
128 Tony Kushner, "The Memory of Belsen," in *Belsen in History and Memory*, 187.
129 Reilly, *Belsen*, 2.
130 IWM 11561.
131 WO 171/4773, Lt-Col. Taylor, DSO, MC, Report, April 1945. According to Taylor, the majority of records had been destroyed on instruction from Berlin prior to the arrival of the Allies.
132 Toby Haggith, "The Filming of the Liberation of Bergen-Belsen and Its Impact on the Understanding of the Holocaust," in *Belsen 1945: New Historical Perspectives*, 109.
133 IWM 11561.
134 National Army Museum, 1994-06-201, Report on Conc. Camp, Belsen (15 April 1945).
135 WO 219/3944A, "Belsen Concentration Camp" by J. Proskie, 22 April 1945.
136 Hardman and Goodman, *The Survivors*, 1.
137 Sington, *Belsen Uncovered*, 47.
138 Liddell Hart Centre for Military Archives, GB 0099 KCLMA, Barnett Papers.
139 R.K. Cameron, "Belsen Concentration Camp: An Eye-Witness Account of an R.C.A.F. Padre," *Front Line* 7, no. 11 (November 1946): 5.
140 Reilly, *Belsen*, 31.
141 A.L. Berney, "The Liberation of Belsen Concentration Camp," BBC, *WW2 People's War* (8 June 2004), http://www.bbc.co.uk/history/ww2peopleswar/user/83/u747283.shtml.

4 A Camp on Exhibit

1 As quoted in Nigel Hamilton, *Monty: Final Years of the Field Marshal, 1944-1976* (New York: McGraw-Hill, 1986), 496. Bernard Montgomery letter to Phyllis Reynolds (29 April 1945), Montgomery Papers, Imperial War Museum, Department of Documents.

2 WO 219/3944A, 21 Army Group: Report on Relief Measures at Belsen (18–30 April 1945).
3 Jeffrey Williams, *Far from Home: A Memoir of a Twentieth-Century Soldier* (Calgary: University of Calgary Press, 2003), 259.
4 WO 219/3944A, 21 Army Group: Report on Relief Measures at Belsen.
5 James E. Young, "Interpreting Literary Testimony: A Preface to Rereading Holocaust Diaries and Memoirs," *New Literary History* 18, no. 2 (Winter 1987): 420.
6 Robert Jay Lifton, *Death in Life: Survivors of Hiroshima* (New York: Random House, 1968), 15.
7 IWM Sound Archives, 11903, interview with Alexander Smith Allan (1991-03-04); italics mine.
8 Ibid.
9 See Julia Kristeva, *Powers of Horror: An Essay on Abjection*, trans. Leon S. Roudiez (New York: Columbia University Press, 1980; 1982).
10 Ibid., 3.
11 Giorgio Agamben, *Remnants of Auschwitz: The Witness and the Archive*, trans. Daniel Heller-Roazen (New York: Zone, 1999), 107.
12 Kristeva, *Powers of Horror*, 4.
13 Ibid.
14 Ibid., 109.
15 Ibid., 2.
16 There are cases of Allied personnel retching and vomiting while in the camp; consequently, some were unable or unwilling to pass through the front gates. For instance, Royal Canadian Air Force mechanic Harry Saltsman recalls travelling to Bergen-Belsen with his brother, future member of Parliament, Max. Harry reveals that after seeing the inmates "in such a deplorable physical state ... I felt faint and was physically sick by the roadside so that I had to sit down." He decided he could go no farther. See Amanda Roberts, "The Saltsman Letters," *Muskoka Times* (ca March 2000). This article first appeared online. My thanks to Amanda Roberts for passing along her article and for sharing her memories of the Saltsman brothers. For other examples, see Ben Shephard, *After Daybreak: The Liberation of Bergen-Belsen, 1945* (New York: Schocken, 2005), 227. Also see Wayne Ralph, *Aces, Warriors and Wingmen: The Firsthand Accounts of Canada's Fighter Pilots in the Second World War* (Mississauga, ON: Wiley, 2005), 199.
17 As quoted in *Remembering Belsen: Eyewitnesses Record the Liberation*, ed. Ben Flanagan and Donald Bloxham (London: Vallentine Mitchell, 2005), 118.
18 Kristeva, *Powers of Horror*, 38.

19 Sylvia Mayer, "American Environmentalism and Encounters with the Abject: T. Coraghessan Boyle's A Friend of the Earth," in *The Abject of Desire: The Aestheticization of the Unaesthetic in Contemporary Literature and Culture*, ed. Konstanze Kutzbach and Monika Mueller (New York: Rodopi, 2007), 222.
20 Kristeva, *Powers of Horror*, 145.
21 Canadian Jewish Congress Charities Committee National Archives, P02/04/6, Gordon George Earle photographs. My thanks to William Earle for additional details.
22 Vancouver Holocaust Centre, Peter Gorst photographs.
23 University of South California's Shoah Foundation Institute, 48192, Larry Mann interview (10 November 1998). Born Louis Libman, he changed his name after the war to Larry D. Mann and became a noted broadcaster, actor, and voice personality.
24 Ibid.
25 IWM Sound Archives, 8253, interview with Richard Leatherbarrow (July 1984).
26 IWM Sound Archive, 7481, interview with William Lawrie (April 1984).
27 George M. Kren Leon Rappoport, *The Holocaust and the Crisis of Human Behavior* (New York: Holmes and Meier, 1980), 18.
28 Ibid.
29 Nesbitt's original name was Max Nezgoraski, which was later shortened to Max Nezgor. His parents, Russian Jews, emigrated from Odessa to Canada at the turn of the twentieth century. Some of Nesbitt's numerous interviews include: Emory University, Special Collections, Woodruff Library, Matthew Nesbitt interview (7 August 1980); as well as box 25, reel 13, William Ned Cartledge and Matthew Nesbitt (4/21/81), series VII – "Witness to the Holocaust" Television Series, Fred Roberts Crawford Witness to the Holocaust Project. Additional interviews with Nesbitt include: USC Shoah Foundation Institute, 28524, interview with Matthew Nesbitt (15 April 1997). Nesbitt also gave a lengthy presentation at the Atlanta World War II Round Table (15 January 1987), as well as an interview with WGST Radio in Atlanta (18 April 1987). My thanks to those individuals who shared with me their memories of Mr Nesbitt, including Dr David Blumenthal, Ms Terry Anderson, Mrs Jackie Metzal, Mr John Kovac, as well as Mr and Mrs Doug and Mary Wilmer.
30 USC Shoah Foundation Institute, 28524, interview with Matthew Nesbitt (15 April 1997). A version of this story is also repeated in Nesbitt's interview with Emory University (7 August 1980) and in his presentation at the Atlanta World War II Round Table (15 January 1987).

31 See Paul Kemp, "The British Army and the Liberation of Bergen-Belsen, April 1945," in *Belsen in History and Memory*, ed. Jo Reilly, David Cesarani, Tony Kushner, and Colin Richmond (London: Frank Cass, 1997), 138.
32 From Nesbitt's presentation at the Atlanta World War II Round Table (15 January 1987).
33 Christopher Browning, *Ordinary Men: Reserve Police Battalion 101 and the Final Solution in Poland* (London: Penguin, 1992; 1998), 170.
34 Ibid., 171.
35 As quoted in *Trial of Josef Kramer and Forty-four Others: The Belsen Trial*, ed. Raymond Phillips (London: W. Hodge, 1949), 145.
36 Karl Jaspers, *The Question of German Guilt*, trans. E.B. Ashton (New York: Fordham University Press, 1947; 2001), 41.
37 Ibid., 25–6.
38 Ibid., 26.
39 For additional information on the Hungarians who worked at Bergen-Belsen, see Cecil D. Eby, *Hungary at War: Civilians and Soldiers in World War II* (University Park: Pennsylvania State University Press, 1998).
40 IWM Department of Documents, 3103, private papers of C.J. Charters.
41 IWM Sound Archives, 11903, interview with Alexander Smith Allan.
42 Glen Hancock, *Charley Goes to War* (Kentville: Gaspereau, 2004), 276–7. Readers should be aware that Mr Hancock's memoir is riddled with significant errors, particularly the chapter titled "The Horror of Belsen Death Camp." I assume that during his background research Mr Hancock confused the Bergen-Belsen concentration camp, which was located in northwest Germany, with details and facts relating to the Bełżec extermination camp, which was located in German-occupied eastern Poland.
43 Ibid., 281.
44 Patrick Gordon Walker, *Patrick Gordon Walker: Political Diaries, 1932–1971*, ed. Robert Pearce (London: Historians' Press 1991), 159.
45 Vancouver Holocaust Education Centre, HVT-3095, Stanley W. Winfield interview (14 November 1990)
46 Morris Janowitz, "German Reactions to Nazi Atrocities," *American Journal of Sociology* 52, no. 2 (September 1946): 141–6.
47 Ibid., 141, 143.
48 Montreal Holocaust Memorial Centre Archives, 2000.10.10, Saul Stein letter (30 April 1945).
49 Tzvetan Todorov, *Facing the Extreme: Moral Life in the Concentration Camps*, trans. Arthur Denner and Abigail Pollak (New York: Henry Holt, 1991; 1996), 123.

50 National Archives, AIR 55/169, Historical Record of Disarmament 84 Group (Part A), 9.
51 Stanley H. Winfield, "Ted Aplin – 'The Angel of Belsen,'" *Zachor* (Vancouver Holocaust Education Centre, May 1994), 5.
52 Among other acts, Aplin helped initiate a system using the armed forces postal service to help survivors contact family and friends outside of Germany. Aplin also assisted in organizing goods collected from Canadian families to be distributed at the camp. In addition, he arranged picnics in the countryside for the children of Bergen-Belsen with the British and Canadian airmen stationed nearby. Among those who attended these picnics were official war artist Mary Kessell and Margaret Wyndham Ward, an aid worker with the British Red Cross. Aplin frequently used air force vehicles from 84 Group for these activities, often without permission. He was threatened with a formal reprimand by his superiors due to a number of these actions. Ultimately, no punishment was issued. My sincerest thanks to Nick Aplin and Attila Clemann for their insight and support regarding the life and war experiences of Ted Aplin.
53 Clara Thomas Archives, York University, F0151, Aplin Family Fonds, Aplin letter to Lillian Sandler (17 June 1945). This particular letter has been published numerous times. For example, see *Battles Lines: Eyewitness Accounts from Canada's Military History*, ed. J.L. Granatstein and Norman Hillmer (Toronto: Thomas Allen, 2004), 379–83, as well as *Archives of the Holocaust*, vol. 15, ed. Paula Draper and Harold Troper (New York: Garland, 1991).
54 Jaspers, *Question of German Guilt*, 26.
55 Clara Thomas Archives, York University, F0151, Aplin Family Fonds, Aplin letter to Lillian Sandler.
56 Quote taken from the description of the "Sandler Gordon Bursary Fund" offered at Osgoode Hall Law School, York University, in Toronto.
57 Vancouver Holocaust Education Centre, HVT-3095, Stanley W. Winfield interview. Winfield wrote numerous letters overseas requesting assistance and advice regarding the situation at Bergen-Belsen, particularly in regards to the camp's orphaned children. He communicated with Canadian Padre Jack J. Eisen and Saul Hayes, national executive director of the Canadian Jewish Congress (via his uncle Harold Weinfeld, a prominent Montreal lawyer), to name a few.
58 As noted, Aplin is well known for his humanitarian efforts at Bergen-Belsen. See Robert Collins, "Angel of Belsen," *Reader's Digest*, November 1990, 69–73. The French version of this article can be found in the same publication in the January 1989 edition. In 2007 a production titled *And Stockings for the Ladies* premiered. The play recounts the experiences of

two Canadian airmen who assisted the survivors at Bergen-Belsen. Based on the letters of Ted Aplin, the award-winning *And Stockings for the Ladies* was written by Attila Clemann, directed by Zach Fraser, and starring Brendan McMurtry-Howlett. Since 2007, the play has had numerous runs across North America. In addition, Ted Aplin is also noted in Derrick Sington's *Belsen Uncovered* (London: Duckworth, 1946), 174, as well as Hetty Verlome's *The Children's House of Belsen* (London: Politico's, 2000; 2004), 247. However, in the latter, Verlome incorrectly calls Aplin a "Reverend" and suggests he entered the camp much earlier than he in fact did.

59 Clara Thomas Archives, York University, F0151, Aplin Family Fonds, Aplin letter to Lillian Sandler (17 June 1945).
60 Jürgen Habermas, "Learning from Catastrophes: A Look Back at the Short Twentieth Century," *The Postnational Constellation: Political Essays*, trans. and ed. Max Pensky (Cambridge, MA: MIT Press, 2001), 38–57.
61 "Interview with Allan [sic] Rose," in *Bitburg and Beyond: Encounters in American, German and Jewish History*, ed. Ilya Levkov (New York: Shapolsky, 1987), 681.
62 Ibid.
63 David Cesarani and Paul A. Levine, "Introduction," in *"Bystanders" to the Holocaust: A Reevaluation*, ed. David Cesarani and Paul A Levine (London: Frank Cass, 2002), 1.
64 Rose participated in video interviews and made speeches regarding his involvement at Bergen-Belsen. Aplin wrote about his experiences. For example, see E.M. Aplin, "I Saw Belsen ... My Conscience Cannot Wait," *Today: An Anglo-Jewish Monthly* 2, no. 5 (April 1946): 18–19, 38.
65 María Pía Lara, *Narrating Evil: A Postmetaphysical Theory of Reflective Judgment* (New York: Columbia University Press, 2007), 4.
66 Berel Lang, *Post-Holocaust: Interpretation, Misinterpretation, and the Claims of History* (Bloomington: Indiana University Press, 2005), 19.
67 For examples of inmates attacking Kapos and local citizenry see Joanne Reilly, *Belsen: The Liberation of a Concentration Camp* (London: Routledge, 1998), 152, 157.
68 See the following interviews held at the Imperial War Museum's Sound Archives, 18046: John Murdoch Cooper interview (1987); 29966, John Randall interview (2002–3).
69 IWM Department of Documents, 4101, private papers of W.J. Barclay (unaddressed letter dated 21 April 1945).
70 Montreal Holocaust Memorial Centre Archives, 2000.10.10, Saul Stein letter (30 April 1945).
71 Lang, *Post-Holocaust*, 20.

72 IWM Department of Documents, 4101, private papers of W J Barclay (unaddressed letter dated 21 April 1945).
73 Sean Longden, *To the Victor the Spoils* (Gloucestershire: Arris, 2004), 285.
74 Ibid.
75 King Whyte, *Letters Home, 1944–1946*, ed. Tanya Nanavati and Maureen Whyte (Toronto: Seraphim Editions, 1996), 55.
76 Ibid.
77 Ibid., 61.
78 Walker, *Political Diaries*, 160 (diary entry dated April 1945).
79 Along with their British counterparts, Canadians were also involved in the Bergen-Belsen war crimes investigation and trials. For example, Raymond Robichaud, of the No. 1 Canadian War Crimes Investigation Unit, was recruited by Lieutenant-Colonel Leopold John Genn to assist in the investigation of war crimes at Bergen-Belsen. Genn served with the Royal Artillery and commanded Britain's No. 1 War Crimes Investigation Team. He later became an assistant prosecutor at the Bergen-Belsen trial in Lüneburg, Germany. After the war Genn became a noted film and stage actor. For additional information on Robichaud, see Patrick Brode, *Casual Slaughters and Accidental Judgments: Canadian War Crimes Prosecutions, 1944–1948* (Toronto: University of Toronto Press, 1997). My thanks to Mr Brode for additional details.
80 See *Trial of Josef Kramer and Forty-Four Others: The Belsen Trial*, ed. Raymond Phillips (London: W. Hodge, 1949).
81 Walker, *Political Diaries*, 161.
82 Jaspers, *Question of German Guilt*, 26.
83 Walker, *Political Diaries*, 159.
84 Frederick Taylor, *Exorcising Hitler: The Occupation and Denazification of Germany* (London: Bloomsbury, 2011), 298. These individuals were Josef Kramer, Irma Grese, Franz Hössler, Dr Fritz Klein, Elisabeth Völkenrath, Peter Weingartner, Karl Francioh, Franz Stofel, Anchor Pichen, Wilhelm Dörr, and Juana Bormann.
85 As quoted in *Remembering Belsen: Eyewitnesses Record the Liberation*, 118.
86 For example, Kochane recalls nurses and various individuals arguing that the news about the atrocities committed by the Germans was likely English propaganda. In addition, in a letter Squadron Leader F.J. Lyons also discusses hearing people call the crimes propaganda. See IWM Department of Documents, 11135, private papers of Squadron Leader F.J. Lyons (Letter in question is dated 18 June 1945).
87 Ontario Jewish Archives, 45, H-24, Alex Pancer photographs (letter dated 15 May 1945).

88 Robert H. Abzug, *Inside the Vicious Heart* (New York: Oxford University Press, 1985; 1987), 128.
89 Larry D. Mann passed away on 6 January 2014. My thanks to his family for their support in writing this book.
90 University of South California's Shoah Foundation Institute, 48192, Larry Mann interview
91 For the Velleman article and Abramson painting see "Belsen," *Flap: 39 Reconnaissance Wing* (Hamburg: Vollmer & Bentlin KG, 1945), n.p. After the war, Velleman became an internationally renowned puppeteer, along with his wife Dora. My thanks to Susan Towers, Kathy Redford, Jamie Ashby, and David Smith for additional details about the life of Leo Velleman.
92 Monty Berger and Brian Jeffrey Street, *Invasions without Tears: The Story of Canada's Top Scoring Spitfire Wing in Europe during the Second World War* (Toronto: Random House of Canada, 1994), 204.
93 These figures were taken from *Canadian Jews in World War II*, ed. David Rome (Montreal: Canadian Jewish Congress, 1947).
94 Ibid., 209.
95 Archives of Ontario, B268404 – F1417, "Application for Duties with Military Government," by F/L G.R.B. Panchuk (24 September 1945).
96 Bohdan Panchuk, *Heroes of Their Day: The Reminiscences of Bohdan Panchuk*, ed. Lubomyr Y. Luciuk (Toronto: Multicultural History Society, Ontario Heritage Foundation, 1983), 87–8. In addition, a field trip organized by 21 Army Group and led by Colonel R.A. Lebon, Chief French Liaison Officer Displaced Persons (SHAEF), travelled to Bergen-Belsen in May 1945. According to a 21 Army Group report, "particular attention was focused on the French deportees, many of whom were interviewed by Col. Lebon concerning their treatment." See 2711/7.1 Displaced Persons Branch, "Field Trip 21 Army Group (3 May – 9 May 1945)," 12 May 1945, Record Group 331, Records of Allied Operational and Occupation Headquarters, World War II, 1907–1966, box 50, file G-5.
97 Testimony of B. Panchuk, Senate of Canada, *Proceedings of the Standing Committee on Immigration and Labour* (29 May 1946), 54. Unfortunately, any existing records accounting for the number of Ukrainian inmates at Bergen-Belsen are in poor condition. In addition, Ukrainian inmates would have been typically listed as either Russian or Soviet. Nevertheless, inmates from the Soviet Union comprised one of the largest group of inmates at Bergen-Belsen, and of that group many were indeed Ukrainian. My thanks to Bernd Horstmann, custodian for the Registry of Names of the Bergen-Belsen Concentration Camp Prisoners at the Research and Documentation Centre, Gedenkstätte Bergen-Belsen, for his assistance on this matter.

98 Wiener Library, 1368/2/2/27, "The Memories of Max Dickson, Formerly Max Dobriner" by Max Dickson, p. 13.
99 Ibid., 16.
100 IWM Department of Documents, 11135, private papers of Squadron Leader F.J. Lyons
101 For examples see Reilly, 66–67.
102 IWM Department of Documents, 11135: private papers of Squadron Leader F.J. Lyons (letter dated 18 June 1945).
103 As quoted in Pearl Sheffy Gefen, "Forty Years Ago as a Frail Israel Fought for Life Our War Heroes Said: 'Lean on Us,'" *Toronto Star*, 2 October 1988, D5.
104 As quoted in Sheldon Kirshner's "Canadian Pilot Witnessed Horrors of Bergen-Belsen," *Canadian Jewish News*, 20 January 2011, 16. My thanks to Brian and Mike MacConnell for additional details.
105 Ibid.
106 Samuel Hynes, *The Soldiers' Tale: Bearing Witness to Modern War* (New York: A. Lane, 1997), 259.
107 WGST Radio (Atlanta), Matthew Nesbitt interview (18 April 1987).
108 Laidlaw Family, Private Collection: Memoir of Ron Laidlaw, RCAF, Public Relations Office, 28. A special thank-you to Lillemor, Peter, and Christian Laidlaw for access to their father's papers and for their support. I also thank Brian Musson for his time, advice, and insight concerning 39 Wing and their encounter at Bergen-Belsen.
109 IWM Department of Documents, 3103, private papers of C.J. Charters (letter dated 15 May 1945).
110 Ibid.
111 USC Shoah Foundation Institute, 48192: Larry Mann interview (10 November 1998).
112 Ted Aplin wrote a moving piece about a seven-year-old girl named Bella, one of the children living at the displaced-persons camp at Bergen-Belsen who attended the Sunday picnics with the Canadian airmen. "Her English was fair and her German good," he writes. "Polish her mother tongue. With Yiddish and Hungarian that makes five languages – did you pick them all up in the camp? Oh yes, but why only five, 'Parlez-vous français?' That is Bella, only seven." See Vancouver Holocaust Education Centre, 96.024.010, the Stanley Winfield Collection. It seems likely that the girl in question is Bella Zajdner (sometimes spelled Bela Seidner), who was born in either 1937 or 1938 in Lodz, Poland. Her mother, Chaja, and father, Jakob, also had a daughter named Pola. See ITS Digitized Collections, USHMM, 0.1, "Central Names Index," Bella Zajdner,

64720044–64720057. My thanks to Ms Jo-Ellyn Decker of the United States Holocaust Memorial Museum for her assistance in locating the identity of Aplin's "Bella." In addition, Bella's older sister (Pola) gave an interview in 1946 while living in the displaced-persons' camp at Bergen-Belsen. See Ghetto Fighters' House Archives, Western Galilee, catalog no. 5595: Pola Zajdner: testimony in the Bergen-Belsen DP camp. A special thank-you to Mr Amos Gonen and Ms Pnina Lifshitz-Aviram for further details.

113 In his subject's official biography, John Coldstream, while not affirming it outright, certainly casts doubt on Bogarde's encounter with Bergen-Belsen, stating, "Nothing is certain." Moreover, in a review of the book, John Carey of the *Sunday Times* writes, "In fact, as John Coldstream showed in his 2004 biography of Bogarde, it is virtually impossible that he [Bogarde] saw Belsen or any other camp. Things he overheard or read seem to have entered his imagination and been mistaken for lived experience." See Coldstream's *Dirk Bogarde: The Authorised Biography* (London: Weidenfeld and Nicolson, 2004), 121–3. Also see John Carey, "*Ever, Dirk: The Bogarde Letters* selected and edited by John Coldstream," *Sunday Times*, 10 August 2008, 2. As this and other chapters have illustrated, a large number of men from the RCAF's 39 Reconnaissance Wing, to which Bogarde was attached, visited the camp in April and May 1945. The Wing's operations record book, its magazine – featuring an article and a painting – along with countless interviews with its personnel – including ones with Bogarde – repeatedly illustrate this fact. Thus, it seems that the overwhelming evidence suggests that Bogarde did encounter the Bergen-Belsen concentration camp near the end of the war. Indeed, in March 2015 John Coldstream reassessed Bogarde's claim that he visited Bergen-Belsen, stating "It is now possible to state with some authority that he did at least set foot inside the camp." See John Coldstream, "Dirk Bogarde and Belsen." Posted in March 2015 to DirkBogarde.co.uk, the official website of the Dirk Bogarde Estate: http://dirkbogarde.co.uk/dirk-bogarde-and-belsen/. My sincerest thanks to Mr Coldstream for taking the time to discuss this issue with me.

114 Dirk Bogarde, *Snakes and Ladders* (London: Chatto and Windus, 1978), 56.

115 Ibid.

116 As quoted in David A. Harris, *In the Trenches: Selected Speeches and Writings of an American Jewish Activist* (Hoboken: KTAV, 2000), 3:144. Furthermore, in *And Peace Never Came* (1997), Holocaust survivor Elisabeth M. Raab notes that any feelings of happiness about liberation never occurred. After being rescued by a group of Americans on her way to being sent to Bergen-Belsen, Raab explains: "A blankness, which is a wall between

me and my feelings, leaves me in despair. I want to call back something that has always been a part of me, but I find that its spot is empty. I have lost a part of myself. I want to cry but the tears won't come. An essential source, an affirmation of life, is gone. Finally I have to resign myself. I ... fall asleep without being able to grasp what freedom means to me." Raab recognizes her good fortune of no longer having to suffer at the hands of Nazi Germany, but she also cannot embrace the joy of her "liberation." See Elisabeth M. Raab, *And Peace Never Came* (Waterloo, ON: Wilfrid Laurier University Press, 1997), 67.
117 As quoted in Wayne Ralph, *Aces, Warriors and Wingmen: The Firsthand Accounts of Canada's Fighter Pilots in the Second World War* (Mississauga, ON: John Wiley and Sons Canada, 2005), 195. A version of this account can also be found in Hugh A. Halliday, *Typhoon and Tempest: The Canadian Story* (Toronto: CANAV, 1992), 162.
118 USC Shoah Foundation Institute, 48192, Larry Mann interview (10 November 1998).
119 Ibid.
120 Elie Wiesel, *The Jews of Silence: A Personal Report on Soviet Jewry*, trans. Neal Kozodoy (New York: Holt, Rinehart and Winston, 1966), 3.
121 Northrop Frye, *Anatomy of Criticism: Four Essays* (Princeton, NJ: Princeton University Press, 1957; 1990), 102.
122 Andrea Reiter, *Narrating the Holocaust*, trans. Patrick Camiller (London: Continuum, 1995; 2000), 171.
123 As quoted in *Legends: Dirk Bogarde Documentary*, prod. Trevor Hyett (Carleton Television, 2000).
124 As quoted in Ian Traynor, "Men Who Showed Belsen Hell to Britain Return," *Guardian*, 15 April 1995, 10.
125 Robert Burns, "Man Was Made to Mourn: A Dirge," *The Poems and Songs of Robert Burns: The Five Foot Shelf of Classics*, ed. Charles W. Eliot (New York: Cosimo Classics, 1909; 2009), 6:66; italics mine.
126 *Portraits of War*, prod. Paul Kemp, 48 minutes (Stornoway Productions, DVD, 2007).
127 For specific reference see Mann's USC interview and MacConnell's interview with the *Canadian Jewish News*. For Rodger's use of the term see his *Time* article, "Belsen," 30 April 1945, 40–1. Hardman's use of the term is in his *The Survivors*, 10.
128 John K. Roth, *Holocaust Politics* (Louisville: Westminster John Knox Press, 2001), 40.
129 Paul Ricoeur, *Time and Narrative*, trans. K. McLaughlin and D. Pellauer (Chicago: University of Chicago Press, 1983; 1984), 1:75.

130 "Rabbi Seeks Wartime 'Friends,'" *Montreal Gazette*, 15 December 1962, 3.
131 "Rabbi Finds Belsen Benefactor," *Windsor Star*, 20 December 1962, 1. Gordon McGregor was awarded the Croix de Guerre with Silver Star by the French government, made Commander in the Order of Orange-Nassau with Swords by the Dutch government, and received the War Cross from Czechoslovakia. He also received a Distinguished Flying Cross and was recognized by the Order of Canada and the Order of the British Empire. For additional details see George Brown and Michel Lavigne, *Canadian Wing Commanders of Fighter Command in World War II* (Langley: Battleline, 1984), 203–18.
132 USC Shoah Foundation Institute, 40440, Bernard Yale interview (14 April 1998).
133 For these examples, see Nesbitt's lecture at the Atlanta WWII Round Table (1987), as well as his USC interview (1997). For their comments about Zündel see Yale's USC interview (1998); Clifford Robb appeared on CFTO News on 25 March 1985. My thanks to Dave Robb for additional details. For Mirsky's confrontation with David Irving see Mervin Mirsky, "I Saw Holocaust Horrors in Person," *Ottawa Citizen*, 18 February 1998, A18.
134 Thompson Family, Private Collection, James Ernest Thompson interview with Nicky Saunders (from the private collection of the Thompson Family, Bowden, Alberta, 1999). My thanks to Donovan Brewster for additional details.
135 Thompson Family, Private Collection, flight logs for F/L Thompson, 437 Transport Squadron.
136 Thompson Family, Private Collection, James Ernest Thompson interview with Nicky Saunders (1999).
137 *Portraits of War*.
138 Ibid. However, in the film, *The Splendour of Order* (Montréal: National Film Board, 1993), Colville's wife, Rhoda, reveals that her husband suffered from nightmares about the experience of working in Bergen-Belsen.
139 As quoted in Kevin Griffin, "Holocaust Horrors Recalled," *Vancouver Sun*, 4 May 1995, B4. His story is also noted in Bronia Sonnenschein, *Victory over Nazism: A Holocaust Survivor's Journey*, ed. Dan Sonnenschein (Vancouver: Deskside, 1998), 59–60.
140 Aplin, "'I Saw Belsen,'" 38.
141 As quoted in Robert Bracken, *Spitfire: The Canadians* (Erin: Boston Mills, 1995), 148. For a detailed description of Wilson's time in the Israeli air force see David J. Bercuson's interview with C.D. Wilson held at the Aliyah Bet and Machal Archives, University of Florida Libraries, Gainesville, Florida.

The interview was conducted by Bercuson during research for his book *The Secret Army* (1983). My thanks to Dr Bercuson and Yael Herbsman for their assistance.

142 Arieh O'Sullivan, "Dad's Army: John Burrows' Search for His Non-Jewish Father's Machal Exploits," *Jerusalem Post Magazine*, 18 May 2001, 10. My thanks to Doreen Bliss of *World Machal* and Stanley Medicks for their assistance.

143 Ibid.

144 Dirk Bogarde, *Cleared for Take-Off* (London: Penguin Group, 1995), 20.

5 The Impossible Real

1 Josef Rosensaft, "Introduction," in *Holocaust and Rebirth: Bergen-Belsen, 1945-1965*, ed. Sam E. Bloch (New York: Bergen-Belsen Memorial Press of the World Federation of Bergen-Belsen Associations, 1965), xlv.

2 *Portraits of War*, prod. Paul Kemp, 48 minutes, Stornoway Productions, 2007, DVD.

3 Imperial War Museum, 7481, interview with William Fairlie Lawrie (1984-04).

4 Lawrence Langer, *The Holocaust and the Literary Imagination* (New Haven, CT: Yale University, 1975), 1.

5 Theodor W. Adorno, "Cultural Criticism and Society," in *Prisms*, trans. Samuel and Shierry Weber (Cambridge, MA: MIT Press, 1990), 34.

6 Ibid.

7 Charlotte Melin, *Poetic Maneuvers: Hans Magnus Enzensberger and the Lyric Genre* (Evanston, IL: Northwestern University Press, 2003), 33. Also see Hans Magnus Enzensberger, "Die Steine der Freiheit," in *Lyrik nach Auschwitz: Adorno und die Dichter*, ed. Petra Kiedaisch (Stuttgart: Reclam, 1995), 73–6.

8 Michael Rothberg, *Traumatic Realism: The Demands of Holocaust Representation* (Minneapolis: University of Minnesota Press, 2000), 3–4.

9 Ibid., 5. Rothberg points to scholars such as Hannah Arendt, Christopher Browning, and Zygmunt Bauman as examples of the "realist" faction.

10 Ibid., 4.

11 Ibid., 5. Rothberg suggests that examples of the "antirealist" side are Elie Wiesel, Claude Lanzmann, and Jean-François Lyotard.

12 Ibid., 6.

13 Ibid., 7.

14 Brett Ashley Kaplan, *Unwanted Beauty: Aesthetic Pleasure in Holocaust Representation* (Urbana: University of Illinois Press, 2007), 2.

15 Ibid., 107.
16 Ibid., 2–3.
17 Ibid., 3.
18 Theodor Adorno, "Commitment," in *The Essential Frankfurt School Reader*, ed. Andrew Arato and Eike Gebhardt (New York: Continuum, 1982), 312.
19 Theodor Adorno, *Negative Dialectics*, trans. E.B. Ashton (London: Routledge and Kegan Paul, 1973), 362.
20 Ziva Amishai-Maisels, *Depiction and Interpretation: The Influence of the Holocaust on the Visual Arts* (Oxford: Pergamon, 1993), 57.
21 Ibid.
22 Ziva Amishai-Maisels, "Art Confronts the Holocaust," in *After Auschwitz: Responses to the Holocaust in Contemporary Art*, ed. Monica Bohm-Duchen (Sunderland: North Centre for Contemporary Art in association with Lund Humphries, 1995), 52.
23 Aharon Appelfeld, "After the Holocaust," in *Writing and the Holocaust*, ed. Berel Lang (New York: Holmes and Meier, 1988), 92.
24 Berel Lang, *Holocaust Representation: Art within the Limits of History and Ethics* (Baltimore: Johns Hopkins University Press, 2000), 18.
25 Laura Brandon, *Art and War* (London: I.B. Tauris, 2007), 45.
26 Brain Foss, *War Paint: Art, War, State and Identity in Britain, 1939–1945* (New Haven, CT: Yale University Press, 2007), 19.
27 Ibid., 31.
28 Roger Tolson, "A Common Cause: Britain's War Artists Scheme," *Canadian War Museum* (2005), 2
29 Laura Brandon, *Art or Memorial? The Forgotten History of Canada's War Art* (Calgary: University of Calgary Press, 2006), xvii.
30 Ibid., xviii.
31 Laura Brandon, "'Doing Justice to History': Canada's Second World War Official Art Program," *Canadian War Museum* (2005): 2.
32 Ibid., 3.
33 As quoted in Wilfred I. Smith, "Introduction," in Peter Robertson, *Relentless Verity: Canadian Military Photographers since 1885* (Toronto: University of Toronto Press, 1973), 14.
34 Ibid.
35 Jon Farrell, "History in the Taking: Some Notes about the Canadian Army Film & Photo Unit," *Canadian Geographical Journal* 30, no. 6 (June 1945): 276–87.
36 Ibid.
37 Timothy Balzar, *The Information Front: The Canadian Army and News Management during the Second World War* (Vancouver: UBC Press, 2011), 2, 8.

38 Department of National Defence, 72/381, "Fighter Wings on the Continent," by Carl Reinke, Flight Lieutenant, Royal Canadian Air Force.
39 Ibid.
40 Kay Gladstone, "The AFPU: The Origins of British Army Combat Filming during the Second World War," *Film History* 14, nos 3/4 (2002): 326.
41 Fred McGlade, *The History of the British Army Film and Photographic Unit in the Second World War* (Solihull: Helion, 2010), 25.
42 Toby Haggith, "Filming the Liberation of Bergen-Belsen," in *Holocaust and the Moving Image*, ed. Toby Haggith and Joanna Newman (London: Wallflower, 2005), 36.
43 Ibid., 37. Both the FPB and the SPECOU received specific instructions on how to cover evidence of war crimes and atrocities in order for the material to be used later at a tribunal. Special attention was to be given to names, dates, and locations.
44 McGlade, *History of the British Army Film and Photographic Unit*, 65.
45 In addition, artists from other countries also worked in and offered reflections on Bergen-Belsen after the camp's surrender. Specifically, Lieutenant Alan Moore, an official war artist from Australia, and Warsaw-born Feliks Topolski, a war artist with the Polish forces in Britain and later commissioned by WAAC as an official war artist.
46 Robert McLaughlin Gallery (Oshawa), Donald Anderson interview by Joan Murray, Oshawa, 23 June 1981, Donald Anderson, artist file, Joan Murray artists' files.
47 After the war, Anderson became involved in commercial and design work in Montreal.
48 In the postwar period, Abramson was selected by the Committee for Education Overseas, under the chairmanship of Vincent Massey, to study in Paris. As part of a cultural project initiated by the French government, Abramson was awarded a scholarship to study at the École des Beaux-Arts, Musée du Louvre, and with modernist painter Fernand Léger. Upon his return to Montreal he founded and directed the Waldorf Galleries and Clayart Studios. He later taught at Dawson College and Concordia University and is noted for having developed "Kinemorphic Imagery," a new photographic system. My thanks to Ronney Abramson for this information.
49 My thanks to Dr Laura Brandon at the Canadian War Museum and Dr Brian Foss, director of the School for Studies in Art and Culture at Carleton University, for their insight on Lamb's encounter with Bergen-Belsen. A special thank-you to Edith Price Bobak and Molly Lamb Bobak for formal confirmation of these details. For further information, see Brian

Foss, "Molly Lamb Bobak: Art and War," in *Molly Lamb Bobak: A Retrospective*, ed. Cindy Richmond (Regina: Mackenzie Art Gallery, 1993).

50 Also of note is Canadian politician, broadcaster, university administrator, and former mayor of Halifax, Edmund L. Morris, a wartime journalist who accompanied Allied troops into Bergen-Belsen in May 1945. He created a sculpture using a piece of granite and wire he took from the camp after a second visit in 1953, along with an empty German cartridge. See Warren Perley, "TV Records Tearful Memories of Holocaust Horror," *Montreal Gazette*, 13 August 1981, 12.

51 Library and Archives Canada, MG30, D292, "Progress Report by LT. D.A. Colville" (1 April – 7 May 1945). According to Saskatoon-born Official Canadian War Artist George Campbell Tinning, he too was supposed to be sent to Bergen-Belsen, but was unavailable for this particular assignment. In response to being unable to work at the camp, Tinning admits that it is "fortunate because I don't know what it would have done to me. I read some fool author the other day who wrote, 'nothing is unforgivable.' Well, I will never forgive the Germans for Belsen and the other camps." See Robert McLaughlin Gallery (Oshawa), Campbell Tinning interview by Joan Murray, 16 May 1979, Campbell Tinning, artist file, Joan Murray artists' files.

52 Historica Dominion Institute, Alex Colville interview (29 April 2010).

53 "Acclaimed Artist Dies at Age 78," *Canadian Jewish News*, 17 May 2001, 32.

54 Hugh Halliday, "Donald Kenneth Anderson: Official War Artist (1920–2009)," *Canadian Military History* 19, no. 4 (Autumn 2010): 56.

55 Robert McLaughlin Gallery (Oshawa), Donald Anderson interview.

56 Foss, "Molly Lamb Bobak," 144.

57 Ulrike Smalley, "Objective Realists? British War Artists as Witnesses to the Liberation of Bergen-Belsen Concentration Camp," *The Holocaust in History and Memory* 2 (2009): 60.

58 Ibid., 55.

59 Ibid., 59.

60 Robert McLaughlin Gallery (Oshawa), Donald Anderson interview.

61 Ron Csillag, "Bayefsky Donates 22 Works to Yad Vashem," *Canadian Jewish News*, 6 April 2000, 5.

62 Veterans Affairs Canada, Government of Canada, interview with Alex Colville, "Heroes Remember" (24 May 1997).

63 As quoted from Philip Kelleway, *Highly Desirable: The Zinkeisen Sisters and Their Legacy* (Suffolk: Leiston, 2008). Letter dated 24 May 1945 from the collection of Captain E.M.G. Johnstone RN (Retd), 75–6.

64 Malcolm Yorke, *Mervyn Peake: My Eyes Mint Gold, A Life* (London: John Murray, 2000), 152.

65 Note that several versions of this poem exist in varying length.
66 Mervyn Peake, "The Consumptive: Belsen, 1945," in *The Glassblowers* (London: Eyre and Spottiswoode, 1950), 15–16.
67 Ibid.
68 Yorke, *Mervyn Peake*, 154–5.
69 Historica Dominion Institute, Alex Colville interview
70 Ibid.
71 Robert Jay Lifton, *Death in Life: Survivors in Hiroshima* (Chapel Hill: University of North Carolina Press, 1991), 31.
72 Robert McLaughlin Gallery (Oshawa), Donald Anderson interview.
73 Lifton, *Death in Life*, 35.
74 See Kelleway, *Highly Desirable*, 75, and G.M. Place, "Artists of Note: Doris Zinkeisen," *The Artist* 39, no. 4 (June 1950), 96.
75 LAC, MG30, D292, "Progress Report by LT. D.A. Colville."
76 As quoted from Kelleway, *Highly Desirable*, 76.
77 Imperial War Museum, Department of Art, WA2/3/183, artist file Leslie Cole.
78 Robert McLaughlin Gallery (Oshawa), Alex Colville interview by Joan Murray (18 December 1978) Alex Colville, artist file, Joan Murray artists' files.
79 Amishai-Maisels, "Art Confronts the Holocaust," 52.
80 As quoted in Csillag, "Bayefsky Donates," 5.
81 Library and Archives Canada, R3940, C.M. Donald interviews Aba Bayefsky (1995–6).
82 Ibid.
83 At the end of war, Bayefsky came into contact with Ted Aplin of 84 Group. Aplin, who was discussed in greater detail in chapter 4, became fascinated by the cultural rebirth being accomplished in Bergen-Belsen by the former inmates now displaced persons (DPs). This artistic renewal included paintings, drawings, music, and the like. Together, Aplin and Bayefsky had the idea of collecting some of the art being done by the DPs and displaying it in exhibitions that they would help set up. The exhibitions would first tour Canada, followed by the United States and England. They both felt that exhibiting the art would help rouse public opinion abroad. Bayefsky travelled to London to speak about it to Vincent Massey, the High Commissioner of Canada to the United Kingdom. According to Bayefsky, staff at Massey's office rejected the idea, telling the Toronto-born artist that it was "none of his business." For further discussion of their plan to showcase the DPs' art, see Library and Archives Canada, R3940, C.M. Donald interviews Aba Bayefsky (7 December 1995), 6–7. Also see Clara

Thomas Archives, York University, F0151, Aplin Family Fonds, Aplin letter addressed to "Darling" and dated 18 August 1945.
84 Ibid.
85 Robert McLaughlin Gallery (Oshawa), Aba Bayefsky interview, by Joan Murray, 27 April 1979, Aba Bayefsky, artist file, Joan Murray artists' files.
86 Eric Taylor, "A Lifetime," in *Eric Taylor: A Retrospective*, exhibition catalogue (Leeds: University Gallery, 1994), 29.
87 Ibid.
88 Kessell was born in London in 1914 and studied at the Clapham Art School and the famed Central School of Arts and Crafts. In 1945 she received a special commission by WAAC to sketch refugees in Germany. See P.L. Heard, "Mary Kessell," in *The Arts*, ed. Desmond Shawe-Taylor, no. 2 (1946–1947): 52–7. It should also be noted that before being commissioned as a war artist, Kessell began a fourteen-year-long love affair with Sir Kenneth Clark, chairman of the War Artists Advisory Committee. See Meryle Secrest, *Kenneth Clark: A Biography* (New York: Holt, Rinehart and Winston, 1984), 166–73.
89 IWM, Department of Documents, "German Diary, August–October 1945," by Mary Kessell.
90 Joanne Reilly, *Belsen: The Liberation of a Concentration Camp* (London: Routledge, 1998), 97–8.
91 Her diary begins with a quote about chaos and disorder from Milton's *Paradise Lost*: "Where Eldest Night / And Chaos, ancestors of Nature, hold / Eternal anarchy, amidst the noise / Of endless wars, and by confusion stand / For hot, cold, moist and dry, four champions fierce / Strive here for Mastery."
92 IWM, Department of Documents, "German Diary, August–October 1945," by Mary Kessell.
93 Ibid.
94 Smalley, "Objective Realists?" 61.
95 Ibid., 62.
96 Christopher Varley, *Aba Bayefsky Revisited: A Retrospective Exhibition* (Toronto: Koffler Gallery, 1989), 13.
97 Bayefsky donated twenty-two of these works to Yad Vashem in Israel; see Ron Csillag, "Bayefsky Donates 22 Works to Yad Vashem," *Canadian Jewish News*, 6 April 2000, 5.
98 Tom Smart, *Alex Colville: Return* (Halifax: Douglas and McIntyre, 2004), 33.
99 For one example see Laura Brandon, "Genesis of a Painting: Alex Colville's War Drawings," *Canadian Military History* 4, no. 1 (Spring 1995): 104.

100 Feliks Topolski, *14 Letters* (London: Faber, 1988), n.p.
101 Sebastian Peake, *A Child of Bliss: Growing Up with Mervyn Peake* (Oxford: Lennard, 1989), 45–51.
102 As quoted from Philip Kelleway, *Highly Desirable*, 76.
103 Robert McLaughlin Gallery (Oshawa), Donald Anderson interview.
104 The many photographs taken by British and Canadian cameramen are held in various public and private archives. The majority of the photographs are held at the National Archives in London and Library and Archives Canada in Ottawa. In addition, numerous collections are held at the Imperial War Museum in London, the Canadian War Museum in Ottawa, as well as the United States Holocaust Memorial Museum in Washington.
105 For a description of Richer and Lattion's encounter at the camp, see Charles H. Richer, "Sgt. Mike Lattion (obituary)," in *1st Canadian Parachute Battalion Association Newsletter* 6, no. 20 (April 1997): 41–3. Richer notes that Lattion produced films of Bergen-Belsen that were later shown in newsreels around the world. However, upon leaving the camp, the two men were ordered to turn over their material to an officer in the War Crimes Committee. My thanks to Patrick Rossiter for providing me with a copy of the newsletter. Mr Rossiter's father, John A. Rossiter, was an intelligence officer in the 1st Canadian Parachute Battalion. It is likely that Rossiter also entered the camp alongside the battalion's commanding officer Fraser Eadie.
106 Laidlaw sent photos of Bergen-Belsen home to his parents. These photos were later displayed in the window of the local newspaper, the *St. Marys Journal Argus*. My thanks to Amy Cubberley, Museum Curator and Archives Assistant at the St Marys Museum for calling my attention to this detail. See "Gruesome Pictures of Concentration Camp," *St. Marys Journal Argus*, 17 May 1945, 12J.
107 Sarah and Chaim Neuberger Holocaust Education Centre, Toronto, Allan Ironside Collection, letter dated 4 May 1945. My special thanks to Dr Nancy Ironside for calling my attention to her father's letters and photographs.
108 Ibid.
109 Andrea Liss, *Trespassing through Shadows: Memory, Photography and the Holocaust* (Minneapolis: University of Minnesota Press, 1998), 1.
110 James McKillop, "British War Film Evidence of the Belsen Horror," *Glasgow Herald*, 6 September 1985, 11.
111 IWM, 4052, private papers of A.N. Midgley (84/50/1).
112 Carol Naggar, *George Rodger: An Adventure in Photography, 1908–1995* (Syracuse, NY: Syracuse University Press, 2003), 136.

113 Lifton, *Death in Life*, 31.
114 As quoted in Naggar, *George Rodger*, 138.
115 Ibid., 140.
116 Ibid., 143.
117 Ibid., 139; my italics.
118 Peter Rodger, *The OMG Chronicles: One Man's Quest to Discover What God Means to People All Over the World* (London: Hay House, 2011), 171.
119 Michael Ignatieff, "Stories of Life after the Shoah," *New Republic*, 14 June 2014. According to Ignatieff, "Sieg grew up, eventually married, had children, and even enjoyed a reunion with the photographer, where they looked at the image together and recalled the scene." Sieg Maandag died in 2013 at the age of seventy-six.
120 Susan Sontag, *Regarding the Pain of Others* (New York: Farrar, Straus and Giroux, 2003), 26.
121 George Rodger, "Belsen," *Time*, 30 April 1945, 40.
122 Cornelia Brink, "Secular Icons: Looking at Photographs from Nazi Concentration Camps," *History and Memory* 12, no. 1 (Spring/Summer 2000): 148.
123 LAC, R5642–0-2-E, interview with Al Calder by Dan Conlin (23 September 1986), Dan Conlin Fonds.
124 Ibid.
125 Laidlaw Family, private collection, Memoir of Ron Laidlaw, RCAF, Public Relations Office, 28.
126 Carol Zemel, "Emblems of Atrocity," in *Image and Remembrance: Representation and the Holocaust*, ed. Shelley Hornstein and Florence Jacobowitz (Bloomington: Indiana University Press, 2003), 202.
127 IWM, Department of Film and Video, A70 308/3-4. See also Haggith, "Filming the Liberation of Bergen-Belsen," 48. Stanislaus Jan Kadziolka was a survivor of Bergen-Belsen. Born in Zembrzyce, Poland, he attended school at the age of ten with Karol Józef Wojtyła, the man who would become Pope John Paul II. Kadziolka was ordained to the priesthood in 1937 for Krakow Archdiocese, Poland. In 1948, he immigrated to Canada, initially settling in Pembroke, Ontario. He received his PhD from the University of Ottawa. Kadziolka was a pastor of Chalk River and Wilno, Ontario. He died in 1986 in Toronto. See "Former Wilno Parish Priest Dies in Toronto at 72," *Ottawa Citizen*, 18 February 1986, D3, and "Kadziolka, Rev. Dr. Stanislaus Jan," *Ottawa Citizen*, 17 February 1986, C4.
128 Mike Lewis, as quoted in Lyn Smith, *Forgotten Voices of the Holocaust* (London: Ebury, 2005), 276.

129 Indeed, contemplating the limits of representation was a preoccupation of many twentieth-century painters, photographers, and their audiences. For example, Belgian surrealist painter René Magritte's iconic image *La trahison des images* (*The Treachery of Images*) depicts a pipe with a caption below that reads, "Ceci n'est pas une pipe" ("This is not a pipe"). Magritte emphasizes that the painting, as an object, is not an actual pipe; rather, it is merely the image of a pipe. He calls our attention to the relationship between an object and a representation of that object. For further discussion see Michel Foucault, *This Is Not a Pipe* (Berkeley: University of California Press, 1983).
130 Zemel, "Emblems of Atrocity," 216.
131 IWM no. BU 3760, photograph by Lieutenant M.H. Wilson, no. 5 AFPU. "Ecce Homo" is Latin for "Behold the Man," a term used by Pontius Pilate at the trial of Jesus Christ. For example see Gerhard Schoenberner, *Der gelbe Stern. Die Judenvernichtung in Europa 1933–1945* (Hamburg: Rütten und Loening, 1960), 196.
132 Canadian War Museum, Photo Archives S 2.6, Bergen-Belsen concentration camp after liberation [graphic material], photos by L. Bloom and L. Thompson, RCAF.
133 Ziva Amishai-Maisels, "Faith, Ethics and the Holocaust: Christological Symbolism of the Holocaust," *Holocaust and Genocide Studies* 3, no. 4 (1988): 478.
134 Scott Watson, *Jack Shadbolt* (Vancouver: Douglas and McIntyre, 1990), 34.
135 As quoted in Ian M. Thom, *Jack Shadbolt: Early Watercolours, July 17 to August 21, 1980* (Victoria: Art Gallery of Greater Victoria, 1980), 8.
136 Jack Shadbolt, *In Search of Form* (Toronto: McClelland and Stewart, 1968), 35.
137 As quoted in Thom, *Jack Shadbolt*, 9.
138 My thanks to Terry Collins for these biographical details. After the war, while with the Reuters news agency in London, Holden was featured in a British Pathé short film titled "Women Going Places" in *Pathé Pictorial Looks at the Modern Woman* (1947). She is considered the first professional female photographer to take General Eisenhower's picture. Also see Michael Posner, "Patricia Holden Collins Was Groundbreaking Wartime Photographer," *Globe and Mail*, 8 December 2011.
139 Historica Dominion Institute, Patricia Collins interview (25 October 2010).
140 Arthur S. Collins, *Before I Forget* (Raleigh: Lulu, 2007), 179–180. Collins was awarded the French Legion of Honour and Distinguished Flying Cross.
141 Historica Dominion Institute, Patricia Collins interview.

142 Ibid.
143 Maurice Blanchot, *The Writing of the Disaster*, trans. Ann Smock (Lincoln: University of Nebraska Press, 1986), 38.
144 Robert McLaughlin Gallery (Oshawa), Donald Anderson interview.

6 Padres, Patients, and Pathologies

1 John W. Thompson letter to Karl Stern n.d. [1945], Karl Stern Papers, Simon Silverman Phenomenology Center, Duquesne University. Also see Paul J. Weindling, *John W. Thompson: Psychiatrist in the Shadow of the Holocaust* (Rochester, NY: University of Rochester Press, 2010), 3. John West Thompson was a neurophysiologist who received his formal education at Stanford, Edinburgh, and Harvard. During the war he served in the Royal Canadian Air Force. He brought attention to medically permitted experiments in Nazi Germany for biological and racial purification. Thompson introduced the term "medical war crimes," which was, at the time, a new concept. It became a category for prosecution, and Thompson's investigations provided the foundation for the Nuremberg medical trials. After the war, Thompson worked for the Field Information Agency Technical (FIAT) and the United Nations Educational, Scientific and Cultural Organization (UNESCO). My thanks to Dr Paul Weindling for sharing his knowledge and expertise concerning Dr Thompson and his efforts at Bergen-Belsen.
2 Imperial War Museum Sound Archive, 30528, recitation by Reverend Leslie Hardman at an open-air service in Hebrew and English at the Bergen-Belsen concentration camp. Hardman is reading a part and a variation of the "Akdamut," an Aramaic liturgical poem recited annually during the Jewish holiday of Shavuos. A common version is as follows: "Were all the skies parchment / And all the reeds pens / And all the oceans ink / And all who dwell on earth scribes / His grandeur could not be told." Taken from Ben Zion Bokser, *The Prayer Book: Weekday, Sabbath, and Festival* (Springfield: Behrman House, 1983). For Hardman this poem suggests a mystical understanding of God; through its recitation one acknowledges that there are no adequate tools to describe the meaning of God. Hardman later reveals that he was criticized by some for repeating the poem during the open-air service. See IWM Sound Archive, 19577, "Images of Belsen," BBC Radio 4 interview with Leslie Hardman (1999).
3 See Debbie Lackerstein, "Medical Responses to the Liberation of Nazi camps, April-May 1945," in *War Wounds: Medicine and the Trauma of Conflict*, ed. Elizabeth Stewart and Ashley Ekins (Auckland: Exisle

Publishing, 2011), 103. Also see Tom Johnstone and James Hagerty, *The Cross on the Sword: Catholic Chaplains in the Forces* (London: G. Chapman, 1996), 247.

4 For example, Paul Weindling, "'Belsenitis': Liberating Belsen, Its Hospitals, and Selection for Re-emigration, 1945–1948," *Science in Context* 19, no. 3 (2006): 401–18. Also see Ben Shephard, "The Medical Relief Effort at Belsen," in *Belsen 1945: New Historical Perspectives*, ed. Suzanne Bardgett and David Cesarani (London: Vallentine Mitchell, 2006), 31–50.

5 As is the case in previous chapters, much of the source material examined stems from the war period. The smatterings of oral interviews, however, were typically recorded decades after the war. For example, many of the interviews explored in this study from the Sound Archive at the Imperial War Museum were recorded post-1990, shortly after a special exhibition on the liberation of Bergen-Belsen was mounted. There were not many opportunities to compare a personal account from the war period with an interview conducted decades later. The few examples that do exist, such as with Glyn Hughes, Alex Colville, and others, show a remarkable similarity in terms of tone and language. A study on the impact of time on an individual's accounts would be of value.

6 Mark Harrison, *Medicine and Victory: British Military Medicine in the Second World War* (Oxford: Oxford University Press, 2004), 8.

7 G.W.L. Nicholson, *Seventy Years of Service: A History of the Royal Canadian Army Medical Corps* (Ottawa: Borealis, 1977), 56.

8 Cynthia Toman, *An Officer and a Lady: Canadian Military Nursing and the Second World War* (Vancouver: UBC Press, 2007), 24.

9 Christopher McCreery, *The Maple Leaf and the White Cross* (Toronto: Dundurn, 2008), 123.

10 Harrison, *Medicine and Victory*, 234.

11 Medical personnel in both the British and Canadian forces, who arrived during the first two days of the camp's surrender (15 and 16 April 1945), were able to offer limited care and attention. For example, see medics from the 1st Canadian Parachute Battalion and the 224 (Parachute) Field Ambulance noted in chapters 2 and 3.

12 Ben Shephard, *After Daybreak: The Liberation of Bergen-Belsen, 1945* (New York: Schocken, 2005), 53–6.

13 Contemporary Medical Archives Collection, Wellcome Library, RAMC 1218/2/13, "Report on Medical Aspects of Belsen" by Brigadier Glyn Hughes, 10; my italics.

14 Imperial War Museum Department of Documents, 3713, private papers of Lieutenant Colonel M.W. Gonin DSO.

15 Myrtle F. Beardwell, *Aftermath* (Ilfracombe: A.H. Stockwell, 1945), 39.

16 Ibid.
17 Joanne Reilly, *Belsen: The Liberation of a Concentration Camp* (London: Routledge, 1998), 35.
18 Ellen Ben-Sefer, "Surviving Survival: Nursing Care at Bergen-Belsen 1945," *Australian Journal of Advanced Nursing* 26, no. 3 (March–May 2009): 105.
19 Hadassah Rosensaft, *Yesterday: My Story* (New York: Yad Vashem and the Holocaust Survivors' Memoirs Project, 2005), 58.
20 See Shephard, *After Daybreak*, 112–13, and Reilly, *Belsen*, 46–7.
21 For additional information about Ms Creelman see Susan Armstrong-Reid, *Lyle Creelman: The Frontiers of Global Nursing* (Toronto: University of Toronto Press, 2014). My thanks to Dr Armstrong-Reid for sharing her insight on the life and experiences of Ms Creelman.
22 For a more detailed discussion of these debates, see Susan Armstrong-Reid and David Murray, *Armies of Peace: Canada and the UNRRA Years* (Toronto: University of Toronto Press, 2008), 249–86.
23 Lyle M. Creelman, "With the UNRRA in Germany," *Canadian Nurse* 43, no. 7 (January 1947): 556.
24 Ibid.
25 United Nations Archive, S-0408–0043, file 3 (Medical-Miscellaneous), "Report: Nursing Personnel for Belsen-Falling Bostel," by Lyle Creelman (10 October 1945).
26 IWM Department of Documents, 9550, "From a Diary Written in Belsen," by M. Silva Jones from the private papers of Miss J. McFarlane (99/86/1).
27 Ibid.
28 IWM, Department of Documents, 1029, private papers of Mrs K.J. Elvidge (letter dated 26 May 1945), 89/10/1.
29 Ibid.
30 The Museum of the Order of St John, 600/136, "A Cog in the Wheel," by A.E. Brown, p. 11.
31 Dr Charles Sutherland Rennie, "Memoir" (private collection). My thanks to R.W. Willer for additional details. Dr Rennie donated photographs he took while working at Bergen-Belsen to the United States Holocaust Memorial Museum (photographs #41271–41276). He also provided a detailed biographical sketch, which I have consulted.
32 Ibid.
33 Thomas Gibson, "Belsen 1945," *Barts and the London Chronicle* 7, no. 1 (Spring 2005): 19. This is an edited version of Gibson's article which originally appeared in August 1945 in the *London Hospital Gazette*.
34 Ibid., 20. Gibson notes that the Canadian airmen also shot two deer in a nearby forest and brought them into the camp for distribution.

35 Typhus, typhoid, and tuberculosis were all present in the camp. Typhus, a highly contagious, louse-borne disease was the primary concern. When he arrived at the camp, the Canadian physician Dr Arthur Riley Armstrong noticed a large number of inmates who were dying from tuberculosis ("galloping consumption," as he called it). See Archive of the Faculty of Health Sciences, McMaster University, 1994.44.11, interview with Dr A. Riley Armstrong, HCM 18–81 (25 November 1981). Dr Armstrong visited the camp approximately ten days after it was surrendered. He was serving with the No. 1 Chemical Warfare Unit, RCAMC, and had been working at a recently discovered chemical warfare camp in nearby Munster, Germany. Born in 1904 in Toronto, Armstrong had a distinguished career in medicine and was a renowned expert on the research and treatment of tuberculosis. Prior to the outbreak of war he worked alongside Sir Frederick Banting and Dr Charles Best, the co-discoverers of insulin.
36 National Archives, WO 222/201, account given to Royal Society of Medicine by Col. Lipscomb (4 June 1945).
37 Contemporary Medical Archives Collection, Wellcome Library, RAMC 1790, "Reflections of 40 Years Ago – Belsen, 1945," by D.T. Prescott.
38 "Prison Occupants Return to Normal," *Saskatoon Star-Phoenix*, 6 May 1946, 6.
39 As quoted in Jean Bruce, *Back the Attack! Canadian Women during the Second World War, at Home and Abroad* (Toronto: Macmillan Canada, 1985), 155. Another Canadian in the 29th General Hospital, Doris Haines (née Murphy), served with the Queen Alexandra's Imperial Nursing Service and repeated comments similar to Deeks, particularly when it came to the psychological burden. See Judy Haines, "Doris Haines," *Globe and Mail*, 26 January 2009, L6. My thanks to Judy Haines and Peter Moyles for their assistance.
40 See Shephard, *After Daybreak*, 110, and Reilly, *Belsen*, 39.
41 As quoted in Virginia Nicholson, *Millions Like Us: Women's Lives in War and Peace, 1939–1949* (London: Penguin, 2011), 299.
42 United States Holocaust Memorial Museum, 2012.367.1, Elsie Deeks collection, letter dated 10 June 1945. My sincerest thanks to Miss Elizabeth Thomson and Judy Thomson Saxerud for their assistance.
43 Ibid.
44 A number of methods were used to help personnel deal with the stresses of working in the camp. Indeed, a variety of different troupes arrived during the summer and autumn of 1945 to entertain British and Canadian personnel working in and around the area. Under the auspices of the Entertainments National Service Association (ENSA), actors Laurence

Olivier and Sir Ralph Richardson, travelling with the Old Vic theatre company, performed for troops across Europe. Presenting George Bernard Shaw's *Arms and the Man*, the company played for personnel at Bergen-Belsen in June 1945. The following month Yehudi Menuhin and Benjamin Britten toured the displaced-persons camps in the British Zone. On 27 July 1945 the duo performed two concerts for the survivors in Bergen-Belsen. On 26 and 27 October 1945, the Halifax Heralds' Concert Party, a civilian troupe of Canadians from Nova Scotia, played for their countrymen at an RCAF station in Celle. Shortly thereafter, the group visited the former site of the Bergen-Belsen concentration camp. An impromptu concert was given to the survivors at the Belsen Hospital. Another civilian concert party, the Repat Review, also played for troops in the area. On 16 November 1945, the RCAF Streamliners, a fifteen-piece dance orchestra, played for personnel in Celle. The group also travelled to Bergen-Belsen. For additional details, see: Lyn Smith, *Heroes of the Holocaust: Ordinary Britons who Risked Their Lives to Make a Difference* (London: Ebury, 2012), 128; Robert Collis and Han Hogerzeil, *Straight On* (London: Methuen, 1947), 66; Toby Thacker, *Music after Hitler, 1945–1955* (Aldershot: Ashgate, 2007), 76; Patrick B. O'Neill, "The Halifax Concert Party in World War II," *Theatre Research in Canada* 20, no. 2 (Fall 1999): 9; Thulasi Srikanthan, "Tradition of Patriotism: As a Young Woman, Yvonne Hamon Served Her Country in WWII," *Toronto Star*, 8 November 2006, A4; and Nicholas Kohler, "Band of Brothers," *National Post*, 11 November 2004, A1.
45 Weiner Library, 01623, "Belsen Concentration Camp, Appendix B," by Brigadier Glyn Hughes.
46 IWM Department of Documents, 3042, private papers of Dr A MacAuslan (95/2/1).
47 For example, see MacAuslan's interview at the Imperial War Museum, 8932/1.
48 National Archives, WO 222/208, "Cases of Starvation in Belsen Camp," by Captain P.L. Mollison, 1945.
49 National Archives, WO 222/201, account given to Royal Society of Medicine by Col. Lipscomb.
50 Ibid.
51 Elaine Scarry, *The Body in Pain: The Making and Unmaking of the World* (New York: Oxford University Press, 1985), 4.
52 Ibid., 5.
53 Ibid., 201.
54 Born in 1904 in Colorado Springs, Colorado, Ancel Keys spent decades studying the impact of diet on health. Among many achievements, he was

responsible for developing the "K-rations," packaged meals consisting of concentrated or dehydrated foods, which were first used by the United States Army during the Second World War. Keys also co-wrote a book with his wife Margaret, *Eat Well and Stay Well* (1959), explaining the benefits and the scientific basis for a Mediterranean-style diet, a meal plan they helped popularize. For more on the life and work of Ancel Keys see Todd Tucker, *The Great Starvation Experiment: Ancel Keys and the Men Who Starved for Science* (Minneapolis: University of Minnesota Press, 2006).

55 Tucker, *The Great Starvation Experiment*, 194.
56 Sir Jack Drummond, "Foreword," in Ancel Keys, Josef Brozek, Austin Henschel, Olaf Mickelsen, and Henry Longstreet Taylor, *The Biology of Human Starvation* (Minneapolis: University of Minnesota Press, 1950), 1: xvi. The issues facing medical teams in Bergen-Belsen are referenced frequently in both volumes of the book.
57 Ibid.
58 After the war, McCreary – who was awarded the Royal Orange Order of Nassau by the government of the Netherlands – became dean of the Faculty of Medicine at the University of British Columbia. For additional information, see Robert Hill, *Jack McCreary: Paediatrician, Pedagogue, Pragmatist, Prophet* (Vancouver: Tantalus Research, 2006). As for Branion, who was born in Brownsville, Ontario, he too was awarded the Royal Orange Order of Nassau. After the war he became dean of graduate studies at the University of Guelph and later, assistant to the president at the university. He was also the former president of the Poultry Science Association. In a letter dated 28 June 1945, Sir Jack Drummond, Ministry of Food, commends the nutritional work done by McCreary and Branion in the Netherlands. See UBC Archive, John McCreary Fonds, box 4-2, letter from J.C. Drummond (28 June 1945). In 1952, upon hearing of the murder of Drummond, his wife, and daughter, McCreary, Branion, and others acknowledged his contribution to Canadian medicine. See H.D. Branion, Gordon Butler, L. Chute, J.F. McCreary, and R.L. Noble, "Sir Jack Drummond, F.R.S.," *Nature* 170, no. 4339 (27 December 1952): 1139. My thanks to Dr Robert Hill, Dr Richard Branion, and Georgia Petropoulos for their assistance concerning Dr Branion and Dr McCreary.
59 University of British Columbia Archives, John F. McCreary Fonds: "Report of Activities of R.C.A.F. Nutrition Group," by J.F. McCreary, Wing Commander
60 These photographs were later donated by Dr McCreary to the Yad Vashem Photo Archive in Jerusalem (Archival Signature 111/4-13).
61 The Empire Club of Canada, Toronto, "The Conditions of Civilians in Western Europe at the Conclusion of the German Occupations," by John

F. McCreary (27 February 1947). In an article which appeared in 1995, Dr Robert Krell, psychiatrist, University of British Columbia professor emeritus, and Holocaust survivor, criticized Dr McCreary, his former colleague at UBC, for his apparent silence on his experience at Bergen-Belsen. Dr Krell writes: "His [McCreary] silence had puzzled me to this day. Wouldn't it have been worthwhile to teach what he had seen?" See Robert Krell, "Children Who Survived the Holocaust: Reflections of a Child Survivor/Psychiatrist," *Echoes of the Holocaust*, no. 4 (June 1995).
62 Ibid.
63 Ibid.
64 For a well-written, lengthy discussion of recapitulation theory, see Stephen Jay Gould, *Ontogeny and Phylogeny* (Cambridge: Harvard University Press, 1977).
65 IWM Department of Documents, 3042, private papers of Dr A MacAuslan (95/2/1).
66 Ibid.
67 Ibid.
68 Leslie Hardman and Cecily Goodman, *The Survivors: The Story of the Belsen Remnant* (London: Vallentine Mitchell, 1958; 2009), 1.
69 Ibid., 10.
70 Alan Robinson, *Chaplains at War: The Role of Clergymen during World War II* (London: Tauris Academic Studies, 2008), 67–70.
71 Joanne Benham Rennick, *Religion in the Ranks: Belief and Religious Experience in the Canadian Forces* (Toronto: University of Toronto Press, 2011), 21.
72 Jacques Castonguay, *Unsung Mission: History of the Chaplaincy Service of the RCAF*, trans. Michael Hoare (Montreal: Institut de Pastorale, 1968), 20.
73 Rennick, *Religion in the Ranks*, 19.
74 Michael Snape, *The Royal Army Chaplains' Department, 1796–1953* (Suffolk: Boydell, 2008), 290.
75 Robinson, *Chaplains at War*, 2. While the author is referring to the RAChD, the same could be said for the other branches in which military chaplains served, as well as for the Canadian perspective.
76 Doris L. Bergen, "Introduction," in *The Sword of the Lord: Military Chaplains from the First to the Twenty-First Century*, ed. Doris L. Bergen (Notre Dame, IN: University of Notre Dame Press, 2004), 2–3.
77 A special thank-you to Monsignor George H. Bourguignon and Dr Jacques Castonguay for sharing with me their memories of Bishop Norman Gallagher. I also thank Roy Piovesana, the archivist and historian with the Roman Catholic Diocese of Thunder Bay, for supplementary details. For additional details about Father Gallagher during the Second World War, see USC Shoah Foundation Institute, 48192, interview with Larry D. Mann

(10 November 1998). My thanks to Reverend Lori Megley-Best, Reverend Ross Connal, Blair Galston and Lea Edgar for additional information concerning Reverend Jack Crees.
78 As quoted in Johnstone and Hagerty, *The Cross on the Sword*, 248. Original citation: Fr H.H. Welchman, SCF (RC) 8th Corps, report to the Principal Chaplain (May 1945), Roman Catholic Chaplains' Department Archives, Bagshot.
79 Isaac Levy, *Witness to Evil: Bergen-Belsen, 1945* (London: Peter Halban, 1995), 12.
80 Hardman and Goodman, *The Survivors*, 16.
81 Leslie Hardman, "Rev. Leslie Hardman," in *Belsen in History and Memory*, ed. Reilly et al. (London: Frank Cass, 1997), 226.
82 Leviticus, chapter 10, verse three.
83 Psalms 30.
84 As quoted in Abraham Joshua Heschel, *A Passion for Truth* (New York: Farrar, Straus and Giroux, 1973), 283.
85 Hardman, "Rev. Leslie Hardman," 226.
86 In letters to his wife, Levy states that when he first found him in the camp, Hardman "fell on my neck and wept like a babe." In another letter to his wife, written four days later, he states that Hardman "is working like a maniac" in Bergen-Belsen. See Levy, *Witness to Evil*, 14–15.
87 As quoted in Johnstone and Hagerty, *The Cross on the Sword*, 248.
88 Ibid., 249. Original citation is as follows: Fr Michael Morrison SJ, "At Belsen," *Interfuse* 41 (1986): 73.
89 Father Michael Morrison SJ, BBC, *WW2 People's War*.
90 Richard Menkis, "Cass, Samuel (1908–1975)," *Encyclopaedia Judaica*, 2nd ed., ed. Fred Skolnik and Michael Berenbaum (Detroit: Macmillan 2007), 4: 507. My thanks to Dr Menkis for sharing his insight into the life of Samuel Cass.
91 Library and Archives Canada, Samuel Cass Fonds, MG 30, D225, vol. 6, "Correspondence: Civilian Affairs in Occupied Northwestern Europe." See letters dated 29 May and 31 May 1945 in particular.
92 Samuel Cass, "Chaplains Thank Canadian Jewry," *Canadian Jewish Chronicle*, 28 December 1945, 11.
93 Operations Record Book, No. 126 Wing, RCAF, April-May 1945. See entries for 30 April, 20 May, and 24 May 1945. For further information about Sanker, see *Service of Praise and Thanksgiving for the Victories of the Allied Nations*. Officiant: The Rev. Dr Louis M. Sanker, Senior Jewish Chaplain, RAF and Tactical Air Force (London: Office of the Chief Rabbi, 1945).
94 IWM Sound Archive, 19577, "Images of Belsen," BBC Radio 4 interview with Leslie Hardman (1999).

95 Hardman has told of his encounter with the Canadian airmen who assisted at Bergen-Belsen numerous times. See his memoir with Goodman, *The Survivors*, 46–8; IWM Sound Archive, 17636, interview with Leslie Hardman, as well as "Rabbi Seeks Wartime 'Friends,'" *Montreal Gazette*, 15 December 1962, 3, and "Rabbi Finds Belsen Benefactor," *Windsor Star*, 20 December 1962, 1.
96 Hardman and Goodman, *The Survivors*, 47.
97 IWM Sound Archive, 19577, "Images of Belsen," BBC Radio 4 interview with Leslie Hardman.
98 Levy, *Witness to Evil*, 25.
99 This was a widespread problem in displaced-persons camps throughout Germany. See Earl Grant Harrison, *The Plight of the Displaced Jews in Europe: A Report to President Truman* (New York: United Jewish Appeal for Refugees, Overseas Needs and Palestine, 1945).
100 Library and Archives Canada, Samuel Cass Fonds, MG 30, D225, vol. 9, "A Record of a Chaplain's Experience – World War II (1942–1946)" by Samuel Cass, Appendix I, 682–5.
101 Ibid., 693.
102 During the time he spent working in Bergen-Belsen, Gelber had not yet been ordained a rabbi and did not work in the military's chaplaincy services. I have included him in this chapter because so much of his writing explores a religious point of view. Gelber considered himself a Reform Jew and spent his life practising and studying Judaism. Indeed, born to parents who were among Canada's leading supporters of Jewish nationalism, Michael Gelber led a remarkable life. An ordained rabbi who also held two PhDs, all of which he obtained after the war, Gelber was also a stockbroker with Bear Stearns; a former dean of the Academy for Jewish Religion; and a professor of religion at NYU. In addition, he was a published author, a playwright, and a practising psychotherapist. His doctoral dissertation at NYU was titled "The Image of the Jew in the Productions of the London Stage from 1919 to 1965" (1967). He is perhaps best known for his book *The Failure of the American Rabbi: A Program for the Revitalization of the Rabbinate in America* (New York: Twayne, 1961). My thanks to Marianne Wientzen Gelber for additional details.
103 A number of Canadians worked with the Joint Distribution Committee (JDC) at Bergen-Belsen. Along with Gelber, most notable were David Wodlinger, who became the JDC's director of the British Zone of Germany, and Ms Lottie Levinson, who later worked on the War Orphans Project, overseeing the required documentation of child refugees.
104 Sholome Michael Gelber, "Wherein Is This Night Different? From Bergen-Belsen, Germany," *Menorah Journal* 35, no. 1 (Jaunary-March, 1947): 21. It

should also be noted that, frustrated by British policy in the camp, Gelber wrote a scathing, anonymous critique titled "Are We Breaking Faith?" which appeared in *New Statesman and Nation* (1946). The piece caused quite a stir and was mentioned in debates in the House of Commons.
105 Ibid., 25.
106 Jacob Neusner and Alan J. Avery-Peck, *The Routledge Dictionary of Judaism* (New York: Routledge, 2004), 86–7.
107 Gelber, "Wherein Is This Night Different?" 30.
108 Canadian Jewish Congress Charities Committee National Archives, "GELBER, Michael (Dr.) – Interview – Rescue & Relief Work UNRAA 1944–45; Post-Holocaust Situation in Bergen-Belsen D.P. Camp," pp. 37–8. Original citation: The Hebrew University of Jerusalem – Oral History Division, (4)51, "Berihah (Organized Escape) and the Camps in Germany 1944–1948," Michael Gelber interview by Aharon Kedar (1964). And like his colleague Ted Aplin, Gelber was willing to break rank to assist at the camp. Of Aplin, upon being asked if he worked in cooperation with Allied military personnel, Gelber said the following: "There was a fellow by the name of Ft.-Lt. Smith and there was a fellow by the name of Ted Applan [sic]. Ft.-Lt. Smith and Applan both came up from 84 Group Disarmament Squad, and they were marvellous in the things they did in order to help people. The liaison with the ordinary soldiers, the Canadian and British soldiers was uniformly harmonious, uniformly sympathetic. Anything that I have said to derogate the policy of the British in Germany is certainly mitigated by the tenderness and goodwill and compassion on the part of the Canadian and British soldiers. They were marvellous men and they did a wonderful job. Everybody liked them and they were very generous with what they did." See the above interview, p. 36. For further discussion of his work assisting survivors escape into Palestine, see Museum of Jewish Heritage, Id no. 1987.T.37, Testimony of Michael Gelber (3 March 1987).
109 Ibid., 2.
110 Hardman and Goodman, *The Survivors*, 36.
111 My thanks to Donald Cameron, Graham Desson, Geordie Beal, Ian McHaffie, Bob Anger, and Kenneth Munro for their help regarding Reverend Cameron.
112 Wilfred H. Dunphy was born in 1904 in Millview, Prince Edward Island. He attended St Augustine's Seminary in Toronto and was ordained in 1931 at Vernon River. He subsequently served in the Diocese of Regina before joining the Royal Canadian Air Force (RCAF) in 1942 as a chaplain. Towards the end of the Second World War, Padre Dunphy became

involved at Bergen-Belsen. He participated in the mass internment and burial services. Afterwards, according to the Operations Record Book of the RCAF's 39 Reconnaissance Wing, Father Dunphy gave a formal talk to the airmen of the wing in the station theatre. Father Dunphy received the Croix de Guerre (avec palme) by the French government. Upon his return to Canada, he continued serving in the air force. He served in both the Halifax and Trenton areas as Command Chaplain of Air Transport Command. He retired from the air force in 1959. After his retirement he was appointed priest at Sacred Heart Parish in Batawa, Ontario. Scholarships were made in his name for students in Batawa-area high schools. Father Dunphy passed away in April 1982. I thank Gorett DaSilva, Simon Lloyd, Donald Moses, Wendy Rayson-Kerr, Heather Candler, Thea Haller, Anne Marie Aquino-Coward, Richard Hughes, and the entire community of Batawa for sharing with me their stories and sources relating to the life of Father Dunphy.
113 R.K. Cameron, "Belsen Concentration Camp: An Eye-Witness Account of an R.C.A.F. Padre," *Front Line* 7, no. 11 (November 1946): 6.
114 Ibid.
115 Ibid.
116 As quoted in Carolyn Purden, "The Two Lives of Ted Light," *Canadian Churchman* (July-August 1969): 10. My thanks to Gordon, Brian, and Gregory Light for their assistance. My thanks also to Ann Benedek.
117 As quoted in Ann Benedek, "Top Official Stands Back to Count Medals," *Canadian Churchman* 105, no. 5 (May 1979): 8.
118 As quoted in Purden, "Two Lives of Ted Light," 10.
119 Ibid.
120 Michael Snape, *God and the British Soldier: Religion and the British Army in the First and Second World Wars* (London: Routledge, 2005), 202.
121 As quoted in ibid., 202. Original citation: IWM Sound Archive, 11572, interview with Harry Levy (1988-11-13)
122 Hardman, "Rev. Leslie Hardman," 232.
123 Ibid., 233.
124 "Ministry Call First Shunned by Cowboy," *Ladner Optimist*, 18 October 1951, 3.
125 Hardman and Goodman, *The Survivors*, 19–21.
126 Ibid., 56.
127 Another Canadian who worked for UNRRA and aided the survivors of Bergen-Belsen was William D. Lighthall of Montreal. A veteran of the RCAF, Wing Commander Lighthall led organization efforts to transfer thousands of survivors from Bergen-Belsen to Sweden for recuperation.

He directed a team of seventeen individuals to undertake this enormous task. A decorated veteran from the First World War, William Lighthall joined UNRRA in 1945 and was initially assigned to Lübeck. For further information see Armstrong-Reid and Murray, *Armies of Peace*, 165–8; Marvin Klemme, *The Inside Story of UNRRA: An Experience in Internationalism* (New York: Lifetime Editions, 1949), 87–113; "Local Men's Work in UNRRA Praised," *Montreal Gazette*, 30 January 1946, 7; and "UNRRA Is Praised for Humane Tasks," *Montreal Gazette*, 19 February 1946, 9. In the Armstrong-Reid and Murray book, Lighthall's name is consistently spelled "Lightall."

128 As quoted in Elmer M. Stanley, "Death Camp Happy Now Toronto Nurses Aid," *Toronto Daily Star*, 19 September 1945, 1.
129 Ibid.
130 Ibid.
131 Hardman and Goodman, *The Survivors*, 108.

Conclusion

1 See Suzanne Bardgett, "The Depiction of the Holocaust at the Imperial War Museum since 1961," *Journal of Israeli History: Politics, Society, Culture* 23, no. 1 (Spring 2004): 146–56, and Donald Bloxham and Tony Kushner, "Exhibiting Racism: Cultural Imperialism, Genocide and Representation," *Rethinking History* 2, no. 3 (1998): 349–58. In 1991 a permanent exhibit concerning the liberation of Bergen-Belsen opened at the Imperial War Museum.
2 Bardgett, "The Depiction of the Holocaust at the Imperial War Museum since 1961," 156.
3 Reesa Greenberg, "Constructing the Canadian War Museum / Constructing the Landscape of a Canadian Identity," in *(Re)visualizing National History: Museums and National Identities in Europe in the New Millennium*, ed. Robin Ostow (Toronto: University of Toronto Press, 2008), 185–6.
4 For example, the testimonies of Mr Duane Daly, secretary, Royal Canadian Legion, Mr Cliff Chadderton, chairman, National Council of Veteran Associations, and Mr Derek Farthing, president, Bomber Command Association of Canada, emphasize the lack of involvement and connection between Canada, its military, and the Holocaust. See Canada, Senate, "Proceedings of the Subcommittee on Veterans Affairs," Issue 4 – Evidence for 3 February 1998 (morning and afternoon sessions respectively).
5 Since the controversy over the proposed gallery at the Canadian War Museum, the Holocaust has been memorialized in other ways in the

country. For example, in 2008 the Canadian Museum for Human Rights in Winnipeg was established by an act of Parliament. At its opening in September 2014 there were ten permanent galleries, one of which examines the Holocaust and other genocides. In March 2011 a National Holocaust Monument Act received royal assent. The bill established a Holocaust monument in Ottawa, Canada's capital. The federal government formally announced the site of the monument in April 2013. It was to be located in a field across from the Canadian War Museum on the LeBreton Flats about a kilometre from Parliament Hill. The winning team included architect Daniel Libeskind and was led by Gail Dexter Lord, co-president of Toronto-based Lord Cultural Resources. The monument is scheduled to open in the autumn of 2015. Until its installation, Canada was the only Allied nation from the Second World War not to have a Holocaust monument in its capital city. Despite these additions, the Holocaust and the liberation of the camps are still not addressed in the Canadian War Museum. For additional information, see Martin Knelman, "Holocaust Monument in Ottawa Corrects 70-Year Mistake," *Toronto Star*, 14 May 2014; Menachem Freedman, "We Can't Let Ottawa's Holocaust Monument Become an Empty Symbol," *Globe and Mail*, 22 May 2014, and John Geddes, "The Monumental Politics behind Ottawa's Newest Memorials," *Maclean's*, 9 January 2015.

6 Michael Berenbaum, "The Nativization of the Holocaust," *Judaism* 35, no. 4 (Fall 1986): 447–57. Also see Berenbaum's *After Tragedy and Triumph: Essays in Modern Jewish Thought and the American Experience* (Cambridge: Cambridge University Press, 1990).

7 As quoted in Tony Curtis, *Welsh Artists Talking to Tony Curtis* (Bridgend: Seren, 2000), 182. My thanks to Peter Jones for his insight on Jonah Jones.

8 Bram D. Eisenthal, "Alan Rose Dies at 74; Was a Leader of Canadian Jewry," *Jewish Telegraphic Agency*, 19 July 1995.

9 Alan Rose, testimony at the Liberators of Nazi Concentration Camps Conference in the State Department, Washington, DC, in October 1981, quoted in *Bitburg and Beyond: Encounters in American, German and Jewish History*, ed. Ilya Levkov (New York: Shapolsky, 1987), 686. Likewise, British Army Major Brian Urquhart claims his direction in life was altered by his encounter at Bergen-Belsen. While working in intelligence, Urquhart came across the camp. "I had seen demolished cities, refugees, people killed in air raids, people killed in battle," he recalls, "but I had never seen anything like Belsen – a great, dusty, open place surrounded by huts with these spectral figures wandering about and a large number of dead people on the ground." After the war he became the Under-Secretary-General of

the United Nations. "Particularly after the Belsen experience," he stressed in a 1996 interview, "I felt extremely strongly that human rights were something which simply had to be developed into an international rule. It simply wasn't good enough to try to rely on people to behave reasonably well: they don't. The Nazis were an extreme, but they are not unique." See Stanford University, Digital Collections, "Preventing Genocide: Interview with Brian Urquhart," conducted by David A. Hamburg (18 March 2008), and Institute of International Studies, UC Berkeley, Conversations with History, Sir Brian Urquhart interview, conducted by Harry Kreisler (19 March 1996).

10 Paul J. Weindling, *John W. Thompson: Psychiatrist in the Shadow of the Holocaust* (Rochester, NY: University of Rochester Press, 2010), 106.
11 Ibid.
12 From a speech to the United Nations given on 29 January 2007 by Mme Simone Veil, president of the Foundation for the Memory of the Holocaust, on the occasion of the International Day of Commemoration in Memory of the Victims of the Holocaust. See Simone Veil, *A Life: A Memoir*, trans. Tamsin Black (London: Haus Publishing, 2007; 2009), 291.

Bibliography

Archival Sources

Abramson Family, Private Collection, Montreal
  Henry S. Abramson Collection
Aliyah Bet and Machal Archives, University of Florida Libraries, Gainesville
  C.D. Wilson interview conducted by David J. Bercuson (10 May 1979)
American Jewish Historical Society, Center for Jewish History, New York
  Machal and Aliyah Bet Records, box 18, file 6: Heaps, Leo
  Machal and Aliyah Bet Records, box 18, file 21: Levine, Abraham (Abe)
  Machal and Aliyah Bet Records, box 19, folder 29: Wilson, Clifford Denny
  Machal and Aliyah Bet Records, box 30, file 1: Manuscript – Heaps, Leo – *Israel, Shalom*
  Machal and Aliyah Bet Records, box 32: Jim McGunigal interviewing Dennis Wilson, Harvey Serulnikov (Serlin), and Harold Katz
Archive of the Faculty of Health Sciences, McMaster University, Hamilton
  Dr Charles Roland Oral History Collection, 1994.44.11 (box 22): interview with Dr A. Riley Armstrong, HCM 18-81 (25 November 1981), Early Canadian Medicine Series
Archives of Ontario, Toronto
  F 1417: Bohdan Panchuk Fonds
  B268404: Application for Duties with Military Government by F/L G.R.B. Panchuk
Archives and Special Collections, University of New Brunswick, Fredericton
  UA RG 340: Joe Stone photographs
Army Medical Services Museum, Aldershot
  RAMC 4/5/22: Belsen Concentration Camp Report by Major R.F. Waldon

Brian Musson Collection, Paris
  Peter Holborne, RCAF, photographs
British Red Cross Museum and Archives, London
  Acc X104: Letters from Miss Enid Fernandes
  T2 WAR: Letters of Miss Margaret Wyndham Ward MBE
Canadian Jewish Congress Charities Committee National Archives, Montreal
  Dr Michael Gelber: Rescue & Relief Work UNRAA 1944–45 and Post-Holocaust Situation in Bergen-Belsen D.P. Camp – interview (1964)
  HDP SV257-SV259: Transcript of Alan Rose Holocaust Documentation Project Interview (17 March 1982), Canadian Jewish Congress Records
  P02/04/6: Gordon George Earle photographs
  P0015: Monty Berger Fonds
  P0127: Alan Rose Fonds
Canadian Parachute Battalion Association Archives, Ottawa
  RF Anderson file 11-2: "From the Rhine to the Baltic" by Ronald Ford Anderson
Canadian War Museum, Ottawa
  Artist file, Alex Colville
  Artist file, Donald K. Anderson: "Donald Kenneth Anderson (draft)" by Hugh Halliday
  19710261-1309: *Belsen* by Donald K. Anderson, Beaverbrook Collection of War Art
  19710261-1393: *Belsen Concentration Camp, Malnutrition Wards* by Aba Bayefsky, Beaverbrook Collection of War Art
  19710261-2033: *Bodies in a Grave, Belsen* by Alex Colville, Beaverbrook Collection of War Art
  19970112-001: *Remembering the Holocaust* by Aba Bayefsky, Beaverbrook Collection of War Art
  Textual Records: 58A 1 279.9: Authorization for Dr Christie to enter Belsen concentration camp
  Photo Archives 52C 4 82.1: Corporal Roy Fergus photograph album [graphic material]
  Photo Archives 52C 4 96.1: Photo album of Squadron Leader Dr.
  Photo Archives, S 2.6: Bergen-Belsen concentration camp after liberation [graphic material], photos by L. Bloom and L. Thompson, RCAF
  Sound Recordings 31 D 5 Colville: interview with Alex Colville, CWM Oral History Project (September 1980)
  Sound Recordings 31D 6 Smith: interview with Theodor (Ted) R. Smith, CWM Oral History Project (24 October 2005)

Bibliography 253

>58A 1 75.22: 84 Group memo regarding closing the medical post at Headquarters by W.A. Nield (26 June 1945)
>58A 1 219.1: War Diary of the 3rd Battalion, North Nova Scotia Highlanders
>58A 1 238.4: Letters written to F/Sgt. J. D. Stennett

City of Victoria Archives, Victoria
>CA CVIC PR 77: Blenkinsop Family Fonds

Clara Lander Library, Winnipeg Art Gallery, Winnipeg
>Henry S. Abramson file

Clara Thomas Archives, York University, Toronto
>F0151: Aplin Family Fonds
>F0520, series S00483: Larry Mann interview (7 September 1995), Knowlton Nash Fonds

Clifford Family, Private Collection, St Catharines
>Reflections on November 11th by William (Bill) Clifford

College of Registered Nurses of British Columbia Archives, Vancouver
>Biographical files: Lyle Creelman

Contemporary Medical Archives Centre, Wellcome Institute, London
>GC186: Vaughan, Dame Janet Collection
>GC76: Hall-Tomkin, Dr Harry Collection
>RAMC92/3/8: Account of the activities of London medical students at Belsen in May 1945, by Dr A.P. Meiklejohn of the Rockefeller Foundation
>RAMC 1103: An Account of the Operations of Second Army in Europe, 1944–1945. Compiled by Headquarters Second Army (Volume II)
>RAMC 1218/2/13: Report on Medical Aspects of Belsen by Brigadier Glyn Hughes
>RAMC 1218/2/18: Memories of a Red Cross Mission by Anny Pfirter
>RAMC 1790: Reflections of 40 Years Ago – Belsen, 1945 by D.T. Prescott

CTV Television Network Archive, Toronto
>Clifford Robb interview (25 March 1985)

Delta Museum and Archive, Delta
>MSS DE 983-165(T): Interview with Norman Jack and Jean Crees

Department of National Defence, Directorate of History and Heritage, Ottawa
>72/381: "Fighter Wings on the Continent" by Carl Reinke, Royal Canadian Air Force
>87/241: "War Diary of Flight Lieutenant Carl Reinke, RCAF"
>Army Headquarters Report No. 17: "The 1st Canadian Parachute Battalion in the Low Countries and in Germany Final Operations" by R.B. Oglesby

Army Headquarters Report No. 19: "Operation 'Plunder': The Canadian Participation in the Assault across the Rhine and the Expansion of the Bridgehead" by 2 Canadian Corps by Paul Augustus Mayer

Army Headquarters Report No. 152: "The Concluding Phase: The Advance into North-West Germany and the Final Liberation of the Netherlands" by W.E.C. Harrison

Canadian Military Headquarters Report No. 99: "Progress of War Artist Programme, Canadian Army Overseas" by C.P. Stacey

Canadian Military Headquarters Report No. 174: "The Canadian Army Occupations Forces in Germany" by C.E. Brissette

Photo Archive, PL-43508, PL-43510, PL-43511, PL-43512, PL-43514, PL-43515, PL-43516: Official photographs of Bergen-Belsen, RCAF

Duquesne University, Simon Silverman Phenomenology Center, Pittsburgh
Karl Stern Papers: John W. Thompson letter to Karl Stern, n.d. [1945]

Emory University, Special Collections, Woodruff Library, Atlanta
Box 25, reel 13: William Ned Cartledge and Matthew Nesbitt. Series VII – "Witness to the Holocaust" television series (4/21/81)

Fred Roberts Crawford Witness to the Holocaust Project: Matthew Nesbitt interview (7 August 1980)

Empire Club of Canada, Toronto
The Conditions of Civilians in Western Europe at the Conclusion of the German Occupations by Wing Commander John F. McCreary (27 February 1947)

E.P. Taylor Research Library & Archives, Art Gallery of Ontario, Toronto
Info D: Henry Abramson file

Getty Images, Seattle
50605938: George Rodger, The LIFE Picture Collection

Ghetto Fighters' House Archives, Western Galilee
Catalog no. 5595: Pola Zajdner: testimony in the Bergen-Belsen DP camp
Photo Archive, 25614: The teaching staff of the school in the Bergen-Belsen DP camp in 1946

Historica Dominion Institute, Toronto
Ronald Andy Anderson interview (1 November 2011)
Marcel Auger interview (3 June 2010)
Alex Colville interview (29 April 2010)
Patricia Collins (née Holden) interview (25 October 2010)

Hopkinson Family, Private Collection, Mount Hope
Fred Hopkinson Collection, RCAF, Public Relations

Imperial War Museum, London
Department of Art, WA2/3/183: Artist file Leslie Cole

Department of Art, 5105: *One of the Death Pits, Belsen: SS Guards Collecting Bodies* by Leslie Cole
Department of Art, 5468: *Human Laundry, Belsen: April 1945* by Doris Zinkeisen
Department of Art, 5587: *A Living Skeleton at Belsen Concentration Camp, 1945* by Eric Taylor
Department of Documents, no catalogue number: German diary by Mary Kessell
Department of Documents, 85/9/1: Brigadier General R.B.T. Daniell, 29 Armoured Brigade
Department of Documents, 67/429/1: Journal of a Horse Gunner by Robert B.T. Daniell
Department of Documents, 1029: Private papers of Mrs K J Elvidge
Department of Documents, 3042: Private papers of Dr A MacAuslan
Department of Documents, 3056: Private papers of E. Fisher
Department of Documents, 3103: Private papers of C.J. Charters
Department of Documents, 3713: Private papers of M.W. Gonin
Department of Documents, 4052: Private papers of A.N. Midgley
Department of Documents, 4101: Private papers of W.J. Barclay
Department of Documents, 9161: Private papers of J. Grant
Department of Documents, 9550: From a Diary Written in Belsen by M. Silva Jones from private papers of Miss J. McFarlane
Department of Documents, 11135: Private papers of F.J. Lyons
Department of Documents, 11561: Private papers of T.J. Stretch
Department of Documents, 13408: Private papers of O.G. Prosser
Department of Film and Video, A70 308/3-4: Lieutenant Mike Lewis, AFPU
Department of Film and Video, FLM 3719: Lieutenant Mike Lewis, AFPU
Department of Photographs, BU 3760: Photograph by Lieutenant M.H. Wilson, No. 5 AFPU
Department of Photographs, HU 75122-35: Photographs by Frank Horner, No. 5 MFPS, RCAF
Sound Archive, 7481: Interview with William Lawrie (April 1984)
Sound Archives, 8253: Interview with Richard Leatherbarrow (July 1984)
Sound Archive, 9542: Interview with James Guy Bramwell (1986-12-07)
Sound Archives, 11903: Interview with Alexander Smith Allan (1991-03-04)
Sound Archive, 17636: Interview with Leslie Hardman (1997-09-22)
Sound Archives, 18046: Interview with John Murdoch Cooper (1987)
Sound Archive, 18175: Interview with John Gourlay Noble (1987-03-07)
Sound Archive, 18177: Interview with Albert Reginald ("Reg") Seekings (1987)

Sound Archive, 19577: BBC Radio 4 interview with Leslie Hardman, "Images of Belsen" (1999)
Sound Archives, 29966: John Randall interview (2002–3)

Institute of International Studies, University of California Berkeley, Berkeley
Conversations with History: Sir Brian Urquhart interview. Conducted by Harry Kreisler (19 March 1996)

Jamieson Family, Private Collection, Toronto
Edgar Jamieson Collection, 84 Group, RCAF

Jewish Public Library Archives, Montreal
ML Archives Bergen-Belsen Survivors: Bergen-Belsen Survivors Association of Montreal JewCan Literature Heaps: Leo Heaps Collection

Joint Distribution Committee Archives, New York
NY AR194554/4/3/6/325: "Report on Bergen-Belsen" by Shalome Michael Gelber (28 June 1946)
NY AR4564/390: "Report on the Activities of the AJDC in the British Zone, Germany, December 8, 1945 to September 20, 1946," by David Wodlinger (20 September 1946)
NY AR194554/4/32/6: Displaced Persons
NY AR194554/4/32/11: Religious, Cultural, and Educational
NY AR194554/4/32/10: Relief Supplies

Laidlaw Family, Private Collection, Toronto
Memoir of Ron Laidlaw, RCAF, Public Relations

Laurier Centre for Military Strategic and Disarmament Studies Archives, Wilfrid Laurier University, Waterloo
No Price Too High Collection, Record Group 2: King Whyte Letters and Photographs

Library and Archives Canada, Ottawa
MG 30, D 225: Samuel Cass Fonds
MG30, D 292, R2111-0-5-E: Progress Report by Lt D.A. Colville (1 April – 7 May 1945)
MG 30 E 283: Gordon Roy McGregor Fonds
MG 31, E 96: Wilfred I. Smith Fonds
MG31-K9: Frank and Libbie Park Fonds, Reports, Correspondence, L.C. Rutherford (Libbie Park), box 20, files 301–2
Operations Record Book, No. 5 Mobile Field Photographic Section, RCAF (May 1945)
Operations Record Book, No. 126 Wing, RCAF (April–May 1945)
Operations Record Book, No. 437 Squadron, RCAF (April 1945)
Operations Record Book, No. 440 Squadron (May 1945)

R10120–0-7-E: Matthew Halton Fonds
R1190–0-3-E: Canadian Broadcasting Corporation Radio War Recordings
R3940: C.M. Donald interviews Aba Bayefsky (1995–6)
R5642–0-2-E: Interview with Al Calder by Dan Conlin (23 September 1986)
R13884–0-9-E: Keith W. MacLellan Fonds
81946: Salsberg, J.B. – Recollections (1970/1979), Paul Kligman Fonds
86195: *L'envers de la Swastika - Atrocités nazies* (*Behind the Swastika – Nazi Atrocities*) (1945), National Film Board of Canada
110624: Proceedings of the CFPU (1986-09-19/21), Dan Conlin Fonds
184951: Halton, Matthew – Report (1945-10-28), CBC Radio
222728: Whyte, King – Report (1945-11-17), CBC Radio
250249: [World War II Comment and Report] (1945-05-09), CBC Radio
250255: [Galloway, Stome] and Warren Wilkes – Comment (1945-05-10), CBC
250589/250591/250595/250597/250642/250649/250651/250668: Fairbairn, Donald B. – Reports (1945-09-19/1945-10-11), CBC Radio
250670/250698: Fairbairn, Donald B. and Benoit Lafleur – Reports (1945-10-12/1945-10-19), CBC Radio
283728: *Alex Colville: The Splendour of Order*: [background interviews] (1983-07-14), Cygnus Communications
325790: Bayefsky, Aba – Interview (1995-12-07), Aba Bayefsky Fonds
435783: [Proceedings of the Convocation Ceremony of St Andrew's College, University of Saskatchewan] (1972-05-03), Emil Fackenheim Fonds
473013: Ouimet, Marcel – Entrevue (1976-11-18), Archives publiques du Canada

Liddell Hart Centre for Military Archives, London
GB 0099 KCLMA: Barnett Papers

Local History and Archives, Hamilton Public Library, Hamilton
R770.92 BLOOM CESH: Lloyd Harold Bloom Collection

McGill University, Department of Rare Books and Special Collections, Montreal
Lighthall Family Collection

McLaughlin Archives, University of Guelph, Guelph
RE1 OAC A0774: General file on Professor Hugh D. Branion, RCAF Nutrition Group

Mervyn Peake Estate, London
Dying Girl at Belsen, 1945 by Mervyn Peake, courtesy of Peters Fraser & Dunlop

Montreal Holocaust Memorial Centre Archives, Montreal
2000.10.10: Saul Stein letter (30 April 1945)
Abraham Brenner Collection

Museum of Jewish Heritage, New York
  ID no. 1987.T.37: Testimony of Michael Gelber (3 March 1987)
  ID no. 1974.T.5: Testimony of Harry Beckenstein (24 November 1974)
  ID no. 1989.T.184: Testimony of Ruth Horak (13 July 1989)
Museum of the Order of St John, London
  600/136: "A Cog in the Wheel" by A.E. Brown
National Archives, London
  AIR 55/108: Operation "Plainfare": A Short History of R.A.F. Celle
  AIR 55/169: Historical Record of Disarmament 84 Group
  WO 171/4306: War Diary, 3rd Parachute Brigade
  WO 171/4697: War Diary, 3/4 County of London Yeomanry
  WO 171/4773: Report on Belsen Camp by Lt-Col. R.I.G. Taylor
  WO 171/5290: War Diary, 4 Battalion, Wiltshire Regiment
  WO 171/7950: War Diary, 224 Military Government Detachment
  WO 171/8035, War Diary, 618 Military Government Detachment
  WO 171/8095: War Diary, 904 Military Government Detachment
  WO 177/360: War Diary, A.D.M.S. 6 Airborne Division
  WO 177/1257: War Diary, 29 British General Hospital
  WO 219/3944A: 21 Army Group: Report on Relief Measures at Belsen (18–30 April 1945)
  WO 219/3944A: Report on Visit to Belsen Camp by ADMG Sups (22 April 1945)
  WO 219/3944A: Belsen Concentration Camp by J. Proskie (22 April 1945)
  WO 222/201: Account given to the Royal Society of Medicine by Lieut-Colonel J.A.D. Johnston
  WO 222/201: Account given to Royal Society of Medicine by Col. Lipscomb (4 June 1945)
  WO 222/208: Cases of Starvation in Belsen Camp by Captain P.L. Mollison (1945)
National Archives and Records Administration, Washington
  100-881 Bergen-Belsen concentration camp, 1945–1948: "Memorandum for Files," n.d., Record Group 153: Records of the Office of the Judge Advocate General (Army), 1792–2010, box 83
  383.7 Public Health Reports Bergen-Belsen: "Memorandum for the Record," 27 April 1945, Record Group 331: Records of Allied Operational and Occupation Headquarters, World War II, 1907–1966, box 66, file G-5
  2711/7.1 Displaced Persons Branch: "Field Trip 21 Army Group (3 May – 9 May 1945)," 12 May 1945, Record Group 331: Records of Allied Operational and Occupation Headquarters, World War II, 1907–1966, box 50, file G-5

Camp Reports, Germany, Ilag Bergen Belsen: "Telegram," 8 August 1944, Record Group 389: Records of the Office of the Provost Marshal General, 1920–1975, box 2143

D238074 and XE238074, Belsen, Jews DP Camp in Bergen: "Reports," June 1948, Record Group 319: Records of the Army Staff, 1903-2009, box 3

Records Relating to Atrocities Committed by the Nazis, compiled 1944–1945: "Extracts from 21 A. Gp. Report on Belsen Concentration Camp," 5 May 1945, Record Group 59: General Records of the Department of State, 1763–2002, box 8

W.C. 31.73 [Belsen Concentration Camp]: "Information Analysis," n.d., Record Group 238: National Archives Collection of World War II War Crimes Records, 1933–1949. box 39, File 31.55

National Army Museum, London
1994–06–201: Report on Conc. Camp, Belsen (15 April 1945)

National Gallery of Canada Library and Archives, Ottawa
Vertical file: Henry S. Abramson

Ontario Jewish Archives, Toronto
45, H-24: Alex Pancer photographs and letters
2010–5/15: Bernard Yale Fonds

Oral History Division, Hebrew University, Jerusalem
Interview no. (4)46: Josef Rosensaft interview (1964)
Interview no. (4)51: Michael Gelber interview (1964)
Interview no. (4)120: H. Levy interview (1978)
Interview no. (4)121: Victor Balfour interview (1978)
Interview no. (25)77: Hagit Lavsky interview (2003)
Interview no. (119)98: Leslie Hardman interview (1975)
Interview no. (156)1: Norbert Wollheim interview (1990)
Interview no. (156)2: Isaac Levy interview (1991)
Interview no. 156(7): Avraham Greenbaum interview (1993)

Powell River Historical Museum and Archive, Powell River
Record of Service, 263: Holborne, A.P. (Pete) – Corporal RCAF Overseas
Record of Service, 609: Vandervoot, Harold – LAC RCAF Overseas

Presbyterian Church in Canada Archives and Records Office, Toronto
Reverend Ross Ketchen Cameron papers

Queen's University Archives, Kingston
1989–001p, V054: Lloyd Thompson Fonds

Research and Documentation Centre, Gedenkstätte Bergen-Belsen, Lohheide
David Rosenthal Fonds: *Unzer Sztyme* (12 July 1945)
William E. Roach Fonds

Robert McLaughlin Gallery, Oshawa
   Aba Bayefsky interview with Joan Murray (27 April, 1979). Aba Bayefsky, artist file. Joan Murray artists' files
   Alex Colville interview with Joan Murray (18 December 1978). Alex Colville, artist file. Joan Murray artists' files
   Donald Anderson interview with Joan Murray (23 June, 1981). Donald Anderson, artist file. Joan Murray artists' files
   Campbell Tinning interview with Joan Murray (16 May 1979). Campbell Tinning, artist file. Joan Murray artists' files

Sarah and Chaim Neuberger Holocaust Education Centre, Toronto
   Allan Ironside Collection
   Clifford Robb Collection

Sound and Moving Image Archive, British Library, London
   C459/41/1-5: George Rodger interview (1992)
   F3378: Janet Vaughan interview (1991)
   V3335/2: Bob Daniell interview (1994)

Stanford University, Digital Collections, Stanford
   Preventing Genocide: Interview with Brian Urquhart. Conducted by David A. Hamburg (18 March 2008).

Stubbs Family, Private Collection, Waterloo
   Photographic collection of James Arthur Stubbs, RCAF

Thompson Family, Private Collection, Bowden
   James Ernest Thompson interview with Nicky Saunders (1999)
   J.E. Thompson Flight Logs, 437 Squadron, RCAF (April–May 1945)

Trent Valley Archives, Peterborough
   Fonds 40: John A.I. Young

United Church of Canada, BC Conference Archives, Burnaby
   Box 1919, file 57: Interview Rev. N.J. Crees (4 February 1977), Heritage Alive Project Fonds

United Nations Archive, New York
   S-0408-0043: UNRRA Germany Mission – British zone headquarters' subject files of regional units and teams
   S-0408-0043, file 3 (Medical-Miscellaneous): "Report: Nursing Personnel for Belsen-Falling Bostel," by Lyle Creelman (10 October 1945)
   S-0408-0042: UNRRA Germany Mission – British zone headquarters' subject files of regional units and teams
   S-0422-0002: Subject files of Assembly Centres and Camps of the Central Registry of the British Zone
   S-0429-0005-01: Subject Files of Area Teams in British Zone / Schleswig-Holstein Region

S-1021-0084-01: UNRRA – Office of the Historian – Monographs, Documents, and Publications

United States Holocaust Memorial Museum, Washington

International Tracing Service (ITS) Digitized Collections, USHMM, 0.1, "Central Names Index," Edward Blenkinsop, 14704159-14704167

ITS Digitized Collections, USHMM, 0.1, "Central Names Index," Violette de Chassaigne, 17090520-17090523

ITS Digitized Collections, USHMM, 2.1.1.1, "Lists of all persons of United Nations and other foreigners, German Jews, and stateless persons; American Zone; Bavaria, Hesse," Robert Jenkinson, 70263290 and 70263696.

ITS Digitized Collections, USHMM, 0.1, "Central Names Index," Keith Mayor, 40812597-40812598

ITS Digitized Collections, USHMM, 0.1, "Central Names Index," Alfred Roe, 34084512- 34084518

ITS Digitized Collections, USHMM, 2.2.2.2., "Official Certificates (marriages and deaths), western zones, general," Alfred Roe, 76849722_0_1-76849722_0_2

ITS Digitized Collections, USHMM, 0.1, "Central Names Index," Bella Zajdner, 64720044-64720057

ITS Digitized Collections, USHMM, 1.1.30, "General Information on Bergen-Belsen Concentration Camp," Report on the Search in Belsen by Lieutenant Francois Poncet (10 June 1946), 8009600, pages 5–62

RG-04.020*01: The Relief of Belsen Concentration Camp Recollections – Reflections of a British Army Doctor by J.A.D. Johnston

RG-09.078: John and Alice Fink collection

RG-09.084: Henry Barson collection

RG-50.234*0024: Oral history interview with Alan Rose

RG-60.3800: "Eyewitnesses and War Correspondents at Plenary," International Liberators Conference (27 October 1981)

1995.A.1138: Ralph Walsh letter regarding Bergen-Belsen

1999.100: Norbert Wollheim collection

2012.367.1: Elsie Deeks collection

Photo Archive, 00818: Dr and Rabbi Michael Gelber of Toronto, Ontario

Photo Archive, 2004.535: Bergen-Belsen liberation photographs by Stanley Brocklebank

Photo Archive, 2009.378: Gerard LaBossiere collection

Photo Archive, 23032: Courtesy of Solomon Bogard

Photo Archive, 25001, 69245, 74929, 74945, 78274: Courtesy of Hadassah Bimko Rosensaft

Photo Archive, 30428: Courtesy of Lev Sviridov
Photo Archive, 41271-41276: Dr Charles Sutherland Rennie photographs
Photo Archive, 46347 and 46348: David Wodlinger of Toronto, Ontario, JDC Chief of Operations in the British zone of Germany
Photo Archive, 55316: Courtesy of Joseph Eaton
Photo Archive, 76491: Courtesy of Arnold Bauer Barach
Photo Archive, 77214: Courtesy of Jack and Iris Mitchell Bolton

University of British Columbia Archives, Vancouver
D805.G3 S66 1945a: Bergen-Belsen by Frank Snowsell (1 May 1945)
4-1: Report of Activities of R.C.A.F. Nutrition Group Detached to S.H.A.E.F. 25 June 1945
John McCreary fonds. Professional affiliation series.
John McCreary Fonds, box 4: Personal files, R.C.A.F. correspondence
Lyle Creelman Fonds, box 2–2: 1944–1945 Record of Service with UNRAA

University of Manitoba Faculty of Medicine Archives, Winnipeg
CA UMFMA Victor_M: Maurice Victor File

University of South California's Shoah Foundation Institute, Los Angeles
05795: Interview with Leslie Hardman (23 November 1995)
08610: Interview with Isaac Levy (30 January 1996)
28524: Interview with Matthew Nesbitt (15 April 1997)
29664: Interview with J. Douglas Paybody (18 May 1997)
39023: Interview with Mervin Mirsky (22 February 1998)
40440: Interview with Bernard Yale (14 April 1998)
40732: Interview with Emmanuel Fischer (12 February 1998)
47651: Interview with Ralph Millman (25 September 1998)
48192: Interview with Larry D. Mann (10 November 1998)
48712: Interview with Leslie Clarke (23 November 1998)

Vancouver Holocaust Education Centre, Vancouver
96.024.010: Stanley Winfield collection
HVT-3095: Stanley H. Winfield interview (14 November 1990)
Peter Gorst Photographs

Veterans Affairs Canada, Government of Canada, Ottawa
"Heroes Remember" Series: Interview with Alex Colville (24 May 1997)

Weiner Library, London
01623: Belsen Concentration Camp Report, Appendix B by Glyn Hughes
1368/2/2/27: The Memories of Max Dickson, Formerly Max Dobriner by Max Dickson
15323: Addresses and Speeches, Commemorative Ceremony of the 50th Anniversary of the Liberation of Concentration Camps, held in the memorial of Bergen-Belsen (27 April 1995)

HA6B-1/20, Jews in Germany Camps: "Bergen Belsen Exhibition, October 1947–April 1948"
WGST Radio, Atlanta
   Matthew Nesbitt interview (18 April 1987)
Wilks Family, Private Collection, Toronto
   Photographic collection of Charles H. Wilks, RCAF
World War II Round Table, Atlanta
   Matthew Nesbitt Lecture at Atlanta's 57th Fighter Group (15 January 1987)
Yad Vashem Archives, Jerusalem
   Photo Archive, 111/4-13: John F. McCreary photos
   Photo Archive, 7036/4, 7036/5, 7036/6: Photographs by Aba Bayefsky
   Photo Archive, 93359: Canadian Zionist Federation photos

Secondary Sources

Abella, Irving. "Canadian War Museum." *Globe and Mail* (22 November 1997): D3.
Abella, Irving, and Franklin Bialystok. "Canada." In *The World Reacts to the Holocaust*, edited by David S. Wyman, 749–81. Baltimore: Johns Hopkins University Press, 1996.
Abella, Irving, and Harold Troper. *None Is Too Many*. Toronto: Lester and Orpen Dennys, 1982.
Absence/Presence: Critical Essays on the Artistic Memory of the Holocaust. Edited by Stephen C. Feinstein. Syracuse: Syracuse University Press, 2005.
Abzug, Robert H. *Inside the Vicious Heart*. New York: Oxford University Press, 1985; 1987.
– "The Liberation of the Concentration Camps." In *Liberation 1945*, edited by Susan D. Bachrach, 23–46. New York: United States Holocaust Memorial Council, 1995.
"Acclaimed Artist Dies at Age 78." *Canadian Jewish News*, 17 May 2001, 32.
Adorno, Theodor W. "Commitment." In *The Essential Frankfurt School Reader*, edited by Andrew Arato and Eike Gebhardt, 300–18. New York: Continuum, 1982.
– "Cultural Criticism and Society." In *Prisms*, translated by Samuel and Shierry Weber, 17–34. Cambridge: MIT Press, 1990.
– *Negative Dialectics*. Translated by E.B. Ashton. London: Routledge and Kegan Paul, 1973.
Afterimage: Evocations of the Holocaust in Contemporary Canadian Arts and Literature. Edited by Loren Lerner. Montreal: Concordia University Institute for Canadian Jewish Studies, 2002.

Agamben, Giorgio. *Remnants of Auschwitz: The Witness and the Archive*. Translated by Daniel Heller-Roazen. New York: Zone, 1999.
Ainsworth, Edgar. "Victim and Prisoner." *Picture Post*, September 1945, 13–17.
Amishai-Maisels, Ziva. "Art Confronts the Holocaust." In *After Auschwitz: Responses to the Holocaust in Contemporary Art*, edited by Monica Bohm-Duchen, 49–77. Sunderland: North Centre for Contemporary Art in association with Lund Humphries, 1995.
– *Depiction and Interpretation: The Influence of the Holocaust on the Visual Arts*. Oxford: Pergamon, 1993.
– "Faith, Ethics and the Holocaust: Christological Symbolism of the Holocaust." *Holocaust and Genocide Studies* 3, no. 4 (1988): 457–81.
Anthropomorphism, Anecdotes, and Animals. Edited by Robert W. Mitchell, Nicholas S. Thompson, and H. Lyn Miles. Albany: State University of New York Press, 1997.
Aplin, E.M. "I Saw Belsen ... My Conscience Cannot Wait." *Today: An Anglo-Jewish Monthly* 2, no. 5 (April 1946): 18–19, 38.
Appelfeld, Aharon. "After the Holocaust." In *Writing and the Holocaust*, edited by Berel Lang, 83–92. New York: Holmes and Meier, 1988.
Archives of the Holocaust. Vol. 15. Edited by Paula Draper and Harold Troper. New York: Garland, 1991.
Armstrong-Reid, Susan. *Lyle Creelman: The Frontiers of Global Nursing*. Toronto: University of Toronto Press, 2014.
Armstrong-Reid, Susan, and David Murray. *Armies of Peace: Canada and the UNRRA Years*. Toronto: University of Toronto Press, 2008.
Arons, Sandrine. "Self-Therapy through Personal Writing: A Study of Holocaust Victims' Diaries and Memoirs." In *The Psychological Impact of War Trauma on Civilians*, edited by Stanley Krippner and Teresa M. McIntyre, 123–34. Westport, CT: Praeger, 2003.
Balzar, Timothy. *The Information Front: The Canadian Army and News Management during the Second World War*. Vancouver: UBC Press, 2011.
Bardgett, Suzanne. "The Depiction of the Holocaust at the Imperial War Museum since 1961." *Journal of Israeli History: Politics, Society, Culture* 23, no. 1 (Spring 2004): 146–56.
Barkin, Kenneth D. "Autobiography and History." *Societas* 6 (Spring 1976): 83–108.
Barnes, James J., and Patience P. Barnes. *Nazi Refugee Turned Gestapo Spy: The Life of Hans Wesemann, 1895–1971*. Westport, CT: Praeger, 2001.
Bartov, Omer. *Mirrors of Destruction: War, Genocide and Modern Identity*. New York: Oxford University Press, 2000.

Battle Lines: Eyewitness Accounts from Canada's Military History. Edited by J.L. Granatstein and Norman Hillmer. Toronto: Thomas Allen, 2004.
Bauer, Yehuda. "On Oral and Video Testimony." *Past Forward* (Autumn 2010): 20–2.
Bayefsky, Edra. "Aba Bayefsky: Life and Work." *Outlook Magazine* (July–August 2012): 7–8, 31.
Beardwell, Myrtle F. *Aftermath*. Ilfracombe: A.H. Stockwell, 1945.
"Belsen Camp Murder of Briton Revealed." *Maple Leaf*, 5 October 1945, 1.
Belsen in History and Memory. Edited by Jo Reilly, David Cesarani, Tony Kushner, and Colin Richmond. London: Frank Cass, 1997.
"Belsen Horrors Recalled: Local Girl Sees Little Chance of Normalcy for Inmates." *Winnipeg Tribune*, 6 May 1946, 4.
Belsen 1945: New Historical Perspectives. Edited by Suzanne Bardgett and David Cesarani. London: Vallentine Mitchell, 2006.
Benarde, Scott R. "How the Holocaust Rocked Rush Front Man Geddy Lee." *Jweekly*, 25 June 2004.
Benedek, Ann. "Top Official Stands Back to Count Medals." *Canadian Churchman* 105, no. 5 (May 1979): 1, 8.
Benjamin, Walter. "Storyteller." In *Theory of the Novel: Historical Approaches*, edited by Michael McKeon, 77–93. Baltimore: Johns Hopkins University Press, 2000.
Ben-Sefer, Ellen. "Surviving Survival: Nursing Care at Bergen-Belsen 1945." *Australian Journal of Advanced Nursing* 26, no. 3 (March–May 2009): 101–10.
Bercuson, David J. *The Secret Army*. Toronto: Lester and Orpen Dennys, 1983.
Berenbaum, Michael. *After Tragedy and Triumph: Essays in Modern Jewish Thought and the American Experience*. Cambridge: Cambridge University Press, 1990.
– "The Nativization of the Holocaust." *Judaism* 35, no, 4 (Fall 1986): 447–57.
Bergen, Doris L. "Introduction." In *The Sword of the Lord: Military Chaplains from the First to the Twenty-First Century*, edited by Doris L. Bergen, 1–28. Notre Dame, IN: University of Notre Dame Press, 2004.
– *War and Genocide: A Concise History of the Holocaust*. Lanham, MD: Rowman and Littlefield, 2003.
"Bergen-Belsen Death Camp Did Not Have Gas Chambers." *Toronto Star*, 20 September 2007.
"Bergen-Belsen: Fr Michael Morrison." *WW2 People's War*, BBC. http://www.bbc.co.uk/history/ww2peopleswar/stories/37/a3953937.shtml.
Berger, Monty and Brian Jeffrey Street. *Invasions without Tears: The Story of Canada's Top Scoring Spitfire Wing in Europe during the Second World War*. Toronto: Random House of Canada, 1994.

Berman, Judith E. "Holocaust Commemorations in London and Anglo-Jewish (Dis-)Unity." *Journal of Modern Jewish Studies* 3, no. 1 (March 2004): 51–71.
Berney, A.L. "The Liberation of Belsen Concentration Camp." WW2 *People's War*, BBC. http://www.bbc.co.uk/history/ww2peopleswar/user/83/u747283.shtml.
Bialystok, Franklin. *Delayed Impact: The Holocaust and the Canadian Jewish Community*. Montreal and Kingston: McGill-Queen's University Press, 2000.
Bishop, Jim. "Anti-Semite Is Unhappy with Self." *Milwaukee Sentinel*, 13 June 1961, 12.
Black, Debra. "Bell Pulls 'Death Camp' Ads." *Toronto Star*, 15 September 2007.
Blanchot, Maurice. *The Writing of the Disaster*. Trans. Ann Smock. Lincoln: University of Nebraska Press, 1980; 1986.
Bloxham, Donald, and Tony Kushner, "Exhibiting Racism: Cultural Imperialism, Genocide and Representation." *Rethinking History* 2, no. 3 (1998): 349–58.
Bogarde, Dirk. *Cleared for Take-Off*. London: Penguin Group, 1995.
– *For the Time Being: Collected Journalism*. London: Viking, 1998.
– *Snakes and Ladders*. London: Chatto and Windus, 1978.
Bok, Sissela. "Autobiography as Moral Battleground." In *Memory, Brain and Belief*, edited by Daniel L. Schacter and Elaine Scarry, 307–24. Cambridge: Cambridge University Press, 2000.
Bokser, Ben Zion. *The Prayer Book: Weekday, Sabbath, and Festival*. Springfield, NJ: Behrman House, 1983.
Bracken, Robert. *Spitfire: The Canadians*. Erin, ON: Boston Mills, 1995.
Brandon, Laura. *Art or Memorial? The Forgotten History of Canada's War Art*. Calgary: University of Calgary Press, 2006.
– *Art and War*. London: I.B. Tauris, 2007.
– "'Doing Justice to History': Canada's Second World War Official Art Program." *Canadian War Museum* (2005): 1–4.
– "Genesis of a Painting: Alex Colville's War Drawings." *Canadian Military History* 4, no. 1 (Spring 1995): 100–4.
– "Reflections on the Holocaust: The Holocaust Art of Aba Bayefsky." *Canadian Military History* 6, no. 2 (Autumn 1997): 62–72.
Brandon, Laura, Peter Stanley, Roger Tolson, and Lola Wilkins. *Shared Experience, Art and War: Australia, Britain and Canada in the Second World War*. Canberra: Australian War Memorial, 2005.
Branion, H.D., Gordon Butler, L. Chute, J.F. McCreary, and R.L. Noble. "Sir Jack Drummond, F.R.S." *Nature*, 27 December 1952, 1139.
Brassett, James. "British Irony, Global Justice: A Pragmatic Reading of Chris Brown, Banksy and Ricky Gervais." *Review of International Studies* 35, no. 1 (2009): 219–45.

Breitman, Richard. *Official Secrets: What the Nazis Planned, What the British and Americans Knew*. New York: Hill and Wang, 1998.
Brink, Cornelia. "Secular Icons: Looking at Photographs from Nazi Concentration Camps." *History and Memory* 12, no. 1 (Spring/Summer 2000): 135–50.
Broadfoot, Barry. *Six War Years, 1939–1945: Memories of Canadians at Home and Abroad*. Toronto: Doubleday Canada, 1974.
Brock, Peter. "'Excellent in Battle': British Conscientious Objectors as Medical Paratroopers, 1943–1946." *War and Society* 22, no. 1 (May 2004): 41–57.
Brode, Patrick. *Casual Slaughters and Accidental Judgments: Canadian War Crimes Prosecutions, 1944–1948*. Toronto: University of Toronto Press, 1997.
Brooks, Jane. "Nursing Typhus Victims in the Second World War, 1942–1944: A Discussion Paper." *Journal of Advanced Nursing* 70, no. 7 (July 2014): 1510–19.
– "'Uninterested in anything except food': The Work of Nurses Feeding the Liberated Inmates of Bergen-Belsen." *Journal of Clinical Nursing* 21, no. 19 (October 2012): 2958–65.
Brooks, Richard. "Images of Belsen that Inspired Peake's Macabre Stories." *Sunday Times*, 26 June 2011.
Brown, George, and Michel Lavigne. *Canadian Wing Commanders of Fighter Command in World War II*. Langley: Battleline, 1984.
Browning, Christopher R. *Collected Memories: Holocaust History and Postwar Testimony*. Madison: University of Wisconsin Press, 2003.
– "German Memory, Judicial Interrogation, and Historical Reconstruction: Writing Perpetrator History from Postwar Testimony." In *Probing the Limits of Representation: Nazism and the "Final Solution,"* edited by Saul Friedländer, 22–36. Cambridge: Harvard University Press, 1992.
– *Ordinary Men: Reserve Police Battalion 101 and the Final Solution in Poland*. London: Penguin, 1992; 1998.
Bruce, Harry. "Death, Art and Alex Colville." *Saturday Night*, May 1972, 30–5.
Bruce, Jean. *Back the Attack! Canadian Women during the Second World War, at Home and Abroad*. Toronto: Macmillan of Canada, 1985.
Burns, Robert. "Man Was Made to Mourn: A Dirge." *The Poems and Songs of Robert Burns: The Five Foot Shelf of Classics*, vol. 6, edited by Charles W. Eliot, 66. New York: Cosimo Classics, 1909; 2009.
Bystanders to the Holocaust. Edited by Michael R. Marrus. Westport, CT: Meckler, 1989.
'Bystanders' to the Holocaust: A Re-evaluation. Edited by David Cesarani and Paul A. Levine. London: Frank Cass, 2002.
Cameron, R.K. "Belsen Concentration Camp: An Eye-Witness Account of an R.C.A.F. Padre." *Front Line* 7, no. 11 (November 1946): 1–6.

Canada, Senate. "Proceedings of the Subcommittee on Veterans Affairs." Issue 4 – Evidence for 3 February 1998.
Canadian Jews in World War II. Edited by David Rome. Montreal: Canadian Jewish Congress, 1947.
"Canadian Labor Groups Oppose Racial Bars in Immigration; Ask Entry of Refugees." *Jewish Telegraphic Agency*, 26 July 1946.
Capon, Alan. "Reconnaissance Picton Photographer Shot for D-Day." *Whig*, 29 August 1985, 1.
Carey, John. "*Ever, Dirk*: The Bogarde Letters Selected and Edited by John Coldstream." *Sunday Times*, 10 August 2008, 2.
Carlson, Don. *R.C.A.F. Padre with Spitfire Squadrons*. Red Deer, AB: D.G. Carlson, 1980.
Carr, David. "The Reality of History." In *Meaning and Representation in History*, edited by Jörn Rüsen, 123–36. New York: Berghahn, 2006.
– *Time, Narrative, and History*. Bloomington: Indiana University Press, 1986.
Cashman, Greer Fay. "All in the Family." *Jerusalem Post*, 25 April 2012.
Cass, Samuel. "Chaplains Thank Canadian Jewry." *Canadian Jewish Chronicle*, 28 December 1945, 11.
– "Rabbi Cass Asks Every Jewish Family to Help." *Jewish Western Bulletin*, 25 January 1946, 2.
Castonguay, Jacques. *Unsung Mission: History of the Chaplaincy Service of the RCAF*. Translated by Michael Hoare. Montreal: Institut de Pastorale, 1968.
Caven, Hannah. "Horror in Our Time: Images of the Concentration Camps in the British Media, 1945." *Historical Journal of Film, Radio and Television* 21, no. 3 (2001): 205–53.
Celinscak, Mark. "Bergen-Belsen in Historical Context." In *… And Stockings for the Ladies*, edited by Attila Clemann, viii–xii. Victoria: First Choice, 2013.
– "Canadians and the Liberation of Bergen-Belsen." Interview with Steve Guthrie. *Newswatch Late Edition*. CHEX Peterborough, 24 February 2014.
– "John Proskie's Story." Interview with Kim Trynacity. *Radio Active*. Canadian Broadcasting Corporation, 26 October 2011.
Celis, Peter. *One Who Almost Made It Back: The Remarkable Story of One of World War Two's Unsung Heroes, Sqn Ldr Edward 'Teddy' Blenkinsop, DFC, CdeG (Belge), RCAF*. London: Grub Street, 2008.
Cesarani, David. *Eichmann: His Life and Crimes*. London: W. Heinemann, 2004.
– "Great Britain." In *The World Reacts to the Holocaust*, edited by David S. Wyman, 599–641. Baltimore: Johns Hopkins University Press, 1996.
Cesarani, David, and Paul A. Levine. "Introduction." In *'Bystanders' to the Holocaust: A Reevaluation*, edited by David Cesarani and Paul A Levine, 1–27. London: Frank Cass, 2002.

Clark, Lloyd. *Crossing the Rhine: Breaking into Nazi Germany, 1944 and 1945.* New York: Atlantic Monthly, 2008.
Clemann, Attila. *And Stockings for the Ladies.* Directed by Zach Fraser and starring Brendan McMurtry-Howlett. Gesamtkunstwerk Project, n.d.
Cohen, Leonard. *Beautiful Losers.* Toronto: McClelland and Stewart, 1966; 2003.
– *The Spice-Box of Earth.* Toronto: McClelland and Stewart, 1961.
Coldstream, John. *Dirk Bogarde: The Authorised Biography.* London: Weidenfeld and Nicolson, 2004.
– "Dirk Bogarde and Belsen." DirkBogarde.co.uk. http://dirkbogarde.co.uk/news/dirk-bogarde-and-belsen/.
Cole, Howard N. *On Wings of Healing: The Story of the Airborne Medical Services, 1940–1960.* Edinburgh: William Blackwood and Sons, 1963.
Collins, Arthur S. *Before I Forget.* Raleigh: Lulu, 2007.
Collins, Robert. "Angel of Belsen." *Reader's Digest*, November 1990, 69–73.
– *You Had to Be There: An Intimate Portrait of the Generation that Survived the Depression, Won the War, and Re-invented Canada.* Toronto: McClelland and Stewart, 1997.
Collis, Robert, and Han Hogerzeil. *Straight On.* London: Methuen, 1947.
Colville, Alex. *Alex Colville: Diary of a War Artist.* Compiled by Graham Metson and Cheryl Lean. Halifax: Nimbus, 1981.
– "Beauty and the Beast." In *Between Ethics and Aesthetics: Crossing the Boundaries*, edited by Dorota Glowacka and Stephen Boos, 251–4. New York: State University of New York Press, 2002.
Cosner, Shaaron, and Victoria Cosner. *Women under the Third Reich: A Biographical Dictionary.* Westport, CT: Greenwood, 1998.
Creelman, Lyle M. "With the UNRRA in Germany." *Canadian Nurse* 43, no. 7 (January 1947): 532, 552–6. Article continued in volume 43, no. 9 (September 1947): 710–12.
Creet, Julia. "On the Sidewalk: Testimony and the Gesture." In *Memory, Haunting, Discourse*, edited by Maria Holmgren Troy and Elisabeth Wennö, 139–59. Karlstad: Karlstad University Press, 2005.
Crerar, Duff. "In the Day of Battle: Canadian Catholic Chaplains in the Field, 1885–1945." *CCHA Historical Studies* 61 (1995): 53–77.
Crew, F.A.E. *The Army Medical Services: Northwest Europe.* Vol. 4. London: Her Majesty's Stationary Office, 1962.
Crownshaw, Richard. "Ethnic Identity and Cultural Heritage: Belsen in the Museum." In *The Media in Britain: Current Debates and Developments*, edited by Jane Stokes and Anna Reading, 295–303. New York: St Martin's, 1999.
Csillag, Ron. "Bayefsky Donates 22 Works to Yad Vashem." *Canadian Jewish News*, 6 April 2000, 5.

Curtis, Tony. *Welsh Artists Talking to Tony Curtis*. Bridgend: Seren, 2000.
Danchev, Alex. *On Art and War and Terror*. Edinburgh: Edinburgh University Press, 2009.
D'Arcy-Dawson, John. *European Victory*. London: Macdonald, 1945.
Davis, W.A. "Typhus at Belsen: Control of the Typhus Epidemic." *American Journal of Hygiene* 46 (1947): 66–83.
Davison, Phil. "Trooper Fred Smith: Soldier Who Helped Liberate Belsen-Bergen." *Independent*, 1 July 2011.
Debates: Official Reports. Canada. Parliament. House of Commons. Vol. 5. Ottawa: Queen's Printer, 1944.
De Grineau, Bryan. "As Dore Might Have Conceived It: Belsen Death Camp." *Illustrated London News*, 5 May 1945, 471–3.
Delaforce, Patrick. *The Black Bull*. Dover: Alan Sutton, 1993.
– *Churchill's Desert Rats: From Normandy to Berlin with the 7th Armoured Division*. Dover: Alan Sutton, 1994.
Derrida, Jacques. "The Law of Genre." Translated by Avital Ronell. *Critical Inquiry* 7, no. 1 (Autumn 1980): 55–81.
Dilthey, Wilhelm. *The Formation of the Historical World in the Human Sciences*. Edited and translated by Rudolf A. Makkreel and Frithjof Rodi. Princeton, NJ: Princeton University Press, 2002.
– *Selected Writings*. Edited and translated by H.P. Rickman. Cambridge: Cambridge University Press, 1976.
Dodick, Mark. "Present, Past Meld in Reunion for Mahal Fliers." *Canadian Jewish News*, 21 August 1986, 19.
Doherty, Muriel Knox. *Letters from Belsen 1945: An Australian Nurse's Experiences with the Survivors of War*. Edited by Judith Cornell and R. Lynette Russell. St Leonards: Allen and Unwin, 2000.
Doniger, Wendy. "Epilogue: Making Animals Vanish." In *Animals and the Human Imagination: A Companion to Animal Studies*, edited by Aaron Gross and Anne Vallely, 349–54. New York: Columbia University Press, 2012.
– "Zoomorphism in Ancient India: Humans More Bestial Than the Beasts." In *Thinking with Animals: New Perspectives on Anthropomorphism*, edited by Lorraine Datson and Greg Mitman, 17–36. New York: Columbia University Press, 2005.
Dow, Helen J. *The Art of Alex Colville*. Toronto: McGraw-Hill Ryerson, 1972.
Drea, Edward J. "Recognizing the Liberators: U.S. Army Divisions Enter the Concentration Camps." *Army History* (Fall/Winter 1992–3): 1–5.
"Dr. J.W. Thompson, Who Aided Concentration Camp Victims, Dead at 59." *Jewish Telegraphic Agency*, 25 August 1965.

Drummond, Jack. "Foreword." In Ancel Keys, Josef Brozek, Austin Henschel, Olaf Mickelsen, and Henry Longstreet Taylor. *The Biology of Human Starvation*. 2 vols. Minneapolis: University of Minnesota Press, 1950.

Eadie, Jim. "Coe Hill Legion Honours Harold and Joan Nash." *Bancroft This Week*, 7 May 2014.

Eakin, Paul John. "The Economy of Narrative Identity." *History of Political Economy* 39 (2007): 117–33.

Eby, Cecil D. *Hungary at War: Civilians and Soldiers in World War II*. University Park: Pennsylvania State University Press, 1998.

"Eight Jews Stabbed, One Shot by Polish Dp's at Bergen-Belsen Camp; Situation Tense." *Jewish Telegraphic Agency*, 19 May 1946.

Eisenthal, Bram D. "Alan Rose Dies at 74; Was a Leader of Canadian Jewry," *Jewish Telegraphic Agency*, 19 July 1995.

Ellis, L.F. *Victory in the West: The Defeat of Germany*. Vol. 2. London: Her Majesty's Stationary Office, 1968.

"The End of Belsen?" *Time*, 11 June 1945, 36.

Engen, Trygg. *Odor Sensation and Memory*. New York: Praeger, 1991.

Enzensberger, Hans Magnus. "Die Steine der Freiheit." In *Lyrik nach Auschwitz: Adorno und die Dichter*, edited by Petra Kiedaisch, 73–76. Stuttgart: Reclam, 1995.

"Even Parachutists Lacking Limbs 'Full of Fight.'" Name of newspaper unidentified. From private collection, Costigan family, ca July 1945.

The Face of the Enemy: British Photographers in Germany, 1944–1952. Edited by Martin Caiger-Smith. Berlin: Nishen, 1988.

Farrell, Jon. "History in the Taking: Some Notes about the Canadian Army Film and Photo Unit." *Canadian Geographical Journal* 30, no. 6 (June 1945): 276–87.

Feinstein, Margarete Myers. "Jewish Women Survivors in the Displaced Persons Camps of Occupied Germany: Transmitters of the Past, Caretakers of the Present, and Builders of the Future." *Shofar: An Interdisciplinary Journal of Jewish Studies* 24, no. 4 (Summer 2006): 67–89.

Fénelon, Fania. *Playing for Time*. Translated by Judith Landry. New York: Atheneum, 1976; 1977.

Ferderber-Salz, Bertha. *And the Sun Kept Shining ...* New York: Holocaust Library, 1980.

Foley, Barbara. "Fact, Fiction, Fascism: Testimony and Mimesis in Holocaust Narratives." *Comparative Literature* 34, no. 4 (Autumn 1982): 330–60.

Forbes, Patrick. *6th Guards Tank Brigade: The Story of Guardsmen in Churchill Tanks*. London: S. Low, Marston, 1946.

"Former Wilno Parish Priest Dies in Toronto at 72." *Ottawa Citizen*, 18 February 1986, D3.
Foss, Brian. "Molly Lamb Bobak: Art and War." In *Molly Lamb Bobak: A Retrospective*, edited by Cindy Richmond, n.p. Regina: Mackenzie Art Gallery, 1993.
– *War Paint: Art, War, State and Identity in Britain, 1939–1945*. New Haven, CT: Yale University Press, 2007.
Foucault, Michel. *This Is Not a Pipe*. Berkeley: University of California Press, 1983.
Fowler, Albert D. "Soldier or Priest? The Experience of Canadian Chaplains in World War II." In *Chaplains in War and Peace: Ethical Dilemmas of Conscience and Conflicting Professional Roles in Military Chaplaincy in Canada*, edited by Michael L. Hadley and Leslie A. Kenny, 33–58. Victoria: Centre for Studies in Religion and Society, University of Victoria, 2006.
Freedman, Menachem. "We Can't Let Ottawa's Holocaust Monument Become an Empty Symbol." *Globe and Mail*, 22 May 2014.
Friedman, Max Paul. "The U.S. State Department and the Failure to Rescue: New Evidence on the Missed Opportunity at Bergen-Belsen." *Holocaust and Genocide Studies* 19, no. 1 (Spring 2005): 26–50.
Frisse, Ulrich. "The 'Bystanders' Perspective': The *Toronto Daily Star* and Its Coverage of the Persecution of the Jews and the Holocaust in Canada, 1933–1945." *Yad Vashem Studies* 39, no. 1 (2011): 213–43.
From the Diary of Anne Frank. Judith Forst et al. Toronto: CBC Records, 2000. Compact Disc.
Frye, Northrop. *Anatomy of Criticism: Four Essays*. Princeton, NJ: Princeton University Press, 1957; 1990.
Geddes, John. "The Monumental Politics behind Ottawa's Newest Memorials." *Maclean's*, 9 January 2015.
Gefen, Pearl Sheffy. "Forty Years Ago as a Frail Israel Fought for Life Our War Heroes Said: 'Lean on Us.'" *Toronto Star*, 2 October 1988, D5.
Gelber, Shalome Michael. "Are We Breaking Faith?" *New Statesman and Nation*, 3 August 1946, 78–9. Article is signed "Canadian Officer," but Gelber is the author.
– *The Failure of the American Rabbi: A Program for the Revitalization of the Rabbinate in America*. New York: Twayne, 1961.
– "Wherein Is This Night Different? From Bergen-Belsen, Germany." *Menorah Journal* 35, no. 1 (January-March, 1947): 21–30.
"Generous Move by RAF Men to Help Belsen Survivors." *Army News*. Darwin: Northern Territory Printing and Press Unit, 25 June 1945, 3.
"German Appeals for Germany." *Windsor Daily Star*, 3 February 1943, 2.

German Concentration Camps Factual Survey. Produced by Sidney L. Bernstein. Restoration produced by David Walsh. 90 minutes. Imperial War Museum, 1945; 2015.
"Germans Still 90 P.C. Nazi Hate Allies, Official Says." *Toronto Daily Star*, 23 August 1946.
Gibson, Thomas. "Belsen 1945." *Barts and the London Chronicle* 7, no. 1 (Spring 2005): 18–20.
Gilbert, Martin. *Churchill and the Jews*. Toronto: McClelland and Stewart, 2007.
– *The Holocaust: The Jewish Tragedy*. London: Collins, 1986.
– *The Second World War: A Complete History*. New York: Henry Holt, 1989.
Gladstone, Kay. "The AFPU: The Origins of British Army Combat Filming during the Second World War." *Film History* 14, no. 3/4 (2002): 316–31.
Glover, Stuart. "Viral Words: Belsen." *New Matilda*, 5 October 2007, 2.
Goatly, Andrew. "Humans, Animals, and Metaphors." *Society and Animals* 14, no. 1 (2006): 15–37.
Gödecke, Monika, Rolf Keller, Thomas Rahe, and Wilfried Wiedemann. *Bergen-Belsen: Explanatory Notes on the Exhibition*. Hannover: Niedersächsische Landeszentrale für Politische Bildung, 1991.
Goldman, Aaron. "Germans and Nazis: The Controversy over 'Vansittartism' in Britain during the Second World War." *Journal of Contemporary History* 14, no. 1 (January 1979): 155–91.
Gollancz, Victor. *Let My People Go*. London: Victor Gollancz, 1943.
– *The Yellow Spot: The Extermination of the Jews of Germany*. London: Victor Gollancz, 1936.
Gould, Stephen Jay. *Ontogeny and Phylogeny*. Cambridge, MA: Harvard University Press, 1977.
Goutor, David. "The Canadian Media and the 'Discovery' of the Holocaust, 1944–1945." *Canadian Jewish Studies*, 4–5 (1996–7): 88–119.
Graham, Andrew. *Sharpshooters at War: The 3rd, the 4th and the 3rd/4th County of London Yeomanry, 1939 to 1945*. London: Sharpshooters Regimental Association, 1964.
Grant, Doris. "Campbell Interrogated Bergen-Belsen Inmates; 60th Anniversary of VE- Day." *Barrie Advance*, 4 May 2005, 5.
Grant, Ian. *Cameramen at War*. Cambridge: Stephens, 1980.
Greary, James. *I Is an Other: The Secret Life of Metaphor and How It Shapes the Way We See the World*. New York: HarperCollins, 2011.
Greenberg, Reesa. "Constructing the Canadian War Museum / Constructing the Landscape of a Canadian Identity." In *(Re)visualizing National History: Museums and National Identities in Europe in the New Millennium*, edited by Robin Ostow, 183–99. Toronto: University of Toronto Press, 2008.

Greenhous, Brereton, Stephen J. Harris, William C. Johnston, and William G.P. Rawling. *The Crucible of War, 1939–1945: The Official History of the Royal Canadian Air Force*. Vol. 3. Toronto: University of Toronto Press, 1994.

Greenspan, Henry. "Survivors' Accounts." In *The Oxford Handbook of Holocaust Studies*, edited by Peter Hayes and John K. Roth, 414–27. Oxford: Oxford University Press, 2011.

Griffin, Kevin. "Holocaust Horrors Recalled." *Vancouver Sun*, 4 May 1995, B4.

Grossman, Atina. *Jews, Germans and Allies: Close Encounters in Occupied Germany*. Princeton, NJ: Princeton University Press, 2007.

"Gruesome Pictures of Concentration Camp." *St Marys Journal Argus*, 17 May 1945, 12J.

Gutkin, Harry. *The Worst of Times, The Best of Times*. Markham, ON: Fitzhenry and Whiteside, 1987.

Habermas, Jürgen. "Learning from Catastrophes: A Look Back at the Short Twentieth Century." In *The Postnational Constellation: Political Essays*, translated and edited by Max Pensky, 38–57. Cambridge, MA: MIT Press, 2001.

Haggith, Toby. "Filming the Liberation of Bergen-Belsen." In *Holocaust and the Moving Image*, edited by Toby Haggith and Joanna Newman, 33–49. London: Wallflower, 2005.

– "The Filming of the Liberation of Bergen-Belsen and Its Impact on the Understanding of the Holocaust." In *Belsen 1945: New Historical Perspectives*, edited by Suzanne Bardgett and David Cesarani, 89–122. London: Vallentine Mitchell, 2006.

Haines, Judy. "Doris Haines." *Globe and Mail*, 26 January 2009, L6.

Halbwachs, Maurice. *On Collective Memory*. Edited and translated by Lewis A. Coser. Chicago: University of Chicago Press, 1992.

Halliday, Hugh. "Donald Kenneth Anderson: Official War Artist (1920-2009)." *Canadian Military History* 19, no. 4 (Autumn 2010): 50–6.

– *Typhoon and Tempest: The Canadian Story*. Toronto: CANAV, 1992.

Hancock, Glen. *Charley Goes to War*. Kentville: Gaspereau, 2004.

Hamilton, Nigel. *Monty: Final Years of the Field Marshal, 1944–1976*. New York: McGraw-Hill, 1986.

Harclerode, Peter. *Fighting Brigadier: The Life and Campaigns of Brigadier James Hill*. Barnsley: Pen and Sword Military, 2010.

– *Go to It! The Illustrated History of the 6th Airborne Division*. London: Bloomsbury, 1990.

Hardman, Leslie. "Rev. Leslie Hardman." In *Belsen in History and Memory*, edited by Jo Reilly, David Cesarani, Tony Kushner, and Colin Richmond, 225–33. London: Frank Cass, 1997.

Hardman, Leslie H., and Cecily Goodman. *The Survivors: The Story of the Belsen Remnant*. London: Vallentine Mitchell, 1958; 2009.
Hardy, Bert. *Bert Hardy: My Life*. London: G. Fraser, 1985.
Hargrave, Michael John. *Bergen-Belsen 1945: A Medical Student's Journal*. London: Imperial College, 2013.
Harris, David A. *In the Trenches: Selected Speeches and Writings of an American Jewish Activist*. Vol. 3. Hoboken: KTAV, 2000.
Harrison, Earl Grant. *The Plight of the Displaced Jews in Europe: A Report to President Truman*. New York: United Jewish Appeal for Refugees, Overseas Needs and Palestine, 1945.
Harrison, Mark. *Medicine and Victory: British Military Medicine in the Second World War*. Oxford: Oxford University Press, 2004.
Hartigan, Daniel R. *A Rising Courage: Canada's Paratroops in the Liberation of Normandy*. Calgary: Drop Zone, 2000.
Harvey, J. Douglas. *Boys, Bombs and Brussels Sprouts*. Toronto: McClelland and Stewart, 1981.
Health and Human Relations in Germany: Report of a Conference on Problems of Health and Human Relations in Germany, Nassau Tavern, Princeton, N.J., June 26–30, 1950. Edited by Jean W. Conti. New York: Josiah Macy Jr Foundation, 1950.
Heaps, Leo. *Escape from Arnhem: A Canadian among the Lost Paratroops*. Toronto: Macmillan, 1945.
– *The Grey Goose of Arnhem*. London: Weidenfeld and Nicholson, 1976.
Heard, P.L. "Mary Kessell." *The Arts*, edited by Desmond Shawe-Taylor, no. 2 (1946–7): 52–7.
Heschel, Abraham Joshua. *A Passion for Truth*. New York: Farrar, Straus and Giroux, 1973.
Hilberg, Raul. *Perpetrators, Victims, Bystanders: The Jewish Catastrophe, 1933–1945*. New York: HarperCollins, 1992.
Hill, Robert. *Jack McCreary: Paediatrician, Pedagogue, Pragmatist, Prophet*. Vancouver: Tantalus Research, 2006.
Hirsch, Marianne. "Editor's Column: What's Wrong with These Terms? A Conversation with Barbara Kirshenblatt-Gimblett and Diana Taylor." *PMLA* 120, no. 4 (October 2005): 1497–1508.
Holocaust and the Moving Image: Representations in Film and Television since 1933. Edited by Toby Haggith and Joanna Newman. London: Wallflower, 2005.
"Holocaust Song Has Cellular Firm Squirming." *Reuters UK*, 15 September 2007.

Hoover, A.J. *God, Britain, and Hitler in World War II: The View of the British Clergy, 1939–1945*. Westport, CT: Praeger, 1999.
Horn, Bernd, and Michel Wyczynski. *Paras versus the Reich: Canada's Paratroopers at War, 1942–45*. Toronto: Dundurn, 2003.
Horowitz, Sara R. *Voicing the Void: Muteness and Memory in Holocaust Fiction*. Albany: State University of New York Press, 1997.
"H.S. Abramson Awarded French Art Scholarship." *Montreal Standard*, 16 March 1946.
Hutcheon, Linda. *Leonard Cohen and His Works*. Toronto: ECW, 1992.
Hynes, Samuel. *The Soldiers' Tale: Bearing Witness to Modern War*. New York: A. Lane, 1997.
Ignatieff, Michael. "Stories of Life after the Shoah." *New Republic*, 14 June 2014.
"Interview with Allan [sic] Rose." In *Bitburg and Beyond: Encounters in American, German and Jewish History*, edited by Ilya Levkov, 680–5. New York: Shapolsky, 1987.
"Introducing the 'Cookie Pusher' of the Montreal St. Andrew Society." *The Journal of the St. Andrew's Society of Montreal* (Fall 1993): 2.
Jackson, G.S. *The Rhine River to the Baltic Sea*. Germany: s.n., 1945.
"Jan Karski to Speak." *Montreal Gazette*, 5 December 1944, 4.
Janowitz, Morris. "German Reactions to Nazi Atrocities." *American Journal of Sociology* 52, no. 2 (September 1946): 141–6.
Jaspers, Karl. *The Question of German Guilt*. Translated by E.B. Ashton. New York: Fordham University Press, 1947; 2001.
"JDC Worker Makes Plea for Victims." *Jewish Western Bulletin*, 14 March 1947, 1.
Johnstone, Tom, and James Hagerty. *The Cross on the Sword: Catholic Chaplains in the Forces*. London: G. Chapman, 1996.
Jones, Jonah. *The Gallipoli Diary*. Bridgend: Seren, 1989.
Jones, Peter. *Jonah Jones: An Artist's Life*. Bridgend: Seren, 2011.
Kadar, Marlene. *Essays on Life Writing: From Genre to Critical Practice*. Toronto: University of Toronto Press, 1992.
"Kadziolka, Rev. Dr. Stanislaus Jan." *Ottawa Citizen*, 17 February 1986, C4.
Kaplan, Brett Ashley. *Unwanted Beauty: Aesthetic Pleasure in Holocaust Representation*. Urbana: University of Illinois Press, 2007.
Kearney, Richard. "Parsing Narrative – Story, History, Life." *Human Studies* 29, no. 4 (December 2006): 477–90.
"Keith MacLellan Honored for Wartime Services." *Suburban*, 2 November 1988, A26.
Kelleway, Philip. *Highly Desirable: The Zinkeisen Sisters and Their Legacy*. Suffolk: Leiston, 2008.

Kemp, Anthony. *The SAS at War, 1941–1945*. London: Penguin, 1991.
Kemp, Paul. "The British Army and the Liberation of Bergen-Belsen, April 1945." In *Belsen in History and Memory*. Edited by Jo Reilly, David Cesarani, Tony Kushner and Colin Richmond. London: Frank Cass, 1997.
– "The Liberation of Bergen-Belsen Concentration Camp in April 1945: The Testimony of Those Involved." *Imperial War Museum Review* 5 (1991): 28–41.
Keys, Ancel, Josef Brozek, Austin Henschel, Olaf Mickelsen, and Henry Longstreet Taylor. *The Biology of Human Starvation*. 2 vols. Minneapolis: University of Minnesota Press, 1950.
Kirshner, Sheldon. "Canadian Pilot Witnessed Horrors of Bergen-Belsen." *Canadian Jewish News*, 20 January 2011, 16.
Klemme, Marvin. *The Inside Story of UNRRA: An Experience in Internationalism*. New York: Lifetime Editions, 1949.
Knelman, Martin. "Holocaust Monument in Ottawa Corrects 70-Year Mistake." *Toronto Star*, 14 May 2014.
Kohler, Nicholas. "Band of Brothers." *National Post*, 11 November 2004, A1.
Kolb, Eberhard. *Bergen-Belsen: From 'Detention Camp' to Concentration Camp, 1943–1945*. 2nd ed. Göttingen: Vandenhoeck and Ruprecht, 1986.
Kostenuk, Samual, and John Griffin. *RCAF Squadron Histories and Aircraft, 1924–1968*. Toronto: A.M. Hakkert, 1977.
Krell, Robert. "Children Who Survived the Holocaust: Reflections of a Child Survivor / Psychiatrist." *Echoes of the Holocaust* 4 (June 1995): 1–3.
Kren, George M., and Leon Rappoport, *The Holocaust and the Crisis of Human Behavior*. New York: Holmes and Meier, 1980.
Kristeva, Julia. *Powers of Horror: An Essay on Abjection*. Translated by Leon S. Roudiez. New York: Columbia University Press, 1980; 1982.
Kushner, Tony. "Different Worlds: British Perceptions of the Final Solution during the Second World War." In *The Final Solution: Origins and Implementations*, edited by David Cesarani, 246–67. London: Routledge, 1996.
– "Editor's Introduction: 'Wrong War, Mate.'" *Patterns of Prejudice* 29, nos 2–3 (April–July 1995): 3–13.
– "The Memory of Belsen." In *Belsen in History and Memory*, edited by Jo Reilly, David Cesarani, Tony Kushner, and Colin Richmond, 181–205. Portland: F. Cass, 1997.
– "Oral History at the Extremes of Human Experience: Holocaust Testimony in a Museum Setting." *Oral History* 29, no. 2, Hidden Histories (Autumn 2001): 83–94.
LaCapra, Dominick. *History in Transit: Experience, Identity, Critical Theory*. Ithaca, NY: Cornell University Press, 2004.

"LAC Blooms on Vegetables." *Maple Leaf*, 22 January 1946, 2.
Lackerstein, Debbie. "Medical Responses to the Liberation of Nazi Camps, April–May 1945." In *War Wounds: Medicine and the Trauma of Conflict*, edited by Elizabeth Stewart and Ashley Ekins, 93–108. Auckland: Exisle, 2011.
Lakoff, George, and Mark Johnson. *Metaphors We Live By*. Chicago: University of Chicago Press, 1980.
Lakoff, George, and Mark Turner. *More Than Cool Reason: A Field Guide to Poetic Metaphor*. Chicago: University of Chicago Press, 1989.
Lane, Ray W. *In Chariots of Iron*. Edmonton: Pagemaster, 2011.
Lang, Berel. *Holocaust Representation: Art within the Limits of History and Ethics*. Baltimore: Johns Hopkins University Press, 2000.
– *Post-Holocaust: Interpretation, Misinterpretation, and the Claims of History*. Bloomington: Indiana University Press, 2005.
Langer, Lawrence, *The Holocaust and the Literary Imagination*. New Haven: Yale University, 1975.
Langlois, Suzanne. "Making Ideal Histories: The Film Censorship Board in Postwar France." In *Secret Spaces, Forbidden Places: Rethinking Culture*, edited by Fran Lloyd and Catherine O'Brien, 107–20. New York: Berghahn, 2000.
Laqueur, Walter. *The Terrible Secret: An Investigation into the Suppression of Information about Hitler's Final Solution*. New York: Henry Holt, 1998.
– *Thursday's Child Has Far to Go: A Memoir of the Journeying Years*. Toronto: Maxwell MacMillian, 1992.
Lara, María Pía. *Narrating Evil: A Postmetaphysical Theory of Reflective Judgment*. New York: Columbia University Press, 2007.
Lavsky, Hagit. *New Beginnings: Holocaust Survivors in Bergen-Belsen and the British Zone in Germany, 1945–1950*. Detroit: Wayne State University Press, 2002.
Law, Cecil. *Kamp Westerbork, Transit Camp to Eternity: The Liberation Story*. Clementsport: Canadian Peacekeeping Press, 2000.
Lawlor, Allison. "Ted Light, Military Chaplain 1914–2005." *Globe and Mail*, 13 June 2005, S6.
Layton, Irving. *Fortunate Exile*. Toronto: McClelland and Stewart, 1987.
Lee, Geddy, and Ben Mink. "Grace to Grace." *My Favourite Headache*. Atlantic, 2000. Compact Disc.
Lee, Geddy, Alex Lifeson, and Neil Peart. "Red Sector A." *Grace under Pressure*. Anthem Records, 1984. Compact Disc.
Legends: Dirk Bogarde Documentary. Produced by Trevor Hyett. Carleton Television, 2000.
Lejeune, Philippe. *On Autobiography*. Edited by Paul John Eakin. Translated by Katherine Leary. Minneapolis: University of Minnesota Press, 1989.

– *On Diary*. Edited by Jeremy D. Popkin and Julie Rak. Translated by Katherine Durnin. Manoa: University of Hawaii Press, 2009.
Levi, S. Gershon. *Breaking New Ground: The Struggle for a Jewish Chaplaincy in Canada*. Edited by David Golinkin. Montreal: Canadian Jewish Congress, 1994.
Levinson, Lottie. "Lottie Levinson in Europe Scores Zionist Nationalism." *Jewish Western Bulletin*, 4 January 1946, 1, 4.
Levy, Isaac. *Witness to Evil: Bergen-Belsen, 1945*. London: Peter Halban, 1995.
Lewinski, Jorge. *The Camera at War: A History of War Photography from 1848 to the Present Day*. London: W.H. Allen, 1978.
Lewis, J.T. "Medical Problems at Belsen Concentration Camp (1945)." *Ulster Medical Journal* 54, no. 2 (October 1985): 122–6.
"The Liberated of Belsen." *OHTWOEE* 3, no. 20 (23 July 1945).
The Liberation of the Nazi Concentration Camps 1945: Eyewitness Accounts of the Liberators. Edited by Brewster Chamberlin, Marcia Feldman, and Robert Abzug. Washington: United States Holocaust Memorial Council, 1987.
Lifton, Robert Jay. *Death in Life: Survivors of Hiroshima*. New York: Random House, 1968.
Liss, Andrea. *Trespassing through Shadows: Memory, Photography and the Holocaust*. Minneapolis: University of Minnesota Press, 1998.
"Local Men's Work in UNRRA Praised." *Montreal Gazette*, 30 January 1946, 7.
Longden, Sean. *To the Victor the Spoils*. Gloucestershire: Arris, 2004.
Louden, Stephen H. *Chaplains in Conflict: The Role of Army Chaplains since 1914*. London: Avon, 1996.
MacAuslan, Rowan. "Some Aspects of the Medical Relief of Belsen Concentration Camp, April–May 1945." Master's thesis, Birkbeck College, University of London, 2012.
MacIntyre, Alasdair. *After Virtue: A Study in Moral Theory*. London: Duckworth, 1981.
Malcolm, Janet. *The Silent Woman: Sylvia Plath and Ted Hughes*. London: Picador, 1994.
Mann, Larry. "Beaching on Normandy Easier a Second Time." *Edmonton Journal*, 9 September 1979, I1.
Mares-Hershey, Victoria. "Distrust of U.N. Shows How Little We Remember." *Portland Press Herald*, 18 October 2005.
Margalit, Avishai. *The Ethics of Memory*. Cambridge, MA: Harvard University Press, 2002.
Margolis, Rebecca. "The Canadian Army Newsreels as a Representation of the Holocaust." In *Lessons and Legacies XI: Expanding Perspectives on the Holocaust in a Changing World*. Edited by Hilary Earl and Karl A. Schleunes, 121–43. Evanston, IL: Northwestern University Press, 2014.

Magritte, René. *La trahison des images*. 1928–29. Oil on canvas. 63.5 cm × 93.98 cm. Los Angeles County Museum of Art, Los Angeles, California.

The Maroon Square: A History of the 4th Battalion, The Wiltshire Regiment. Compiled by A.D. Parsons, D.I.M. Robbins, and D.C. Gilson. London: Franley, 1955.

Martin, Sandra. "Lyle Creelman, Nurse and Administrator, 1908–2007." *Globe and Mail*, 10 March 2007, S9.

"Mass Murderess: Woman Leader of Nazi Guards at Belsen Camp Sets Record for Evil." *Life*, 8 October 1945, 40.

Mayer, Sylvia. "American Environmentalism and Encounters with the Abject: T. Coraghessan Boyle's A Friend of the Earth." In *The Abject of Desire: The Aestheticization of the Unaesthetic in Contemporary Literature and Culture*, edited by Konstanze Kutzbach and Monika Mueller, 221–4. New York: Rodopi, 2007.

McCooey, David. *Artful Histories: Modern Australian Autobiography*. Cambridge: Cambridge University Press, 1996.

McCreery, Christopher. *The Maple Leaf and the White Cross*. Toronto: Dundurn, 2008.

McGill, Robert. "The Life You Write May Be Your Own: Epistolary Autobiography and the Reluctant Resurrection of Flannery O'Connor." *Southern Literary Journal* 36, no. 2 (Spring 2004): 31–46.

McGlade, Fred. *The History of the British Army Film and Photographic Unit in the Second World War*. Solihull: Helion, 2010.

McKillop, James. "British War Film Evidence of the Belsen Horror." *Glasgow Herald*, 6 September 1985, 11.

Meisels, Leslie. *Suddenly the Shadow Fell*. Toronto: Azrieli Foundation, 2014.

Melin, Charlotte. *Poetic Maneuvers: Hans Magnus Enzensberger and the Lyric Genre*. Evanston, IL: Northwestern University Press, 2003.

Memory of the Camps. Directed by Sidney Bernstein. 56 minutes. PBS *Frontline*, 1985.

Menkis, Richard. "'But You Can't See the Fear that People Lived Through': Canadian Jewish Chaplains and Canadian Encounters with Dutch Survivors." *American Jewish Archives Journal* 60, nos 1–2 (2008): 24–50.

– "Cass, Samuel (1908–1975)." *Encyclopaedia Judaica*, 2nd ed., vol. 4, edited by Fred Skolnik and Michael Berenbaum, 507. Detroit: Macmillan, 2007.

Menkis, Richard, and Ronnie Tessler. *Canada Responds to the Holocaust, 1944 to 1945*. Vancouver: Vancouver Holocaust Education Centre, 2005.

Mikel, Melissa Dawn. "Pebbles for Peace: The Impact of Holocaust Education." Master's thesis, University of Toronto, 2014.

Milberry, Larry, and Hugh A. Halliday. *The Royal Canadian Air Force at War, 1939–1945*. Toronto: CANAV, 1990.

Milton, Sybil. "The Camera as a Weapon: Documentary Photography and the Holocaust." *Simon Wiesenthal Center Annual* 1 (1984): 45–68.

"Ministry Call First Shunned by Cowboy." *Ladner Optimist*, 18 October 1951, 3.

Mirsky, Mervin. "I Saw Holocaust Horrors in Person." *Ottawa Citizen*, 18 February 1998, A18.

Modes of Individualism and Collectivism. Edited by John O'Neill. London: Heinemann, 1973.

Monnon, Ernest, and Mary Ann Monnon. *"Right on, you got the elbow out!": Wartime Memories of the R.C.A.F.* Toronto: Dundurn, 1990.

Montgomery, Bernard. "21st (British) Army Group in the Campaign in North-West Europe, 1944–45." *Journal of the Royal United Service Institution* 90, no. 56 (November 1945): 431–54.

Moorehead, Caroline. *Dunant's Dream: War, Switzerland and the History of the Red Cross*. London: HarperCollins, 1998.

Morse, Jennifer. "War Art: Aba Bayefsky." *Legion Magazine*, 1 May 1998.

Mortimer, Gavin. *Stirling's Men: The Inside History of the SAS in World War II*. London: Cassell, 2004.

Naggar, Carol. *George Rodger: An Adventure in Photography, 1908–1995*. Syracuse, NY: Syracuse University Press, 2003.

Nazi Germany, Canadian Responses: Confronting Antisemitism in the Shadow of War. Edited by L. Ruth Klein. Montreal and Kingston: McGill-Queen's University Press, 2012.

"Nazi Underground Seen Future Evil." *Montreal Gazette*, 18 November 1944, 19.

"Nazi Underground to Be Best of All." *Regina Leader-Post*, 18 November 1944, 16.

Neumann, Klaus. *Shifting Memories: The Nazis Past in the New Germany*. Ann Arbor: University of Michigan Press, 2000.

Neusner, Jacob, and Alan Jeffery Avery-Peck. *The Routledge Dictionary of Judaism*. New York: Routledge, 2004.

Nicholson, G.W.L. *Seventy Years of Service: A History of the Royal Canadian Army Medical Corps*. Ottawa: Borealis, 1977.

Nicholson, Virginia. *Millions Like Us: Women's Lives in War and Peace, 1939–1949*. London: Penguin, 2011.

Night Will Fall. Directed by André Singer. 75 minutes. British Film Institute, 2014.

Nijboer, Donald. *No 126 Wing RCAF*. Oxford: Osprey, 2010.

Nolan, Brian. *Airborne: The Heroic Story of the 1st Canadian Parachute Battalion in the Second World War*. Toronto: Lester, 1995.

Norman, Andrew. "Telling It Like It Was: Historical Narratives on Their Own Terms." *History and Theory* 30, no. 2 (May 1991): 119–35.

Novick, Peter. *The Holocaust and the Collective Memory: The American Experience*. London: Bloomsbury, 2001.
Official History of the Canadian Medical Services, 1939–1945: Organization and Campaigns. Vol. 1. Edited by W.R. Feasby. Ottawa: Queen's Printer and Controller of Stationary, 1956.
O'Hanlon, Betty. *Finding a Familiar Stranger*. Edmonton: Plains, 1988.
Olick, Jeffrey K. *In the House of the Hangman: The Agonies of German Defeat, 1943–1949*. Chicago: University of Chicago Press, 2005.
Olney, James. *Metaphors of Self: The Meaning of Autobiography*. Princeton, NJ: Princeton University Press, 1972.
O'Neill, Patrick B. "The Halifax Concert Party in World War II." *Theatre Research in Canada* 20, no. 2 (Fall 1999): 1–16.
O'Sullivan, Arieh. "Dad's Army: John Burrows' Search for His Non-Jewish Father's Machal Exploits." *Jerusalem Post Magazine*, 18 May 2001, 10.
Palamountain, Edgar W.I. *Taurus Pursuant: A History of 11th Armoured Division*. Germany: 11th Armoured Division, 1945.
Panchuk, Bohdan. *Heroes of Their Day: The Reminiscences of Bohdan Panchuk*. Edited by Lubomyr Y. Luciuk. Toronto: Multicultural History Society, Ontario Heritage Foundation, 1983.
"Paratrooper Remembered on Banff Avenue." *Banff Crag and Canyon*, 10 November 2009, 7.
Parry, Nigel. "British Graffiti Artist, Banksy, Hacks the Wall." *Thresholds*, 1 October 2006.
Pathé Pictorial Looks at the Modern Woman. Film ID 1341.29, Tape PM1341 (29 September 1947).
Paybody, Douglas. "The Liberator." *Observer*, 9 January 2005.
Peake, Mervyn. "The Consumptive: Belsen, 1945." In Meryn Peake, *The Glassblowers*, 15–16. London: Eyre and Spottiswoode, 1950.
– *Titus Alone*. Harmondsworth: Penguin, 1970.
Peake, Sebastian. *A Child of Bliss: Growing up with Mervyn Peake*. Oxford: Lennard, 1989.
Perl, Gisella. *I Was a Doctor in Auschwitz*. New York: International Universities Press, 1948.
Perley, Warren. "TV Records Tearful Memories of Holocaust Horror." *Montreal Gazette*, 13 August 1981, 12.
Perlove, B. "Don't Forget! Fifty Forum Reporter Sees Horrors of Belsen." *Fifty Forum*, 17 August 1945, 1.
Photographs, Histories, and Meanings. Edited by Marlene Kadar, Jeanne Perreault, and Linda Warley. New York: Palgrave Macmillan, 2009.
Piovesana, Roy. *Hope and Charity: Diocese of Thunder Bay*. Thunder Bay: Roman Catholic Bishop of Thunder Bay, 2002.

Place, G.M. "Artists of Note: Doris Zinkeisen." *Artist* 39, no. 4 (June 1950): 86, 95–6.
Pocock, Tom. *The Dawn Camp up Like Thunder*. London: Collins, 1983.
Popkin, Jeremy D. *History, Historians, and Autobiography*. Chicago: University of Chicago Press, 2005.
– "Holocaust Memories, Historians' Memoirs: First-Person Narrative and the Memory of the Holocaust." *History and Memory* 15, no. 1 (Spring/Summer 2003): 49–84.
Portraits of War. Produced by Paul Kemp. 48 minutes. Stornoway Productions, 2007. DVD.
Posner, Michael. "Patricia Holden Collins Was Groundbreaking Wartime Photographer." *Globe and Mail*, 8 December 2011.
Prayer for the Dead: Herzl Kashetsky. Produced and directed by Lisa Lamb. New Brunswick Museum, Saint John Jewish Historical Museum and Fundy Community Television, 1997.
"Prison Occupants Return to Normal." *Saskatoon Star-Phoenix*, 6 May 1946, 6.
Probing the Limits of Representation: Nazism and the "Final Solution." Edited by Saul Friedländer. Cambridge, MA: Harvard University Press, 1992.
Purden, Carolyn. "The Two Lives of Ted Light." *Canadian Churchman*, July-August 1969, 10, 12.
Raab, Elisabeth M. *And Peace Never Came*. Waterloo, ON: Wilfrid Laurier University Press, 1997.
"Rabbi Finds Belsen Benefactor." *Windsor Star*, 20 December 1962, 1.
"Rabbi Seeks Wartime 'Friends.'" *Montreal Gazette*, 15 December 1962, 3.
Ralph, Wayne. *Aces, Warriors and Wingmen: The Firsthand Accounts of Canada's Fighter Pilots in the Second World War*. Mississauga, ON: John Wiley and Sons Canada, 2005.
Randall, John and M.J. Trow. *The Last Gentleman of the SAS*. New York: Random House, 2014.
Ravvin, Norman. "A Museum, War Art and Canadian Identity." *Canadian Jewish News*, 31 August 2006, 41.
Rawling, Bill. *Death Their Enemy: Canadian Medical Practitioners and War*. Ottawa: Bill Rawling, 2001.
Reagan, Charles E. *Paul Ricoeur*. Chicago: University of Chicago Press, 1996.
Reilly, Joanne. *Belsen: The Liberation of a Concentration Camp*. London: Routledge, 1998.
– "'With Waving Flags': Bergen-Belsen and the Myth of Liberation." *Patterns of Prejudice* 29, nos 2–3 (April–July 1995): 61–74.
Reinisch, Jessica. "Introduction: Relief in the Aftermath of War." *Journal of Contemporary History* 4, no. 3 (2008): 371–404.

Reiter, Andrea. *Narrating the Holocaust*. Translated by Patrick Camiller. London: Continuum, 1995; 2000.
- "Narrating the Holocaust: Communicating the End or the End of Communication?" *Patterns of Prejudice* 29, no. 2–3 (April–July 1995): 75–87.

The Relief of Belsen, April 1945: Eyewitness Accounts. Compiled by Paul Kemp. London: Imperial War Museum, 1991.

Remembering Belsen: Eyewitnesses Record the Liberation. Edited by Ben Flanagan and Donald Bloxham. London: Vallentine Mitchell, 2005.

Rennick, Joanne Benham. *Religion in the Ranks: Belief and Religious Experience in the Canadian Forces*. Toronto: University of Toronto Press, 2011.

Richer, Charles H. "Sgt. Mike Lattion (obituary)." In *1st Canadian Parachute Battalion Association Newsletter* 6, no. 20 (April 1997): 41–3.

Ricoeur, Paul. *Critique and Conviction: Conversations with François Azouvi and Marc de Launay*. Translated by Kathleen Blarney. New York: Columbia University Press, 1995; 1998.
- *Oneself as Another*. Translated by Kathleen Blamey. Chicago: University of Chicago Press, 1992.
- *The Symbolism of Evil*. Translated by Emerson Buchanan. Boston: Beacon, 1970.
- *Temps et récit*. 3 vols. Paris: Seuil, 1983.
- *Time and Narrative*. 3 vols. Translated by K. McLaughlin and D. Pellauer. Chicago: University of Chicago Press, 1983; 1984.

Ricoeur, Paul, David Carr, and Charles Taylor. "Discussion: Ricoeur on Narrative." In *On Paul Ricoeur: Narrative and Interpretation*, edited by D. Wood, 160–87. New York: Routledge, 1991.

Roberts, Amanda. "The Saltsman Letters." *Muskoka Times* (ca March 2000)

Robinson, Alan. *Chaplains at War: The Role of Clergymen during World War II*. London: Tauris Academic Studies, 2008.

Rodger, George. "Belsen." *Time*, 30 April 1945, 40.

Rodger, Peter. *The OMG Chronicles: One Man's Quest to Discover What God Means to People All Over the World*. London: Hay House, 2011.

Rose, Alan. "Testimony at the Liberators of Nazi Concentration Camps Conference." In *Bitburg and Beyond: Encounters in American, German and Jewish History*, edited by Ilya Levkov, 686–7. New York: Shapolsky, 1987.

Rosensaft, Hadassah. *Yesterday: My Story*. New York: Yad Vashem and the Holocaust Survivors' Memoirs Project, 2005.

Rosensaft, Josef. "Introduction." In *Holocaust and Rebirth: Bergen-Belsen, 1945–1965*, edited by Sam E. Bloch. New York: Bergen-Belsen Memorial Press of the World Federation of Bergen-Belsen Associations, 1965.

Rosensaft, Menachem. "Bergen-Belsen: The End and the Beginning." In *Children and the Holocaust: Symposium Presentations*, 117–36. Washington: United States Holocaust Memorial Museum, 2004.

– "The Mass-Graves of Bergen-Belsen: Focus for Confrontation." *Jewish Social Studies* 41, no. 2 (Spring 1979): 155–86.
Rosenthal, David. "Our Voice: The First Jewish Periodical in Germany after Liberation: The Story of *Undzer Shtimme* in Bergen-Belsen." *Jewish Frontier* 63, no. 5 (September/October 1996): 19–21.
Rosse, Captain the Earl of, and Colonel E.R. Hill. *The Story of the Guards Armoured Division*. London: Geoffrey Bles, 1956.
Roth, John K. *Holocaust Politics*. Louisville: Westminster John Knox, 2001.
Rothberg, Michael. *Traumatic Realism: The Demands of Holocaust Representation*. Minneapolis: University of Minnesota Press, 2000.
Rousset, David. *L'univers concentrationnaire*. Paris: Éditions de Pavois, 1946.
Rughani, Pratap. "Are You a Vulture? Reflecting on the Ethics and Aesthetics of Atrocity Coverage and Its Aftermath." In *Peace Journalism, War and Conflict Resolution*, edited by Richard Lance Keeble, John Tulloch, and Florian Zollmann, 157–71. New York: Peter Lang, 2010.
Sapir, Edward. *Culture, Language and Personality*. Berkeley: University of California Press, 1962.
"Saul Laskin Describes Belsen Camp." *Daily Times Journal*, 26 March 1946.
Saunders, Tim. *Operation Varsity: The British and Canadian Airborne Assault*. Barnsley: Pen and Sword, 2008.
Savage, Jon. *England's Dreaming: Anarchy, Sex Pistols, Punk Rock and Beyond*. New York: St Martin's Griffin, 1991; 2011.
Scarry, Elaine. *The Body in Pain: The Making and Unmaking of the World*. New York: Oxford University Press, 1985.
Schoenberner, Gerhard. *Der gelbe Stern. Die Judenvernichtung in Europa 1933–1945*. Hamburg: Rütten und Loening, 1960.
Schulze, Rainer. "'Keeping Very Clear of Any 'Kuh-Handel': The British Foreign Office and the Rescue of Jews from Bergen-Belsen." *Holocaust Genocide Studies* 19, no. 2 (Fall 2005): 226–51.
Scott, Joan. W. "The Evidence of Experience." *Critical Inquiry* 17, no. 4 (Summer 1991): 773–97.
Sebald, W.G. *On the Natural History of Destruction*. Translated by Anthea Bell. Toronto: Alfred A. Knopf Canada, 1999; 2003.
Secrest, Meryle. *Kenneth Clark: A Biography*. New York: Holt, Rinehart and Winston, 1984.
Seger, Gerhart. *A Nation Terrorized*. Chicago: Reilly and Lee, 1935.
Senate of Canada. *Proceedings of the Standing Committee on Immigration and Labour* (29 May 1946).
Service of Praise and Thanksgiving for the Victories of the Allied Nations. Officiant: The Rev. Dr. Louis M. Sanker, Senior Jewish Chaplain, RAF and Tactical Air Force. London: Office of the Chief Rabbi, 1945.

Shadbolt, Jack. *In Search of Form*. Toronto: McClelland and Stewart, 1968.
Shanahan, Noreen. "Belsen Diarist Hated Medicine and Loved Writing." *Globe and Mail*, 29 March 2013.
Shapiro, Marshall. "Adath Israel Honours Jewish War Vets." *Jewish Tribune*, 10 November 2005.
Shephard, Ben. *After Daybreak: The Liberation of Bergen-Belsen, 1945*. New York: Schocken, 2005.
– "The Medical Relief Effort at Belsen." In *Belsen 1945: New Historical Perspectives*, edited by Suzanne Bardgett and David Cesarani, 31–50. London: Vallentine Mitchell, 2006.
Shields, Roy. "Gallery 'With a Purpose' Opened by Artist Couple." *Monitor*, 26 February 1953.
Sington, Derrick. *Belsen Uncovered*. London: Duckworth, 1946.
Smalley, Ulrike. "Objective Realists? British War Artists as Witnesses to the Liberation of Bergen-Belsen Concentration Camp." *Holocaust in History and Memory* 2 (2009): 53–67.
Smart, Tom. *Alex Colville: Return*. Halifax: Douglas and McIntyre, 2004.
– "A Broken Neck, a Shattered Heart." *Telegraph-Journal* (New Brunswick), 5 May 2012, F3.
Smith, Lyn. *Forgotten Voices of the Holocaust*. London: Ebury, 2005.
– *Heroes of the Holocaust: Ordinary Britons Who Risked Their Lives to Make a Difference*. London: Ebury, 2012.
Smith, Michael. "Bletchley Park and the Holocaust." In *Understanding Intelligence in the Twenty-First Century*, edited by L.V. Scott and P.D. Jackson, 111–21. London: Routledge, 2004.
Smith, Sidonie, and Julia Watson. *Reading Autobiography: A Guide for Interpreting Life Narratives*. Minnesota: University of Minnesota Press, 2001.
Smith, Ted. "Horror Beyond Belief." In Paul Hunter and Jim Rankin, *Never Forget: More Stories from the Conflict Zones*, 57–60. Toronto: Star Dispatches, 2013.
Smith, Wilfred I. *Code Word CANLOAN*. Toronto: Dundurn, 1992.
– *Experiences of a CANLOAN Officer, 1944–1945*. Ottawa: Public Archives, 1977.
– "Introduction." In Peter Robertson, *Relentless Verity: Canadian Military Photographers since 1885*, 8–33. Toronto: University of Toronto Press, 1973.
Snape, Michael. *God and the British Soldier: Religion and the British Army in the First and Second World Wars*. London: Routledge, 2005.
– *The Royal Army Chaplains' Department, 1796–1953*. Suffolk: Boydell, 2008.
Snell, Adrian. "Kaddish for Bergen Belsen." *Alpha and Omega*. DaySpring Records, 1985.

Sommer, Robert, and Barbara A. Sommer. "Zoomorphy: Animal Metaphors for Human Personality." *Anthrozoos: A Multidisciplinary Journal of the Interactions of People and Animals* 24, no. 3 (September 2011): 237–48.

Sonnenschein, Bronia. *Victory over Nazism: A Holocaust Survivor's Journey*. Edited by Dan Sonnenschein. Vancouver: Deskside, 1998.

Sontag, Susan. *Regarding the Pain of Others*. New York: Farrar, Straus and Giroux, 2003.

The Splendour of Order. Directed by Don Hutchison. Montreal: National Film Board, 1993.

Srikanthan, Thulasi. "Tradition of Patriotism: As a Young Woman, Yvonne Hamon Served Her Country in WWII." *Toronto Star*, 8 November 2006, A4.

Stacey, C.P. *The Victory Campaign: The Operations in North-West Europe, 1944–1945*. Vol. 3. Ottawa: Queen's Printer and Controller of Stationery, 1960.

Stanley, Elmer M. "Death Camp Happy Now Toronto Nurses Aid." *Toronto Daily Star*, 19 September 1945, 1.

Steiner, George. *Language and Silence: Essays on Language, Literature, and the Inhuman*. New York: Atheneum, 1967; 1974.

"Stettler Doctor Returns to Describe Crossing of Rhine with Paratroopers." *Edmonton Journal*, 4 July 1945, 1 and 5.

Stevens, Gordon. *The Originals: The Secret History of the Birth of the SAS*. London: Ebury, 2005.

Stone, Dan. *History, Memory and Mass Atrocity: Essays on the Holocaust and Genocide*. Portland: Vallentine Mitchell, 2006.

Stratton, Jon. "Punk, Jews, and the Holocaust – The English Story." *Shofar: An Interdisciplinary Journal of Jewish Studies* 25, no. 4 (Summer 2007): 124–49.

Strong, Anna Louise. "Mass Murder!" *Maclean's*, 1 September 1944, 11, 39–41.

Struk, Janina. *Photographing the Holocaust: Interpretations of the Evidence*. London: I.B. Tauris in association with European Jewish Publication Society, 2004.

Stubbs, Andrew. *White Light Primitive*. Regina: Hagios, 2009.

Stuchen, Philip. "Mass-Employment for Displaced Persons." *Queen's Quarterly: A Canadian Review* 54, no. 3 (Autumn 1947): 360–5.

– "The Problem of Palestine." *Queen's Quarterly: A Canadian Review* 54, no. 4 (Winter 1947–8): 413–20.

"Study in Evil: The SS Women of Belsen." *Daily Mail*, 23 April 1945, 3.

Taylor, Eric. "A Lifetime." In Derek Hyatt, *Eric Taylor: A Retrospective, Exhibition Catalogue*, 29–31. Leeds: University Gallery, 1994.

Taylor, Frederick. *Exorcising Hitler: The Occupation and Denazification of Germany*. London: Bloomsbury, 2011.

Terraine, John. *The Right of the Line: The Royal Air Force in the European War, 1939–1945*. London: Hodder and Stoughton, 1985.

Thom, Ian M. *Jack Shadbolt: Early Watercolours, July 17 to August 21, 1980*. Victoria, BC: Art Gallery of Greater Victoria, 1980.
Thompson, Lloyd E. *At Face Value: Portraits by Lloyd E. Thompson*. Picton, ON: Picton Gazette, 1976.
Tibbs, David J. *Parachute Doctor: The Memoirs of Captain David Tibbs*. Edited by Neil Barber. Sevenoaks: Sabrestorm, 2012.
Todorov. Tzvetan. *Facing the Extreme: Moral Life in the Concentration Camps*. Translated by Arthur Denner and Abigail Pollak. New York: Henry Holt, 1991; 1996.
Toews, John E. "Intellectual History after the Linguistic Turn: The Autonomy of Meaning and the Irreducibility of Experience." *American Historical Review* 92, no. 4 (October 1987): 879–907.
Tolson, Roger. "A Common Cause: Britain's War Artists Scheme." *Canadian War Museum* (2005): 1–5.
Toman, Cynthia. *An Officer and a Lady: Canadian Military Nursing and the Second World War*. Vancouver: UBC Press, 2007.
The Topography of the Bergen-Belsen Camp: Six Maps. Edited by Monica Gödeck. Stuttgart: Druck and Design, 2008.
Topolski, Feliks. *14 Letters*. London: Faber, 1988.
Traynor, Ian. "Men Who Showed Belsen Hell to Britain Return." *Guardian*, 15 April 1995, 10.
Trepman, Paul. *Among Men and Beasts*. Translated by Shoshana Perla and Gertrude Hirschler. New York: Bergen Belsen Memorial Press, 1978.
Trial of Josef Kramer and Forty-four Others: The Belsen Trial. Edited by Raymond Phillips. London: W. Hodge, 1949.
Tucker, Todd. *The Great Starvation Experiment: Ancel Keys and the Men Who Starved for Science*. Minneapolis: University of Minnesota Press, 2006.
Turner, Kevin. "Nazi Death Camp Photos Record the Unimaginable." *News Leader* (Fernandina Beach, Florida), 5 January 2005, 1A, 8A.
"23,000 Hungry at Belsen Fed by Canadian Expert." *Toronto Daily Star*, 18 July 1945, 24.
Tyrer, Nicola. *Sisters in Arms: British Army Nurses Tell Their Stories*. London: Weidenfeld and Nicolson, 2008.
"UNRRA Is Praised for Humane Tasks." *Montreal Gazette*, 19 February 1946, 9.
Urquhart, Brian. "Belsen: There Are Things We Must Never Forget." *Montreal Gazette*, 1 May 1985, B3.
– *A Life in Peace and War*. New York: Harper and Row, 1987.
– "Shameful Neglect." *New York Review of Books*, 25 April 2002, 12–14.
"Vancouver Jewry Subscribe $40,000 to External Welfare." *Jewish Western Bulletin*, 3 May 1946, 1.

Van Straubenzee, Alexander. "The Stench of Death." *Spectator*, 9 April 2005.
Varley, Christopher. *Aba Bayefsky Revisited: A Retrospective Exhibition*. Toronto: Koffler Gallery, 1989.
Veil, Simone. *A Life: A Memoir*. Translated by Tamsin Black. London: Haus Publishing, 2007; 2009.
Velleman, Leo. "Belsen." *Flap: 39 Reconnaissance Wing*. Hamburg: Vollmer and Bentlin KG, 1945: n.p.
Verlome, Hetty. *The Children's House of Belsen*. London: Politico's, 2000; 2004.
Victory from Above: The 1st Canadian Parachute Battalion. Produced by Lance Goddard. Written by Peter Kent. Koch International, 2002. 88 minutes.
Visual Culture and the Holocaust. Edited by Barbie Zelizer. New Brunswick, NJ: Rutgers University Press, 2001.
"Volunteers Fight Battle of Winter in Germany." *Mercury* (Hobart Town), 7 January 1946, 3.
Walker, Patrick Gordon. *Patrick Gordon Walker: Political Diaries, 1932–1971*. Edited by Robert Pearce. London: Historians' Press 1991.
War Diary of the 1st Canadian Parachute Battalion. Compiled and edited by Walter Romanow, Morris Romanow, Helene MacLean, Rosalie Hartigan, and Bill Dickson. Calgary: Bunker to Bunker, 2006.
Watson, Scott. *Jack Shadbolt*. Vancouver: Douglas and McIntyre, 1990.
Watts, Sybil. "Windsor Woman Saw Buchenwald, Belsen." *Windsor Daily Star*, 4 September 1945, 16.
Weinberg, Gerhard L. *A World at Arms: A Global History of World War II*. Cambridge: Cambridge University Press, 1994.
Weindling, Paul. "Belsenitis: Liberating Belsen, Its Hospitals, UNRRA, and Selection for Re-emigration, 1945–1948." *Science in Context* 19, no. 3 (2006): 401–18.
– *John W. Thompson: Psychiatrist in the Shadow of the Holocaust*. Rochester, NY: University of Rochester Press, 2010.
– "The Origins of Informed Consent: The International Scientific Commission on Medical War Crimes, and the Nuremberg Code." *Bulletin of the History of Medicine* 75, no. 1 (Spring 2001): 37–71.
– "Victims, Witnesses, and the Ethical Legacy of the Nuremberg Medical Trial." In *Reassessing the Nuremberg Military Tribunals: Transitional Justice, Trial Narratives, and Historiography*, edited by Kim C. Priemel and Alexa Stiller, 74–103. New York: Berghahn, 2012.
Weintraub, Karl J. "Autobiography and Historical Consciousness." *Critical Inquiry* 1, no. 4 (June 1975): 821–48.
– *The Value of the Individual: Self and Circumstance in Autobiography*. Chicago: University of Chicago Press, 1978; 1982.

White, Hayden. *The Content of the Form*. Baltimore: Johns Hopkins University Press, 1987.
– *Tropics of Discourse*. Baltimore: Johns Hopkins University Press, 1978.
Whitlam, George. "Palestinians Should Be Helped." *Toronto Star*, 7 January 1993, A16.
Whyte, King. *Letters Home, 1944–1946*. Edited by Tanya Nanavati and Maureen Whyte. Toronto: Seraphim Editions, 1996.
Wiesel, Elie. *The Jews of Silence: A Personal Report on Soviet Jewry*. Translated by Neal Kozodoy. New York: Holt, Rinehart and Winston, 1966.
Wieviorka, Annette. *The Era of the Witness*. Translated by Jared Stark. Ithaca, NY: Cornell University Press, 2006.
Williams, Jeffrey. *Far from Home: A Memoir of a Twentieth-Century Soldier*. Calgary: University of Calgary Press, 2003.
Winfield, Stanley H. "Ted Aplin – "The Angel of Belsen." *Zachor* (Vancouver Holocaust Education Centre, May 1994), 5.
Winnett, Robert. "Lord Taylor of Warwick: 'I have a role to play in House of Lords.'" *Telegraph*, 8 November 2011.
Wiseman, Debbie. "Bergen-Belsen." *The Promise*. MGM / Silva Screen, 2011.
Wodlinger, David. "An UNRRA Field Supervisor Looks Back." *Canadian Welfare* (April 1948): 12–16.
Women, Autobiography, Theory: A Reader. Edited by Sidonie Smith and Julia Watson. Madison: University of Wisconsin Press, 1998.
Wood, E. Thomas, and Stanisław M. Jankowski, *Karski: How One Man Tried to Stop the Holocaust*. New York: J. Wiley and Sons, 1994.
Wright, Stephen L. *The Last Drop: Operation Varsity, March 24–25, 1945*. Mechanicsburg: Stackpole, 2008.
Yorke, Malcolm. *Mervyn Peake: My Eyes Mint Gold, A Life*. London: John Murray, 2000.
– *Today I Worked Well – The Picture Fell Off the Brush: The Artistry of Leslie Cole*. Upper Denby: Fleece Press, 2010.
Young, James E. "Interpreting Literary Testimony: A Preface to Rereading Holocaust Diaries and Memoirs." *New Literary History* 18, no. 2 (Winter 1987): 403–23.
– "Toward a Received History of the Holocaust." *History and Theory* 36, no. 4 (December 1997): 21–43.
– *Writing and Rewriting the Holocaust: Narrative and the Consequences of Interpretation*. Bloomington: Indiana University Press, 1988.
Zammito, John H. "Reading 'Experience': The Debate in Intellectual History among Scott, Toews, and LaCapra." In *Reclaiming Identity: Realist Theory and*

the Predicament of Postmodernism. Edited by Paula M.L. Moya and Michael R. Hames-Garcia. Himayatnagar: Orient Longman, 2000.

Zander, Ulf. "To Rescue or Be Rescued: The Liberation of Bergen-Belsen and the White Buses in British and Swedish Historical Cultures." In *The Holocaust on Post-war Battlefields: Genocide as Historical Culture*, edited by Klas-Göran Karlsson and Ulf Zander, 343–82. Malmö: Sekel, 2006.

Zelizer, Barbie. *Remembering to Forget: Holocaust Memory through the Camera's Eye*. Chicago: University of Chicago Press, 1998.

Zemel, Carol. "Emblems of Atrocity." In *Image and Remembrance: Representation and the Holocaust*, edited by Shelley Hornstein and Florence Jacobowitz, 201–19. Bloomington: Indiana University Press, 2003.

Index

1st Canadian Parachute Battalion (Canadian), 24–5, 27–30, 33, 36, 44–5, 52–3, 60–1, 68, 71, 129, 146, 192–3, 205n33, 212n49, 234n105
1 Chemical Warfare Unit (Canadian), 240n35
1 Commando Brigade (British), 26
1st Parachute Army (German), 33
1st Special Air Service (British), xiv, 26, 28–9, 34, 45, 52, 54, 65, 69, 96, 195–6n4, 204–5n29, 206n47
1 Vascular Injuries Research Section (British), 172
1 War Crimes Investigation Team (British), 222n79
1 War Crimes Investigation Unit (Canadian), 222n79
2nd Special Air Service (British), 28, 30
3rd Infantry Division (Canadian), 38
3rd Parachute Brigade (British), 27, 29–30, 33
3 (X) Troop, 10 (Inter-Allied) Commando (British), 103
3rd/4th County of London Yeomanry (British), 36, 51

4th Battalion, Wiltshire Regiment (British), 40
5 Army Film and Photographic Unit (British), 38, 96, 110, 116, 126, 146, 152
5 Mobile Field Photographic Section (Canadian), 38, 126, 147
6th Airborne Division (British), 24, 27–8
6 Group (Canadian), 186
6 Mobile Field Photographic Section (Canadian), 38, 126, 147
7th Armoured Division (British), 24–5, 28–9, 36, 51, 95, 193, 206n45
7th Brigade, 72nd Battalion (Israel), 114
7th Brigade, 79th Battalion (Israel), 114
7 General Hospital (Canadian), 40
7 Mobile Bacteriological Laboratory (British), 38
VIII Corps (British), xiii–xiv, xvi, 28, 30, 33, 36–7, 44–5, 57, 77, 160–1
8th Parachute Battalion (British), 27, 34
8th Royal Tank Regiment (British), 83, 101

Index

9th Brigade (Israel), 114
9th General Hospital (British), 39
9th Parachute Battalion (British), 27
10 Garrison (British), 37, 53, 80
11th Armoured Division (British), 25, 28–9, 36–7, 96, 146, 204–5n29
11th Light Field Ambulance (British), xv, 57, 165, 170
12 Field Dressing Station (Canadian), 211n35
13 Regiment, Honourable Artillery Company (British), 204–5n29
14 Amplifying Unit (British), 36, 56, 195–6n4
15th Scottish Division (British), 30
21 Army Group (British), 24, 26–7, 37, 78–9, 125, 163, 172, 223n96
21 Light Field Ambulance (British), 63
22 Field Transfusion Unit (British), 39
29th Armoured Brigade (British), 28, 34, 204–5n29
29th General Hospital (British), 169, 171, 240n39
30 Field Hygiene Section (British), 38, 80
30 Field Transfusion Unit (British), 39
32 Casualty Clearing Station (British), 37, 63, 69, 80, 170
35 Casualty Clearing Station (British), 39
37 Kinema Section (British), 90
39 Reconnaissance Wing (Canadian), 28, 31, 38, 40, 58, 84, 102, 107, 125–7, 128–9, 146, 180, 185, 208n70, 223n91, 225n113, 246–7n112
63rd Anti-Tank Regiment (British), xiv, 33–4, 37, 45, 53, 69, 204–5n29
76 Field Hygiene Section (British), 37
83 Group (British), 27

84 Group (British), 40–1, 91–2, 94, 220n52, 232–3n83, 246n108
101 Squadron (Israel), 114
113 Light Anti-Aircraft Regiment (British), 37, 80–1, 90
126 Wing (Canadian), 26, 28, 31, 40, 86, 92, 103, 112, 183, 188
127 Wing (Canadian), 31, 38, 127, 129
143 Wing (Canadian), 27, 31, 40
224 Military Government Detachment (British), 37, 67, 80
224 Parachute Field Ambulance (British), 36, 61, 193
249 Oxfordshire Yeomanry Battery (British), 53
402 Squadron (Canadian), 105
408 Squadron (Canadian), 91
411 Squadron (Canadian), 105
420 Squadron (Canadian), 186
425 Squadron (Canadian), 186
437 Squadron (Canadian), 39
439 Squadron (Canadian), 108
440 Squadron (Canadian), 40
618 Military Government Detachment (British), 37
649 Company Royal Army Services Corps (British), 96
817 Military Government Detachment (British), 37
904 Military Government Detachment (British), 37
8402 Disarmament Wing (Canadian), 41, 92
8501 Disarmament Wing (British), 104

Aaron (prophet), 181–2. *See also* Nadab and Abihu; David, King of Israel
abjection (concept), 81–5

Abramson, Henry S., 103, 127–9, 137, 208n70, 230n48; *untitled* (painting), 127–8, 137
Adorno, Theodor, 118–21
Ainsworth, Edgar, 128, 131, 138, 208n70
Aitken, Sir Max (Lord Beaverbrook), 123
Akdamut (poem), 237n2
Alighieri, Dante, 59, 110; *Divina Commedia* (poem), 110
Allan, Maj Alexander Smith, 81, 90–1
Allied Control Commission, 174
Alt, Dorothy, 99. *See also* Whyte, King (husband)
American Field Photographic Branch (FPB), 126, 230n43
Amersfoort concentration camp, 199n15
Anderson, F/O Donald K., 38, 127, 129–31, 135, 146, 159, 207–8n66, 230n47; *Belsen* (painting), 127, 130
Anderson, Sgt Ronald Ford (Andy), 52, 205n33
Aplin, S/L Edwin Miller (Ted), 41, 92–5, 114, 220n52, 220–1n58, 221n64, 224n112, 232–3n83, 246n108
Appelfeld, Aharon, 122
Arab-Israeli War (1948), 114–15, 193
Arendt, Hannah, 228n9
Armstrong, Dr Arthur Riley, 240n35
Army Film and Photographic Unit (British), 38, 61, 85, 96, 110, 116, 126, 146, 152, 236n131
Army Medical Services (British), 162
associative clusters, 102, 109. *See also* Frye, Northrop
Auschwitz concentration camp, 139, 41, 50, 118, 120–1

Babi Yar massacre, 48
Badgley, Frank C., 125
Banksy, xv, 198n9
Banting, Sir Frederick, 240n35
Barclay, Sgt W.J., 96, 99
Barnett, Maj Benjamin, 34, 67, 69, 75
Bartsch, Louise C., 189
Bauman, Zygmunt, 228n9
Bayefsky, F/L Aba, 38, 127, 129, 131, 137–8, 140–1, 143, 157, 207–8n66, 232–3n83, 233n97; *Belsen Concentration Camp, Malnutrition Wards* (painting), 141; *Epilogue* (collection), 143; *Remembering the Holocaust* (painting), 144
Beardwell, Myrtle, 166
Bell Canada, xvi
Belsen (Germany), 200–1n29
Belsen trial ("Trial of Josef Kramer and 44 others"), xiv, 73, 100, 147, 195n3, 222n79; executions, 222n84
"Belsen Was a Gas" (song), xv–i, 197n7. *See also* Sex Pistols
Bełżec extermination camp, 210n10, 219n42
Bergen (Germany), 78
Bergen-Belsen concentration camp: alcohol and cigarettes, 40, 87, 170–1, 183, 193; burial of the dead, 78, 179–81, 246–7n112; cannibalism, 60, 67; death rate, 42, 61, 161, 166, 175, 179; descriptions of, 53–9; disparity, 136–7, 159; donations of supplies, 40, 80–1, 92, 129, 170, 182–3, 239n34; ethnicity of inmates, 42, 75, 111; food supply, 36–7, 40, 59, 66–7, 69, 75, 80–1, 92, 129, 177, 183, 190, 215n106; humour, 85, 102, 171; illness, Allied personnel, 170, 217n16; illness, inmates 42, 60, 65,

170, 172, 176–7, 190; kapo (prisoner functionary), 62, 96, 101, 221n67; liberation, 31–7; religious services, 152, 177, 179, 190; smell, 54–7, 59, 76, 212n49; starvation, 42, 59, 66–7, 70, 172–6, 242n56; surrounding area, 29–34, 37, 41, 53–4, 69, 79–80, 91, 93, 102, 160, 165, 170, 183, 194; typhus, xiv, 33, 36, 53, 60–1, 99, 136, 160, 170, 240n35; water supply, 36, 59, 61, 66, 80, 160
Bergen-Hohne Hospital (Glyn Hughes Hospital or Belsen Hospital), 38–9, 132, 136, 145, 148, 167, 170, 189, 192, 240–1n44
Bergen-Hohne Training Area, 29
Berger, Monty, 103
Berney, Maj A.L., 37, 77
Bernstein, Sidney, xv, 196n5. See also *German Concentration Camps Factual Survey* (film)
Best, Dr Charles, 240n35
Blanchot, Maurice, 159; *The Writing of the Disaster* (philosophy), 159
Blenkinsop, S/L Edward (Teddy), 195–6n4
Bletchley Park, 46; Government Code and Cipher School, 46
Bloch, Sam E., xviii
Bloom, LAC Lloyd H., 147, 154, 156
Bogaerde, Capt Derek Van den (Dirk Bogarde), 107, 110, 115, 225n113
Bohnekamp, Lt Col Hans, 33
Branion, Dr Hugh, 174, 242n58
Bricha, 184
Britain: Holocaust, public awareness, 47–50; House of Commons, 48, 245–6n104; Parliament, 48
British Army of the Rhine (BAOR), 104

British Broadcasting Corporation (BBC), xv, 46, 50–1, 91, 99
British Mandate for Palestine, 45, 114–15
British Red Cross Society, 39, 197–8n9
Brittain, Donald, xvi. See also *Memorandum* (film)
Britten, Benjamin, 240–1n44
Brooke, FM Alan, 27
Brown, Ada Evelyn (Lyn), 169
Browning, Christopher, 5–6, 17, 87–8, 228n9
Brunstein, Esther, 42–3
Buchenwald concentration camp, 101, 104
Burns, Robert, 111; "Man Was Made to Mourn: A Dirge" (poem), 111
Burrows, John, 115

Calder, Sgt A.H., 146, 150, 152
Calgary Highlanders (Canadian), 79
Cameron, Chaplain Ross K., 76, 179, 185–6
Canada: Holocaust, public awareness, 47–5; Parliament of Canada, 49, 65, 217n16, 248–9n; Senate of Canada, 103, 191–2
Canadian Broadcasting Corporation (CBC), 196–7n6, 207n60
Canadian Chaplain Service (CCS), 178
Canadian Club (Toronto), 48
Canadian Film and Photo Unit (CFPU), 38, 125, 146, 150
Canadian Government Motion Picture Bureau, 125
Canadian Jewish Congress, 23, 34, 51, 194, 206n45, 220n57
Canadian Military Headquarters, 157, 182

Canadian Museum for Human Rights (Winnipeg), 248–9n5
Canadian War Memorials Fund (CWMF), 123
Canadian War Museum (Ottawa), 127, 191, 234n104, 248–9n5; Holocaust gallery debate, 191–2
Canadian War Records (CWR), 123–4
Canadian War Records Office (CWRO), 123
Canadian Women's Army Corps, 124
CANLOAN program, 40, 65, 209n88
Capa, Robert (Endre Ernö Friedmann), 148–9
Carr, David, 8–12, 20
Cartier-Bresson, Henri, 148
Cass, Chaplain Samuel, 179, 182–4
Casualty Air Evacuation Unit (Canadian), 111
Celle (Germany), 30–1, 33, 36, 40–1, 44, 65, 75, 90, 92, 94, 101–2, 171, 184, 240–1n44; Celler Hasenjagd ("Celle hare hunt"), 30
Central Ukrainian Relief Bureau (CURB), 103
Chadderton, Hugh Clifford (Cliff), 248n4
Charters, Cyril J., 90–1, 106–7
Chassaigne, Violette de, 195–6n4
Chełmno extermination camp, 48
Churchill, Prime Minister Winston, 27, 46
Clark, Sir Kenneth, 123–4, 233n88
Clyne, Sgt Eric, 36
Cohen, Leonard, xvi, 198n12
Coldstream Guards (British), 30
Cole, Leslie, 38, 127, 131, 136, 207–8n66; *One of the Death Pits, Belsen*: *SS Guards Collecting the Bodies* (painting), 136, 138
Collins, Arthur Stewart, 158. *See also* Holden, Patricia May (wife)
Colville, Lt Alexander (Alex), 38, 113, 116, 127, 129, 131–2, 134–7, 143, 145, 157, 207–8n66, 227n138, 238n5; *Bodies in a Grave, Belsen* (painting), 134–5
Committee for Education Overseas (Canadian), 230n48
Cossman, Howard, 114
Costigan, Capt Patrick Gerald, 36–7, 60–1, 71, 192, 213n71, 213n79
Cottrell, Leonard, xv. *See also Man from Belsen, The* (play)
Crawford, Dr Fred Roberts, 86; Witness to the Holocaust Project, 86, 218n29
Creelman, Lyle, 39, 167, 189, 192
Crees, Chaplain Norman Jack, 179, 188
Crerar, Gen Henry, 27

Daily Telegraph (London), 48
Daintree-Johnson, Maj H., 207n55
Daly, Duane, 248n4
Daniell, Brig Robert B.T., 34, 204–5n29; *Journal of a Horse Gunner: India to the Baltic via Alamein*, 34
David, King of Israel, 181. *See also* Aaron; Nadab and Abihu
Deeks, WO Elsie May, 39, 170–1, 240n39
Demjanjuk, John, 113
Department of Psychological Warfare (Canadian), 99
Dickson, Max (Max Dobriner), 103–4
Dilthey, Wilhelm, 13, 19

Directorate of Public Relations (British), 126
distance (theme), xiv, 53, 61, 76, 85, 150, 156, 193–4, 198n12
Doerksen, John, 113–14
Doherty, Muriel Knox, 167
Druillenec, Harold Osmond Le, xiv
Drummond, Sir Jack, 174, 242n58
Dunphy, Chaplain Wilfred H., 179, 185, 246–7n112

Eadie, Lt Col Fraser, 36, 44, 234n105
Earle, Cpl Gordon George, 84
Eden, Anthony, 46
Eichmann, Obersturmbannführer Adolf, 16, 18
Einsatzgruppen, 48. *See also* Babi Yar massacre
Eisen, Chaplain Jack J., 220n57
Elvidge, Katherine J., 168–9
Empire Club of Canada (Toronto), 174
Entertainments National Service Association (British), 240–1n44
Enzensberger, Hans Magnus, 119, 121

Fallingbostel prisoner of war camp (Stalag XI-B), 199n15
Farthing, Derek, 248n4
Fenby, Charles, 131
Fénelon, Fania, xiii
Field Information Agency Technical (FIAT), 237n1
First Canadian Army, 24, 26, 54, 182
Fisher, Pte Emmanuel, 69
Flanagan, Michael, 115
Flap (magazine), 103, 127
Forst, Judith, 196–7n6
Francis, Robert (Bob), 103

Frank, Anne, 42, 196–7n6
Frank, Margot, 42
Frankfurter, Supreme Court Justice Felix, 47
Franks, Col Brian, 26
Frye, Northrop, 102, 109. *See also* associative clusters

Galbraith, Chaplain George, 179
Gallagher, Chaplain Norman, 102, 179, 243–4n77
Gear, F/L Victor Le, 108
Gelber, Shalome Michael, 184–5, 245nn102–3, 245–6n104, 246n108
General Headquarters Liaison Regiment ("Phantom"), 34, 36, 63
Genn, Lt Col Leopold John, 222n79
Georgia Commission on the Holocaust, 87
German Concentration Camps Factual Survey (film), xv, 196n5
Gibson, Thomas, 170, 239n34
Gilmore, Maeve, 132. *See also* Peake, Mervyn (husband)
Glen, Iain, xvi
Globe and Mail (Toronto), 49
Gollancz, Victor, 49; *Let My People Go* (pamphlet), 49; *The Yellow Spot: The Extermination of the Jews of Germany* (book), 49
Gonin, Lt Col Mervin Willett, xv, 37, 57, 165, 197–8n9
Gorst, Peter, 84
Grant, Sgt Ian, 146
Grant, Capt J., 63
Gray, Capt John W., 34, 63, 71, 75, 206n47
Grese, Helferin Irma, 72–3, 222n84
Grineau, Bryan de, 128, 208n70

Guards Armoured Division (British), 25
guilt, German, 85–95. *See also* Jaspers, Karl

Haeckel, Ernst, 175. *See also* ontogeny recapitulates phylogeny (theory)
Haganah, 115, 194
Haines, Doris, 39, 240n39
Halifax Heralds' Concert Party (Canadian), 240–1n44
Hancock, Glen, 91, 219n42
Hardman, Chaplain Leslie, 20, 40, 59–60, 64–5, 75, 111–12, 160–1, 177, 179, 181–5, 187–90, 226n127, 237n2, 244n86, 245n95; *The Survivors: The Story of the Belsen Remnant* (memoir), 60, 64–5
Hardy, Sgt Bert, 146
Hardy, Justin, xvi. See also *Relief of Belsen, The* (film)
Hartigan, Cpl Daniel, 53, 68
Hayes, Saul, 220n57
Haywood, Sgt Harold, 147
Heaps, Abraham A., 65
Heaps, Lt Leo, 65, 70–1, 114
Heidekaserne, 30
Henson, Herbert Hensley (Bishop of Durham), 49
Herzogenbusch concentration camp (Camp Vught), 199n15
Hilberg, Raul, 17, 95
Hill, Brig James, 27
Himmler, Reichsführer Heinrich, 33, 46
Hitchcock, Alfred, xv, 196n5. See also *German Concentration Camps Factual Survey* (film)
Hitler, Führer Adolf, 48, 51, 86, 90, 93, 95, 158, 194

Höhne – Displaced Persons' Centre (Bergen-Belsen Displaced Persons' Camp), 131, 141, 143, 167, 183, 224–5n112, 232–3n83, 240–1n44
Holborne, Corp A.P. (Pete), 180
Holden, Patricia Mary, 158–9, 236n138
"Holidays in the Sun" (song), 197n7. *See also* Sex Pistols
Holocaust: artistic symbolism, xvi, 61–3, 66, 82, 120–1, 137, 152–3, 158–9; International Day of Commemoration in Memory of the Victims of the Holocaust, 194; media coverage, 47–50; nativization (concept), 193; use of term, 52
Holocaust Educational Trust, 190
Hopkinson, P/O Fred, 57–8, 146
Hughes, Brig Hugh Llewellyn Glyn, xvi, 36, 39, 57–8, 161, 163–5, 172, 195–6n4, 238n5
Hungarian Army, 33, 68–70, 90, 169, 219n39

Illustrated London News, 49, 128
Imperial War Museum (London), 124, 128, 131, 191, 196n5, 234n104, 238n5, 248n1; Holocaust exhibition, 191
International Tracing Service (ITS), xiv
Ironside, F/L Allan, 147
Irving, David, 20, 113
Isaiah (prophet), 184
Israel (state), 114, 184, 233n97
Israeli Air Force (IAF), 114, 227–8n141
Israelites (ancient), 184
Izbica Lubelska (Poland), 46, 210n10. *See also* Karski, Jan

Jamieson, Edgar, 94
Janowitz, Morris, 91
Jaspers, Karl, 88–90, 93, 100–1; *The Question of German Guilt* (philosophy), 88
Jenkinson, 195–6n4, 206n47; Robert Jenkinson, 195–6n4
Jesus Christ, 153, 185, 236n131
Jewish Chronicle (London), 48–9
Johnson, Mark, 66
Johnston, Lt Col James A.D., 37, 56, 63
Joint Distribution Committee (JDC), 184, 245n103
Joint War Organisation (British), 161–2
Jones, Beatrice Mary (Molly) Silva, 167–8
Jones, Jonah, 61, 193

Kaddish, 179, 181, 196–7n6
Kadziolka, Father Stanislaus Jan, 152–3, 235n127
Kaplan, Brett Ashley, 120, 156. *See also* unwanted beauty (concept)
Karski, Jan, 46–7, 95, 210n10. *See also* Izbica Lubelska
Kashetsky, Herzl, xvi; *A Prayer for the Dead* (exhibit), xvi
Kearney, Richard, 11
Kelly, Col Mike, 198–9n14
Kessell, Mary, 38, 127, 131, 140–1, 188, 207–8n66, 220n52, 233n88
Keys, Dr Ancel, 173–4, 241–2n54; *The Biology of Human Starvation* (book), 174. *See also* Minnesota Starvation Experiment
Kindertransport (Refugee Children's Movement), 103
Klein, Dr Fritz, 139, 222n84

Kochane, Louis, 83, 101, 222n86
Kramer, Hauptsturmführer Josef, 33, 69–70, 73, 88, 100–1, 147, 149–50, 222n84
Krell, Dr Robert, 242–3n61
Kristeva, Julia, 81–3. *See also* abjection (concept)

Laidlaw, P/O Ron, 3, 106, 146, 152, 234n106
Lakoff, George, 66, 215n104. *See also* metaphors, Great Chain of Being
Lamb, Lt Molly (Molly Bobak), 124, 127, 157, 208n70
Lanzmann, Claude, 228n11
Lattion, Sgt Mike, 146, 234n105
Laufer, Bernard, xvi
Lawrie, Sgt William, 85, 116, 146–7
Layton, Irving, xvi
Lazecko, Jean, 189
Leader (magazine), 131, 133
Leatherbarrow, Sgt Richard, 85
Lebon, Col R.A., 223n96
Lee, Geddy, 196–7n6; "Grace to Grace," 196–7n6
Léger, Fernand, 230n48
Lemkin, Raphael, 149; *Axis Rule in Occupied Europe* (book), 149
Levine, Abraham (Abe), 114
Levinson, Lottie, 245n103
Levy, Senior Chaplain Isaac (Harry), 179, 181, 183, 185, 187, 244n86
Levy, Ruth. *See* Flanagan, Michael
Lewis, Sgt Mike, 85, 146–7, 152–4, 156
Liberty (magazine), 48
Life (magazine), 117, 148–9, 151
Lifton, Robert Jay, 81, 134–5, 148. *See also* psychic closing-off (concept)
Light, Chaplain Edwin S., 179, 186–8
Lighthall, William D., 247–8n127

Lincoln's Inn Fields, 158
Linder, Bert, 109
Lindsay, Nigel, xvi
Lipscombe, Lt Col F.M., 170, 172
Lobauer, Hilde ("S.S. woman without uniform"), 73
Luftwaffe (German), 92–3
Lüneburg Heath, xvii, 6, 21, 25, 29–31, 40, 53, 79, 81, 105
Luther, Martin, 91
Lyons, S/L F.J., 104, 222n86
Lyotard, Jean-François, 228n11

Maandag, Sieg, 149, 235n119
MacAuslan, Alan, 172, 175–6
MacConnell, Brian, 105, 226n127
Machalnik (Machal), 114–15
MacInnis, A.J. (Scotty), 68
Maclean's (Toronto), 49
MacLellan Lt Keith W., 34, 192, 206n45
Magritte, René, 236n129; *La trahison des images* (painting), 236n129
Majdanek concentration camp, 49
Malindine, Capt E.G., 146
Man from Belsen, The (radio play), xv
Mann, Larry D. (Louis Libman), 84, 102–3, 107–9, 111, 218n23, 223n89
Massey, Charles Vincent, 124, 129, 230n48, 232–3n83
Mayor, AB Keith, xiv, 195n3
McCreary, W/C Dr John F., 40, 174–5, 242n58, 242–3n61
McCurry, H.O., 124
McDougall, Maj Jack, 125
McGregor, CO Gordon, 112, 227n131
medical students (British), 39, 162, 169–70, 176
Melvin, Brig J., 36
Memory of the Camps (film), 196n5

Menuhin, Yehudi, 240–1n44
Menzies, Tobias, xvi
metaphors, 8, 61–8, 71, 76, 85, 92, 176, 189, 198–9n14; animal, 57, 62–6, 71, 76–7, 85, 189; Great Chain of Being, 66, 215n104; supernatural, 71, 77, 86, 92; zoomorphism, 62–3, 85. *See also* ontogeny recapitulates phylogeny (theory)
Michie, Lt Col A.M., 161
Midgley, Sgt Norman, 96, 146–7
Miles, Maj W.H., 37
Milton, John, 233n91; *Paradise Lost* (poem), 233n91
Ministry of Information (British), 123, 131
Minnesota Starvation Experiment, 173
Mirsky, Lt Col Mervin, 20, 54, 113, 227n133
Mollison, Capt P.L., 172
Montgomery, FM Bernard, 26–7, 29, 78, 125, 163
Moore, Lt Alan, 230n45
Morawetz, Oskar, 196–7n6; "From the Diary of Anne Frank" (composition), 196–7n6
Morden, LAC Harold, 111, 113
Morgensztern, Rabbi Menachem Mendel (Kotzker Rebbe), 181–2
Morris, Edmund L., 231n50
Morrison, Chaplain Michael, 152–3, 179, 182

Nadab and Abihu, 181. *See also* Aaron, Prophet; David, King of Israel
National Gallery (London), 123
National Gallery of Canada (Ottawa), 124

National Holocaust Monument (Ottawa), 248–9n5
National Holocaust Monument Act (Canada), 248–9n5
Nesbitt, Sgt Matthew (Max Nezgoraski or Max Nezgor), 86–7, 106, 113, 218nn29–30, 227n133
Neuengamme concentration camp, 195–6n4
Night Will Fall (film), 196n5
Noble, John Gourlay, 52
Norris, Sgt Peter, 146
Nuremberg trials, 198–9n14, 237n1
Nutrition Group, RCAF (Canadian), 40, 174

Oakes, Sgt Harry, 146
Old Vic (theatre company), 240–1n44
Olivier, Laurence, 240–1n44
ontogeny recapitulates phylogeny (theory), 175–6
Operation Archway, 26
Operation Checkmate, xiv
Operation Plunder, 23–8, 192
Operation Varsity, 26–7
Oranienburg concentration camp, 48
Order of St John, 161–2
Ordnungspolizei (German), 87
Osborne, Edna, 189
O'Sullivan, Thomas, 115

Palestine, 45, 114–15, 184, 193, 246n108
Pancer, Alexander, 101, 103
Panchuk, Gordon Bohdan, 103, 223nn96–7
Panzer Training School, 163, 165
Paybody, Lt Col J. Douglas, 44, 55
Peake, Mervyn, 127, 131–4, 145, 208n70; "The Consumptive: Belsen, 1945" (poem), 132; *Dying Girl at Belsen* (painting), 132–3, 145; *Titus Alone* (novel), 145; "The Victims" (poem), 145
Peake, Sebastian, 145
Phelps, Dr Peter, 198–9n14
Picture Post (London), 128, 131
Pinewood Studios, 126
Pocock, Tom, 131
Pontius Pilate, 236n131
Prescott, Dr D.T., 170
Proskie, S/L John, 37, 67, 75, 192, 207n60, 215n106
Prosser, O.G., 53
psychic closing-off (concept), 134–5, 140, 148

Queen Alexandra's Imperial Military Nursing Service (QAIMNS), 162–3, 168

Raab, Elisabeth M., 225–6n116
Radio Luxembourg, 91, 99
RAF Celle, 30–1
Randall, Lt John, 34, 54–5, 69
RCAF Public Relations Department (Canadian), 158
RCAF Streamliners (Canadian), 240–1n44
RCAF Women's Division (Canadian), 158
recapitulation (biogenetic law or embryological parallelism), 175–6, 243n4; *See also* Haeckel, Ernst
Red Cross (British), 39, 131, 161–2, 166–7, 197–8n9, 207–8n66, 220n52
Redgrave, Corin, xvi
Redgrave, Jemma, xvi
Reichstag, 48
Reinke, Carl, 103

Relief of Belsen, The (film), xv
Rennie, Dr Charles Sutherland, 39, 169–70, 239n31
Repat Review (Canadian), 240–1n44
responsibility: Allied governments, 94, 96; German government, 91, 94, 96; individual, 20, 89, 94, 96, 153
Rhine River, xvii, 21, 23–8, 41
Richardson, Sir Ralph, 240–1n44
Richer, Lt Charles H., 146, 234n105
Ricoeur, Paul, 6, 8, 10–12, 19, 112, 200–1n29
Robb, LAC Clifford, 20, 113, 227n133
Roberts, L/Cpl Sidney, 36
Robichaud, Raymond, 222n79
Rodger, George, 111, 117, 148–51, 156, 226n127
Rodger, Peter, 149
Roe, PO Alfred John, xiv, 195n2
Roosevelt, President Franklin D., 47
Rose, Alan, 23, 25, 51, 56, 95, 193, 206n45, 221n64
Rosensaft, Dr Hadassah, 108, 166
Rosensaft, Josef, xvi, 116. *See* World Federation of Bergen-Belsen Survivors (Associations)
Rossiter, IO John A., 234n105
Rothberg, Michael, 119, 121; realist and antirealist (concepts), 119, 228n9, 228n11
Rousset, David, 57; l'univers concentrationnaire (concept), 57, 76
Royal Air Force (British), 26, 47, 126; Bomber Command, 26
Royal Air Force Chaplains' Branch (British), 178
Royal Army Chaplains' Department (British), 177–8, 243n75
Royal Army Medical Corps (British), 37, 53, 162, 170

Royal Canadian Air Force (Canadian), 6, 26, 28, 80, 103, 125
Royal Canadian Army Medical Corps (RCAMC)
Royal Engineers (British), 179, 38, 71, 127, 131, 140
Royal Engineers (Canadian), 211n35
Rubenstein, Manya (Mary), 196–7n6
Rush (band), 196–7n6; "Red Sector A" (song), 196–7n6. *See also* Lee, Geddy; Rubenstein, Manya

Sachs, Nelly 119
Sachsenhausen concentration camp, xiv
Saltsman, Harry, 217n16
Saltsman, Max, 217n16
Sandbostel concentration camp, 39, 199n15
Sandler, Lillian, 93–4
Sanker, Senior Chaplain Louis, 40, 183
Sauve, WO J.R.F., 174
Scarry, Elaine, 173, 175
Scheuen (Germany), 40, 92
Schmidt, Col Hans, 33
Schutzstaffel (SS, German), 30, 33, 42, 69–70, 73, 98–99, 136, 138–9; descriptions of, 70–1, 72–3, 150; female, 71–3, 150, 179; male, 71, 179; violence against, 69, 71, 96, 99; violence by, 43, 62
Scots Guards (British), 30
Second British Army, 24, 26, 205n33
Second Tactical Air Force (TAF), 40, 183
Seekings, Sgt Reginald, 34, 54, 69
Seger, Gerhart H., 48, 95; *A Nation Terrorized* (account), 48

Senate Subcommittee of Veteran Affairs (Canada), 191–2
Sesia, Maj A.T., 129
Sex Pistols, xv–i, 196–7n6, 197n7. *See also* "Belsen Was a Gas" (song); "Holidays in the Sun" (song)
Seymour, David (Chim or Dawid Szymin), 148–9
Shadbolt, Jack, 157–8; *Aftermath and Terror of a Street* (painting), 157; *The Dogs* (painting), 157; *Sketch for "The Yellow Dogs"* (painting), 158; *Victim* (painting), 157
Shavuos (Jewish holiday), 237n2
Shaw, George Bernard, 240–1n44; *Arms and the Man* (play), 240–1n44
Singer, André, 196n5. See also *Night Will Fall* (film), 196n5
Sington, Derrick, 36, 56–7, 59, 61–3, 70, 75, 195–6n4, 220–1n58; *Belsen Uncovered* (memoir), 56, 75, 195–6n4, 220–1n58
Smith, Lt Wilfred I., 40, 209n88
Snell, Adrian, 196–7n6; "Kaddish for Bergen Belsen" (song), 196–7n6
Sobibór extermination camp, 41, 49
Soltau (Germany), 31, 36, 185
Special Coverage Unit (SPECOU), 126, 230n43
Spotton, John, xvi. See also *Memorandum* (film)
Stein, Saul, 92, 97
Stewart, Lt Col Hugh, 110
St John War Organisation (British), 131, 207–8n66
St. Marys Journal Argus, 234n106
Stone, Sgt Joe, 58, 146
Stretch, Chaplain T.J., 66, 71, 74, 179
Stubbs, LAC James Arthur, 147

Supreme Headquarters Allied Expeditionary Force (SHAEF), 99, 174, 223n96
Swift, Chaplain Edmund, 179
Sylvestre, Chaplain J.P.E.M., 179

Taharah (ritual), 181
Taylor, Sgt Eric, 38, 127, 131, 138, 140, 142, 207–8n66; *A Living Skeleton at Belsen Concentration Camp* (painting), 142
Taylor, John (Baron Taylor of Warwick), 198–9n14
Taylor, Lt Col Richard (R.I.G), xiv, 33–4, 36, 216n131
Thompson, F/O James Ernest 113
Thompson, S/L John W., 41, 94, 160, 194, 237n1
Thompson, LAC Lloyd E., 147, 154, 156
Time (magazine), 149–50
Times, The (London), 49
Tinning, George Campbell, 231n51
Tonkin, Maj John, 28–9, 34, 206n47
Topolski, Feliks, 143, 145, 208n70, 230n45; *The Memoir of the Century* (installation), 143
Toronto Daily Star, 49
Traverner, Joy (Joy Trindle), 171
Treblinka extermination camp, 41, 50
Turner, Mark, 66, 215n104. *See also* metaphors, Great Chain of Being

Ukrainian-Canadian Servicemen's Association, 103
Union of Soviet Socialist Republics, 41, 49–50, 223n97; Red Army, 41, 49, 203n2

United Nations, 149, 194, 249–50n9; Convention on the Prevention and Punishment of Genocide (CPPCG), 149
United Nations Educational, Scientific and Cultural Organization (UNESCO), 237n1
United Nations Relief and Rehabilitation Administration (UNRRA), 39, 161–2, 167, 184, 189, 247–8n127
United States Holocaust Memorial Council, 24
United States Holocaust Memorial Museum, 34, 204–5n29, 234n104
unwanted beauty (concept), 120. *See also* Brett Ashley Kaplan
Urquhart, Maj Brian, 249–50n9
US Army Center of Military History, 24

Vanderwell, Janet, 189
Vandivert, William, 148
Veil, Simone, 194
Velleman, Leo, 103, 223n91
Vicious, Sid, xv. *See also* "Belsen Was a Gas (song); "Holidays in the Sun" (song); Sex Pistols
Victor, Maurice, 50–1, 57, 211n35
Vistula-Oder Offensive, 203n2
Volkssturm, 30
Voluntary Aid Detachments (British), 162, 169
Voluntary Aid Detachments (Canadian), 163, 170

Wagner, Richard, 71; *Der Ring des Nibelungen* (opera), 71
Waldon, Maj R.F., 69

Walker, Patrick Gordon, 91, 99–101
Wannsee Protocol, 18, 202n62
War Artists' Advisory Committee (WAAC), 123–4, 131, 207–8n66, 230n45, 233n88
War Artists' Committee (WAC), 124
Ward, Margaret Wyndham, 220n52
War Orphans Project, 245n103. *See also* Levinson, Lottie
Wehrmacht (German), 29–30, 38, 68, 87–8, 90, 166
Weichmann, Herbert, xvi
Weinfeld, Harold, 220n57
Weizman, Ezer, 114
Welchman, Senior Chaplain Herbert H., 161, 179, 182
Werwolf (werewolves), 30, 204n28
Westerbork transit camp, 199n15
White, Hayden, 3, 7–11, 22
White Paper on German Atrocities (report), 45
Whyte, King, 99
Wiesel, Elie, 109, 228n11
Wiles, Deputy Assistant Chaplin O.D., 179
Williams, Capt Jeffrey, 78
Williams, Capt W.R., 36
Wilson, F/O Clifford Denzel (Denny), 105, 114, 227–8n141
Wilson, Lt Martin H., 146, 153–4, 236n131
Winfield, Sgt Stanley, 41, 91, 94, 220n57
Winnipeg Free Press, 49
Winwood, Maj T.C.M., 88
Wiseman, Debbie, 196–7n6; "Bergen-Belsen" (song), 196–7n6
Wodlinger, David, 245n103

Wojtyła, Karol Józef (Pope John Paul II), 235n127
World Federation of Bergen-Belsen Survivors (Associations), xvi, xviii, 116
Wunstorf (Germany), 29, 31, 87, 105

Xanten (Germany), 27

Yad Vashem (Israel), 233n97, 242n60
Yale, Bernard, 94, 113, 227n133

Zajdner, Bella (Bela Seidner), 224–5n112
Zajdner, Pola, 224–5n112
Zinkeisen, Doris, 38, 127, 131–2, 135–8, 145–7, 207–8n66; *Human Laundry, Belsen: April 1945* (painting), 136–7
zionism, 114, 184, 245n102
Zündel, Ernst, 20, 113, 227n133

www.ingramcontent.com/pod-product-compliance
Lightning Source LLC
Chambersburg PA
CBHW020353080526
44584CB00014B/1006